BEETHOVEN

THE MAN WHO FREED MUSIC

BEETHOVEN

THE MAN WHO FREED MUSIC

BY

ROBERT HAVEN
SCHAUFFLER

TUDOR PUBLISHING CO.
NEW YORK   1946

"HE WHO TRULY UNDERSTANDS MY MUSIC
MUST THEREBY GO FREE OF ALL THE MISERY
WHICH OTHERS BEAR ABOUT WITH THEM"

BEETHOVEN

In abridged form Part One of this book has appeared serially in "The Outlook and Independent."

Contents

CONTENTS

CONTENTS

CONTENTS

CONTENTS

CONTENTS

CONTENTS

CONTENTS

CONTENTS

CONTENTS

CONTENTS

CONTENTS

thoven Takes Him to Gneixendorf, September, 1826 — A
Trying Guest — Homely Brother Johann — Beethoven's
Habits of Composition Too Much for Cook — The Vine-
Dresser Valet's Account — What the Natives Thought of
Him — *"A Bissel Stada!"* — Friction.

CONTENTS

CONTENTS

List of Illustrations

Introduction

For a long time I had been hoping to discover a particular type of book in English about the man who, more fully and variously than any other, freed music. I wanted one built on a more balanced and unified plan than the volumes at hand. These were of three kinds: the wholly biographical,[1] the wholly musical,[2] and the combination which treated both these themes in separate sections of the same work, strongly featuring either the man[3] or his art.[4]

I wanted a trustworthy account correlating the great emancipator's music with his highly interesting life and slighting neither. I wanted a view of his achievement, illumined by "the man in relation to his times"[5]—in relation also to the art of music and the battle ground of æsthetics.

After a vain search I was tempted, four years ago, to undertake such a biography myself. This book aims to interweave in a running narrative the life, personality, and contribution of Beethoven and to give these factors equal attention.

Thayer relates[6] how, in planning for the first official biography of the Master, Schindler fell out with Ries because the latter "contended that to tell the whole truth about great men was right and could do them no injury." In holding this liberal view Ries

---

[1] E. g., those by Rolland, Ludwig, and that giant, Thayer.
[2] E. g., Walker.
[3] E. g., Turner and Grace.
[4] E. g., Bekker.
[5] Goethe, *Wahrheit und Dichtung.*
[6] Vol. III, p. 198.

was well in advance of his age, and even in advance of the admirable but somewhat puritanical Thayer, who thought fit to suppress certain facts of importance.

From Schindler's day to this, the literature of Beethoven has often shown a strong mythopœic tendency, a trend away from established fact, a leaning toward sentimental rhapsody. This school of biographers might well take as its motto M. Romain Rolland's dauntless ejaculation: "Let us inhale the breath of heroes!"[7] It looks upon the composer of the *Hymn to Joy* and the *Missa* as, almost *ipso facto,* a seraphic being who could do no wrong. The movement has recently culminated in Bartels's[8] attempt to transfigure the music maker of Bonn into the founder of a new religion—a triumphant competitor of Jesus Christ!

Mr. Ernest Newman,[9] on the other hand, briefly presenting the Master's less edifying aspect, unrelieved by the all-palliating context, falls in with the derogatory tendency now fashionable in biography.

As between the deifiers and the detractors, however, Beethoven has suffered far more from the former. This man is too mighty to fear being portrayed, like Cromwell, "warts and all." And no writer need apologize for telling, as he sees it, that "whole truth" for which Ries contended.

This book is a grateful beneficiary of the recent Centenary literature, which has shed new light on many phases of the Master's life and work and facilitated judicial conclusions on such controversial matters as his health and his relations with women.

If in the following pages the angle of approach differs somewhat from that of other biographers, it may be because for years I observed Beethoven's music from the special viewpoint of the

---

[7] *Beethoven,* 1923, Introd., p. v.
[8] *Beethoven* (undated), Borgmeyer, Hildesheim.
[9] In *The Unconscious Beethoven,* 1927.

professional violoncellist and grew intimate with his orchestral works from the successive vantage of each choir of the orchestra. This specialization, however, has been partially modified by long and close intimacy with pianists whose bible, in thirty-two chapters, starts with *Genesis* in F minor and ends with *Revelation* in C minor.

Few words will be devoted to Beethoven's least interesting compositions or to the sort of commentary often found in program notes. Unless accompanied by a concert, detailed analysis of music is usually wearisome, unprofitable, and almost incomprehensible without frequent interruptions to consult scores. The reader will search these pages in vain for descriptions of how the third bassoon, inverting the theme in the relative minor, is overwhelmed by furious viola arpeggii in F sharp, and staccato chords from the brass choir. Nor will he be urged to believe that the flute, announcing the tender second subject, can only mean a tiny rift of blue amid the menacing storm clouds through which glides a solitary sunbeam to glorify the uplifted shield (*"empor strebend"*) of a knight in armour.

A few compositions, like the *Eroica,* have been given unusual space in order to bring out sources or relationships which may heighten enjoyment of the music, and which seem to have escaped the comment of other writers.

To avoid the considerable margin of error and infelicity to be found in the standard English versions, all foreign letters and documents quoted in this book have been freshly translated.

Part II is a study of Beethoven's creative processes. Though it is the more original portion of the book, it owes much for method and inspiration to that brilliant disclosure of Coleridge's mind in action, *The Road to Xanadu.*[10] As the reader will find, if he persists to the closing chapter, a certain melodic pattern has been uncovered. Beethoven used this in his principal themes with aston-

---

[10]By John Livingston Lowes, 1927.

ıshing frequency, investing it at each recurrence with a disguise sufficiently varied and effective to have preserved its incognito up to the present day.

This man's music wears like Bessemer steel. But, unlike that reliable substance, it is an inexhaustible treasure trove of surprise and delight. I am confident that any music lover who can lay aside all preconception and prejudice and acquaint himself with the best of Beethoven will feel not only a fresh enthusiasm for this composer but a new and more vital relationship to the whole art. To know Beethoven is to know the heart of music.

To the kindness of that eminent musicologist, the late Oscar G. Sonneck, I owe two careful readings of the manuscript. One of the last acts of his generous life was to jot down valuable criticisms and suggestions which amounted in themselves to a small volume. His counsel induced me to postpone publication for a year in order to enlarge and recast the book upon a more serviceable and interesting plan.

For reading and criticizing these volumes while in manuscript sincere thanks are due to Mrs. Grace Hazard Conkling, Professor John Erskine, Mr. Lawrence Gilman, Dr. Otto Kinkeldey, Mr. Julius Mattfeld, Mr. Gustave Reese, Mr. Frederick N. Sard, Mrs. Vieva D. Smith, Mr. George Stevens, and Mr. Lyman Beecher Stowe. Special gratitude is due Miss Marion Bauer for repeated readings of manuscript and proofs, for help in making the Glossary, in the selection and special arrangement of several musical examples, and for communicating certain of her notable discoveries.

Invaluable aid must be acknowledged from an unexpected source—the electrical recordings of Beethoven's chief orchestral and chamber works which have recently been made for the new phonograph, and the autographic reproductions of his sonatas for the player-piano. Studying these discs and rolls, score in hand, with no limit to the repetition of any desired passage, one can discover, from dawn to dusk, more well-hidden details in a given composition than during a lifetime of casual attendance at concerts.

I have to thank Miss May Seymour for help in handling the musical examples. For information, advice, and other kind assistance, grateful acknowledgment is made to: Mr. Harold Bauer, Mr. Francis Rufus Bellamy, the Von Breuning family of Vienna, Mr. Carl Engel, Professor Max Friedländer of Berlin University, Miss Dorothy Lawton, Mr. C. B. Oldman of the British Museum, Dr. Alfred Orel, Mynheer Julius Roentgen, Miss Marion Rous, my brother Mr. Lawrence Schauffler, Dr. Ludwig Schiedermair of Bonn University, Mr. Dwight Shouse, Mr. William C. Smith of the British Museum, Miss Muriel Tankard, and Mevrouw Jo van Ammers-Küller; also to the Beethoven Association of New York, the *Beethovenhaus* in Bonn, and the music libraries of Berlin, Bonn, Vienna, London, Boston, Washington, and New York.

R. H. S.

New York City, June, 1929.

PART I

HIS LIFE AND WORKS ·

BEETHOVEN THE LIBERATOR

Most of the music his young ears had known
  Was lackey-made, obsequiously neat,—
A pleasing toy, a powdered wig of tone
  To grace the chat of gentry after meat.
But when he touched the strings, the rabble surged
  Into the palace among the guests, to find
Their joy and pain, their calm and passion merged
  In universal measures for mankind.

Then to his ears the applauding world went dim—
  And, on the lonely Patmos of the brave,
He heard the future's choiring Seraphim
  Transporting men sprung out of slime and cave
    And the dark age that merely could adore
    Great music like the Fifth and Leonore.

R. H. S.

THE NICKNAME

THE small boys of Bonn, with whom he played marbles and practised archery and robbed Frau Fischer's hen roost, nicknamed Ludwig *"der Spangol."* If they had talked English, they would have called him "Spanish" or "Spangy."[1]

The familiar names which youngsters invent for one another the world over are not often high-flown or pleasing to their victims. They are usually based with uncompromising directness on some salient physical peculiarity. Seldom do they wander far from the type of Skinny, Carrots, Runt, Lefty, and Squinter.

The creator-to-be of the Fifth symphony was in all likelihood called "Spangy" on account of that swarthy complexion which neighbour Fischer described as "black-brownish." For his comrades could hardly have known about the musical castles in Spain that used to beckon him from the playground.

But these soon came to be the most real and important things in the boy's life. Far more than the colour of his cheeks—if the other boys had but known it—the musical

---

[1]*"Der Spangol"* was a boyish corruption of *"der Spagnol"* ("the Spaniard").

castles justified the curious nickname. Posted at his favourite hiding place in the attic window young Ludwig could make them out, beyond that broad current of the Guadalquivir which stupid folk stubbornly miscalled the Rhine—perched on the summit of those violet Segovian crags close to the horizon, which prosaic souls, as yet uninitiated, used merely to know as the Siebengebirge.

There in the attic he would sit hour after hour, attending to the Spanish castle tunes that sang themselves in his head; until the shuffle of an unsteady step would break into the music. Father would come with an alcoholic breath and a loud voice. And Spangy would be hauled downstairs to pound the piano or scratch the fiddle.

These instruments, though, were not half bad if the grown-ups would only leave him alone. For he could have fun playing himself the latest Spanish castle tunes. But too often he would be frightened, at his fiddling, by a sudden snarling voice:

"What's all this nonsense you're scratching again? You there—scratch according to the notes or I'll fetch you a clout on the ear!"

One should not be too hard on Father Johann. With all his folly, perhaps he did more for the art of music than an intelligent and sympathetic father would have done. Young Spangy's gift for invention was stimulated by his revolt from the paternal admonition to "scratch according to the notes."

On the contrary one should feel indebted to Johann van Beethoven. Unwittingly he reënforced the lad's affection for his Spanish castle music. At Ludwig's most impressionable age the pedantic drunkard invested creative art for him with the glamour of forbidden fruit. Without meaning to do so Johann taught the boy that printed melodies are sweet but those unprinted are sweeter.

One morning Frau Fischer came through the courtyard and saw the lad in the window of his bedroom, his head propped on his hands, staring at something invisible to her.

"Well, Ludwig, how do things look?"

No answer.

When she saw him again she took him to task: "You know, Ludwig, no answer is also an answer."

"Oh, no; I didn't mean that! Please excuse me. I was taken up just then with such a beautiful deep thought that I couldn't bear to be disturbed."

It is probable that Ludwig's unique talent for improvisation and composition, as opposed to the uncreative virtuoso's career of pounding or scratching according to the notes, was partly due to what the psychological jargon of our day would call a mechanism of escape from the arid literalism of his impossible father.

When the boy became a man he even went so far in his revolt against visible notation that he would sometimes play the piano part of one of his own concertos from a few leaves sparsely scrawled over in a sort of private musical stenography. And amid all his preoccupations he had a grin of *Schadenfreude* to spare for the unhappy bewilderment of the young disciple whose duty it was to turn pages. Who can doubt that when the disciple made a slip the Master would nudge him and growl—in full-flavoured compensation for his own youthful miseries: "You there—turn according to the notes!"

On one side the van Beethoven[2] family was Flemish, from near Louvain. It was no mere accident that Ludwig's paternal grandfather was both wine merchant and singer; that his great-great-grandfather dealt in wine too; that his maternal grandfather was head cook in a castle; his father a singer and connoisseur of wine; and that the Flemish branch of the family boasted painters and a sculptor. For head cooks and artists are masters of good taste and form and colour, while wine merchants and singers deal in products dear to Dionysus, the god of creative fertility. The wine merchant strain in Beethoven was apotheosized by Bourdelle, whose head of the Master,[3] in the Metropolitan Museum, bears these words of Beethoven, selected and liberally translated from those reported by Bettina Brentano: "I am the Bacchus who presses out for men this glorious wine, and intoxicates their souls."[4]

His two Flemish great-grandparents made Beethoven a compatriot of that proud band of Northern colourists and masters of form who ranged from the Van Eycks and Memling through Rubens, Van Dyke, and Teniers the Younger, to Alfred Stevens and Meunier.

With such blood in his veins it is natural that Beethoven should have given, in his *Pastoral* symphony, the first

[2]In Flemish, *Beet* means "beet," and *hoven*, "garden"; so van Beethoven signifies "of the beet garden." (See E. Closson, *L'Elément Flamand dans Beethoven*, 1928, p. 21.)

[3]See List of Illustrations.

[4]See p. 273.

notable modern impulse to that sort of tone-painting we call program music. It is also characteristically Flemish that he should have given this impulse not crudely but subtly—the only way a composer legitimately can. Flemish too is that impatience of authority and that proud independence which were presently to assist him in freeing musicians from the status of lackeys and making professional men of them.

When Ludwig's paternal grandfather, Ludovicus van Beethoven, was still a boy he showed his independence by quarrelling with his family and leaving home never to return.[5] In 1733, a brilliant lad of twenty-one, he was appointed court musician to Clemens August, Elector of Cologne. But he did not go to the city of smells and famous architecture. Almost five centuries before, proud Cologne had cast forth its reigning archbishop. And ever since, the ecclesiastical Electors had been obliged to rule from the smaller city of Bonn. Whereupon Bonn became so exclusively a court town that seven eighths of its people were understood to be fed from the castle kitchen.

Ludovicus promptly made an unhappy marriage. His wife, who had been Maria Josepha Poll, bore him two babies who died in infancy. Then, towards the close of 1739, came Johann, a son destined to turn out badly. That is to say, if a bad end may properly be claimed for anyone who gives the world its chief musician.

Maria Josepha took to drink: an obvious thing to do if

---

[5] Just as young Lalo, the French composer, was to run away from Lille, near by, more than a century later. Note in passing that Lille was once a Flemish town.

one is unhappy and one's husband, when not disporting himself upon the operatic stage, is conducting a small wine business. The poor woman was shut up as a hopeless dipsomaniac to end her days in a cloister in Cologne.

Ludovicus throve. Beginning with 300 florins a year, a high salary for a young singer in those days, he served the Elector four decades with such increasing success that, in 1761, he was invited to the honourable post of *Kapellmeister*, or head of the court music.

The son Johann inherited his mother's love of a good time and her weakness of character. Though he had but small talent for music he followed a long way behind his fine old father as a court singer.[6] And he did a little fiddling at odd times.

Drink soon ruined whatever modest chance he had of a successful career. On account of his wild habits he was nicknamed by his father Johannes der Läufer. And it is probable that he was even more appropriately known by the neighbours as "Johannes der Säufer." This frivolous play upon the name of Salome's famous victim, the Baptist,[7] may be approximated in English only by some such phrase as "John the Gullet-Baptist."

In 1767 Maria Magdalena Kewerich, twenty-year-old daughter of the Ehrenbreitstein castle cook, and widow of a valet, married this ne'er-do-weel Johann. She was gentle,

---

[6]Professor Schiedermair has recently discovered a fact which shows what a good name Ludovicus had left behind in Belgium. A few weeks before the birth of young Ludwig his father was offered a post as singer in the cathedral at Liége. The hero of this book narrowly missed growing up a Belgian. (*Der Junge Beethoven*, 1925, p. 97.)

[7]*Johannes der Täufer.*

hard-working, amiable, and tactful. It is reported that no one ever saw her smile. She did the best she could with her worthless husband. But that was not much. Submerged by hard work, frequent pregnancies, poverty and shame, she could not give her children the care which her tenderness prompted. Neither could she draw solace and inspiration from any proud realization of what a treasure she had given the world.

Chapter II

A TOWN OF MUSIC LOVERS

Ludwig's Birth, December 16, 1770 — No. 20 Bonngasse — Family Misery — A Musical Atmosphere — How the Elector Sacked the Classics — The Elector's Love of a Practical Joke — 1780, Max Franz, a Fiddling Elector — A Street of Music Lovers — Early Trios Op. 1, 3, 8, and 9 — Second-Violin Trouble — "Man, Help Thyself!" — A Rich Period for the Arts — Teachers

IN DECEMBER, 1770, Ludwig was born in Bonn.[1] No one knows the exact date, but he was christened December 17th, and at that time it was a Rhenish custom to baptize children within twenty-four hours of their birth. His mother was twenty-four years old and his father, thirty. He was their second child.

The infant, who was to be worshipped as "the saviour of music" by wise men yet unborn, first made himself heard in a room assuredly more lowly and probably more picturesque than the manger of Bethlehem. A man of average height must stoop under the beams of the little mansard chamber in No. 20 Bonngasse.[2] On the wall outside an old crane still hangs, and a splendid vine with a stem now thick as a man's leg. In the garden there is a portentous pendulum pump four yards tall.

---

[1] There must have been something emancipatory about 1770, for in this same year was born William Wordsworth, the man who was to free English poetry from its moss-covered conventions.

[2] In 1770 it was No. 515 Bonngasse.

For Ludwig himself it was unlucky to have been born under such conditions. Poverty and family misery bore harder on him as a child than they ever have on any other great composer, not excepting Haydn. But for the world it was a huge piece of luck that he descended from a cook, a valet's widow, and a poor drunken singer and had ancestors with liberty-loving Flemish blood in their veins. If he had been born into the German "society" of the day he might never have emancipated music from the bonds of fashion.

Bonn has long stood as the typical small German city. It is appropriate that the standard exemplar of the typical German art should have come from there.

At once little Ludwig began to breathe a thoroughly musical atmosphere and to imbibe a tradition of creativeness—such as it was—agreeably spiced with honesty.

Half a century before the boy's birth Joseph Clemens, the Elector up in the big castle, was a forward-looking composer. His equipment and methods were identical with those of the modern composer-prince, Mr. Israel Baline, who is better known as "Irving Berlin."

As Clemens did not know his notes he would sing, to a sort of stenographer-composer in his employ, whatever came into his head. This functionary put the tunes on paper, adding appropriate harmony. Like Berlin, Clemens pilfered freely from the classics. "The *methodum* which I use," he confessed, "is that of the bees who extract and carry away the honey from the most toothsome flowers; so I also have taken all my compositions from excellent masters whose *Musikalien* pleased me. Though some deny their thefts, and try to get credit for what they steal from others, you see that I frankly confess my own. So, let nobody be wroth if he hears old arias in my work, for, as they are beautiful, the old is not deprived of its praise. . . . I attribute everything to the grace of God who enlightened me, the unknowing, to do these things."

From which it may be seen that the loathsome habit of openly sacking the classics is no more confined to the jazz age than it was to the baroque. But the jazz age has made one welcome improvement. It no longer attributes these crimes "to the grace of God"!

Perhaps, however, Clemens said that last bit—as our own Samuel Clemens might have said it later on—with his tongue in his cheek. He was an old boy who dearly loved his practical joke. And he intensively cultivated a brand of horseplay which may have set a standard Bonn tradition. For the like of it, as we shall later see, was pursued with gusto by Beethoven himself.

Shortly after his consecration as archbishop, Clemens publicly announced that on the first of April he would deliver a sermon in church. When the time came he climbed solemnly into the pulpit, bowed ceremoniously, made the sign of the cross, then suddenly shouted, "April fool!" and hastened out, shaking with mirth, amid a mocking tucket of trumpets and rattle of drums.

All the successors of this sportive Elector, until they were done away with in 1794, were friendly to the cause of good music. It was a fortunate thing. One shudders to reflect what the art might have lost if "Spangy" had been born and raised in, say, the Russian slum and the Bowery cabarets that stepmothered Irving Berlin.

Max Franz, who succeeded to the Electorship in 1780, when Ludwig was going on ten, was a generous patron of the arts. He helped music most of all, on account of being an ardent amateur viola player. He often had musical evenings up at the castle, and sometimes invited the public to listen. Naturally his subjects patterned after him. In the Bonn of 1780 the family string quartet or orchestra was as common a sight as it is rare in the Pittsburgh of to-day.

If all other sources of information had been destroyed we could deduce this intimate musical atmosphere from the first published compositions which Ludwig, soon after leaving home, dignified by opus numbers. One could tell that the creator of the piano trios (Op. 1) and the string trio in E flat (Op. 3) had been born and bred in a street where, as in the typical pipe dream of the impassioned chamber-music "fan," you had only to whistle some well-known string quartet tune (say the Eighteenth Century equivalent of what the beginning of Beethoven's Seventh quartet is for us) and eager heads would pop out of windows on both sides of the street. Down towards the Rhine and up towards the *Münster,* enthusiastic counter tunes would come whistling back, with all degrees of in-tuneness, from a whole neighbourhood of puckered lips.

Yes, the Bonngasse was a highly musical street. In the same house with the Beethovens lived the Salomons. The father fiddled in the opera. The two daughters sang at

[11]

court. But their chief joy and pride was Johann, the son who was away carving out a brilliant career as violinist in Berlin and London. He graduated into a successful impresario and, in 1790, persuaded Haydn to visit England. Later on he was destined to further Ludwig's interests there. Grandpa Ludovicus van Beethoven, the chapelmaster, had a house nearly opposite. Next to him lived that thoroughly musical establishment, the Rieses'. Ludwig took violin lessons from Franz the father.[3] A little down the street lived Simrock, the hornist, who later on was to be one of Ludwig's publishers.

The three trios for violin, violoncello, and piano (Op. 1) are still necessary staples in chamber-music circles when pianists with no more technic than they should have, join the strings. The string trio in E flat (Op. 3) is an earlier work. Its first draft was almost certainly written before Beethoven left Bonn for good in 1792. This delightful composition reveals its maker as a young chap who had plumbed the distressful vicissitudes of the amateur string quartet party. He knew it for what it was, an institution which almost always developed second-violin trouble, either through exhaustion, boredom, "fiddle-neck," envy, hurt pride, or friction with brother viola. Ludwig, himself a viola player of sorts, had evidently encountered this difficulty. He resolved by a bold stroke to make amateur fiddlers forever independent of the inevitable worst.[4] The "fans" of

---

[3] Years afterwards he repaid them by accepting Ferdinand, the son, as pupil and disciple-of-all-work.

[4] Mozart, it is true, had in 1788 written a *divertimento* in E flat for violin, viola, and violoncello. But the piece was too much for the technic of most amateurs—and is to this day.

Bonn must have been grateful to him for filling that bitter want. One can see what an enthusiastic reception opus 3 must have had from the fact that opus 8 and 9 consisted of a serenade and three more trios for string-quartet-minus-absentee.

Writing these trios and making them almost as full and rich as the ordinary string quartet was an act of such characteristic self-reliance as had, at an early date, been drilled into Ludwig by the poverty and drunkenness of his father. This manly quality was reënforced by his love and pity for his poor mother and by a responsible executive job which he won at twelve years. This was to sit at the cembalo in the orchestra, read from score, and come to the rescue of any faltering player. One of the most famous *mots* of his maturity was to be: "Man, help thyself!" "Spangy" had already begun to practise this bit of preaching under the form of "Boy, help thyself!"

Beethoven's youth fell in a rich period for the German arts. In rapid-fire succession there appeared Lessing's *Minna von Barnhelm* and *Nathan the Wise*; Goethe's *Werther* and *Goetz*; Schiller's *The Robbers* and *Don Carlos*; Gluck's epoch-making operas *Orpheus* and *Alceste*; Mozart's *Abduction from the Seraglio,* his finest symphonies and quartets; and some of Haydn's best chamber music.

A weaker personality than Beethoven's would have been cowed by all this brilliance into chronic imitativeness. But without crushing him in the least it only stimulated the young musician. True, for a few years he played the "sedulous ape" to Haydn and Mozart. But that was only to get up momentum. He soon learned to borrow so creatively as to cover his loans.

The paternal ambition to make "Spangy" another such gold-coining infant prodigy as Mozart had been, combined with the paternal weakness for elbow-lifting, very soon transformed a natural, fun-loving small boy into a temporarily serious and careworn little adult who walked with a preoccupied stoop.

His first teachers were his father and an old organist named Van den Eeden. But at nine he was turned over to a royal good fellow named Pfeiffer, Johann's boon companion and associate gullet-baptist. The pair used sometimes to reel into the small house in the small hours, pull "Spangy" whimpering out of bed, and give him a severe piano lesson that lasted until dawn, with plenty of blows for a sleep-drunken little boy who was not quite up to the mark.

Chapter III

THE SPANISH CASTLE TUNES

*Neefe, the Music Master, 1779 — Hiller's Æsthetic Ideas
— Music vs. Literature — The Bagatelles of 1782 — Start-
ing the Ball of Romanticism — Becomes Court Organist,
1784 — Visits Vienna, 1787 — Praise from Mozart —
Mother's Death — A Second Home at the Von Breunings
— Slow Ripening — Count Waldstein — Improvisation —
Head of the Family — Encouragement from Haydn, 1792
— Name First Joined with Those of Mozart and Haydn*

No WONDER "Spangy" began to put away the glorious
follies of youth at an age when he should have embraced
them with both arms. No wonder he began at nine to lay
the foundations of a shy, morose, irritable, suspicious, uncouth, misanthropic manhood. No wonder he turned to his
engrossing reveries full of Spanish castle tunes, as an escape
from the harsh actualities of life.

But help was at hand in the person of a real teacher.
Christian Gottlob Neefe, when he arrived in Bonn in 1779,
was a composer of moderate celebrity, a good organist, and
an excellent all-around musician.

His middle name, Gottlob, means "Praise God!" Music
lovers echo it when they consider the happy chance that
gave Ludwig such a mentor and friend before he was eleven
and had stopped school. For at this impressionable age he
was most in need of inspiration and guidance.

Neefe played an invaluable part in forming the man who was to free music. He was a small, stoop-shouldered tailor's son from Chemnitz, a touching figure. If we knew nothing else about him we could guess at his unusual intelligence from the fact that he gave "Spangy" Bach's *Welltempered Clavichord* to study when that now famous work was still in manuscript.

It was not long before Neefe made of the lad a better pianist, organist, and composer than he himself was. He did something more important. He started him on the way towards adopting a new philosophy of music, destined to play an important rôle in revolutionizing the art.

He filled the boy with the ideas of his friend and master, Johann Adam Hiller. Hiller was partly responsible for that revolution by which the æsthetic ideas of the Nineteenth Century were drastically to break with those of the Eighteenth. According to the latter the duty of music was to reflect concrete ideas and definite pictures of the world —to be both illustrations and musical settings of the text of life.

But Hiller was one of the useful band of pioneers who were groping towards the truth that music can never be definite and concrete like words or pictures. Dimly he saw that its chief glory is its indefinite, abstract, universal quality, and that whatever tends to constrict that glory to the concrete function of illustrator sins against the art.

With the exception of such advanced spirits as Johann Sebastian Bach and Mozart at his greatest,—men who were not in full sympathy with their own epoch and were more or less ignored by it,*—the Eighteenth Century tended to see a piece of music as a single picture. The Nineteenth came to look upon it more as a frame suitable for any one of millions of pictures painted in a certain mood. The composer furnishes the frame; the imagination of the creative listener supplies its own picture. Those naïve books about "the meaning of music" which inform us that the C minor symphony can only depict fate thundering at the door of human life, or that the C sharp minor sonata exclusively indicates a moonlit garden with a deaf Beethoven making love to the Countess Giulietta Guicciardi, are in tune with the spirit of the Eighteenth Century but are unfit for our times.

The Eighteenth Century was more disposed to ask music, "What do you mean?" the Nineteenth, to ask, "What do you mean to me?" The Eighteenth tended to think the abstract, universal element of music its worst weakness; the Nineteenth, to see in this element its supreme strength.

Neither Hiller nor Neefe personally went as far as this. But they started Beethoven on his Promethean way, towards freeing music from the bonds of the literal. Small wonder that, all his life long, the composer's unconscious trend was away from the necessary concreteness of vocal music towards the imaginative liberty of instrumental.

The first drafts of most of the Bagatelles known as opus 33 were probably written in 1782. Here we have the first glimpse of Beethoven in his rôle as emancipator of music. The lad of eleven actually sounded a new note in the

---

*Although popular, Haydn. the innovator was also an exception.

history of piano literature. These little pieces, though not so remarkable in content as was Beethoven's highly original use of the word "Bagatelle," were destined to be powerful factors in freeing the piano from its slavery to the larger forms exclusively. The Bagatelles founded the family which was to boast such progeny as the Schubert *Impromptus*, the Chopin *Preludes*, the Schumann *Kinderscenen*, the Brahms *Intermezzi*, and Debussy's *Arabesques*.

At thirteen "Spangy" blossomed out into the precocious dignity of court organist. Through Frau Fischer's eyes we see him dressed up for a function at the Castle, "in sea-green tailcoat, a flowered waistcoat of white satin, green knee-breeches with buckles, white silk stockings, black rosetted shoes, with his crush hat under his left arm, his dagger at his side, and crowned with curls and a pigtail of real hair."

This is her description of the boy himself: "Short, stocky, broad shoulders, short neck, thick head, round nose, black-ish brown complexion."

At sixteen Ludwig visited Vienna. We know little about his short stay there except that he played for Mozart. At first he made small impression on this young master and saw that Mozart felt he had prepared his improvisations. Piqued, the lad demanded an original theme. The famous composer gave him one with a catch in it[1]—a melody so well hidden that only a musical intelligence of a high order could discover it. Ludwig pounced instantly upon this hidden tune and improvised on it with such brilliant inspiration

---

[1] See Sir George Grove, *Beethoven and His Nine Symphonies*, 1896, p. 252, n.

that the great man walked into the next room exclaiming: "Watch that chap! Some day he'll make the world talk about him."

He was recalled to Bonn by his beloved mother's last illness and reached there only in time for the end. All his life long he was to fear for himself the tuberculosis which killed her. John the Gullet-Baptist immediately sold her clothes to the peddlers in order to buy further libations. And Ludwig had the shame of seeing his mother's dresses hawked about in the market-place. The boy had always ardently loved this fine woman with the sad eyes which had never been known to smile; and he took her loss deeply to heart.

Towards the end of 1787, he fortunately secured two pupils in a cultured patrician family, the Von Breunings. In the son Stephan, four years younger, he found a lifelong friend, as well as in the daughter Eleonore, who was two years his junior.[2] Frau von Breuning became his second mother. This most tactful and understanding lady took him lovingly in hand, rounded off many of his sharper corners, introduced him to literature and cultured society. Soon he looked upon the Von Breunings' house as his alternative home.

Before 1792, the year he settled permanently in Vienna, Ludwig did not compose anything particularly noteworthy. For early brilliance he was never in the same class with Mozart, who, as a lad of nineteen, wrote *La Finta Giardiniera;* nor with Schubert and Mendelssohn, who at seven-

---

[2] Professor Ludwig Schiedermair states that Eleonore was the object of Ludwig's first serious passion. (*Der Junge Beethoven,* 1925, p. 207.)

teen tossed off respectively *Gretchen at the Spinning Wheel* and the *Midsummer Night's Dream* overture.

Like Bach, Wagner, Brahms, and Franck, who never found their start until they had passed twenty, Beethoven belonged among the late developing geniuses. Wagner, indeed, did not write *The Flying Dutchman* until he was thirty; and Franck waited until forty-eight before creating his first masterpiece, *The Beatitudes*. The slowly ripening fruits are usually better. They have more juice.

"One must be something in order to accomplish something," said Goethe. And here in the fruitful valley of the Rhine was slowly ripening a tremendous personality, magnetic, incalculable, of infinite richness, of inexhaustible interest. All the best of his work was destined to be a direct reflection of that personality.

Among his best friends in Bonn were Franz Wegeler, who afterwards married Eleonore von Breuning, and Count Ferdinand von Waldstein, whom he was to immortalize by an important dedication. The Count became his first patron, saving his pride by conveying badly needed funds to him so tactfully that they seemed to be presents from the Elector.[3]

---

[3]Count Waldstein, Ludwig's senior by eight years, had been reared in the Bohemian castle of Dux. In 1785, a year or two before he left for Bonn, the famous Casanova had arrived and had been appointed librarian of Dux. This rake of sixty, expelled from most of Europe and worn out by his escapades, had settled down there to write his memoirs. One wonders what sort of influence the magnetic old man exerted on the sensitive character of young Waldstein, and whether any of that influence, transmitted perhaps to Ludwig by his first patron, may have been responsible for his physical misfortunes. In her *Memories* Countess Lulu Thürheim says that Waldstein was "the plaything of scoundrels who frequently compromised his honour. He often miserably smirched his glorious name . . . and approached the dirt too closely to escape being sprinkled with mud." (Quoted in Schiedermair, *Der Junge Beethoven*, p. 179.) We

Waldstein was the first to realize what a genius Bonn had produced. And he was the first to develop Ludwig's extraordinary talent for improvising on a given theme, an accomplishment which was to prove a useful entering wedge in the Vienna days to come. Ludwig soon became a master of this sort of playing and began to pour into it at twenty that original emotional power which was destined to free music from the toils of rococo fashion.

In a journal by Carl Ludwig Junker, Prince Hohenlohe's chaplain, we have a vivid impression of how that power struck a contemporary.

I also heard one of the greatest of pianists, the dear good Bethofen [sic]. . . . I heard him extemporize in private; yes, I was even invited to propose a theme for him to vary. The greatness of this amiable, light-hearted man, as a virtuoso, may in my opinion be safely estimated from his almost inexhaustible wealth of ideas, the altogether characteristic style of expression in his playing and the great execution which he displays. I know, therefore, no one thing which he lacks, that conduces to the greatness of an artist. I have heard Vogler[4] upon the pianoforte . . . and never failed to wonder at his astonishing execution; but Bethofen, in addition to the execution, has greater clearness and weight of idea, and more expression—in short, he is more for the heart—equally great, therefore, as an *Adagio* or *Allegro* player. Even the members of this remarkable orchestra are, without exception, his admirers, and are all ears when he plays. Yet he is exceedingly modest and free from all pretension. . . . His style of treating his instrument is so different from that usually adopted, that it impresses one with the idea that by a path of his own discovery he has attained that height of excellence on which he now stands.

know that Beethoven's friendship for the Count had cooled years before 1823, when Waldstein died in poverty at Vienna.

[4]This was the Abt Vogler of Robert Browning's famous poem.

Ludwig was now the head of the family. By court order he directly drew half of the paternal Gullet-Baptist's salary "besides the salary which he now draws, and the three measures of grain for the support of his brothers." For four years he played viola in the theatre orchestra. This experience was to prove invaluable to him as a symphonist. He fell violently in love with two young girls, Jeanette d'Horvath and Marie Westerhold, and promptly fell out again.

One day in 1792 Haydn passed through Bonn. Then the world opened wide before Ludwig; for Haydn encouraged the young man to visit Vienna and study with him. Count Waldstein thought highly of the scheme and used his influence with the Elector. Finally all was arranged. Beethoven was to have his chance. Waldstein obtained him a long leave of absence with salary and sent him a charming and inspiring farewell letter. It ended with the exhortation: "Receive Mozart's spirit from the hands of Haydn."

This letter was noteworthy, not as an accurate prophecy, but because it associated for the first time the three musical names which have since come to form a classic trinity. The fact is, the Count's last sentence flew wide of the target. For, as usual, Beethoven bettered his well-meaning friend's idea. He acted on his life principle, "Man, help thyself!" He went in for nothing second-hand. Instead, as his Sketch Books reveal, he worked out his own salvation with agony and grim fortitude. Result: something that transcended even Haydn's genial craftsmanship and Mozart's luminous spirit. Out of it was to emerge the focal personality of the art of music—and its emancipator.

Chapter IV

YOUNG PYGMALION AND THE PLASTER CASTS

Vienna, 1792 — Social Success — Dress and Dance —
Haydn's Neglect — Lessons from Schenck Sub Rosa —
Studies with Albrechtsberger, 1793–1795 — Fugues and
the Breath of Life

ON THE 10th of November, 1792, Bonn's great man, not yet twenty-two, arrived in Vienna to seek his fortune. He was small, thin, homely, pock-marked, unkempt, morose-looking. His protruding front teeth forced his lips out at an awkward angle. He had an uncouth gait and a low-comedy Rhenish accent. His purse was light. Though the Elector promised to continue his small organist's salary, only a minute portion of this was ever paid, and it soon turned spectre-thin and died.

His only assets were a strong personality, a few letters of introduction from Count von Waldstein—and genius. With these he soon had the Viennese nobility at his feet.

Young Beethoven possessed one startling gift which instantly struck the Austrian fancy. It is almost pathetic that the attention of Vienna was first caught and its imagination first excited, not by the intrinsic merit of Beethoven's compositions,—for opus 1 was not published until 1795, three years later,—but by his ability to improvise on any theme whatever.

The banality of most of his first sketches would suggest that his improvisings could not have been as creatively brilliant as they have been reported. Either his contemporaries were dazzled and made less critical by the personal authority and charm of the man, or the performances were mentally prepared in advance to a greater extent than they realized. His melodramatic "stunts," like improvising fluently from Steibelt's upside-down violoncello part[1] must have astonished people too much to let them soberly assay the actual worth of the music.

On such a gift was built up the fame of "Blind Tom," the negro idiot. To prize a Beethoven exclusively for it was like valuing a gold mine for the size of the sunflowers that grow around the shaft entrance.

There is a danger inherent in this endowment. A brilliant sight reader is apt to despise technical grind and neglect finish, so that, as the saying goes, he reads better than he plays. Similarly the composer who can improvise is tempted to be frivolous and superficial—to relinquish the "lamp at midnight hour" in favour of the pinwheel.

Beethoven's calibre was large enough to avoid this danger. He was that almost mythical person—a brilliant improvisator who could, and did, take infinite pains. An inspiring commentary on these pains is offered by his Sketch Books, now in the Prussian State Library in Berlin. They furnish thrilling evidence that at least one improvisator of the first order could rewrite a tune ten, twenty, fifty times, until it assumed the one inevitable final form.

---

[1]See pp. 72–73.

Ludwig's first thought on arrival in Vienna was to make himself presentable. For a gentleman this was harder and more expensive then than now. "I must buy an entirely new outfit," we read in his notebook, with exact entries of the prices he had paid for silk stockings, boots and shoes. After that the address of the dancing master from whom this lord of rhythm tried (actually in vain!) to learn how to oblige his feet to follow the dictates of his head.[2]

Haydn did not go back on the letter of the promise he had made in Bonn. He gave the young student instruction in harmony and counterpoint. Nor did the most famous living composer overcharge him. "*Haidn 8 Groschen*" is an entry in his notebook for December 12, 1792. This fee was the equivalent in present buying power of about $3.20. What would Stravinsky, Strauss, Schoenberg, or Ravel charge to-day for a single private theory lesson?

It was not long before Beethoven found that his genial but somewhat toplofty master was giving him scant attention and correcting few of the many errors in his exercises. M. D'Indy strives to justify this neglect on the ground that Beethoven was studying composition with Haydn and that

---

[2]That Beethoven could never manage to dance in time is strange, but no more so than that Tennyson, Swinburne, Matthew Arnold, and our own Robert Frost should have had no ear for music. Tennyson's lack of musical common sense comes out in that curious passage where, in "Maud," he rhymed a weirdly compounded orchestra consisting of

"flute, violin, bassoon,"

with an even more impossible factor:

"the dancers dancing in tune."

Besides owning legs that would not obey a rhythmical brain, Beethoven probably had, even before his deafness, a poor ear for music, so far as pitch was concerned. Amenda relates that when the Master once undertook to play the violin for him the result was so fantastically out of tune that he had to yell for mercy.

a teacher of composition cannot be bothered by the small grammatical details of harmony and counterpoint.[3] But after weighing all known manuscripts and authorities that bear on this point Nottebohm and Thayer concluded that counterpoint and the theory of harmony were what Beethoven was studying and that Haydn was not conscientious with him.

If this had happened later on, when deafness had made him morose and recognition had made him imperious, Beethoven would most likely have thrown the exercise book at his old master's head. But in 1792 the student still had his way to make; and so he performed prodigies of tact and self-mastery. Instead of treating Haydn to violence he treated him to drinks, as witness these entries in the diary: "Coffee 6 kreutzer for Haidn and me"; and again: "22 kreutzer for Haidn and me, chocolate."

To balance the famous man's neglect he took theory lessons in secret from the now forgotten composer Johann Schenck. But so closely did he follow the path of prudence as to recopy the exercises Schenck had corrected, before submitting them to Haydn. This farce continued until the latter left for London, at the end of 1793, turning his pupil over to the renowned Albrechtsberger.

With astonishing and commendable self-control Beethoven kept hard at counterpoint, although the Spanish castles—now more full of sirens than those rocks which Ulysses almost failed to pass—kept charming him with their most seductive tunes. He was wild to compose real music.

---

[3] Vincent D'Indy, *Beethoven*, 1913, pp. 16–17.

Yet until April, 1795, he turned up doggedly three times a week at the grim old master's door.

There is no doubt that the excellent professor gave Beethoven much highly useful information and desperately needed discipline. He also did his conscientious best to interest the future composer of the C sharp minor quartet in the art of casting, in dead, cold, white plaster, what Beethoven afterwards described as "musical skeletons."

Long afterwards, in recalling these days, the latter remarked to Holz that there was "no art in making a fugue." The difficulty was to let 'imagination also claim its rights' —to breathe into the thing the breath of life—to endow it with "a truly poetic element."[4]

Shattering thought! Why, if any pupil had dared to try endowing a fugue with a poetic element in the old professor's presence, Herr Albrechtsberger would have been as profoundly shocked as if, in passing through the museum of antique casts, he had accidentally noticed some young Pygmalion luring the flush of life to the cheek of a plaster Galatea.

---

[4]See p. 374.

Chapter V

THE MUSICIAN MOVES ABOVE
THE SALT

*Discipline — Revolt — Studies with Salieri — Attic to
Palace — A Talented Nobility — Privileges at Court —
Outwitting the Musical Parasites — Proud Independence*

THIS sort of discipline was just what Beethoven needed.
His early training had been sketchy. After infancy licence
to follow his musical whims had been liberally accorded
the boy prodigy of Bonn. The new regimen was excellent
for him.

All the same, he reacted vigorously against Albrechtsberger's sacrosanct pedantries. Now and then, along the
road to Parnassus, when a silver-haired old rule, half asleep
in the sun, saw the chariot of Beethoven's creative inspiration bearing down, it had to jump wildly for a doorway or be flattened out by the thundering wheels and
hooves.

The old professor was somewhat shaken by his contact
with young Pygmalion. A few years later he was heard to
growl, with a sad shake of the head, words to this effect:
"No, Beethoven never learned anything; and what's more,
he never *will* write anything worth while." This was much
the attitude that Cherubini was destined to adopt toward
Berlioz; and the dignitaries of the Milan Conservatory
toward young Verdi.

Ferdinand Ries, who personally knew all of Beethoven's teachers, said they were unanimous in declaring the young fellow was always so headstrong and self-willed that he had to learn many things by bitter experience which he never was willing to learn from a lesson.

And a very good thing too. If he had been more docile he could never have been the man to set music free. The wonder is that, at twenty-two, an age when his personality was already powerfully developed and his own ideas clamouring for utterance, he could have found the self-mastery to learn one half of all he learned from Haydn, Schenck, and Albrechtsberger about theory, and last of all from Salieri about song-composition and the musical setting of Italian words.

In a moment of extreme revolt Beethoven once remarked that Haydn had never taught him anything. And his attitude towards Albrechtsberger was somewhat cold and formal. But at the height of his fame he expressed himself towards old Schenck with charming gratitude. An episode which occurred long after showed one of the pleasantest sides of his nature: Calling on the aged Salieri one afternoon in 1809 and finding him out, he left a slip of paper with these words scrawled in huge characters: "The pupil Beethoven was here." The pupil Beethoven! And this was the celebrity who had already written the *Eroica* and Fifth symphonies, the *"Appassionata"* sonata, the *"Emperor"* concerto, and *Fidelio*.

Financially and socially Beethoven fast made his way. On his arrival he lodged in an attic. Soon he was able to move to the ground floor. And in little more than a year he was living in the palatial home of Prince Lichnowsky, more as son than guest. With the charm which he sometimes put into words as well as tones he once remarked of his hostess: "The Princess was within one of enclosing me in a glass bell, so that the unworthy might neither touch nor breathe upon me!"

These so sympathetic, intelligent, and impressionable aristocrats must have had a strong influence upon the sensitive young fellow. The Prince was an ardent Anglophile and loved to give himself, as M. de Hevesy quaintly says,[1] "*l'aspect et la contenance*" of a lord. This may help to explain the origin of the composer's steadfast love of England and those exaggerated ideas of her perfection, which he never lost, even after George IV ignored his gift of the "*Battle*" symphony.

As soon as the Viennese nobility realized Beethoven's genius—and they were quick to do so—they gave him an enthusiastic welcome. Their palaces flew open. The young musician entered and held court. He realized his good fortune. A living income with intelligent sympathy and appreciation for his music were what he wanted; and these patricians seemed able and willing to furnish such things.

Many of them were excellent musical amateurs. The Lichnowskys were capable pianists; Baroness von Ertmann, an admirable one. Prince Lobkowitz was a clever fiddler. Prince and Count Esterhazy played respectively the bary-

---

[1] André de Hevesy, *Beethoven, Vie Intime*, 1926, p. 12.

ton[2] and the oboe, while Count Brunswick was a dependable violoncellist.

These were the folk who had supported and appreciated Haydn, Mozart, and the other composers—and had made servants of them. Beethoven was of different calibre. In his teens the Von Breunings and Count Waldstein had accustomed him to mingle with aristocrats on terms of perfect equality. He knew that his genius was a thing of more nobility than all the hereditary titles of Vienna taken in a lump. And the bearers of those titles were compelled by the sheer power of that genius, and of his imperious personality, to accept him at very much his own valuation.

This sudden bridging of social gulfs bears testimony to the compelling charm of the plebeian lad. Unaided by this magnetic power his musical qualities alone would never have been able to win a strategic social position for himself and his successors.

It was too bad that Walt Whitman and his "Poem of Joys" had not yet appeared among men. With what authentic conviction and authority Beethoven could have set to music such a passage as:

O the joy of a manly self-hood! . . .
To confront with your personality all the other personalities
    of the earth.

He had a pleasant friendship with Prince Lobkowitz, but under the express stipulation that he should hold up his end of a discussion "as though they were of equal birth."

---

[2] A sort of *viola da gamba* fitted with sympathetic strings. Haydn wrote many baryton compositions for the Prince, his master.

We shall see how he complained to his imperial pupil, the Archduke Rudolph, of the court officials' pedantry and flatly refused to be bullied and taught etiquette by them. One day the Archduke kept Beethoven waiting before a lesson, and the Master, in revenge, gave the young prince's fingers a severe twisting.

RUDOLPH: Why are you so impatient?

BEETHOVEN: You wasted my time in the anteroom.

It never occurred again.

Beethoven's independent blood would not tolerate the docile position which society had always imposed on the maker of music. The court of Stuttgart might compel Spohr to fiddle while the audience played cards; the Saxon court might make Moscheles play the piano during the dinner hour. But Beethoven was of a more mettlesome breed. Once while performing with Ries at Count von Browne's in Baden he was disturbed by Count von Palffy's loud voice in the next room. Instantly he sprang up from the instrument and cried in a still louder voice: "For such swine play I not!"

He was probably the first member of his craft to oppose a ferocious front to those parasites who insist on the musician giving them his professional services for nothing. The young man from Bonn became so rudely obdurate that the spongers were driven to all manner of ruses.

One was to herd the guests into the next room and leave the virtuoso alone with the piano. If that did not work the crafty host would spirit out of the way all but one chair and the piano stool. He would occupy the chair, and Beethoven, by a process of elimination, the stool. His absent-minded hand would strike a chord or two. Then, before he knew it, he would be in the mid-tide of improvisation.

One host always left music paper about, hoping to reap some composition as a souvenir. The Master often wrote on it, but invariably remembered to fold it up and carry it away.

Beethoven led the musical leeches a hard life. It was no uncommon thing for titled ladies to go down on their knees, beg him to play—and be refused.

Though he accepted Lichnowsky's hospitality he was quixotically independent. One day he heard the Prince direct his valet that in case he himself and his guest should ring at the same time, the guest must be served first. Without hesitation Beethoven engaged a servant. He wanted to ride. The Prince offered him the freedom of his stables. The proud young musician retorted by setting up a horse of his own.

On the patriarchal dining tables of feudal times the large saltcellar marked an important social boundary. The gentry sat above, the common people below, the salt. Here and now, in the person of this compelling young man of the proud and fiery charm, the musician suddenly cast off his inferiority and moved above the salt.

Chapter VI

HE COMES, HE PLAYS, HE CONQUERS

Musical Conditions in Vienna — First Public Appearance in Vienna, 1795 — B Flat Piano Concerto — Presence of Mind at Rehearsal — Making Money — Father's Death — Sends for Brothers — Trios, Op. 1 — Haydn's Attitude towards Them — "Joseph Vance" Tunes — Ambition

THE art of music has so recently evolved its elaborate material setting that conditions in the world's most musical city a century and a third ago seem primitive to us to-day. In 1795 there was scarcely any public criticism of music outside of London. Vienna had no symphony orchestras except scratch affairs hastily assembled and sketchily rehearsed for special occasions. There were almost no public concerts except those functions called "Academies." These were given by composers to advertise their own compositions, or by well-known virtuosos or prodigies. "Stunt" improvising and trials of skill between composers and pianists were all the rage. Advertising was still in the early embryonic period. Executants and composers instinctively used the servants' entrance.

The man who was already beginning to emancipate these unhappy people and their art actually lived in Vienna for two and a half years, and enjoyed overwhelming success in private, before he had a chance to be heard in public.

This chance came on March 29, 1795, at a concert for

the benefit of the widows and orphans of the Society of Musicians. His old friend Dr. Wegeler tells how he characteristically put off writing the new piano concerto he was to perform until only two days were left for the *finale*. This crisis was complicated by a severe attack of colic. Beethoven worked on the concerto; the doctor worked on the colic; while four copyists toiled in the anteroom, pouncing upon each wet sheet of manuscript and writing out the orchestral parts.

The first rehearsal was held in Beethoven's rooms the day before the concert. There the Master gave an exhibition of musical presence of mind. His pianos usually had something seriously wrong with them. His absent-minded habit of upsetting the inkwell upon the strings could have done them no particular good. This piano turned out to be half a tone lower than the wind instruments. Unhesitatingly the Master had the orchestra tune to the pseudo B flat of the discouraged *Klavier* and played his own part a semitone higher than he had written it.[1]

This was like the feat with which, many years later, a certain young Johannes Brahms was to win the startled admiration of his audience in Celle. Brahms and the violinist Remenyi found a piano too low in pitch to suit the violinist. Instantly the young composer transposed the piano part of Beethoven's C minor violin sonata from memory, a semitone higher. It is appropriate that history should have

[1]Thayer shows that this concerto was the one in B flat (Op. 19), not that in C, as Wegeler thought. So that the Master actually transposed it at sight to the key of B with its five awkward sharps. This reference to Thayer, and those to follow, mean the American edition, the standard three-volume source book of information about Beethoven's life, edited and finished from Thayer's papers by Henry E. Krehbiel, 1921.

doubly repeated itself by bringing a Beethoven composition into this incident.

Ludwig's finances were decidedly improving. He was no longer anxiously noting down the stray coppers invested in temperance drinks "for Haidn and me." Money came in fast—but no faster than he could lavish it on his friends. All was—apparently—right with his world.

His father, John the Gullet-Baptist, had, in 1792, died of too zealous baptistry, without causing much filial grief.[2]

Ludwig had sent for his brothers, promising to establish them in Vienna and life. And he had kept his word. Czerny described the two boys as follows: "Karl: short, red-haired, ugly; Johann: large, dark, a handsome fellow and an absolute dandy." Karl became a third-rate musician; Johann, a druggist. They were destined to be two thorns in their brother's flesh.

In 1795, with three trios for violin, violoncello, and piano (Op. 1), Beethoven made his bow as a regular composer. And a portentous bow it was. These compositions instantly overshadowed all that Haydn and Mozart had ever composed in that form. The older trios had been written with one eye upon the fashionable taste of the Austrian aristocracy. Opus 1, on the other hand, while keeping many a rococo characteristic, was written with an eye single to the expression of strongly personal feeling. It has pages where one can almost overhear the proud commoner exulting in his own mental and spiritual resources.

[2] When the Elector Archbishop heard this news he allowed himself a pleasantry in a letter to Court Marshal von Schall: "The revenues from the liquor excise have suffered a loss in the deaths of Beethoven and Eichhoff."

Ries records that during an evening party at Prince Lichnowsky's Beethoven played these trios to Haydn, from manuscript. The old master said a number of complimentary things about the first two. But he counselled his pupil not to publish the third, in C minor.

This surprised Beethoven, since he considered the third the best of the trios, and it is still the one which gives the greatest pleasure and makes the most effect.

In consequence, Haydn's remark left a bad impression on Beethoven, and led him to suppose that Haydn was envious, jealous and ill-disposed towards him. I confess that when Beethoven told me of this I took small stock in it. So I made an opportunity to ask Haydn himself about it. But his answer confirmed Beethoven's idea; he said he had had no idea that this trio would be so quickly and easily grasped and so well received by the public.

Ries was wrong in concluding that Haydn's statement confirmed Beethoven's idea about his master being jealous and ill disposed. The fact was, the old gentleman did not understand this dazzling new music. Naturally he felt that nobody else would and that the better part of valour would be suppression.

When opus 1 was first tried over by the circle of eminent chamber musicians who met at Tompkinson's piano warehouse in London, J. B. Cramer, the pianist, cried: "This is the man who is to console us for the loss of Mozart!"

One imagines that these prophetic words might have been spoken after the slow movement of the D major trio. It was the newest note, and the most consoling, that had sounded in music for many a long day. This *Largo con espressione* was the first example in Beethoven's work of what admirers of the novelist De Morgan might call the "Joseph Vance" type of melody. "How often have I said to myself, after hearing some especially convincing tune of Beethoven's, 'Why, if that is so, there can be no occasion to worry.'"[3]

This movement was the pioneer in that long line of comforting, reassuring melodies in which Beethoven stood, and stands, supreme. They include the slow movement of the *Pathétique* and *"Appassionata"* sonatas, the second theme of the *"Waldstein's"* opening movement, the *Andante con moto* of the B flat trio (Op. 97), the *Adagio* of the Ninth symphony, and the *Cavatina* of the B flat quartet (Op. 130).

The trios were sold by subscription, and at once netted their composer the tidy sum of 878 gulden, almost six times his wraith-like organist's salary. But success did not in the least go to his head. He resolutely put aside all temptation to capitalize himself by writing down to the popular taste. Instead he scribbled on the margin of a Sketch Book:

Courage! Despite all the weaknesses of the body, my spirit shall rule! Here I am, twenty-five years old. This year must bring out the complete man.—Nothing must remain over.

Surely a heaven-storming program. Not for many a day did the young composer's wagon reach anything like the altitudes of the star he had selected for hitching purposes. But at least, during 1796, it often left the ground.

[3]"I . . . have . . . regarded [Beethoven] as being not so much a Composer as a Revelation. His music always seems to me to explain everything that I can understand, and to supply exhaustive conclusions in all the crucial questions of life and death; and I am satisfied that, when I don't understand, it is my fault, not his." (William de Morgan, *Joseph Vance*, p. 406.)

Chapter VII

"THE GREAT MOGUL"

1796, First Piano Sonatas — First Violoncello Sonatas — Disgusted by Listeners' Tears — His One-Way Sense of Humour — 1797, E Flat Sonata — New Friends — Strength, His Morality — Was Beethoven Conceited? — Haydn and Prometheus — Humility towards Forerunners — Socialistic Ideas — "I too Am a King!" — Ridicules Prince Lobkowitz — Describes Friends as "Instruments on Which I Play" — Quick Alternations of Mood — Jekyll and Hyde

IN 1796 Beethoven published, as opus 2, the first three of his thirty-two piano sonatas.

The first, in F minor, begins imitatively with that familiar formula which was nicknamed, from its contour and its place of origin, "the Mannheim rocket." Mozart had already touched this rocket off in a place of honour, the *finale* of the G minor symphony. Beethoven was to offer it a still loftier distinction in the *scherzo*[1] of the Fifth.[2]

The F minor sonata was probably written in Bonn. It goes along tamely enough, echoing its predecessors, up to the sombre and violent *finale*. At that point, however, Bee-

---

[1]No intelligent discussion of music can be carried on without the use of a certain number of technical terms. These, however, may be so quickly and easily mastered by consulting any book on the appreciation of music, or the Glossary in the Appendix of this work, that no apology will be offered for the occasional use of such words as 'scherzo," "coda," and "development."

[2]See p. 222.

thoven breaks with the rococo tradition that a closing movement should be a suavely cheerful affair, guaranteed to put the aristocrats into a good temper. Without offering much of purely musical interest these pages are prophetic.

The next two sonatas bear the unmistakable stamp of Vienna. They were chiefly intended for the display of their composer's virtuosity as pianist. This they accomplished in a fashion that took the wind out of Haydn's and Mozart's sails and established a new standard of sonata technic.

But their display element was still obviously unsublimated. In later sonatas, the *"Moonlight,"* the *"Waldstein,"* and the *"Appassionata,"* we shall find virtuosity the obedient and intelligent slave of the emotional and intellectual factors.

The A major (Op. 2, No. 2) is remarkable for a *Largo appassionato* shaken by such a depth charge of emotion as had never yet been encountered by a piano sonata. To us of to-day its harmonic idiom is admittedly somewhat outworn, but to 1796 it was an amazing portent. We can have small conception how such revolutionary music stirred the souls of men when these old chords were new.

The opening movement of the C major sonata (Op. 2, No. 3), like the *Adagio* of the F minor, was elaborated from a boyish quartet and shows an astounding advance over its original. The third movement is the first true *scherzo* (with coda) among the sonatas; although the A major contains an *allegretto* movement labelled *"Scherzo,"* a forerunner of the form which was to be one of the Master's most original contributions to his art.

In spite of its obtrusive virtuosity this C major sonata overflows with the laughing exultation of a young provincial, sound in body, emotionally exuberant, conscious of superiority, who came and played, and conquered the musical capital of the world.

Opus 2 was dedicated "*A Mr. Joseph Haydn Docteur en musique.*" "Papa" wished the younger man to describe himself on the title page as "pupil of Haydn." But Beethoven demurred. He felt that the old master's very moderate exertions on his behalf had not entirely justified the claim.

Having taken Vienna by storm in 1795, the following year Beethoven tried Berlin. For use on this trip he wrote two violoncello and piano sonatas (Op. 5) and dedicated them to Friedrich Wilhelm II, King of Prussia.

These sonatas were constructed on the curious plan (afterwards abandoned as monotonous) of two fast movements with a long, slow introduction. The F major breathes the freshness of youth—and some of its faults. Its reach exceeds its grasp. It is comparatively callow and superficial. But the G minor (Op. 5, No. 2), although its light, gay, closing rondo seems something of a misfit, is the most fiery, moving, and impressive sonata for violoncello which had up to that time appeared on earth.[3]

Beethoven played at the court of Berlin and was rewarded by a gold snuffbox filled with louis d'or—"no

---

[3]The reader may object: "How about the sonatas of Johann Sebastian Bach?" The six famous compositions popularly known as the "violoncello suites" were originally composed for the violoncello piccolo, a five-stringed cross between the viola and the violoncello, invented by the Father of Music. Of his three so-called "violoncello and piano" sonatas, Bach wrote those in D major and G minor for *viola da gamba* and cembalo; and the first, in G major, for two flutes and cembalo, afterwards arranging it for *gamba*.

ordinary snuffbox," he proudly explained, "but the sort usually given ambassadors."

On two occasions he improvised at the Singakademie. The audience, profoundly moved, paid him the tribute of tears, which only disgusted the young Master. "That's not what we artists want," he explained long afterwards, in recalling the scene. "We want applause!"

An incident which happened during this trip showed his one-way sense of humour. In a duel of improvisation with the well-known pianist, Himmel, Beethoven let the latter play for a time, then remarked: "But look here, when are you going to begin?" Himmel, furious, finally made it up with him but resolved to get even. After Beethoven's return to Vienna the Berliner wrote that everybody was talking about the latest invention, a lamp for the blind. Swallowing the bait, Beethoven eagerly demanded more details, only to receive a coarse epistolary horse laugh that filled him with unforgiving rage.

The fourth piano sonata, in E flat (Op. 7), appeared in 1797. It showed a still unclouded exuberance and zest in life, with a considerable advance in freedom of part writing, in the fusing of technic with emotion and the conscious with the unconscious. Though the so-called "*Appassionata*" is by no means an erotic composition one finds it hard to agree with Czerny's feeling that this E flat sonata glows with an emotion so much more ardent that it, and not opus 57, should have received that famous name.

The young composer had now collected around him a

number of devotedly adoring friends: Carl Amenda, a young theological student and fiddler; Ignaz Schuppanzigh, the fat violinist whom he nicknamed "Milord Falstaff"; Freiherr Nikolaus Zmeskall von Domanovecz, a Bohemian nobleman who wielded an agile violoncello bow and was only too happy to fetch and carry for such a man.

Like many others, Zmeskall was often so cringingly humble to his master that the latter noted in his most famous love letter: "The humility of men to men,—it pains me." (See p. 299.)

But when the factotum took heart and ventured so far from humility as to read the celebrity a lecture for his own good, it seemed to pain him still more. And he countered with: "Devil take you! I want to hear nothing of your moral ideas. Strength is the morality of men who show themselves superior to others, and it is mine." This outburst may have inspired Nietzsche, some years later, in the construction of his "superman."

Beethoven was now nearing twenty-eight, and his friends noticed that he began to lose the more quiet, retiring manner of his youth, and to take a somewhat high tone. His enemies, and even others, called him conceited. Papa Haydn referred to him, with a twinkle, as "The Great Mogul."

If Beethoven was conceited he entertained a more favourable opinion of himself than the facts would warrant. But did he?

One day in 1801, just after the opening of *The Creations of Prometheus,* he met Haydn, who caught hold of him and said: "I heard your ballet yesterday and liked it very much."

"Dear Papa," replied Beethoven, who could seldom resist a pun of any sort, "you are awfully good, but it's a long way from being a *Creation*."

Haydn was surprised by this answer. He was almost ruffled. After an awkward pause he responded: "True, it's no 'Creation.' What's more, I scarcely think it ever will be." They parted with mutual embarrassment.

On his deathbed Beethoven received two presents: a picture of Haydn's birthplace and the complete works of Handel. He cherished the former as a small boy cherishes a red tin submarine and called out to a visitor: "See this little house; and in it such a great man was born!" Of Handel he said: "To him I bow my knee!" Of himself he confessed: "It seems to me as though I hadn't written anything yet."

The following incident shows his attitude toward Mozart. One day in 1799 he attended a promenade concert in the Augarten with Cramer. They were walking slowly about, listening to Mozart's C minor concerto. At a particularly fine passage Beethoven pulled up short, exclaiming: "Cramer, Cramer,—we'll never be in a position to make the like of that!" And this from the man who had already written the C minor trio, the G minor violoncello sonata, and the piano sonatas in E flat, D major, and C minor: works which surpassed anything that Mozart had done in these particular forms. In these incidents where was "The Great Mogul"?

Such humility in genius strikes a sonorously sympathetic chord in the breasts of most of us. We are at once objective bears and subjective bulls. Our complaints about egotism in others are often unconscious confessions of egotism in ourselves. The truth of the matter seems to be that young Beethoven overvalued himself less than most people do. On the other hand, as might be expected from a person of his intelligence, he undervalued himself less. Instances of such exaggerated humility as have just been mentioned were rare. As a general thing he saw himself neither smaller nor larger than he was—in other words, very much as we now see him a century after his death.

Like most intelligent and lower-class young men Beethoven had socialistic ideas.

I wish [he wrote to Hofmeister the publisher] that things could be arranged differently in this world. There simply ought to be a central world-depot of the arts, where the artist need only bring his work in order to take what he required.

He had not been long in Vienna when, talking in this strain to a gentleman at Prince Lobkowitz's palace, he showed a vigorous realization of his own significance. He said he wished he could find some such person as Goethe and Handel had found, who would take over the right to publish all his compositions and give him in return an income for life.

"My dear young man," responded the other, "you are neither a Goethe nor a Handel, and it is not likely that you ever will be; for such masters will not be born again."

Beethoven glared in silent wrath, and Lobkowitz tried clumsily to placate him: "The gentleman did not mean to wound you. It is an established maxim, with which most men agree, that the present generation cannot possibly produce such mighty spirits who have already earned their fame."

"So much the worse, Your Highness," Beethoven retorted; "but with men who will not believe and trust in me because I am still unknown to universal fame, I cannot hold intercourse."

He ended a letter to Baron von Türkheim thus: "Goodbye dear *Freiherr* and . . . remember that, though not in name, I too am a *Freiherr*!!!!"[4] Which anticipated a later remark when he took exception to the cheap ring sent him by the ruler of Prussia. "But realize," said a friend, "it is the present of a king." "I too am a king!" growled Beethoven.

He did not like it when the exalted ones of earth seemed to realize their own exalted state. In a note to Zmeskall he once called Prince Lobkowitz *"Fitzliputzly."* This was a satirical Viennese way of referring to the toplofty character of Huitzlipochtli, the over-god of the Aztecs.

It speaks vividly for the personal authority of the man that, in spite of taking such a high line, he managed to win and hold the sympathetic assent, or at least the forbearance, of so many of his more intelligent contemporaries. For at that time none of them could possibly have realized in the Beethoven of the first period one half of the greatness which we now find in him.[5] Nor could they have had any sus-

---

[4]One of Beethoven's puns: *Freiherr* means "baron," and more literally, "free master."

[5]He was comparatively late in developing. By Miss Catharine Morris Cox, assisted by three other psychologists, the Beethoven of twenty-six years old is rated only 121st among the world's 300 most eminent young men. (*The Early Mental Traits of 300 Geniuses*, being Vol. II in Genetic Studies of Genius, 1926.)

picion that this same high line was destined to be the first important factor in freeing the musician from the status of a servant and lifting him to that of a professional man.

Even to us at this distance, however, various defects of his qualities are unpleasantly apparent. He was frankly cynical enough to set down, black on white, a brutally utilitarian attitude towards certain devoted and apparently intimate friends. "I value them," he wrote, "merely by what they do for me. . . . I regard them simply as instruments on which I play when I please."

In mitigation of our sentence let us take into account that none but a musical mind could associate on congenial terms with Beethoven, and that no other living musician was his equal. Spiritually he was of necessity a lonely man. But he was a kind and generous man too, and usually tried to render good for good and service for service.

In his relations with humanity Beethoven knew little of the golden mean. He seldom played the tune of friendship upon the pedestrian and well-worn centre of the keyboard. He was either evoking seraphic and ecstatic *Benedictus* harmonies from the loftiest strings, or at a bound was clawing furiously among the thickest, angriest bass notes.

> *Himmelhoch jauchzend,*
> *Zum Tode betrübt,*

> (Exulting to heaven,
> Dejected to death,)

is the Goethean way of describing his lightning-like alterations of altitude. But the vignette of the little girl with the little curl hits him off even more accurately.

He was as hard to keep within the bounds of moderate conduct and equable intimacy as a panther cub compressed under a small boy's sweater. Here are two epistles which he wrote on consecutive days in 1799 to his young friend J. N. Hummel,[6] who was to be famous as a composer:

He is to keep away from me! He is a false cur and may the devil fly away with false curs.

BEETHOVEN

Nazy of my Heart! You are an honourable fellow and I now see that you were in the right. So come to me this afternoon. You will find Schuppanzigh too, and both of us will ruffle and shuffle and scuffle you to your heart's content. Here is a kiss from your

BEETHOVEN
alias, SOUR DUMPLING

This pendulum movement runs through nearly all his correspondence with friends, moistened by the Jean-Paul-ine gush of the period. Talk of this kind would brand a man to-day as hopelessly sentimental. At the close of the Eighteenth Century it meant nothing of the sort.

A limited command over his emotions was natural in a highly temperamental person who had been brought up as a prodigy by a drunken father and a discouraged, over-burdened mother. His sudden importance and authority as a twelve-year-old cembalist and his intimate association with the actors and actresses of those days could not have helped him materially towards self-control. Nor did he find anyone who might have taught him to rule his spirit

---

[6] T. Frimmel (*Beethoven Handbuch*, 1926, Vol. I, pp. 229, 235) thinks these letters were more probably addressed to Seyfried or Schuppanzigh. He has evidently overlooked the mention of Schuppanzigh in the second one. Thayer states positively that they were written to Hummel and preserved by him.

until, at seventeen, almost too late, he was admitted to the wholesome influence of the Von Breuning circle.

And so he grew up into a person forever alternating between the limits of an almost insane wrath and a correspondingly exaggerated penitence; between flashes of hauteur and sentimental, grovelling humility; between the wastefulness of a man who has never known the value of money and the avarice of one who has never known its essential worthlessness; between the omniscience of a monster of resolution who will take no counsel from man, god, or devil, and the invertebrate mushiness of a craven who cannot make up his own mind.

It must have been most uncomfortable for the human environment of this piece of incarnate quicksilver. None the less, one thanks "whatever gods may be" that he was not as other folks. The very unexpectedness, the passionate intensity, of this incurable adolescent, though they made him almost impossible as a temporal friend to any individual, were powerful factors in forming him into the eternal friend of humanity. One reason why his music is many times more popular to-day than during his lifetime is that one never can foresee which way this Ariel's fancy is going to dart. It is always vivid, always fresh, always surprising. One cannot outguess Beethoven.

Like many of his appreciators, this man suffered from the disease of dual personality. And both the Jekyll and the Hyde phases were high powered. But let him who is wholly without dissociation among us cast the first stone at Mr. Hyde!

Chapter VIII

CATASTROPHE FINGERS THE KNOCKER

1798, Approach of Deafness — Despairing Music — Sonatas Op. 10 — Courage — 1799, Sonate Pathétique — Pianistic Depths and Modernity — The Epoch-Making Germ-Motive — Its Interlocking of Movements — Its Far-Reaching Influence — The Source-Motive — Groups of Compositions Thematically Interlocked — Emotional Extremes in His Music

AFTER all, the really important thing about Beethoven—his music—is largely pure Jekyll. And his rhymes admirably with his sensitive, kind heart, his noble aspirations, his wide sympathy for greatness and goodness everywhere, his generosity, the complete sportsmanlike celerity with which he often owned himself in the wrong, his steadfastness in adversity, his heroism and even good cheer under the rods of calamity.

Early in 1798 the young Master suffered a shock that at first nearly prostrated him. With rapidly growing apprehension he noticed that something was wrong with his hearing. For years he was to guard the trouble, so horrible to a musician, as a shameful and ridiculous secret.

The first impulse of this man of passionate extremes was to retire from the world and yield to despair. His next was to give battle.

Although it is nearly always poor psychology to see in an artist's works a diary of his emotional life, the novelty and poignance of the tragic note that now suddenly sounded in Beethoven's music makes it reasonable to suppose that this note was caused by his deafness and his consequent fight with himself. The writer is convinced that out of this battle came the most sublimely heartbreaking music the world had yet heard: the *Largo e mesto* of the D major piano sonata (Op. 10, No. 3),

Ex. 1

the first part of the *Sonate Pathétique* (Op. 13) and the *Adagio affettuoso ed appassionato* of the first string quartet (Op. 18), which he himself associated with the tomb scene in *Romeo and Juliet*. This is indeed music eternally fit for the tragic parting of lovers—the parting of the music maker from his noblest sense.

But Beethoven was made of the same Antæan stuff as Johnnie Armstrong of the old ballad:

> Said John, "Fight on, my merry men all,
> I am a little hurt, but I am not slain;
> I will lay me down for to bleed a while,
> Then I'll rise and fight with you again."

Beethoven rose and began that superb series of piano sonatas beginning with the C minor (Op. 10, No. 1), and only ending with the E flat (Op. 31, No. 3) when he had mastered the larger medium of the symphony.

These sonatas constituted at once his spiritual outlet and his armour against desperation. So far beyond mere defiance do they go that they can even smile, laugh, and play. They can soothe and reassure. They can float us to iridescent caverns east of the sun and west of the moon.

If one motto could stand for the general cast of Beethoven's spirit as he wrote this music, it might take form in some words from a letter about his deafness, written later, to his friend, Dr. Franz Wegeler, and given more fully in chapter XII: "I will seize fate by the throat; most assuredly it shall not get me wholly down—oh, it is so beautiful to live life a thousandfold!"

In the *Sonate Pathétique* (Op. 13) it is possible to see—as one of a thousand equally valid interpretations—an epitome of the characteristic way in which Beethoven reacted to the menace of deafness. The introduction might well suggest a stricken wail; the first movement a grim fight for courage. The *Adagio cantabile* is one of the deepest and surest of all musical consolations in sorrow. And the rondo-*finale*, despite the minor key of its principal refrain, almost verges on gaiety.

In its idiomatic technical treatment of the keyboard, the *Pathétique* stands as the first truly modern sonata. Its predecessors sound to us to-day somewhat as if they had originally been written for string ensembles and then arranged for harpsichord, clavichord, or piano. No one but Mozart, in his fantasies in C major and C minor, had ever sounded anything like such pianistic depths as these.

This sonata is even more noteworthy as one of the first elaborate examples in Beethoven's work of an important device for which there is no adequate word in English. Not wishing to resort to foreign expressions like *Ur-Motif* or *Gestaltungsprinzip*, the writer has been driven to coin the term germ-motive, meaning a germinal phrase cyclically used to interlock the parts of a sonata or symphony into a unified whole. In developing this mechanism Beethoven fathered the leitmotif of Wagnerian music-drama. Such a device for securing musical economy and unity was all but unknown in that period. True, the idea of introducing the same or a similar phrase into different movements of a large work had already been sketchily put into operation by Vivaldi in his program music, by Johann Sebastian Bach in various suites, cantatas, and Passions, by Handel in his suites, by Haydn, as in the minuet and *finale* of his short B major symphony and in *The Seasons*, by Mozart in his A major piano concerto (Köchel No. 414),[1] in his G major trio (Köchel No. 496), and in his D major string quartet (Köchel No. 575). But before the *Pathétique* it had never been so systematically used nor on a scale large enough to warrant any such designation as germ-motive.

The first definite appearance of this device, in the

---

[1] For this observation about the Mozart concerto the writer is indebted to his friend Mr. C. B. Oldman, the Mozart authority of the British Museum.

Pathétique, is impressive. Out of the C–D–E flat theme of the slow introduction

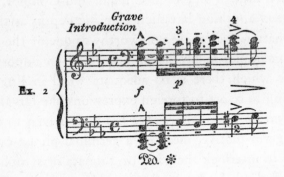

is developed the B flat–E flat–F–G flat of the second subject of the *Allegro di molto.*[1a]

And even the first subject is faithful to this pattern in all but the second of its first five notes.

The opening three notes of this motive appear (marked by a bracket) in the third bar of the *Adagio cantabile.*

[1a] Beethoven had recently used the same phrase (E–A–B–C) in his C minor string trio (Op. 9, No. 3, *Adagio con espressione,* first subject).

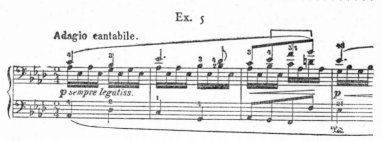

Ex. 5

Adagio cantabile.

The little tune comes again, turned end for end (marked by a bracket), in the second subject;

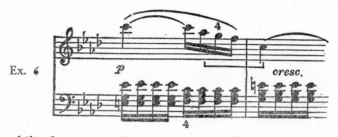

Ex. 6

while the principal refrain of the closing rondo echoes it note for note—G–C–D–E flat—in the original key of the first movement.

Ex. 7

Allegro.

In chap. LV, p. 566 ff., we shall see this same germ-motive used in so many later compositions that it becomes what we shall call a source-motive.

The popularity instantly won by the *Pathétique*, with its new structure, helped to lift the sonata from its rut and to establish the novel principle that this form should represent a logical organic unit, rather than be a more or less haphazard assemblage of four pieces. It prepared the way for such cyclic works as the Fifth and the Ninth symphonies. It stretched a hand down the years to give Berlioz his *idée fixe*, Loewe the motives that recur in his ballads and lend them such an epic quality, and to knit together the parts of Dvořak's *"New World,"* Tschaikowsky's Fifth, and Franck's D minor symphonies.

From the *Pathétique* dates not only the full inner homogeneity of the sonata, but Beethoven's occasional practice of tying together thematically whole groups of compositions. The motives which produced the effect of unity in such groups, we shall, for convenience, call "source-motives." For instance, the second subsidiary theme of the *Pathétique*'s rondo

Ex. 8

reappears almost note for note as the second subject of the *finale* of the A major string quartet (Op. 18, No. 5).

Ex. 9

There is more than a first cousinship between the opening of the *Allegro ma non troppo* of the quintet for piano and wind instruments (Op. 16)

Ex. 10

and the first piano tune in the Horn sonata (Op. 17),

Ex. 11

and the second theme of the first movement of the C minor string quartet (Op. 18, No. 4).

Ex. 12

We shall often meet this device again.

In looking through a thematic catalogue of his works one can see his tendency to emotional extremes. After a gloomy composition one is nearly sure to find a piece full of serene happiness or sparkling exuberance or boisterous laughter. The light-hearted clarinet trio (Op. 11) and the three optimistic violin sonatas (Op. 12) follow hard upon the tragic *Largo e mesto* of the D major sonata. The latter, indeed, ends with serenity and humour. And after the *Pathétique*, the two piano sonatas in E major and G major (Op. 14) lift their cheery voices as if to say: "Well, after all, fate may seal the outer ear, but it cannot close up the ears of a musician's mind!"

Chapter IX

BEETHOVEN HUGS THE
CONTRABASS

*Learns from Virtuosos — Plays with Dragonetti, 1799 —
Original Cure for a Financial Crisis — The Beethoven
Myth — Hurls Dish at Waiter — Fun in His Music*

LIKE most geniuses Beethoven hungered and thirsted for
perfection in his art and never lost an opportunity to learn
from a specialist. His position as a youthful fiddler in the
Bonn orchestra had brought him an unusual and invaluable
insight into the characteristics and potentialities of the
different instruments. This gave him an immense advantage over many of his successors who, like Moussorgsky, had
so little of such practical experience that in actual performance many of their orchestral effects are lost. His contact
with Bernhard Romberg in Bonn, and later with Duport
in Berlin, had allowed him to absorb from two of the leading
virtuosos of their day the last word in up-to-date violoncello technic.

Now, in 1799, Dragonetti, the Paganini of the contrabass, visited Vienna. And Beethoven eagerly sought another
opportunity to learn. The great bassist came by invitation
to call on the composer. Thinking to scare him, Beethoven
proposed that they play his own G minor violoncello sonata.
But Dragonetti negotiated the nimble passage work, on
his leviathan, with the easiest dexterity. The composer's

delight grew until, when the Italian failed to trip over the arpeggio stumbling blocks in the rondo, Beethoven surged up from the piano and enclosed man and bass in a bear hug which anticipated the comprehensive embracings of the *Choral* symphony.

In return he received inside information on technic which has, ever since, made operators of the Falstaffian fiddle perspire, especially in the Trio of the *scherzo* of the Fifth symphony. Seeing the poor basses bent double and with thyroid eyes, frantically defending their honour, one remembers Dragonetti's "scab" action in showing the Master what doughty deeds his short thick bow could accomplish when on its mettle.

In these days, before his deafness had made him sour and suspicious, he could sometimes be cornered without a fatal explosion of temperament. The man had small idea of the value of currency, but passed it out with both hands to indigent friends. Whenever the spirit moved him he changed his lodgings, and occasionally found himself in the position of paying for three or four sets of rooms at the same time. This encouraged financial crises.

One day he remarked to his crony Amenda: "The rent is due, and I have no idea how to meet it."

"That's easy," said the resourceful Amenda. "Now, here's a theme, '*Freudvoll und Leidvoll.*' Just write some variations on it. I'm going to lock you in, and you must have made a start when I come back."

In three hours Amenda opened the prison: "Well, have you started?"

BEETHOVEN HUGS THE BASS

A rather crusty Beethoven tossed over a paper, growling: "There's the rag!" (*"Da ist der Wisch!"*)

Friend Amenda rushed it to the landlord. "Carry this to a music publisher. He will pay you well for it."

The incredulous landlord hesitated for a while, but hastened back exultant to inquire whether there were any more scraps of paper like that going begging. One shudders to think how rich Beethoven (who, as we shall see, was the real inventor of jazz) might have become if he had lived a century later, thirty-five hundred-odd miles to the west, and had possessed a somewhat less rigorous artistic conscience.

Homely episodes like this, and other incidents to be told as our story goes on, are what confound the literary mythologists and the more fanciful painters and sculptors, who, sedulously suppressing all that they have considered trivial and vulgar, have turned the short, swarthy, stocky, pockmarked provincial, with the comic-strip accent, into an alabaster demigod and made him much the sort of personage that Parson Weems made of that extremely human and fallible gentleman who set America free.[1]

Others have evolved for us a gloomy, Byronic Beethoven, stalking into the night with a dæmonic furrow between his blazing orbs, his hand thrust desperately into his small-clothes, and his whole awful person as alien to common humanity as his Jovian locks were to a comb. A little more and one might expect the Delphic oracle to give

---

[1] Washington said *vale* to the United States about the time that Beethoven's first symphony and first string quartet said *ave* to the world.

tongue from the depths of that curious dimple in his chin.

After consulting some of these authorities it is almost a shock to look at the facts and discover a hero capable of hurling a dish of lungs and gravy at the waiter's head, and suddenly changing his wrath into roars of laughter when he noticed that the poor man's scolding tongue was silenced by having to lick up the gravy that ran down his chops. This was a hero who could fly into a fury because he imagined he had been short-changed half a cent. As a matter of fact he rarely knew for certain anything about money, but was so far from the bounds of mathematical genius that in order to find out the product of 13 x 24 he had to add thirteen twenty-fours.[2]

Discounting the excesses of hero worship we also find a good fellow with a tender heart, a portentous weakness for the same bad puns, a practical joker, a person normally bubbling over with high spirits and drollery. This last trait can be deduced by anyone with half an ear, from such music as the Sixth and Eighth symphonies, the introduction to the *finale* of the First, the *scherzos* of the Sixth, Seventh, and Thirteenth string quartets, the *presto* of the sixth piano sonata, the *scherzo* of the fifth violin sonata and the variations of the clarinet trio.

---

[2]This sum appears, in Beethoven's hand, on the first page of the autograph score of the *Coriolanus* overture.

Chapter X

FINDING HIS MEDIUM

Cautious Approach to New Forms — 1800, First Symphony — Septet — The String Quartet as a Vehicle — The Lobkowitz Quartets, Op. 18 — The First Piece of Jazz — His First Real Chef d'Œuvre — The Schuppanzigh Quartet — Lichnowsky Gives Beethoven Cremona Fiddles and an Annuity

BEETHOVEN always approached a new form cautiously, methodically, and attempted it only after elaborate preparation. Before writing his first symphony he did not, it is true, wait as long as his great successor, Brahms. But he was thirty, a vivid contrast to Mozart, who composed his forty-first symphony at the age of thirty-two.

The First symphony, in C major (Op. 21), was given its début on the second of April, 1800. In it Beethoven leaned heavily on the more rococo qualities of Haydn and Mozart. This procedure held true of his first work in other media, whether piano or duet sonatas, trios, quartets, or masses. While he was feeling his way to easy mastery in an untried field he was reminiscent. Only at the second or third attempt did he become the original thinker we know.

He has confessed that he never gave any thought to being an innovator. "The new and original," he once remarked, "is born of itself without one's thinking of it." So soon as his mind ceased to be careful and troubled, like

Martha's, about technical matters, and could devote itself to "the better part," originality came quite unconsciously.

The dominant seventh chord which opened the First symphony

Adagio molto.

Ex. 13

was denounced by the critics as wildly iconoclastic. In reality this and many other striking features of the C major were merely borrowings from certain of his predecessors.

But the fact remains that this work, tentative though it was, surpassed all other existing symphonies except a handful of Mozart's and Haydn's.

That boldly dissonant opening chord was a prophecy of the career of the man who, after he had found his symphonic legs, was to free music from the fashionable set patterns of the rococo world. Significantly enough, opus 21 appeared in 1800—the great divide between the Eighteenth and the Nineteenth centuries.

Hard on this prophecy followed the septet (Op. 20), which proved Beethoven's first popular "hit" in chamber music.[1] It is simple, clear, and sparkling. Everyone can understand it at a first hearing. It is as engagingly and

[1]Just as Brahms's first "hit" was to be the *"Spring"* sextet (Op. 18).

brilliantly representative of Germany's rococo period as the paintings of Watteau are representative of that period in France. Perhaps for this very reason the mature Nineteenth Century Beethoven disliked the popularity of the piece and could not hear it mentioned without a flare of impatience. "The septet," he once whimsically observed, "was written by Mozart." "There is, of course, feeling in it, but little art," he quite unjustifiably remarked to Carl Holz. Outside of his orchestral work, he never wrote anything more for wind instruments in the larger forms.

At the turn of the century a far more sympathetic vehicle, the string quartet, began to absorb him. Halfway between the intimate diary of his more or less improvised piano sonatas and the quasi-public utterances of his symphonies, these heart-to-heart conversations between four intellectual and spiritual equals, the two violins, viola and violoncello, came to form the very heart of Beethoven's music. Into the string quartet, far more than into solo, operatic, or oratorio forms, and even more than into the symphony, the Master came to pour the concentrated essence of all that was truest and finest in himself.

Divorced from any adventitious element of the virtuoso's technical exhibitionism, or of the falsifying impact of crowd psychology, the democratic little group of strings offered him the perfect medium. Perfect too in intonation. For when a keyboard instrument like the piano is "tuned" it is put scientifically out of tune. The same black key is made to do duty both for a sharp and for a flat, although, if mathematically correct, the former should sound higher than the latter. In this way the orchestra, also, must compromise with expediency.[2]

On the other hand, the string quartet, when left to itself, can give each note with absolutely pure intonation. This advantage, together with its flexibility, variety in unity, and absence of distracting sensuous appeal, made it the logical vehicle for the best in Beethoven. Such an austere medium bears much the same relation to the colourful orchestra as an etching bears to an oil painting.

Beethoven's first six compositions for two violins, viola, and violoncello are usually called the Lobkowitz quartets, after the prince to whom they were dedicated. Their creator had not yet fully mastered the form. And like all his ventures in a new field, they leaned somewhat on the arm of the past. None the less, how could any quartet party, amateur or professional, struggle on without them? This somewhat tentative venture of the young fellow of thirty has become almost the backbone of quartet literature.

Why? For one thing, because it is such fun to explore. Its kaleidoscopic unexpectedness rewards you. The wit and humour is dovetailed—or rather, dove-necked—with elusive attitudes of such iridescent loveliness. The hidden treasure caches are forever yielding something so new in ground you have already passed over a hundred times, ground every inch of which you supposed you had by heart.

In the last three Lobkowitz quartets there are distinct

[2]This compromise is known as "equal temperament." The chief trouble with it is, as Mr. T. F. Stuart Harris explains, in his *Handbook of Acoustics*, "that overtones, which should be coincident, are not so, but produce audible beats." Which means that the upper partials clash in aërial warfare above the apparently amicable promenade of their respective fundamentals.

thematic echoes, almost borrowings, from the rococo masters.[8] But the first three are much more consistently in the spirit of these masters. The opening movement of the F major (No. 1) is more cut and dried than anything else in the whole series;[4] although at the 30th bar it brings to light a charming example of a concealed counter subject— one of those subtly hidden tunes which, as a lad, he had so brilliantly detected in the theme given him by Mozart for improvisation. But the intensity of tragic passion in the great *Adagio* is a worthy forerunner of the *Adagio* of that other F major quartet, the First Rasoumowsky.

Opus 18, No. 2, is known as the *Komplimentierungs* or "Compliment" quartet, because its opening

Ex. 14

---

[3] See p. 515.

[4] But in the development of this first movement one finds the true Beethovenian touch in the four-measure alternation of minor and major, beginning at the 151st bar.

might suggest an elaborate reception at some rococo court, like Schoenbrunn, or Nymphenburg, or Potsdam. Some early commentator felt that at (a) the arriving guest might be supposed to sweep a grand curtsey, which is answered at (b) by his host. Whereupon at (c) the double doors sweep grandly open and all hands ceremoniously parade, with countless "after-yous," to the banquet hall.

Ex. 15

The gem of the Fourth quartet (in C minor) is the opening movement. Though the principal theme bears a close resemblance to the basic tune of the *Sonate Pathétique*,[5] there is nothing *pathétique* about this virile, self-assured music. It is the precursor of the Ajax-defying-the-thunder mood we are to meet with in the first movements of the *Eroica* and C minor symphonies.

Here was an utterance straight from the innermost heart of the young Master. A new note had been struck. A deeper level of the psyche, heretofore voiceless, had been reached and set free for musical expression.

In the *scherzo* of the B flat quartet (No. 6) we catch Beethoven in the act of stealing the Twentieth Century's thunder by inventing the first piece of jazz. For this *scherzo*

Ex. 16

is brimful of the subtle, catchy syncopations, the bizarre wit, and the perversely independent part-writing which most people imagine to be the popular invention of the 1920's. One need only substitute for the first violin a saxophone with an effective caterwaul; add a myriad-minded drummer equipped with one half of the items in the catalogue of Messrs. Sears, Roebuck & Co.; daub the classical

[5] See the beginnings of Ex. 3, p. 54, and Ex. 7, p. 55.

beauty of the original with a vermilion splotch or two of cave-man war paint; cease abruptly at the third measure from the end—and behold, music worthy of the proudest and loftiest traditions of the Great White Way.

From start to finish of the Lobkowitz quartets one can see Beethoven progressively drawing away from his musical forbears and coming easily, naturally into his own. He was perfectly right about the new and original being born of itself. This young man took no more thought for it than did the lilies of the field—though he met with considerably greater success than they. His originality was the product of the perfect relaxation of a genius.

Certain tone colours, certain emotional strata, appear at this point for the first time in quartet literature. And a daring hand shows crisply here and there through the traditional form. The *Adagio* of the G major (No. 2) is interrupted by a pert little *scherzo* episode. And the curious slow introduction to the *finale* of the B flat (No. 6), which is not too happily named *La Malinconia*, reappears twice amid its rollicking Ländler-like tunes. Like *Romeo and Juliet*, written just two centuries before, opus 18 was the first real *chef d'œuvre* of the youth of a supreme creative artist. And this correspondence lends added appropriateness to the fact, mentioned in a former chapter, that when conceiving the slow movement of the First quartet, Beethoven had in mind the Tomb Scene from Shakespeare's early play.

This music was composed with a quartet of talented boys in view. They were all about sixteen years old. Their leader.

fat Ignaz Schuppanzigh, was destined all his life to practise Beethoven quartets with the ink still wet. He served
the Master as Joachim was to serve Brahms. These boys
played every Friday morning at the palace of Prince Lichnowsky. Opus 18 had its first reading there. The Prince
was enthusiastic, and, before the six epoch-making works
were done, he munificently settled on Beethoven an annuity
of 600 gulden, "until such time as he should find a fitting
official position." In addition, before 1802, he gave him
the four precious Cremona instruments which still hang,
seductive but mute, in the *Beethovenhaus* at Bonn, and
tempt all true fiddlers to toy with the idea of grand larceny.

Chapter XI

PROMETHEUS WRITES A BALLET

IN THE spring of 1800 Beethoven entered into a contest
of skill with a charlatanesque musician named Steibelt.
The two met at Count Fries's house. While Beethoven
merely played the rather simple piano part of his clarinet
trio (Op. 11) Steibelt brought out a showy quintet of his
own. And he improvised, tickling the ears of the groundlings with his tremolos, which at that time were a piquant
novelty.

Beethoven [wrote Ries] could not be induced to play again.
A week later there was another concert at Fries's; Steibelt once
more played a quintet which had a good deal of success. He also
played an improvisation (which had been previously prepared),
and chose the same theme on which the Master had written the
variations in his trio. This incensed Beethoven and his admirers.
He had to go to the pianoforte and improvise. He went in his
usual (I might say, ill-bred) manner to the instrument, as if half

pushed, taking the violoncello part of Steibelt's quintet in passing, placed it (intentionally?) upon the stand upside down, and with one finger drummed a theme out of the first few measures. Insulted and angered, he improvised in such a manner that Steibelt left the room before he had finished, would never again meet him and, indeed, made it a condition that Beethoven should not be invited, before he would accept an invitation.

Not long after Beethoven came to Vienna, Franz I, the new Emperor of Austria, laid aside the wig and adopted the frock coat. This was, as the sprightly M. de Hevesy remarks, the *"seul et unique changement qu'il daigna admettre"* (the sole and unique change which he deigned to concede).[1]

With his First symphony and Second quartet Beethoven also laid aside the musical wig. Not only his music and manners, but even his attire, came to express a profound independence of public opinion. He often dressed, not in a frock coat, but in a costume appropriate to a shipwrecked mariner. Perhaps he felt that he was a sort of musical Robinson Crusoe, the sole and lonely denizen and monarch of his own world. His pupil Czerny was fond of pointing out the resemblance of one of his more shaggy and unconventional costumes to the goatskin habit of Defoe's famous hero.

An eccentric, uncouth, ugly, small provincial, he had abruptly descended upon the musical capital and had, in the turn of a hand, attained such a social and artistic position as few great musicians had ever won in a lifetime of

---

[1] André de Hevesy, *Beethoven, Vie Intime,* 1926, p. 12.

struggle. Here was a difficult personality, excitable, unrestrained, with lofty standards and small tolerance for the foibles of society or the shortcomings of his colleagues.

He was an outspoken man, with a tongue that could become, on slight provocation, like a whiplash soaked in vitriol. He even went so far as to call a number of the leading local organists and conductors "hand-organists." Small wonder that the rank and file of Viennese musicians revenged themselves with strident contempt and ridicule on this foreigner, this utterly irregular fellow who had dropped from heaven knew where, to steal their prestige and elbow them aside. Except such outstanding persons as Weigl, Gyrowetz, Salieri, and Eybler, few of them treated him worthily.[2] Even Papa Haydn, as we have seen, was not quite spacious in this respect. When Koželuch heard the C minor trio (Op. 1) he flung it upon the floor and remarked to Haydn: "We would have managed that differently, wouldn't we, Papa?" And Haydn answered with a smile: "Yes, we would have managed that differently."

In January, 1801, Beethoven sent the B flat piano sonata (Op. 22) to his publisher with the enthusiastic comment: "This sonata, my dearest Mr. Brother, will wash" (*"hat sich gewaschen"*). His prophecy has been justified. The surf of time has beaten upon it for more than a century and a quarter without causing its bold colouring to fade very noticeably. And yet opus 22 hints at reactionary tend-

---

[2] "Every great man . . . who has sought to bring new birth to the souls of men has learned that nothing more surely provokes the hatred of the world than the knowledge that he is steering by a star they cannot see." John Middleton Murry, *Jesus—Man of Genius*, 1926, p. 317.

encies. There is an old-fashioned absence of coda in the first movement. Its emotional side shows less than usual of that depth and individuality which was in process of freeing music from the urbanities of the rococo. And there is more virtuosity for its own sake than one would expect from the Beethoven who was now launched into the Nineteenth Century.

The D major piano sonata (Op. 28), sometimes called the *"Pastoral"* sonata, is one of the first of a number of compositions—their archetype was to be the *Pastoral* symphony—reflecting that intense solace which the deaf often draw from nature. The opening movement might well recall those lines by Walt Whitman:

Afoot and light-hearted I take to the open road,
Healthy, free, the world before me,
The long brown path before me leading wherever I choose. . . .
I think I could stop here myself and do miracles.

Beethoven was an enthusiastic out-of-doors person. He once declared that he loved a tree more than a man. Even if his music did not proclaim his passion for the open, one could infer it from his Sketch Books, where, scrawled among the staves, one finds such ejaculations as: "It is as though, out in the country, every tree said to me: '*Holy, holy.*'" Each summer he spent as much time as he could manage in the unspoiled woods of the suburbs: Hetzendorf, Heiligenstadt, Baden, and Mödling. There, rain or shine, he would wander composing, or lie on the soaked ground, too absorbed to notice that he was cold or wet and was planting the seeds of illness. Through the woods and meadows he stormed, waving his arms, shouting and singing at the top of a none too agreeable voice. The peasants looked upon him as crazy, and the very beasts of burden often took fright at the apparition.

Amid all his abstract writing Beethoven found relaxation in composing *The Creations of Prometheus*, a ballet for Salvatore Vigano. This dancer held in 1801 much the same commanding position that Nijinsky and Pavlowa were to win more than a century later.

It was appropriate that Beethoven should have written the *Prometheus* music at the time when he himself was about to become the Prometheus of music. For this man was destined to bring clearer light, greater warmth, and larger freedom to a groping art, too often chilled and fettered by fashion, and to expiate his benign audacity through terrible suffering.

Significantly enough, the chief melody of this ballet was later on to figure in three of his other works, one of which was the theme of the variations that end the sublimities of the *Eroica* symphony. It seems almost as though Beethoven, dimly conscious of his own Promethean nature, used this melody somewhat as a sign manual.

The authorized edition of the charming string quintet in C major (Op. 29), Beethoven's only complete original composition in this form, was published by Breitkopf and Härtel in 1802. Simultaneously, as Ries records, it

was stolen in Vienna and published by A. [Artaria] and Co. Having been copied in a single night it was full of errors. . . .

Beethoven's conduct in the matter is without parallel. He asked A. to send him for correction fifty copies which had been printed, but at the same time instructed me to use ink on the wretched paper and as coarsely as possible; also to cross out a number of lines so that it would be impossible to make use of a single copy or sell it. The scratching out was particularly in the *scherzo*. I obeyed his instructions implicitly.

This affair was the forerunner of that long series of regrettable business deals in which Beethoven's Mr. Hyde was to assume charge of affairs, with much play of ill-founded suspicion and little sportsmanship. He rushed into print, angrily accusing the two publishers, Mollo and Artaria, of having stolen the manuscript of his quintet in order to pirate it. This involved him in the turbulent sort of complications from which his life was destined to be seldom free. When it developed that Mollo had nothing to do with the matter Beethoven took back the charges against him. Whereupon Artaria summoned the composer into court and secured a judgment, condemning the latter publicly to retract his charges. But his independent Flemish blood obstinately refused to do any such thing, court or no court. These bickerings dragged on until, in 1805, the good-natured Artaria let him off, agreeing to assume all the costs of the trial. In return Beethoven promised to write, and let Artaria publish, another quintet, with some musical trifle for good measure. This quintet was never finished. Later Beethoven rather shabbily fobbed off in its place a trio for two oboes and English horn which he had written in 1794 as one of his studies in the use of orchestral instruments. The trifle was published in 1806, as opus 87.

In the three piano sonatas (Op. 26 and 27, Nos. 1 and 2), published in 1802, Beethoven made one of his many minor fresh starts as a stylist in commencing to handle the form more freely. He began all three slowly: two *andantes* and an *adagio*. In the last he reduced the number of movements from four to three. He labelled both the E flat and the C sharp minor sonatas (Op. 27, Nos. 1 and 2) "*quasi una fantasia.*" He made several movements flow into one another. And he interrupted the opening *Andante* of the E flat with a short *Allegro*. These were tactics in Prometheus's campaign to free the art from the clasp of frozen forms.

Not that the slow beginnings of these sonatas were any more of an absolute innovation than his use of the term *scherzo,* or his substitution in the C minor quartet of a slowed-down *scherzo* for the usual *adagio*. The rococo masters had made tentative beginnings along this line. Mozart had commenced his A major piano sonata with a slow theme and variations. And Haydn, in his C major quartet (Op. 66) had substituted an *Allegretto scherzando* for a slow movement. The spirit of these Beethoven sonatas, however, was an absolutely new thing in the world. The Mozart and Haydn movements had the gay, sportive, often trifling tone of the old-fashionable rococo culture. Even their pathos went scarcely more than skin deep.

But Beethoven began the A flat sonata (Op. 26) with a theme of what has, earlier in this book,[3] been called the "Joseph Vance" type.

[3]See p. 38.

Ex. 17

Its third and fourth variations offered prophetic witness that here was a man who, recreating Bach's miracle of the Goldberg variations, should shatter the old variation to bits and build in its place something profoundly significant.

He found it one of the most superficially conventional of all musical forms. Developing it little by little, in the *Eroica*, the "*Appassionata*," the Fifth symphony, the B flat trio, the E major and C minor sonatas, the Ninth symphony, and the last string quartets, he made it an infinitely flexible, subtle, sensitive, and eloquent medium for expressing the innermost mysteries of his being.

The variations of the A flat sonata are delicious. But the high light of the composition is the "Funeral March on the Death of a Hero." Here we have no mere transcript of history. This hero never lived except in the supervital world of Beethoven's imagination. Originally the Master began this composition simply in order to out-funeral-march an ephemeral but popular composition by Paer, an opera scribbler of the day. But, once started, Beethoven's crescent fancy soon made the situation so real to him that he created a piece which remains the ideal type by which all other funeral marches are judged. And this in spite of the realism of those muffled drums which would have drummed any other composer backwards off the field.

The Minuet of the A flat is a crisp first cousin to the Minuet of the First symphony. While the *finale* is a charmingly graceful half parody, half complimentary commentary on the flowing style of Beethoven's virtuoso rivals, Clementi and Cramer.[4]

Yet, in one way, this sonata marks a retreat rather than an advance. It shows no such unity of mood, of emotional logic, or of theme as had fused the *Pathétique* and poured it bubbling into a single mould. It strikes one somewhat more as a chance assemblage of piano pieces. One thinks of a scarcely congenial family of four splendid individuals, sprung from an unusually fortunate marriage of convenience, who have little in common but a name.

There are almost as many and as foolish legends current about Beethoven as about another emancipator contemporary with him—George Washington. Some sentimentalist has invented a popular myth about the so-called "*Moonlight*" sonata (Op. 27, No. 2). There are several versions. One of the more imaginative holds that Beethoven was wandering the moonlit streets of Vienna when he saw a

---

[4]The humorous elements of this movement and, as we shall see, of the *Pastoral* symphony's *scherzo*, laid the foundation for that art of musical parody which flourishes to-day with the whimsical connivance of Messrs. Richard Strauss, Edward Ballantine, Sigmund Spaeth, Daniel Gregory Mason, and others.

blind youth leaning on the arm of his beautiful sister and lamenting that he should never see the greatest of all musicians. Beethoven accosted them, went to their humble home, seated himself at the poor piano, and inspired by the sightless orbs of the boy, by the *beaux yeux* of the maiden, and by the moonlight pouring in at the casement—improvised the C sharp minor sonata. Then, rising to his full five feet five, he revealed his identity, embraced them, and rushed forth to dash down the inspiration. A variant of this tale makes Beethoven pass the blind boy's window, overhear him bungling the F major sonata (Op. 10, No. 2) and expressing a wish that he could hear the composer play it. Then it makes the latter push his way in unannounced, play it correctly, and fall to improvising opus 27, No. 2.

As a matter of fact, the composition named in this legend should be called the "Moonshine" sonata. Moonlight was first mentioned in connection with it by Rellstab, the leading German critic of the day. He remarked in a review that the first movement made him feel as though he were seeing moonlight upon the waves of the Vierwaldstätter See. This was enough for that incorrigible urge, the popular mythopœic impulse.

Might not this movement have just as suitably suggested to Rellstab the atmosphere of a thick pine forest at noon? Or a father pondering darkly over the future of his genius of a daughter who is entering upon a doubtful marriage? Or the sunken bell? Or a homesick poet lost on a glacier? Or an earthbound spirit regretting love and laughter? Or perhaps a prenatal dream of past bliss?

One incomparable thing about music is that a bit of it, within certain wide limits, may mean almost anything to almost anybody. The romancer who, by playing on mankind's juvenile weakness for bedtime stories, seeks to belittle, localize, and imprison the universal immensity of music within the narrow concrete walls of a single fiction, does the art an almost blasphemous wrong.

A feature of this C sharp minor sonata which means vastly more in the history of the arts than its possible literary significance is the way in which the great arpeggios of the *finale* are freed at a stroke from the superficiality and exhibitionism which had traditionally been associated with arpeggios, and informed with a highly emotional personality of their own. So that they become no more than a means to a purely musical but deeply felt end. Farther on, in connection with the composer's love life, we shall hear more of this composition.

Except the early pieces for wind instruments Beethoven's violin and piano sonatas are, on the whole, the least attractive items in the roster of his chamber music. Besides the *"Kreutzer"* (Op. 47), only three others (in F major, Op. 24; in C minor, Op. 30, No. 2; and in G major, Op. 96) stand out as the product of an inner urge. The others fall into the class of those less vital "occasional" works which Beethoven sometimes wrote for special reasons other than because he could not help it.

The violin sonata in F major (Op. 24) is a bright, gay, bubbling, almost burbling little work, which has been more or less appropriately renamed the *"Spring"* sonata. Its easy unity suggests that it came in a single gush. It has an infectious smile, does not go very deep, and is the too apparent progenitor of Grieg's violin sonata in the same key. We shall see, however, that Beethoven's F major, and its predecessor in A minor (Op. 23) were pioneer exponents of the germ-motive in chamber music.[5]

The C minor violin sonata (Op. 30, No. 2) is sometimes called the "*Eroica*." In eloquence and depth of inspiration it ranks next to the "*Kreutzer*." One cannot quite agree with Herr Ernest in calling it "*grossartig*" and "one of the high points of Beethoven's creativeness." But the dramatic power of the first *Allegro con brio* foreshadows that which was to open the Fifth symphony; while the first theme itself—

Ex. 18

—is a minor version of how the Eighth symphony was to open a decade later.

Ex. 19

(Transposed to C major for comparison)

And two decades after, this motif's rhythmical plan may well have suggested to Schubert the opening of his string quartet in D minor.

Far greater works than these were soon to come—the defiant answer of a creative hero to catastrophe.

[5] See pp. 534–535.

Chapter XII

LE GRAND SOURD

*The Rift in the Lute — First Admissions of Deafness —
1801, Letter to Amenda — Letters to Wegeler — Antæan
Resilience — Relations with Brothers — Insults Prince
Lobkowitz — 1802, Heiligenstadt Testament — Effects of
Deafness — Frees Creative Music from Composer-Execu-
tant Tradition — and from Taint of Virtuosity — Causes
of Deafness — Nature of His Disease*

WE HAVE already seen how, early in 1798, the curse of
deafness came to Beethoven. It flashed like the handwriting
on the royal wall into a scene of plenty, happiness, and
triumph.

He had made fame, money, and friends, although he
sought to give away all but the fame with both hands and
with both fists. He was the darling of the aristocracy. He
could afford to be extravagant about apartments and to
set up a valet and a riding horse. The publishers competed
sharply for his manuscripts. He was the favourite piano
virtuoso of the day.

But all this time the menace kept whispering *crescendo*
into his ear words scarcely more reassuring than the
"memento mori!" which the Roman slave was bidden
murmur into the ear of the general celebrating his triumph.
In spite of everything that the limited medical science of
the day could do, his hearing grew steadily worse.

Naturally Beethoven kept the trouble secret as long as he well could. He felt about his poor ears as a beautiful but aging woman feels about her poor cheeks and eyes and throat. When, on June 1, 1801, he knew the absolute need of a confidant he sat down and wrote to an intimate friend who lived far away—Carl Amenda, then a pastor in Kurland:[1]

MY GOOD AMENDA, MY LOYAL FRIEND: How often do I wish you were with me, for your Beethoven lives very unhappily, in constant conflict with nature and his Creator; oftentimes I have cursed the latter for making his creatures the sport of the most terrible chance, so that often the most beautiful blossoming is thereby destroyed and crushed; know then that my noblest faculty, my hearing, has sadly deteriorated. When you were still with me[2] I had intimations of this, but said nothing about them; now it has been growing steadily worse, and whether it can be cured remains to be seen, the trouble probably comes from the condition of my abdomen; as regards the latter, I am almost completely cured, will my hearing grow better? I hope it indeed, but doubtfully, such diseases are the most incurable. What a sorrowful life I must now live, avoiding all that is dear and precious to me; and, too, among such miserable egotistical people as . . . etc. Oh how happy would I be if my hearing were completely restored . . . but as it is I must draw back from everything, and the most beautiful years of my life will take wings without accomplishing all the promise of my talent and my powers! . . . Sorrowful resignation, in this must I find refuge; I have of course resolved to raise myself above all this; but how will that be possible? . . . My affliction causes me the least trouble in playing and composing, the most in association with others. . . . I beg you to keep

---

[1]In the translations of Beethoven's letters his unconventional ideas of punctuation, capitalization, and spelling of proper names have been faithfully followed.
[2]1798–1799.

this matter of my deafness a profound secret and confide it to no one, no matter whom. . . . Your loyal friend who really loves you,

L. v. BEETHOVEN.

Note that even such a mind as Beethoven's could be so far unbalanced as to describe his physical ear as: "my noblest faculty." Only after some years did he come to realize that his ears stood to his imagination in somewhat the same humble relation in which Maelzel's Mechanical Trumpeter stood to a Stradivarius violin.

To his old friend Dr. Wegeler he wrote on June 29, 1801, after a description of his prosperity:

The only pity is that my evil demon, my bad health, is continually putting a spoke in my wheel, by which I mean that my hearing for the last three years has grown steadily worse. . . . My ears whistle and buzz continually night and day. I can say that I am living a wretched life; for two years I have avoided almost all social gatherings because it is impossible for me to say to people: "I am deaf." If I belonged to any other profession it would be easier, but in my own it is an awful state, the more since my enemies, who are not few, what would they say? In order to give you an idea of this curious deafness of mine I must tell you that in the theatre I must get very close to the orchestra in order to understand the actor. If I am a little distant I do not hear the high tones of the instruments and singers, and if I be but a little further away I do not hear at all. Often I can hear the low tones of a conversation, but not the words, and as soon as anybody shouts it becomes intolerable. It seems singular that in conversation there are people who do not notice my condition at all, attributing it to my absence of mind.

Some months later he wrote again to Wegeler:

I am living more pleasantly now since I began to mingle more with people. You will scarcely believe how lonely and sad my life was for two years; my bad hearing haunted me everywhere like a ghost, and I fled from mankind and seemed like a misanthrope, though I was far from being one. This change has been wrought by a *dear, fascinating* girl, who loves me and whom I love. I have had a few blessed moments within the last few years and for the first time I feel that marriage might bring me happiness; she is, alas! not of my station—and now—I certainly could not marry; —I must get out and lustily knock about the world.—There is no greater joy for me than to pursue and produce my art. . . . oh if I were only rid of this affliction I could embrace the world! I feel that my youth is just beginning, and have I not always been a sickly person? . . . Every day I approach nearer the goal which I feel but cannot describe. Only therein can your Beethoven live. No thought of peace! No! I cannot endure it! I will seize fate by the throat; most assuredly it shall not get me wholly down—oh it is so beautiful to live life a thousand-fold! ("*das Leben tausendmal leben!*")

Later on we shall see more of the "dear, fascinating girl" referred to in this letter.

The man had such terrific vitality that even in the lowest depths of despair he did not wholly lose his fighting spirit, nor his whimsicality, nor even his gaiety and sparkle. Consider the infectious jollity of the fugato *finale* which ends the F major piano sonata (Op. 10, No. 2).

Ex. 20

This was written shortly before the tragic *Largo e mesto* (Op. 10, No. 3). Think of the serene brightness of the minuet, and the humour of the rondo which followed that cry of agony. Only the greatest geniuses have enough resilience to raise them from such sorrow as breathes through the *Grave* and the *Allegro di molto* of the *Sonate Pathétique*, and at once to make such a joyful noise as is contained in the movements which open and close opus 14, which close opus 15, which is heard in each of the Lobkowitz quartets (Op. 18), in the First symphony, the F major violin sonata, the first half of the A flat piano sonata (Op. 26), the opening of the E flat sonata (Op. 27, No. 1), and even in the *Allegretto* of the *"Moonlight"* sonata itself. This was a man whom nothing could down; a man who could walk through the valley of the shadow of death and turn the croakings of its ravens into a rollicking canon.

There is evidence, however, that many of Beethoven's statements about his own deafness were exaggerated; and that as late as the Eighth symphony, written in 1812, his ears enjoyed many a good day when they heard speech and music with almost normal clarity.

As his trouble grew worse he naturally looked more and more for help and comfort to his only living blood relations, his brothers. At the same time his natural absent-mindedness, greed, suspicion, and irascibility increased. From this period in his life on it must have been no simple feat to maintain pleasant fraternal relations with Ludwig so much as a fortnight. A man who was capable at any moment of turning savagely upon his most intimate friends would not be likely to mince matters with his younger brothers. (He once referred to Johann as a "relative in no wise related.") The fact that they avoided any permanent rupture with him is to be written down on the credit side of their ledger. And the great man's many lamentations and accusations against them are only to be swallowed with pinches of salt.

For was he not the irresponsible genius who once took violent offence at a perfectly innocent remark of his dear friend and patron, Prince Lobkowitz? Beethoven was frothing at the mouth over the absence of the third bassoon from one of the *Fidelio* rehearsals. Prince Lobkowitz tried to appease him by pointing out that the orchestra might be able to pull through for the present with the first and second bassoons. This made the composer so wild that on his way home he ran to the Prince's palace, thrust his head inside the great doors, and to the stupefaction of the lackeys bellowed: *"Lobkowitz, donkey!"*

On the other hand no quantity of salt can disguise the fact that scarcely a single word has come down to us from Beethoven's contemporaries in favour of his brothers. The pair seem to have generously shared most of his defects without coming in for his qualities. True, Thayer's great-hearted though not entirely convincing apologia cleared them of certain heavy accusations; but it remains well established that Johann and Karl tried to get Ludwig into their own power and alienate his friends. They robbed him, gave out for publication compositions of which he was ashamed, and generally behaved like true sons of that bounder, John the Gullet-Baptist. There is no doubt that they materially intensified the tragedy of his life.

Karl, however, despite his dishonesty, was an invaluable aid to Ludwig as private secretary. His business letters are destined to add to the gaiety of music lovers. For he took his pen in hand and hawked about the lunar rainbows of sonatas and the crepuscular surf of symphonies like so many measures of parsnips or pigs of iron.

Beethoven spent the summer of 1802 in that quaint village near Vienna which gave its name to his famous Heiligenstadt Testament. He wrote it there on October 6th. In thus pouring out his feelings he cleansed his stuffed bosom of that perilous stuff which preyed upon his heart. Reading these tortured pages, one feels that at this time, but for the Master's consciousness of the indestructibility of the creative force within him, he would surely have laid violent hands upon himself. Herr Ernest comments on the document:

The loftiest purity of sentiment and the most unselfish goodness, despair about life and undiminished enthusiasm for art, deep despondency and firm resolution, are here fused into a truly affecting whole, the impression of which is further heightened by language which, as so often when the agonies of his heart struggled for expression, rises to almost poetic beauty.[8]

TESTAMENT.

FOR MY BROTHERS CARL AND BEETHOVEN.
O you my fellow-men, who take me or denounce me for morose, crabbed, or misanthropical, how you wrong me! you

---

[8]*Beethoven*, 1920, p. 136.

know not the secret cause of what seems thus to you. My heart and my disposition were from childhood up inclined to the tender feeling of goodwill, I was always minded to perform even great actions; but only consider that for six years past I have fallen into an incurable condition, aggravated by senseless physicians, year after year deceived in the hope of recovery, and in the end compelled to contemplate a *lasting malady,* the cure of which may take years or even prove impossible. Born with a fiery lively temperament, inclined even for the amusements of society, I early was forced to isolate myself, to lead a solitary life. If now and again I tried for once to give the go-by to all this, O how rudely was I repulsed by the redoubled mournful experience of my defective hearing; but not yet could I bring myself to say to people "Speak louder, shout, for I am deaf." O how should I then bring myself to admit the weakness of *a sense* which ought to be more perfect in me than in others, a sense which I once possessed in the greatest perfection, a perfection such as few assuredly of my profession have yet possessed it in—O I cannot do it! forgive me then, if you see me shrink away when I would fain mingle among you. My misfortune gives me double pain in making me misunderstood. Recreation in human society, the more delicate passages of conversation, confidential outpourings, none of these are for me; all alone, almost only so much as the sheerest necessity demands can I bring myself to venture into society; I must live like an exile; if I venture into company a burning dread falls on me, the dreadful risk of letting my condition be perceived. So it was these last six months which I passed in the country, being ordered by my sensible physician to spare my hearing as much as possible. He fell in with what has now become almost my natural disposition, though sometimes, carried away by the craving for society, I let myself be misled into it; but what humiliation when someone stood by me and heard a flute in the distance, and I heard *nothing,* or when someone heard *the herd-boy singing,* and I again heard nothing. Such occurrences brought me near to despair, a little more and I had put an end to my own life—only it, *my art,* held me back. O it seemed to me impossible to quit the world until I had produced all I felt it in me to produce; and so I reprieved this wretched life—truly wretched, a body so sensitive that a change of any rapidity may alter my state from very good to very bad. Patience—that's the word, she it is I must take for my guide; I have done so—lasting I hope shall be my resolve to endure, till it please the inexorable Parcæ to sever the thread. It may be things will go better, may be not; I am prepared—already in my twenty-eighth year forced—to turn philosopher: it is not easy; harder for an artist than for anyone. O God, Thou seest into my inward part, Thou art acquainted with it, Thou knowest that love to man and the inclination to beneficence dwell therein. O my fellow-men, when hereafter you read this, think that you have done me wrong; and the unfortunate, let him console himself by finding a companion in misfortune, who, despite all natural obstacles, has yet done everything in his power to take rank amongst good artists and good men.—You, my brothers Carl and   , as soon as I am dead, if Professor Schmidt is still alive, beg him in my name to describe my illness, and append this present document to his account in order that the world may at least as far as possible be reconciled with me after my death.—At the same time I appoint you both heirs to my little fortune (if so it may be styled); divide it fairly, and agree and help one another; what you have done against me has been, you well know, long since forgiven. You, brother Carl, I especially thank for the attachment you have shown me in this latter time. My wish is that you may have a better life with fewer cares' than I have had; exhort your children to *virtue*, that alone can give happiness—not money, I speak from experience; that it was which upheld me even in misery, to that and to my art my thanks are due, that I did not end my life by suicide.—Farewell, and love each other. I send thanks to all my friends, especially *Prince Lichnowski* and *Professor Schmidt*. I want Prince L.'s instruments to remain in the safe keeping of one of you, but don't let there be any strife between you about it; only whenever they can help you to something more useful, sell them by all means. How glad am I if even under the

sod I can be of use to you—so may it prove! With joy I hasten
to meet death face to face. If he comes before I have had an opportunity to unfold all my artistic capabilities, he will, despite
my hard fate, yet come too soon, and I no doubt should wish him
later; but even then I am content; does he not free me from a
state of ceaseless suffering? Come when thou wilt, I shall face
thee with courage. Farewell, and do not quite forget me in death,
I have deserved it of you, who in my life had often thought for
you, for your happiness; may it be yours!

LUDWIG VAN BEETHOVEN.

Heiglnstadt,

6th October, 1802.

Seal.

For my brothers
Carl and
to read and to execute after my death.

Heiglnstadt,[4] 10th October, 1802. So I take leave
of thee[5]—sad leave. Yes, the beloved hope that I
brought here with me—at least in some degree to
be cured—that hope must now altogether desert me.
As the autumn leaves fall withered, so this hope too
is for me withered up; almost as I came here, I go
away. Even the lofty courage, which often animated
me in the lovely summer days, has vanished. O Provi-
dence, let for once a pure day of joy be mine—so
long already is true joy's inward resonance a stranger
to me. O when, O when, O God, can I feel it once
again in the temple of Nature and of Humanity.
Never? No—O that were too cruel!

The italics are Beethoven's. Consider the touch of
coquetry involved in giving his age as four years too young.
In this he was only following the lead of Father Johann,

---

[4]Heiligenstadt is spelled Heiglnstadt by Beethoven, in both places.

[5]By "thee" he means "joy." Already he was planning that setting of Schiller's "Ode to
Joy" with which he was to end the *Choral* symphony more than two decades later.

who had once publicly declared the boy prodigy to be two years younger than he was.

Notice the significant omission of one brother's name. Perhaps Johann had been unusually trying in those days. And observe in the style of the postscript, stammering and almost incoherent from excessive emotion, the counterpart in words of those moving measures in the *adagios* of the tenth, thirteenth, and sixteenth quartets, where the Master's too full heart seemed to falter in his own natural language of tones. Grove thought the postscript might have been addressed, not to the brothers, but to some woman with whom he was in love at the time.

The suicidal gloom of this document represented merely a passing mood. And after all, its lamentations were not for any possible effect of his deafness upon the thing that mattered most to him—his creative work—but because it hampered his outer relations with the world. From these depths he rebounded to the ebullience of one of his most fecund periods.

Beethoven's irascibility and tendency to suspect all and sundry were sorely inflamed by his affliction. Unless one has suffered from it, a normal person can scarcely realize how deafness affects disposition and emotional balance. For ten days, following an operation, the writer once had the experience of total deafness. His whole idea was to escape from people. When with them he felt certain that they were all ridiculing him or conspiring against him.

For so prominent a personage as Beethoven was at thirty-one, this effect would have been greatly intensified. He had the illusion that nearly all the world was at war with him. And more and more he came to feel that certain questionable actions were fair in war, especially when the odds stood: one against the world.

It is hard to overestimate the gain which resulted for music from Beethoven's deafness. It weaned him away from the distractions of piano virtuosity, just as the accidental injury to Robert Schumann's finger was to wean him, some decades later. It threw him wholly into composition. So, by chance, Beethoven provided an example which freed creative music from the evil old tradition that composer and interpreter should be one and the same person. Voluntarily this emancipator freed the composer from the disadvantage of being a servant. Involuntarily he freed him from the incubus of being an executant. Thus he prepared the way for non-virtuoso composers like Berlioz, Schumann, Wagner, Ravel, and Stravinsky.

His deafness freed music in yet another way. When he ceased to play the piano Beethoven stopped writing solo pieces with any "occasional" taint—pieces for the advertisement and display of his own dexterity at the keyboard. This change was also dictated by the independent quality of his powerful personality. Most of the compositions of Bach, Haydn, and Mozart had been strongly influenced, if not activated, by their own personal virtuosity and by the posts they held. Mozart, it is true, had made a beginning, toward the end of his career, in composing from pure inclination. But Beethoven was the first important composer to throw the full weight of his influence towards establishing the art on a basis of music for music's sake. He was the first to refuse orders which did not rhyme with inspiration, and he refused not a few. In struggling free of outer compulsion, and writing the bulk of his work from inner compulsion alone, and without regard to considerations of virtuosity, he signed music's declaration of independence.

There have been many theories about the immediate cause of Beethoven's deafness. The Fischer manuscript says it began when he came in overheated one day in 1796, undressed to his trousers, and cooled off in a draught.

Writing in 1814,[6] Dr. Weissenbach attributed it to a severe attack of typhus which Ludwig may have had at adolescence. In a letter to Wegeler, Beethoven, as we have seen, blamed it upon those troubles in the abdomen which started in the Bonn days. But in 1815 he provided Charles Neate, the English pianist, with the least plausible account of all. He told him, in the course of writing an opera, "not *Fidelio*,"[7] he had trouble with the first tenor, who insisted upon having his part changed. Finally the fellow knocked at the door once too often.

> I sprang up from table under such an excitement of rage, that, as the man entered the room, I threw myself upon the floor as they do upon the stage [here Beethoven spread his arms and made a gesture of illustration], coming down upon my hands. When I arose I found myself deaf and have been so ever since. The physicians say, the nerve is injured.

[6] *Reise zum Congress.*

[7] Frimmel (*Beethoven Handbuch*, Vol. II, p. 303) thinks that Neate may have misheard "oratorio" as "opera," or that Beethoven may have thought of *The Mount of Olives* as a sacred opera.

Ever since the Great War brought us into starker contact with grosser reality we have laid aside much of the prudery with which we formerly evaded the discussion of venereal disease. "With greater social frankness on the subject," writes Mr. Ernest Newman, "has come a welcome tendency to put moral judgments on one side and to see it mainly as a question of hygiene, individual and social."[8] We now feel it decent to call a spade a spade, whereas the earlier biographers felt they must call it an instrument for the manipulation of indecent matter and for beating about the bush.

A body of literature has grown up about the questions: Did Beethoven suffer from some venereal disease? And, if so, what were its reactions upon his body and mind? Space forbids a discussion of the voluminous arguments pro and con. From a study of the available documents[9] the writer has formed the following conclusions:

(1) Beethoven was highly sexed and nonascetic.

(2) Strong circumstantial evidence, coupled with frequent outbursts of a despair unwarranted by circumstances known to us, make it extremely probable, though not certain, that he suffered from some venereal disease, acquired or inherited.

(3) Which, it is impossible, with our present data, to specify. Before Ricord's tests in 1838 the different venereal diseases were confused with one another in origin and more or less in treatment.

---

[8] *The Unconscious Beethoven*, 1927, p. 38.
[9] See Bibliography, pp. 638–639. Also: Springer: *Die Geniale Syphilitiker*, 1928; and Carl Engel: "Views and Reviews," *Musical Quarterly*, Oct., 1927, pp. 650–658.

(4) The cirrhosis of the liver of which he died in 1827 may have been caused, wholly or in part, by a venereal disease. But it is almost certain that his deafness was not so caused.

(5) His nervous irritability and hatred of his notoriously light sisters-in-law, which rose at times to the blind intensity of a sexual obsession, must have been aggravated by the circumstances surrounding the origin of any venereal disease he may have contracted.

In weighing the evidence the writer has diligently borne in mind one fact. In spite of the solid advance in medical science during the last century the doctors of to-day are admittedly at fault in diagnosing something like two patients out of three. This alarming percentage of error would naturally increase where the patient has been a hundred years dead. Exactly what was wrong with Beethoven's health we shall probably never know with certainty.

Chapter XIII

THE MORTAL BELOVEDS

Beethoven's Virility — Puritanism of Biographers — Attitude toward Women — Rudeness to Servant and Countess Guicciardi — Magdalena Willmann — Therese Malfatti — The Brunswicks — Bettina Brentano — Beethoven as a Lover — Sublimation and Compensation — Handicaps — His Loss, Our Gain

LIKE most geniuses, Beethoven was highly susceptible to the appeal of sex. From an early age he was always in a state of emotion due to one love affair or another. "There was never a time," according to his boyhood friend Dr. Wegeler, "when Beethoven was not in love, and that in the highest degree." Occasionally he "made a conquest which would have been difficult if not impossible for many an Adonis." In touching on his relations with women most of Beethoven's biographers suddenly purse up their lips and mumble their words. Thayer, for example, becomes stilted and mutters: "Let such matters, even if details concerning them were more obtainable, be forgotten." This suggests a bigoted puritanism which must somewhat impair the truth of any biography.

M. Vincent D'Indy writes of him as "a being eminently chaste." He "could not conceive sensual love otherwise than according to the commandments of God—solely in marriage." Herr Paul Bekker, too, would almost like to unsex Beethoven and his music.

Beethoven's relations with women arose naturally from his friendly impulses. . . . Love was never the driving force in his purposes. . . . His music is outside the realm of sexual impulses.

As if any lasting art product could exist outside this realm! Particularly the music of a man so exuberantly vital as Beethoven. Later on Herr Bekker, growing dimly conscious of his error, adds, without realizing the contradiction:

The erotic instinct in him, sublimated, soars to the heights.

The kernel of truth in the contentions of those who would make a Galahad of Beethoven is that he undeniably had loftier sexual ideals than most men. In one of his Sketch Books for 1817 we find this entry:

Sensual gratification without union of souls is and remains bestial. One experiences afterwards no trace of a noble sentiment; on the contrary only penitence.

Ferdinand Ries, who knew the Master during his prime, declared that Beethoven

was fond of the company of women, especially if they had young and pretty faces, and generally when we passed a somewhat charming girl he would turn back and gaze keenly at her through his glasses, and if he noticed that I was observing him, he would laugh or grin. He was frequently in love, but generally only for a short period. Once when I twitted him about his conquest of a pretty woman he admitted that she had held him in the strongest bonds for the longest time, viz. fully seven months.

A great deal of mythological balderdash has been written about Beethoven's affairs of the heart. The plain fact is that these adventures never played any prominently important or long-continued rôle in his scheme of things.

One of the first anecdotes which we have of his relations with women exhibits that rude factor of moral priggishness which all through his letters is like grit in the eyes of those who care for his music. In his late teens Beethoven made a trip with some friends who knew his peculiarities. They bribed a waitress to flirt with him. Meeting with no encouragement, the girl showed more and more initiative. Then suddenly Beethoven turned—and gave her a sonorous box on the ear.

This ungallant incident occurred in 1787. Thirty-six years later a written conversation of the deaf man with his factotum, Schindler, revealed much the same conduct. But this time it was shown towards a woman whom he had passionately loved. With it we find an unpleasing sort of exhibitionist rectitude towards her husband.

The lady was the Countess Gallenberg, who, as young Countess Giulietta Guicciardi, had figured in Beethoven's famous letter of 1801 to Wegeler as "a dear, fascinating girl who loves me and whom I love." It is probable that Giulietta was for a short time engaged, or as good as engaged, to Beethoven; but that the match was opposed by her father, who knew that the virtuoso was going deaf, and may have known still more about his health. A little later, at about the time when Beethoven realized that he could never be her husband, he dedicated to her the *"Moonlight"* sonata (Op. 27, No. 2).[1] And here is the condensed conversation of 1823, translated from the *mélange* of German and bad French in which it was scribbled:

BEETHOVEN: I was well loved by her—more than her husband ever was. However he [Count Gallenberg] was more her lover than I, but through her I learned of his poverty and I found a man of means who gave me the sum of 500 florins to help him out. He was always my enemy. That was precisely the reason why I did him all the good in my power. . . . She was his wife before her journey to Italy. Arrived in Vienna,[2] she came to me in tears, but I despised her.

SCHINDLER: Hercules at the crossroads!

BEETHOVEN: And if I had wished to expend my vital powers on that life, what would have remained for that which was nobler and better?

Which looks uncommonly like an expert piece of rationalizing.

Beethoven had many other flames. Several of them, at one time and another, he tried to marry. To Fräulein Magdalena Willmann, an opera singer from his home town, he wrote in 1795 a proposal of marriage. She scornfully left it unanswered, "because he was ugly and half crazy." Pearls before swine! True, but the pearls would have made

---

[1] Although, if any girl caused the sadness and despair reflected in this music, her name was not, in all likelihood, Giulietta. For the composition Beethoven originally intended dedicating to the Countess Gallenberg was the not particularly ardent Rondo in G major (Op. 51, No. 2). At the last moment, however, wishing to inscribe this piece after all to the Countess Lichnowsky, he asked it back, and dedicated the C sharp minor to Giulietta instead. There is no good reason to suppose that his devotion to her lasted more than a few months. In her old age the Countess spoke of Beethoven without affection, as a person who had composed some "crazy" music. Then, an afterthought, with sudden animation: "But his playing—it was heavenly!"

Behrend comments on these words: "A characteristic statement, which . . . shows from what angle these circles admired Beethoven—that is, as a piano virtuoso."

[2] The words "arrived in Vienna" were interpolated by Schindler for clarity.

a most ill-starred wedding gift. A sound instinct underlay Magdalena's stupid words. No woman could have lived for six months with a man of Beethoven's violent and erratic temperament,—a man to whom the relief of frequent tempests of unreasoning rage was a physical necessity,—a man who could brook neither regularity nor monotony nor restraint of any kind.

Therese Malfatti, a girl of fifteen, whom at thirty-nine he wished to marry, had the same sound instinct. He was also in love, at various times, with two sisters, the Countesses Therese Brunswick and Josephine Deym, with the fascinating Bettina Brentano who captured Goethe's fancy, and with others. But such relations were on the whole not very satisfying. They yielded him more bitterness than sweetness. There is reason to believe that as a lover he was crude and *gauche*, that he was "too rash, too unadvised, too sudden." Naturally this increased his difficulties with the ladies, and forced him, through sublimation, to lavish on his art more energy than he would have chosen. He was enabled to write his greatest works by the psychic mechanism of compensation. Deaf, ill, eccentric, lonely, unattractive, he was in urgent need of a woman's loving companionship. By sublimating his physical creativeness and making supreme beauty out of it compensation took the credit and let the cash go.

Before he had been long in Vienna he became such a grotesquely conspicuous figure that it required all of a girl's courage to be seen in public with him. And few were brave enough to take a second walk by the Master's side.

With the years he lost whatever mitigation of his ugliness the freshness of youth had lent him. His relations with women grew correspondingly more difficult. His loss; our gain. If he had possessed Casanova's face, figure, health, and hypnotic power over women the world would in all likelihood be the poorer to-day by the *Eroica,* the violin concerto, the "*Appassionata,*" the *Missa,* and the C sharp minor quartet. But if he had been the coolly sexless sort of person that many of his biographers would like to make him out, he would never have had any biographers.

Chapter XIV

"A FRESH START"

Le poëte, l'artiste, le saint, disent sans cesse "Encore plus haut."
—ABBÉ ROUX, Pensées.

1803, Sonatas, Op. 31 — A New Style — "Read Shake-speare's Tempest" — April 5, 1803, a Beethoven Program — Concert Conditions Then and Now — First Performance of C Minor Concerto — A Terrible Rehearsal — Second Symphony — The Beethovenian Scherzo — Thematic Interlocking of Movements — The Triad, a Source-Motive as well as a Germ-Motive — The Mount of Olives — The Gellert Songs — "Kreutzer" Sonata — May, 1803, First Performance by Bridgetower, a Mulatto — Dedicated to the Unappreciative Kreutzer

"I AM not at all satisfied with my work so far, and I mean to make a fresh start from to-day." According to Czerny, Beethoven said these words to Krumpholz, his faithful factotum, not long before the appearance of the piano sonatas, opus 31, the first two of which were published early in 1803. This resolution ushered in the second period of his creative life. He probably made it after the actual composition of the first two sonatas. There is nothing revolutionary in the light-hearted G major, with its Haydn-ish *Adagio grazioso*. Nor is the tragic D minor,[1] which is a

---

[1]This is sometimes called the *"Recitative"* sonata, from the recurrent recitative-like figure with which it opens.

musical companion piece to the Heiligenstadt Testament, more than a bridge to the suburbs of the next period.

The new phase begins with the *scherzo* and *finale* of the E flat major sonata (Op. 31, No. 3). This, instead of being grouped with the two preceding works, belongs more naturally with the sets of variations (Op. 34 and 35) and the two virtuoso sonatas, the *"Waldstein"* (Op. 53) and *"Appassionata"* (Op. 57), which follow it.

Of these variations Beethoven wrote to his publishers, Breitkopf and Härtel:

Both are handled in an entirely new manner . . . usually I hardly realize when my ideas are new, and hear of it first from others; but in this instance I can myself assure you that I have done nothing in the same manner before.

The novelty of this style consisted in bringing back into his piano works the elements of virtuosity which had recently been subordinated to the direct poetic expression of emotion. But here virtuosity and poetry were so wholly fused as to form not two elements but one. To the mind of the writer, the E flat sonata (Op. 31), in the midst of which this miracle took place, is one of the loveliest creations of the Master; while the two sets of variations somehow lack that flash of power which can shock a pleasing assemblage of notes into a masterpiece.

The limpid, almost ecstatic beauty of the E flat may be a possible commentary on the exaltation into which this titan fought his way after struggling with despair. We have seen how the grievous *Largo e mesto* of opus 10, No. 3, was followed by two movements of sunny serenity and humour. We have seen how the bright spirits of opus 14 followed the *Pathétique;* and we shall see how the Master was to rally from the despair following the collapse of his hopes for *Fidelio;* how he pulled himself together and lost himself in the humours, the exuberances, and the golden glow of the G major concerto, of the Rasoumowsky quartets, the *"Spring"* symphony, and the monarch of all violin concertos. What other human has ever shown more resilience under the hammers of adversity?

And now, in the period at which we have arrived, we find the happy lyric tenderness of the E flat sonata following hard upon the lamentations of the *"Recitative."* Incidentally, this D minor is the sonata which Beethoven's factotum Schindler once coupled with the *"Appassionata."* He naïvely asked what they meant. And the Master replied: "Read Shakespeare's *Tempest."*

Many have thought this a harmless mystification intended to seal the mouth of a bore. Regarding the *"Appassionata,"* chapter XVIII will suggest a different explanation. As for opus 31, did the Master possibly think of the *Allegro* and Minuet of the E flat sonata as a Ferdinand and Miranda love episode, following the shipwreck of the *"Recitative"*?

The unbelievable fertility of this period pushed Beethoven's private life to the wall. He had no time to live outside the kingdom of heaven that was within him. Happily inspired geniuses, like happy nations, have no history —or scarcely any.

April 5, 1803, is a momentous date in the history of

music. At the Theater an der Wien the Master brought to a hearing the wealth of works he had created or finished within a year. But *what* a hearing! We moderns find it hard to realize our good fortune in having the C minor concerto played by Gieseking on a modern concert grand, with Stokowski and the Philadelphia orchestra, or Toscanini and the Philharmonic. We scarcely appreciate the privilege of hearing an orchestra which has been daily rehearsed and has been rigorously weeded out and recruited from among the best players in the world. Between a concert by such an organization and that of April 5, 1803, there is a shocking contrast.

The solo part of the C minor concerto was played on a miserable little box of wires, hardly more sonorous than a spinet. The virtuoso was Beethoven himself, whose deafness and creativeness had already made sad inroads on his technic. There had not been time for him even to write out his own part. He played it from a few sheets of self-invented musical shorthand. And these a frantic young satellite had to "turn according to the notes."

The orchestra was a hastily improvised affair, recruited from the highways and hedges for this occasion only. It had to appear without even a single completely adequate rehearsal. In such circumstances a smaller person than Beethoven would have been disheartened. But this man was sustained by his prophetic vision and the knowledge that he was working for distant generations. Born into a day of small things he helped the day to expand by giving it creations beyond the scope of its available means of expression.

So it was literally forced to improve these means and thus to grow with them—a method much used by emancipators of humanity.

The concert programs of those days were of such stupendous proportions that they could be digested only by an audience of musical ostriches. This program included the First and Second symphonies, the C minor piano concerto, (Op. 37), and a whole oratorio, *The Mount of Olives.*

To aggravate matters the general rehearsal began at eight on the morning of the concert. Ries reported it a terrible occasion. By half-past two everybody was exhausted and more or less disgruntled. In this crisis Lichnowsky proved himself every inch a prince. Dispatching an emergency call to a caterer he saved the day with free sandwiches and wine. After this things went better.

The concert was a success and brought Beethoven 1,800 gulden. But the press proved none too favourable, complaining especially that the Second symphony was a laboured striving for originality. The *finale,* which sounds so harmless to us to-day, seemed to the ears of 1803 an outrageous straining after novelty at any price. One critic likened it to "a repulsive monster, a wounded dragon, throwing its unwieldy body about, and lashing wildly with its tail as it stiffens in its death agony."

It seems hardly possible that only a year could have separated the Second symphony (Op. 36) from the First. In the First everything spoke of Haydn, Mozart, the rococo, and the gropings of an apprentice hand. In the Second Haydn and Mozart began to blow faint as the horns of elfland. The colour was glowing, the outlines sure. It was a frontier work, with one foot on the formal Eighteenth and the other on the romantic Nineteenth Century slope of the great divide. Here first we see Beethoven, touching a prelude upon the mature instrument which was to sound the universal chords of the Third, Fifth, and Ninth symphonies.

The most significant thing about the Second is that here the typical Beethoven *scherzo*

Ex. 21

first tentatively entered the symphony. In this form Beethoven's early manhood was destined to strike out its most characteristic and lasting contribution to the art.

The relationship between the *scherzo* and the *Larghetto*[2] of the Second is so close as to remind one of the thematic oneness we have noticed in the *Sonate Pathétique*,[3] from which work, indeed, as we shall see, these movements borrow the germ-motive that unifies it. Among all the movements, however, there is a much more general thematic unity than this. Everyone knows that the Fifth symphony is founded, to a certain extent, on the half-triad G–G–G–E flat. But it is not generally realized that in a much more

---

[2] See Ex. 236, p. 555.
[3] See pp. 53-55.

literal sense the Second symphony is built upon the whole triad. Take the first subject of the first movement, strip it of ornaments, and reduce it to lowest terms. It amounts to no more than the mere tonic chord the notes of which are starred in the following example:

Ex. 22

Likewise, though less frankly, the triad germ-motive is found to be the basis of all the other principal themes of the first movement, *Larghetto* and *scherzo*, and of the tune which opens the *finale*, after the two-measure wink of its mock-heroic introduction. As for the other two *finale* themes, they are as nakedly and unashamedly triads as the opening of the *Eroica* or of the C minor concerto.

Now the triad is a fundamental thing in music, and one of its mysteries.

. . . here is the finger of God, a flash of the will that can,
  Existent behind all laws, that made them and, lo, they are!
And I know not if, save in this, such gift be allowed to man,
  That out of three sounds he frame, not a fourth sound, but a star.
Consider it well: each tone of our scale in itself is naught:
  It is everywhere in the world—loud, soft, and all is said:
Give it to me to use! I mix it with two in my thought:
  And there! Ye have heard and seen: consider and bow the head![4]

The triad played a larger rôle than that of a mere germ-motive used to tie together the movements of a single work. It was also one of those basic motives which gave Beethoven

---

[4] Robert Browning, "Abt Vogler."

so little peace and which managed to insinuate themselves so often into the very fountainhead of his creativeness, and into so many of his subjects, that we shall, for convenience, and in default of existing terminology, call them source-motives. For truly Beethoven drew from such sources an important part of his material.[5]

Apart from its historical and technical interest and significance, the Second is not a very highly satisfying symphony. It is much more of a pioneer work than the First. And pioneer works are seldom finished products. Beethoven's imagination usually kept somewhat ahead of his technic. But the Second is a rare instance of the contrary. Here his manner was more advanced and significant than his matter.

A word about the rest of that interminable program. The C minor was the last concerto which Beethoven was to treat in the time-honoured manner as a display piece for a soloist. The three which were to follow, two for piano and one for violin, were more like the symphonies for orchestra with solo instrument obbligato, which Schumann and Brahms were to develop.

The oratorio *The Mount of Olives* (*Christus am Ölberge*) (Op. 85) is one of Beethoven's weakest works. It must have been insufferable when added to that Gargantuan feast of April 5th. In composing this oratorio Beethoven was almost as much handicapped by the unpoetic text as if he were setting Stubbs's *Ecclesiastical Polity*, or *Who's Who*. It is evident that the music was made, not born.

[5]For a discussion of the triad as source-motive see pp. 575-577.

The reverse happened when next he tried vocal music. The six religious lyrics of Gellert, which he set as opus 48, inspired him as much as *The Mount of Olives* had repelled him. The *"Song of Penitence"* and *"The Praise of God in Nature"* are the best of these. They are perhaps the most powerful and elemental short pieces that this unvocal composer ever wrote for the voice.

The *"Kreutzer"* sonata (Op. 47) is less a sonata than a sort of double concerto for violin and piano, unaccompanied. This occasional work was written at the request of the famous mulatto violinist, Bridgetower, for his concert in May, 1803. The exciting tarantelle-like *finale*

Ex. 23

had been written the year before for the A major violin sonata. But Beethoven recognized that it did not belong there. He plucked it from that ugly duckling as if it were a bunch of pure gold tail-feathers. So late was he in finishing the work that the frantic Bridgetower had to read the variations at sight on the platform from Beethoven's hopelessly blind manuscript.

It implies no great compliment for the other nine to call this the best of Beethoven's violin sonatas. True, it is a consistent whole, like a Whistler painting which is covered by a single skin. But in the matter of sincerity and emotional depth the *"Kreutzer"* here and there betrays that it was written for a special occasion. After the moving intimacy of the slow movement's theme

Ex. 24

the superficiality of the variations is a surprise and a disappointment. One feels that the composer has not quite kept faith. But technically the work is of keen interest as regards the thematic interlocking of the different movements by means of a germ-motive.[6]

Beethoven promised Bridgetower the dedication of this sonata. Then he quarrelled with him "over a girl" and inscribed the work instead to the eminent violinist, Rudolph Kreutzer. But Kreutzer could never bring himself to play the sonata because he felt that it was so "outrageously unintelligible!"[7] In offering him this dedication Beethoven had, for once, cast guineas before guinea pigs.

[6]See pp. 536–538.
[7]Berlioz, *Voyage Musical*, Vol. I, p. 261.

By this time the Master was well launched on the "fresh start." Soon his growing momentum was to carry him into one of the most consistently and superbly creative periods that any artist has ever known.

Chapter XV

BEETHOVENISM

Each age is a dream that is dying
Or one that is coming to birth.

—ARTHUR E. W. O'SHAUGHNESSY, "The Music Makers."

What Are Classicism and Romanticism? — Beethoven Simultaneously Embodies Both — Political Revolution and Romanticism — The Young Æsthetic Radicals — Formlessness as the Law of Form — Creators and the Golden Mean — Beethoven Harmonizes Extremes — Breadth of His Interests

▲▲

ALTERNATING through the story of the arts run the rhythms of two opposing but complementary impulses: classicism and romanticism. One is the architectonic, clarifying, the other is the adventurous, enriching impulse.

The writer knows no clearer description of the workings of the law of periodicity in art than the one given by Dr. Daniel Gregory Mason:[1]

For a while it [art] develops its power of synthesis until it is able to present a few simple factors of effect in clear, salient unity. This is what is called a period of classicism. Then, dissatisfied with its attainment, desiring a richer reflection of the great whirl of experience, it reaches out after novel effects; its vision is for a while more extended than clear, and, presenting many effects which it cannot yet unify, it becomes brilliant, suggestive, fragmentary, turgid, inchoate. There has been a sacrifice of the old

---

[1]*From Grieg to Brahms*, 1927, p. 217 ff.

simple clarity for a richer chaos, or, in the trite terminology, a romantic movement. Now, however, technical skill and synthetic power of thought again advance, and a new and complexer order supervenes on the temporary confusion. Unity of effect is regained, art is classic once more (but with increased wealth of meaning), and the time is ripe for another burst of romanticism.

To make Dr. Mason's explanation more vivid we might think of the romanticist as the child who finds the house stuffy, runs out to romp on the sunny beach, and wanders far, having all kinds of strange and enlivening experiences, until he falls into a quicksand. And the classicist is his learned father, the renowned professor, who pulls the lad out and carries him home to bed. Thereupon he empties the little pockets and discovers—among the bits of kelp and sea urchins and curious pebbles and shreds of jellyfish— three or four absolutely new and priceless specimens to add to his incomparable, but somewhat dusty, shell collection. It is exactly the impulse he needs, and he gets out the feather duster and sets to work with renewed enthusiasm.

It is good to realize that these two are quite necessary to one another. For, if the man steadies and saves the lad, the lad freshens up the man and enriches his life.

Beethoven embodied in his one person the ideals of both classicism and romanticism and held the balance true between them. He was at once the eternal sage and the eternal youth. If any artist of any sort can ever be said to have brought one age to a close and inaugurated the next, Beethoven was that artist. More than any other one man's his influence ended the rococo period of classicism in music and created the romanticism with which we are familiar. Indeed, this was so largely his unaided achievement that the new musical movement which began the Nineteenth Century should perhaps be called, not romanticism, but Beethovenism.

In the rococo age form was all in all—beautiful, smoothly rounded, superficial form, which covered with fashionable éclat no little poverty of content and of emotion; graceful form which harmonized with the frivolous elegance of gentry, blind and insensible to the misery of the masses.

Then the revolution exploded. "Liberty, equality and fraternity" was projected in splashes of blood and fire across the heavens of Europe and America. The fierce revulsion called romanticism set in. Led by such hot-headed young æstheticians as Tieck, Schlegel, and Novalis, the romanticists proposed in the interests of liberty to cast form into outer darkness and set up emotion in its place.

"Down with the Bastille of form!" they shrieked. "Long live content, as determined by the personal emotions of the artist!" In the way of young literary radicals they began by drawing up into a program the articles of their faith. They had no notion they themselves were proposing that the plough should precede the ox. For the gospel according to art commences, not "In the beginning was the word," but "In the beginning was the deed." The laws of art are deduced from works of art; not vice versa.

These terrible infants of romanticism made very much the mistake which was repeated in America, more than a century later, by the so-called *Imagistes*. With pomp and circumstance Tieck and his friends announced their great deeds to the world before the fact. As Herr Ernest phrases it, they "proclaimed formlessness as the one law of form, and believed that by this denial of the old they had already created something new. One forgot, or ignored, the fact that true originality consists not in being different from others, but in being wholly in harmony with one's self." And so it comes that we are to-day more interested in what Tieck, Schlegel, and Amy Lowell have to say about other artists than we are in their original work.

Great creators almost never spring from the ranks of the violent revolutionists or of the crustacean conservatives. They are not, as Pope expressed it,[2]

> . the first by whom the new are tried,
> Nor yet the last to lay the old aside.

Their home is with truth, somewhere near the golden mean.

Beethoven grew up amid the hard-shell formalism of the classical age. He was almost six years old when the Liberty Bell gave forth that first peal of romanticist music from the belfry of Independence Hall in Philadelphia. He was almost nineteen when the Bastille fell with a crash heard round the world. His early manhood welcomed with enthusiasm the rousing call of the French Revolution.

But he kept his head. He steered his artistic career successfully between Scylla and divine Charybdis. On the one hand he realized the shortcomings of the feudal and aristocratic past. On the other he perceived that the æsthetic philosophy of the extreme "reds," if carried to a

[2] *An Essay on Criticism,* l. 335.

logical conclusion, would end in obliterating the frontier between art and nature—would, in fact, destroy the very things that make art art.

He saw too, very clearly, the contradiction into which Tieck and his comrades fell when they acknowledged freedom and the emotion of the unconscious as the sources of all art, and then proceeded to fetter themselves by laying down conscious, a priori principles to be followed in their own subsequent creative work.

Beethoven's chief contribution lay in harmonizing these two extremes. He dug the old forms out of their rut, remoulding them nearer to the age's need. And he instinctively felt that the age's need coincided with his own heart's desire. As we have before remarked, he never consciously strove for originality. Anyone who assumes the air of having said or done the unique is usually self-deluded. The Master's uniqueness came of itself when he set the old forms free for the reception of a more profound charge of sincere and personal emotion than they had ever felt. The music was new, not because he deliberately tried for novelty, but because nearly every bar of it was freely saturated with his unusual and powerful personality.

Although Beethoven had had almost no formal schooling this personality of his was laid out on a broader intellectual scale than can be found in any of his forerunners. These men had usually been servants. They had taken an interest in little besides their own "shop."

Beethoven's interest embraced the universe. He once wrote pompously to his publishers:

There is no dissertation which would be too learned for me. Without setting up the smallest pretension to real learning, I have from childhood on always endeavoured to grasp the significance of the better things and of the wise productions of every age. Shame on any artist who does not feel himself obliged to do at least as much!

Standing at the junction of two epochs Beethoven became the leading spirit of each. His romanticism made him the greatest of the classicists, for it inspired him to play Pygmalion to the plaster casts of music and flush them with the warmth of his own superb vitality. At the same time his classicism made him the greatest of the romantics, for it led him to temper the fantastic excesses of the young extremists into a reasonable working philosophy, of far-reaching influence.

More than any other leading figure in the history of the arts Beethoven was responsible for that mystical marriage between two opposed systems of æsthetics wherein, as Herr Ernest expresses it, "each yielded up something of its own nature so that they might unite into a single new and higher form of being." Too bad that the Master could not have been one of those "long-livers" portrayed in *Back to Methuselah!* He might have held the romantic and classical impulses in equilibrium, on into the coming age of the one-sixteenth tone scale.

However, let us give thanks for what he actually accomplished. It takes a colossal genius to be at once a leading representative of classicism and of romanticism. This was Beethoven's achievement. Let us see what came of it.

[121]

Chapter XVI

PROMETHEUS BRINGS FIRE

Napoleon and the Eroica, 1803 — *Absurd Poetic Programs of Early Critics — Beethoven on Napoleon's Death — His Possible Attitude towards the* Scherzo — *The Germinal* Prometheus *Tune — Bekker on the* Prometheus *Idea — Momentousness of the* Eroica — *One Gigantic Set of Variations — The Hero Theme a Germ-Motive — Derived from the* Prometheus *Tune — Resemblances in Mozart — Other Thematic Liaison Work — Interlocking of Movements Deliberate — Novelty of the* Eroica — *The Epochmaking Beethovenian* Scherzo — *Finale Inadequate — Sonata-Form Freed — The Episode — Burning His Bridge-Passages — Sonata-Form Fused — The Symphony Unified — Press Unfavourable*

THE unconscious mind of a musical genius can usually be counted upon to create something more universal than any concrete poetic idea which his conscious mind may happen to associate with his music.

In 1803 young Europe regarded Napoleon I as its Messiah and apostle of liberty, very much as it was destined for a short time, one hundred and fifteen years later, to regard Woodrow Wilson. It was in this year that Beethoven began his third sonata for orchestra. He called it the *Eroica,* or *Heroic,* symphony.

In it he intended to celebrate the personality of the Corsican. But before he had finished one page the music had shot far above the levels of a work about any one personality. So that when, angered by Napoleon's imperial ambitions, Beethoven struck his name from the title page of the completed symphony, he made the music not less, but more, true to itself. For the *Eroica* is laid out on a vast scale. Its program, if program there must be, should aim at nothing smaller than an apotheosis of the heroic in mankind.

Some guides to musical appreciation are positive that the Funeral March dealt with the death of the English General Abercrombie at the battle of Alexandria. Others claim that it had to do with the false report of Nelson's death at Aboukir. But even supposing that Beethoven had had either of these men in mind (which is not so) it would prove nothing against the generic quality of the music.

The earlier critics took this symphony with extreme literalness. Lenz[1] was convinced that the thirty-two great bangs in the syncopated portion of the development of the first movement meant that the hero, whoever he was, perished, like Cæsar in the Capitol, of thirty-two dagger thrusts! This of course would transpose the second half of the *Allegro* to the ethereal heights of the Hereafter.

Oulibischeff[2] recognized in the first movement the galloping of Napoleonic squadrons and felt sure they had arrived in Egypt by the time the development had been reached, because its Episode (see Ex. 43, p. 135) was decidedly "a tune of oriental colouring"!

[1] Wilhelm von Lenz, *Beethoven*, 1858, Vol. III, p. 295 ff.

[2] Alexander Oulibischeff, *Beethoven, seine Kritiker und seine Ausleger*, translated into German, 1859, p. 184 ff.

As a matter of fact when, in 1821, Beethoven heard of Napoleon's passing at St. Helena, he remarked with the satisfaction of a successful seer: "I composed the music for that sad event some seventeen years ago." But, like his critics, the composer was mistaken. His music is too universal for the narrow scope of any one sad event. His unconscious mind builded better than he knew.[3]

The *scherzo*,[4] on the other hand, might conceivably be taken as a broad, brilliant fresco of common life. Possibly Beethoven's conscious mind may have thought of it as depicting the Dionysiac dance in which man's immortal will to live—carrying on in defiance of no matter what death and destruction—hands on the torch of exuberantly heroic vitality from generation to generation. Or, more concretely, the close relation of these principal themes with those of the first movement suggests that Beethoven may have had in mind an excited crowd of hero worshippers at a public festivity. To them enters the hero amid wild acclamations and turns toward them the most genial and human side of his rugged personality.

But does it really matter *what* concrete image the Master's conscious mind played with as long as his unconscious gave us something that so far transcends any poetic image? Richard Wagner spoke more modestly and more truly than any who have commented on this symphony:

[3]Supposing the Funeral March were expressible in poetic terms, it might more fittingly be described as a dirge for all humanity. "If a nation—yes, if all mankind were laid to rest it would need no more sublime strains. If the *Eroica* glorifies any one hero, it is Beethoven himself." (From an unpublished lecture by Dr. Max Friedländer of Berlin University.)

[4]See Ex. 37, p. 132, and Exs. 28–30, p. 128.

THE BOURDELLE BEETHOVEN
In the Metropolitan Museum of Art

MOZART

Who said of young Beethoven, "Watch that chap!
Some day he will make the world talk about him"

BEETHOVEN'S GRANDFATHER, LUDOVICUS

BEETHOVEN'S BIRTHPLACE AT BONN

"SPANGY"

Beethoven at sixteen years of age in court dress

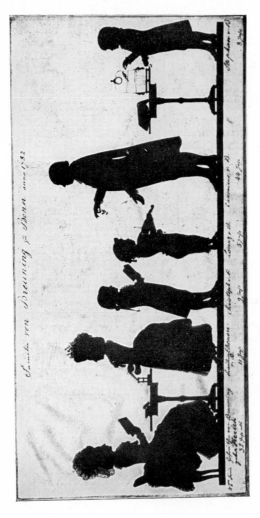

SILHOUETTE OF THE VON BREUNING FAMILY

Eleanore is second, facing her mother, who made Ludwig a second home.
Stephan is feeding the bird

I   II

IV   V

BEETHOVEN'S TEACHERS

I Johann Albrechtsberger   II Antonio Salieri

III Joseph Haydn

IV Joseph Schenck   V Christian Gottlob Neefe

JOHANN NEPOMUK HUMMEL
Whom Beethoven called "Nazy of my Heart"

I

II

TWO OF BEETHOVEN'S SUMMER RETREATS
I Heiligenstadt
II Mödling: Courtyard of the Haffner House

THE MORTAL BELOVEDS
I Therese Malfatti   II Countess Giulietta Guicciardi
III Countess Therese Brunswick
IV Amalie Sebald   V Bettina von Arnim, *née* Brentano

BEETHOVEN IN 1803
From the miniature by Hornemann

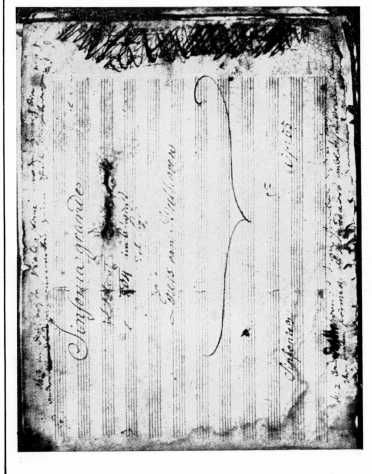

THE EROICA SCORE

Title-page, with Napoleon's name obliterated as shown in centre

BEETHOVEN IN 1804
After the Mähler portrait from the copy in possession
of the Beethoven Association, New York

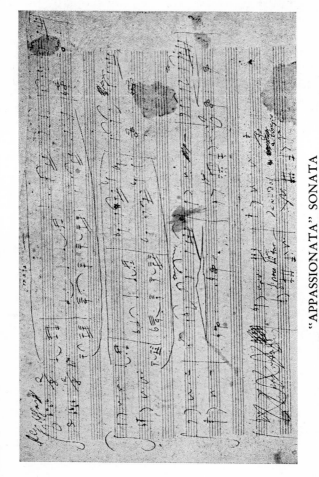

"APPASSIONATA" SONATA

Reduced facsimile from the original rain-spotted manuscript

I   II

III   IV

EARLY INTERPRETERS OF BEETHOVEN'S MUSIC

I Baroness Dorothea von Ertmann   II Carl Czerny
III Ferdinand Ries   IV Ignaz Schuppanzigh

BEETHOVEN'S LETTER TO THE "IMMORTAL BELOVED"
Beginning of the second section of the letter

In none but the Master's language of tones could be expressed that inexpressible which words may manage to indicate with only the utmost embarrassment and difficulty.[5]

As we shall presently see, the theme of the *finale* was probably the germ of the entire work. Beethoven composed it in 1801 as the chief tune in his *Prometheus* ballet. When, two years later, he began to create the symphony of heroism it was natural to borrow musical material from his own treatment of the heroic legend. There he had depicted the

lofty spirit who found the men of his day in a state of ignorance and civilized them by giving them the sciences and arts. Starting from this idea . . . the ballet shows us two statues, vivified and made susceptible to all the passions of human life by the power of harmony.[6]

Following in the literal footsteps of Lenz and Oulibischeff, Professor Bekker seeks to interpret the *Eroica finale* as Beethoven's "true Prometheus poem . . . for which the ballet and the pianoforte variations(Op. 35) were merely preparatory." He sees the introduction's downward hurtling figure in G minor as

the fall of the Titans, while through Prometheus' word of power the first statue begins to stir with life. A simple theme (hesitating between the dominant and the tonic) appears, representing the germ of the movement and also the first primitive form of life. The second figure imitates the clumsy, difficult motion of the first. The theme becomes clearly more definite and conscious,

---

[5]Richard Wagner, *Gesammelte Schriften*, Vol. V, p. 172.

[6]Quoted from the official theatre playbill, which gives virtually all we know of the action of the ballet. The original text of the work has been lost.

symbolizing life's will to form, and suddenly assumes a different aspect. . . . The great act of creation seems to take place before our eyes, the creative will calling up an endless multiplicity of forms, till a supernatural triumph of mind is achieved, flooding the universe with light.[7]

Such literalism as this is one of the chief natural foes of music.

When Beethoven created the *Eroica,* he became a modern Prometheus and brought to mortal music a hitherto un-dreamed-of fire. The momentousness of such a feat would seem to justify discussing this symphony in more detail than any other work of the Master.

Here and elsewhere[8] much attention will be paid to the varied origins and inter-relationships of his subject matter. For the benefit of the wary reader who instinctively shies away from diagrams of the inexplicable the writer would disclaim any fatuous idea of "explaining" a piece of music when he traces the descent or consanguinity of its themes. This is done merely in the hope of shedding more light upon Beethoven's creative processes, particularly upon his mastery of economy of material and variety in unity.

In a liberal sense of the term, this whole *Eroica* symphony is simply one gigantic set of variations, including the *finale's* set as a smaller wheel within its enormous one. As long as Beethoven himself wrote the label *Eroica* on the flyleaf of the symphony we may legitimately designate its opening tune as the Hero theme.

---

[7]*Beethoven,* 1925, p. 165.
[8]See especially chaps. LIII–LVI.

Allegro con brio.

Ex. 25

This heroic tune, which appositely consists of a bugle call transposed into the baritone register, can be traced, under various appropriate disguises, in every movement. It runs throughout the work as one of the early instances of the germ-motive, though far more ingeniously varied than when we met with that invention in the *Sonate Pathétique* and the Second symphony.

Dr. Charles Wood discovered that if we take the first two full measures of the Funeral March,

Ex. 26

undress them of their mere ornaments, revise their rhythm, and hum them backwards (a proceeding fit for music about death, which is a reversal of the forward drive of life) — we have the beginning of the Hero theme, appropriately transposed to the minor, and sounding like this:[9]

Ex. 27

[9]On the margin of the manuscript of this book the late Oscar G. Sonneck noted his impression that "the Hero theme appears in the Funeral March somewhere in the lower or middle regions, quite recognizably, without having to divest Istar of her veils." Search revealed among the middle voices of bars 87–92 the familiar tune C–E–C–G–C–E–G–C. But it is rhythmically so distorted and is divided up so cleverly between the first and second horns as to be almost unrecognizable unless one already knows it is there.

We have the germ-motive again, brutalized and roughly handled, in the syncopated second theme of the *scherzo*.

Ex. 28

And it is interesting to find, in looking through Beethoven's *Eroica* sketches, that one of his early ideas for the Trio of this *scherzo* was the following variant of the Hero theme:

Ex. 29

In the Sketch Books the composer rarely bothered to write down any signature. Here the reader must supply the three flats. Fortunately he soon thought better of this crude idea, and gave us instead the present enlivening outburst of hunting horns.

Ex. 30

As for the *finale*, if one will half shut that which in the inner ears corresponds to the outer eyelids and will hum the *Prometheus* theme of the variations,

Ex. 31

its general outline will be recognized as resembling that of the germ-motive. It is evident that Ex. 31 is such an elaboration of Ex. 25 as would be appropriate for the theme of a set of variations, especially if one considers the second and third measures of Ex. 31 as an amplification of its first three notes. If we eliminate these two measures by telescoping the tune the *Prometheus* theme will read:

Ex. 32

Melodically this amounts to Ex. 25 minus its fourth note and its very end; which would come to this:

Ex. 33

The resemblance of the two tunes is brought still closer by the horn's version of Ex. 25 in the coda of the first movement (at measure 631), with its repeated high B flats.

And the idea that Ex. 25 may have been derived from Ex. 31 is made still more plausible by the assurance of Czerny that the original Hero theme went as follows:

Ex. 34

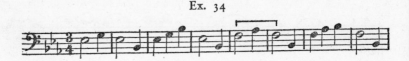

Notice how the bracketed F–A flat–F in this Sketch version follow the F–A flat–F in the second and third bars of Ex. 31. This strongly suggests that the Hero theme was originally more like an almost unabridged version of the *Prometheus* theme and was telescoped only as a happy afterthought.

The fact that Beethoven used Ex. 31 in his *Prometheus* ballet as early as 1801 would appear to indicate that this may have been the germ of the *Eroica*. Although the *Prometheus* tune now seems to us like an elaboration of the germ-motive the writer is inclined to believe that Beethoven worked backwards and arrived at Ex. 25 by telescoping and simplifying Ex. 31.[10]

Of course there remains the suspicious resemblance, or rather identity, of Ex. 25 with the opening of the twelve-year-old Mozart's operetta, *Bastien et Bastienne*.

Ex. 35

---

[10]The *Prometheus* tune, in its turn, may have been derived from the very similar melody at bar 136 of the *finale* of the First string quartet (F major, Op. 18, No. 1).

There is also a speaking—or rather, singing—likeness to a part of the same germinal composer's E flat symphony (opening Allegro, bar 29, ff.).[11] If this was stealing it was the regal kind that "blesseth him that gives and him that takes." It would remind one of the way Shakespeare borrowed his *Julius Cæsar* from the desiccated pages of Plutarch. It would recall the brilliant result as well. For both Shakespeare and Beethoven put the unremarkable, alloy-like material through their Midas machines, and it came out pure gold.

But it is doubtful if Beethoven had ever heard *Bastien*. Sir George Grove thought he may have, in his Bonn days. Thayer was positive that he never had. Even if he had, the Mozart tune probably influenced him quite unconsciously when he was telescoping the *Prometheus* tune into the Hero theme. At any rate, this latter was the sort of elemental, inevitable theme which might occur independently to more than one genius, just as the idea of the telephone occurred to three inventors at once.

The prevalence of the Hero germ-motive by no means exhausts the inter-movement theme relationships of this closely knit symphony.

Just as the second subject of the *scherzo* (see Ex. 28, p. 128) is a variant of the Hero theme, so the *scherzo's* first subject, if one may coin a needed word, is a "scherzification" of the end of the second subject of the first movement. Compare the second half of Ex. 36 with the first theme of

---

[11]And to the first subject of the *Allegro assai* of Joseph Reicha's D major symphony.

Ex. 36

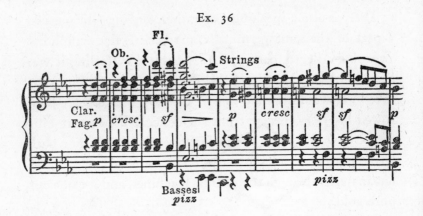

the *scherzo*, which is purposely given with its introduction. Consider in both of these examples the upward chromatic progression followed by the four-note passage which runs downward in eighths.

Ex. 37

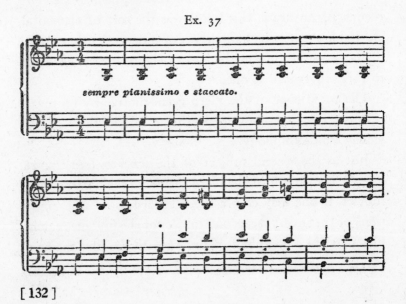

Before leaving Ex. 36, let us notice that its first half also has a cousin in another movement. If its high flute voice is dropped down an octave to the plane of the other instruments and its repeated notes are fused into one the tune reads:

Ex. 38

And what is this but a transposition of the start of the *Prometheus* tune?

Ex. 39

The fugato in the Funeral March

Ex. 40

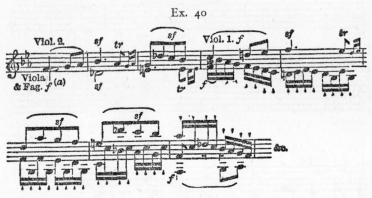

begins with an inversion of the second theme of this movement,

Ex. 41

which reminds one of the B natural–C–D–E flat at the beginning of the March,[11a] and the extraordinarily eloquent little slurred run of the double-bass accompaniment to the first theme which lends such a subtly mysterious colour of distant muffled drums to the opening. But the beginning of this fugato is also tied up to the first movement by its close resemblance to the clarinet phrase at the latter's 57th measure,

[11a]See Ex. 26, p. 127, first two full bars.

and to that of the violoncello in the Episode at bar 287.

Just as the short development ends, the violoncellos and basses start a figure

that vividly recalls their own giant stridings in the development of the first movement.

It may be objected that Beethoven did not mean a large part of these subtle imitations and analogies—that they were merely accidental. But it is hard to believe that such a mighty improvisator could have overlooked many of the possibilities of his chief subjects, especially of such well worked and often used material as the *Prometheus* tune.

The artist Mähler has related how he once heard the composer improvise for two hours on the closing portion of the *Eroica finale*. Could such a finished expert in the development of subjects have failed to experiment, for instance, with telescoping the *Prometheus* theme? Could he have neglected to try it in the minor, reversed, inverted, or scherzified? It seems highly improbable.

That the *Eroica* could have been written, as it was written, only one year after the Second symphony is hardly credible. It burst upon the world with the abruptness of an exploding mine. The first three movements were overwhelmingly new phenomena. Nothing like the broad lines or the terrific intensities of the first movement had yet been known.[12] Creating it must have been a stupendous experience. Indeed, as one surveys the battle ground of the Sketch Books, one seems to discern a heroic form locked in struggle with a huge winged figure, and to catch the desperate cry: "I will not let thee go, except thou bless me!"[13] Whatever else from the Master's hand may have aged, these measures are as fresh and luminous with terrible light as the day they were finished.

No such poignant and noble funeral march as the second movement had ever been heard, nor has ever been heard. In those days it was a startling innovation to put such a piece into a symphony. And it was even more startling to introduce the conventional old device of a fugato,[14] and

---

[12]"The excellence of every art is its intensity, capable of making all disagreeables evaporate from their being in close relationship with Beauty and Truth."—JOHN KEATS. (Quoted in Colvin's *Life of Keats*, p. 253.)

[13]Genesis XXXII, 26.

[14]See Ex. 40, p. 134.

then inform the thing with a passion and compelling poetry that made it shine as the glory of the movement—that is to say, if one excepts the truly seraphic breath of consolation at the beginning of the coda.

Ex. 46

The brazen footfalls of this fugato, solemnly, implacably advancing, brought to the mind of Felix Weingartner "the chorus in a tragedy of Æschylus."

A more startling novelty was the introduction of the first of those tremendous *scherzos* which constituted perhaps the most original, individual, and epoch-making contribution that Beethoven ever made to the forms of music. Though Haydn invented the charming name and applied it to a speeded-up minuet, his successor invented the thing itself. If this *scherzo,* this "huge spout of life,"[15] were blotted out of the literature of music, along with its mighty successors in the Fifth and Ninth symphonies, the B flat trio, the *Hammerklavier* sonata, the First Rasoumowsky, and C sharp minor quartets, the art would be unthinkably impoverished.

It was, of course, an unusual proceeding to end a symphony with variations. But a more momentous innovation was the poetic and symbolic significance attained by the Master in mixing their unheard-of colours on his new

[15]As Mr. Lawrence Gilman has aptly called one of these *scherzos.*

orchestral palette, and by vividly individualizing the different instruments.

Yet for all its germinal quality and its undeniable charm, this movement is a disappointment, as *finales* and last acts often are. It is almost as unworthy to complete such a titanic first movement and march and *scherzo* as the charming legs of a ballet dancer would be to terminate a statue of Hercules. One has the same sense of anticlimax as is given by the *finale* of the tremendous B flat trio and by that setting of Schiller's drinking song *de luxe* which ends, but does not finish, the Ninth symphony.

Here one is sometimes strongly tempted to try a little surgery and enjoy these works as glorious torsos. Surely they can do without inadequate legs as well as Our Lady of Milo can do without adequate arms!

But the most revolutionary thing about the *Eroica* was the liberation it gave sonata-form in the first movement. Beethoven freed it for the reception of a more consistent, more closely knit logic and a more poignant emotion than it had ever before known. One way by which he made sonata-form spacious for the welcoming of fresh ideas was by introducing the lovely, wistful, and apparently new E minor Episode into the development section of this movement.

Ex. 43

The "working-out" portion of a sonata had heretofore been as jealously taboo to new ideas as the mind of a fundamentalist to new theological doctrine. VERBOTEN was posted on the sacred enclosure. Then Beethoven came striding roughshod over the forbidden threshold, leading in this radiant novelty.

And yet, the more you make friends with the interloper, the more convincingly it seems to fit into the logical scheme of the symphony—the more it begins to sound like an animated and ornate version of the second principal subject.[16] The likeness becomes marked in the descending run at the end of both tunes. And the D sharps which the first violin repeats for four measures by way of ushering in the Episode add to the resemblance. It is as though Beethoven had written the poetic second subject in austere blank verse, neglected it, and later, repenting of this neglect, had embellished it with rhyme, enriched it with allusion, and brought it in again, under the pseudonym of Episode.

The word "allusion" refers to that phrase in the violoncello part of the Episode (in its second appearance, bar 323)

Ex. 47

which is a rhythmic variant of the transitional motive

Ex. 48

---

[16] See Ex. 36, p. 132.

beginning at bar 45 of the first movement and leading towards the second subject. This is evolved, in turn, from the phrase

Ex. 49

with which the violoncellos continue the Hero motive at the 6th bar.

Which brings us to a most significant invention in this so inventive symphony. It was a device here used for the first time in symphonic writing and was destined to cause a sensational change in the character of sonata-form—to make it more of an organic unit than ever before.

The device consisted in doing away with the arbitrary but conventional bridge-work passages which had always led from the first to the second subjects in this form (Wagner labelled them "the clatter of dishes between the courses of a meal"), and in constructing the approach, instead, out of materials taken from the first subject itself. When Beethoven built an approach out of Ex. 48,[17]—the child of Ex. 49,[18] he literally burned his symphonic bridges behind him.

The approach came out as follows:

Ex. 50

---

[17]See p. 139.
[18]See last-given example.

and it in turn evolved a second approach.

Ex. 51

This, when undressed of its passing notes, amounts to

Ex. 52

which is the child of the passage marked (a) in Ex. 50.

Burning his bridges made it possible for Beethoven to carry out strictly the new method which was his chief gift to Romanticism. This consisted in the ordered and convincing progress of thematic logic[19] from the first to the second subject and beyond. This was sharply opposed to the more fortuitous hit-or-miss methods of his rococo predecessors.[20]

The *Eroica's* crowning invention consisted in fusing the sonata-form movement into an absolutely organic unity. Before Beethoven such a movement had been more like a

---

[19]Various musical forms bear a close correspondence with the mechanisms of the science of logic. The sonata, for example, is inductive; the variation form, deductive. Expressed in a logical formula:

Sonata-form : Induction : : The Variation : Deduction.

In the *Eroica* symphony Beethoven fused both of these forms into a kind of wordless superlogic.

> "But God has a few of us whom he whispers in the ear;
> The rest may reason and welcome; 'tis we musicians know."
> (ROBERT BROWNING, "Abt Vogler.")

[20]Another of this symphony's inventions is a marked increase in the importance and length of the development section and of the coda. The development section here is three times the length, and its coda more than twice the length, of corresponding portions of the Second symphony. In all his other symphonies the development is no longer than the exposition, while in the *Eroica* it is almost twice as long.

book of short stories with a connecting thread of interest. At one clap, in opus 55, he turned it into a novel so highly organized and closely reasoned that you would mar it by cancelling "half a line." And exactly as he unified the sonata-form movement he unified the symphony itself. He found it an anthology. He left it an epic. These were the changes which the emancipator had to accomplish in order that musical romanticism might be freed to deliver its direct message.

Amateur contemporary criticism did not like the *Eroica*. During the first performance a lamentable howl became audible from the peanut gallery: "I'd give another kreutzer if it would only stop!"

The press was no more favourable. It complained that the work was grotesque, bizarre, and lacking in all unity. This is exactly what the press, which lives for the moment, complains, oftener than not, about epoch-making master-pieces. In spite of the fact that its *finale* is not as great as the other sublime movements of the *Eroica* we now know that no work so closely knit, so consistently organic, and so incandescent with Promethean fire had ever before been written in symphonic form.

Chapter XVII

THE PRACTICAL JOKER

Beethoven Carries On the Torch of Freedom — Psychological Insight — Allows Consecutive Fifths — "I May Do it, but Not You" — Rooms with Von Breuning, May, 1804 — Illness — Quarrel — Reconciliation — Von Breuning's Letter to Wegeler, September, 1804 — Beethoven Enjoys Shocking the Reactionaries — A Musician's Practical Jokes — Baton Technic — Confuses the Orchestra — Baits an Angry Oboist — Plays Pranks on Singers — A Poor Sportsman — The "Andante Favori" and His Revenge on Ries — The First Quartet Concerts, 1804 — Beethoven's Disconcerting Behaviour

WE HAVE seen how Beethoven began to free music from its more or less menial position as satellite of fashion and to reveal it as an independent world. He did this in part by transforming and liberating its chief forms so that they might be hospitable to the profoundest emotion and intellect of humanity.

It is, of course, true that in the preceding century Johann Sebastian Bach had poured his intellect and emotion freely into such forms as his early days offered. He had made so many bold departures from the established harmonic rules, for example, that nearly all modern harmony is to be found in his pages. But his influence was slight until after Beethoven, the Martin Luther of music, had nailed his theses upon that portal of the future, the *Eroica* symphony. For the older man was neglected until so long after his death that the boldness of Beethoven won authority with young composers long before the boldness of Bach. Strangely enough, the contemporaries of the latter regarded him as a pedantic throw-back to an earlier age. And, though a small portion of his work was familiar to Beethoven and had a certain influence upon him, Bach remained almost unknown to the world until Mendelssohn had preached for years the gospel according to J. S. B.

Handel was limited by his predominant interest in the more restricted field of vocal music. The beginnings of intellectual and emotional freedom may be traced here and there in the greater works of Haydn and Mozart. But, even if they had the latent capacity, these masters were too handicapped by their dependent positions below the salt at noblemen's tables to cut an important figure as emancipators.

Perhaps Beethoven could not have succeeded in the formidable task of socially reconstructing the musician had he not been enough of a psychologist to appreciate the reasons for its difficulty. A letter written to nephew Karl two years before his death shows his shrewd realization of how the top dog instinctively opposes the rise of the under dog. "These so-called grand gentlemen do not relish seeing an artist, who is otherwise their equal, also well-to-do."

Beethoven was once advised by his pupil, Ferdinand Ries, of two consecutive fifths which the young fellow had discovered in the C minor quartet.[1] At first Beethoven denied

---

[1]Op. 18, No. 4. In point of fact, the fifths were well covered.

their existence. But confronted with the score he inquired: "Well, who has forbidden consecutive fifths?"

"Marpurg, Fux . . . all the authorities on theory."

"Well," answered Beethoven, "*I* allow them thus." By which he meant, "when used as I have used them here."

In the authoritative accents of this new lawgiver there is an echo of the way in which Jesus sometimes talked to his disciples. One is reminded that Beethoven once remarked: "My kingdom is in the air," and that Hans von Bülow, the enthusiast, called him "The Saviour of Music."

But, unlike Jesus, he was inclined to recommend a democratic code to others while he himself observed an aristocratic one. Czerny recalled that Anton Halm

once brought him a sonata he had composed. When Beethoven pointed out certain errors, Halm retorted that the Master also allowed himself many violations of the rules. "I may do it, but not you," was the answer.

Early in May, 1804, Beethoven left his own apartment and went to live with his boyhood's friend, Stephan von Breuning. Almost at once he came down with a serious illness which left behind it an obstinate intermittent fever. His friend nursed him devotedly. Finding that he still had to pay rent for his abandoned lodging Beethoven blamed Von Breuning for not having given the necessary notice, quarrelled with the customary violence, and left in high dudgeon.

Some months later the young men met by accident and made things up. The composer sent his friend the ivory miniature of himself by Hornemann—and a sheet of good words:

Behind this picture, my dear Steffen, let us hide forever, all that for a while passed between us. I know that I have torn your heart. For that deed, the feelings within me, which you must have noticed, have punished me sufficiently. It was not wickedness that I felt towards you. No, if it were that I should never again be worthy of your friendship,—passion on both sides; but mistrust of you rose in me; and there came between us men unworthy of us. . . . Forgive me if I have wounded you; I suffered no less. When I saw you no longer near me, for the first time I vividly felt how dear to my heart you are and always will be. Surely you will once more fly to my arms as in past days.

Von Breuning showed himself a true sportsman. On November 13, 1804, he wrote uncomplainingly to their common friend Wegeler without a word about the quarrel:

The friend of my youth here, is often largely responsible for my being forced to neglect the absent. You wouldn't believe, dear Wegeler, what an indescribable, I might say fearful effect the gradual loss of hearing has had on him. Picture to yourself how unhappiness must affect one of his violent temperament; in addition to his reserve and suspicion, often towards his best friends, and in many matters the inability to make up his mind! Most of the time, with only a few exceptions when he spontaneously gives vent to his original feelings,—association with him is a real exertion, at which one can scarcely trust oneself. . . . Anxiety and the care of him have used me rather severely. Now he is quite well again.

Beethoven immensely enjoyed shocking the musical scribes and pharisees. Hearing of their consternation and rage over such revolutionary phenomena as the dissonant opening of the First symphony, and the discordant battle-like climax in the development of the *Eroica*, he rubbed his hands together in high glee and exclaimed: "Yes, yes, they marvel and put their heads together and peer into all the books. But they'll not find these things in any school of thorough-bass!"

Their state of mind tickled his impish love of practical jokes. He was forever playing them on friend and foe alike and even on the interpreters of his works. At the very end of the development in the *Eroica* he made the French horn begin the Hero theme in the tonic against a dominant seventh chord sketched in tremolo by the violins. Of course, until ears began to be modernized in preparation for our own enlightened age this passage always sounded as though the unfortunate hornist had made a false entry. (Though when, at the rehearsal, the rash Ries thought so and said so he barely escaped a box on the ear.)

And there is another apparently innocent passage, in the 175th measure of the *scherzo,* which Beethoven made so diabolically difficult for the second horn that the hapless manipulator of that ticklish instrument has seldom announced it, to this day, without a disastrous quack.

At Prince Lobkowitz's, the celebrated oboist Ramm once took part in a private performance of the *Eroica* under the baton of its creator. Now composers are notoriously poor executants and conductors. Though Beethoven was a splendid pianist before he became too deaf, he was a less efficient leader. Spohr related that it was his custom

to indicate expression to the orchestra by all sorts of curious bodily movements. At *piano* he crouched down lower and lower, according to the degree of softness he desired. At a *crescendo* he gradually rose again, and at the entrance of the *forte* jumped into the air. Sometimes too he unconsciously shouted to strengthen the *forte.*[2]

These acrobatics must have interfered with the effect intended. For at the *Eroica* performance, during the savagely syncopated climax of the development (the part which represented to Lenz the thirty-two dagger thrusts), Beethoven got out, and threw the orchestra into such confusion that he had to stop and start again.

Perhaps Ramm may have been so indiscreet as to smile. Perhaps the Master saw the smile and meditated revenge. At any rate, in the *Notizen* Disciple Ries relates that

on the same evening he played his Quintet for Pianoforte and Wind Instruments with Ramm as oboist. In the last *Allegro* there are several holds before the theme is resumed. At one of these Beethoven suddenly began to improvise, took the Rondo for a theme and entertained himself and the others for a good while,—but not the other players. They were displeased and Ramm even very angry. It was really very ludicrous to see them, expecting the performance to be resumed at any moment, putting their instruments to their lips, only to take them down again. At last Beethoven was satisfied and dropped into the Rondo. The whole company was in transports of delight.

Like many absolute musicians, Beethoven was not overfond of singers. He was extraordinarily pleased when he could play a practical joke on one of them. As boy accom-

---

[2]*Manuscript note by the late Oscar G. Sonneck:* "What Beethoven did you can see done by any competent conductor-technician to-day. In Beethoven's time that sort of thing was new and violated custom. The musicians were not used to it, and Beethoven, not having enough practice to get absolute baton mastery, would upset the apple cart at a critical point. However, I have a suspicion that as an *interpretative* conductor he was much better than his contemporaries realized."

panist at the Court of Bonn he had once earned from the Elector a smiling reprimand for having, with a fantastic improvisation on the piano, thrown out a conceited tenor who plumed himself on being able to hold any note, no matter what antics his young friend should cut. But Ludwig had done it fairly, with the singer's consent, and while conscientiously strumming the proper cue with the little finger of his right hand.

In 1805 Mozart's egotistic brother-in-law, Sebastian Meier, sang the rôle of Pizarro in *Fidelio* (or *Leonora*, as it was then called). Beethoven decided to take him down a peg. At the place where Pizarro significantly declaimed:

> Soon will his blood be flowing,
> Soon will the poor worm writhe,

Beethoven wrote a trick passage, making the strings play in unison an appoggiatura of a minor second below each note the singer uttered,

Ex. 53

an effect which the fiddlers mischievously overemphasized. This tied Mozart's relative up hand and foot in his own vocal cords. Foaming with rage he shrieked at the composer: "My brother-in-law would never have written any such damned nonsense!"

Beethoven, however, was a poor sportsman. Whenever the shoe was on the other foot he grew furious. His law about practical joking was the one that he had laid down for Halm in connection with breaking rules of grammar: "I may do it, but not you."

One day Ries happened in just as the so-called *"Andante Favori"*[8] was finished. Beethoven played it twice to him. The young disciple had such an excellent memory that on his way home he stopped in at the Lichnowsky palace and reproduced the piece, out of his head, to the Prince. Next day the latter called on Beethoven and jocularly remarked: "Just hear what I have composed. It's not bad." "I don't want to hear it," was the blunt answer. But the Prince, not to be denied, rattled off parts of the *"Andante Favori."* Beethoven was beside himself. When he learned what Ries had done, he vowed never to play for him again. And, despite Lichnowsky's most diplomatic entreaties, he kept his vow.

The only practical joke which he allowed people to play on him was a recurrent one of which he was wholly unaware. When his clothes had reached a certain point of

---

[8] This piece was originally written for the *"Waldstein"* sonata (Op. 53). Beethoven probably took it out for the same reason that Brahms gave, in excising the slow movement from his E minor violoncello sonata—because he found the latter was "stuffed too full of music."

disreputability his friends would creep into his bedroom at night and substitute for them a brand new outfit. In the morning Beethoven dressed—and never noticed anything different.

In 1804 the Schuppanzighs had the audacity to undertake what Hanslick assures us was the first series of public string quartet concerts ever given. To us it seems almost incredible that such an indispensable part of civilized life should be a strictly modern institution, only a century and a quarter old.

Queer things went on in those concerts. Schuppanzigh tramped time for the players with his foot. And whenever Beethoven did not like a tempo he would rise and stamp heavily from the hall with angry snorts. An inveterate punster like him would perhaps have admitted that to the poor fiddlers such behaviour was disconcerting.

Chapter XVIII

BEETHOVEN'S "TEMPEST"

1804, "Waldstein" *and* "Appassionata" — *A Well-Known Source-Motive* — *Schindler Asks Meaning of* "Appassionata" — "Read Shakespeare's Tempest" — *Did the Critics Read the Play?* — *Growing Popularity* — *Visit from a Nameless Beauty* — *His Music Massacred* — *Origin of the Joy Theme*

In 1804 Beethoven was engaged both on the *"Waldstein"* sonata (C major, Op. 53) and on the work which came unofficially to be called the *"Appassionata"* (F Minor, Op. 57). These are the most brilliant of the piano sonatas. Like the *"Kreutzer,"* they are almost concertos without orchestral accompaniment. In them, even more than in the G major and *"Emperor"* concertos, virtuosity is successfully fused with creative inspiration.

As is often the case in the long list of Beethoven's works, these two form a pair in vivid emotional contrast. The *"Waldstein"* is bright, serene, happy. More acceptably than most of this composer's music, it may be performed by pianists who incline to coldness, dryness, and superficiality. Not so the *"Appassionata."* Its last section might well pass for a struggle between a Nietzschean superman and ghouls of despair. Notice how the rhythm of the C minor symphony's opening motive pounds menacingly in the bass, at the portal of the first movement.

Ex. 54

And in the life-and-death *finale* the sinister visitants, whoever they are, come out victorious. It may be that the despair of these pages reverberated those passionate disappointments of his over Napoleon and over Giulietta Guicciardi, which recall a phrase in his letter of November 2, 1803, written to the painter Macco: "There are times in a man's life that must be got through somehow."

These three short notes followed by a longer one constitute, rhythmically, one of those basic motives which[1] we have ventured to christen source-motives. The rhythm of this particular source-motive is best known in the so-called "Fate motive" which opens and permeates the Fifth symphony. But it recurs early and late in Beethoven's writing: at the start of the four-handed sonata (Op. 6); in the beginning of the *finales* of the C minor (Op. 10, No. 1) and *"Recitative"* sonatas (Op. 31, No. 2),[2] and on almost every page of the *finales* of the D major and A major quartets (Op. 18, Nos. 3 and 5). There is a strong infusion of it in the *finale* of the *"Moonlight"* (Op. 27, No. 2). It figures in the opening of the G major concerto.[3] The

[1] On pp. 56 and 111–112.
[2] See Ex. 86, p. 226.
[3] See Ex. 69, p. 192.

[153]

"*Harp*" quartet (Op. 74) uses it at the commencement of the first movement's coda, as well as to provide the main subject for the elaborate *scherzo.*[4] And it reappears as late as the *Alla Danza Tedesca* of the B flat quartet (Op. 130). In chapter LVI we shall see how, in his principal subjects, Beethoven used another source-motive still more lavishly and managed to conceal the fact of its existence until a century after his death.

Some years after it was written Schindler was artless enough to ask Beethoven "the meaning" of this "*Appassionata*" sonata. "Read Shakespeare's *Tempest*," was the laconic reply.[5] Commenting on these words a critic once asserted that Beethoven could surely never have read beyond the title of Shakespeare's play or he would not have made such a senseless remark. And nearly all subsequent critics have echoed this observation.

Perhaps these writers themselves could not have read *The Tempest* with much imaginative intensity. If it is necessary to paste literary labels on masterpieces of music the first movement of the "*Appassionata*" might well characterize a benignant amateur sorcerer like Prospero. The tempest and trouble in it are indulgent make-believe.

> PROSPERO (*Lays down his mantle and speaks to Miranda*):
> Lie there, my art. Wipe thou thine eyes; have comfort.
> The direful spectacle of the wreck, which touch'd
> The very virtue of compassion in thee,
> I have with such provision in mine art
> So safely ordered, that there is no soul,

---

[4]See Ex. 99, p. 245.
[5]See p. 107.

> No, not so much perdition as an hair
> Betid to any creature in the vessel
> Which thou heard'st cry, which thou saw'st sink.

In reality one feels that "All's right with the world" because Ferdinand and Miranda "have changed eyes." One can almost hear the kindly old father chuckle with satisfaction, and murmur (aside):

> They are both in either's powers: but this swift business
> I must uneasy make, lest too light winning
> Make the prize light.

The lovely, serene vision of the variation movement might well have been inspired by such words as these from Act III, Scene II:

> Be not afeard; the isle is full of noises,
> Sounds and sweet airs, that give delight and hurt not. . . .
> Will hum about mine ears; and sometimes voices,
> That, if I then had waked after long sleep,
> Will make me sleep again.

Or by this page of Act IV, Scene I, surely a passage of as royal a purple as literature can boast:

> These our actors,
> As I foretold you, were all spirits, and
> Are melted into air, into thin air:
> And, like the baseless fabric of this vision,
> The cloud-capp'd towers, the gorgeous palaces,
> The solemn temples, the great globe itself,
> Yea, all which it inherit, shall dissolve,
> And, like this insubstantial pageant faded,
> Leave not a rack behind. We are such stuff
> As dreams are made on; and our little life
> Is rounded with a sleep.

This slow movement starts

Ex. 55

Andante con moto.

p e' dolce.   *ten*

with no more apparent melody to it than the opening of
the *Allegretto* of the Seventh symphony,[6] or that other
Allegretto which constitutes the fifth variation in the
C sharp minor quartet (Op. 131).[7] Here is harmony rather
than melody; suggestion rather than speech. Or rather, one
might almost say, the harmony *is* the melody. And in all
three cases Beethoven knew that those lines of monotonous
upper notes were the lids of treasure caskets soon to open
upon the irised flames of jewels and the suffused radiance
of pearls fit for Miranda's bosom.

When he had thus far followed his poetic peer, Beethoven
—one may well fancy—was overcome by the grievous contrast between the happy ending of this fictitious tempest
and the fury of the real one raging within himself. We can
imagine him rushing blindly to pour all his acrid despair
into that *finale* whose sudden outburst still reminds us of
the voice of the man of Avon. For there is a Shakespearean

---

[6]See Ex. 117, p. 308.
[7]See pp. 461 and 466.

grandeur in these ferocious ravings. It is as if we were over-hearing the incoherence of a desperate Lear as he shouted:

Blow winds and crack your cheeks! rage! blow!

Ries was in at the birth of this movement. Beethoven was spending the summer at Döbling, near Vienna. Every morning after breakfast he would say: "Come, Ries, let's take a few minutes' walk." Which usually meant that after several steps the Master would be seized with an inspiration and would chase it all day

Thorough bush, thorough brier, over park, over pale,

with poor hungry Ries slogging along stubbornly in his wake. On this particular day they did not get back until nearly eight at night.

He had all the time been humming and sometimes roaring to himself, high and low, but without singing any actual notes. When I asked him what was up, he said: "I have just thought of a theme for the last movement of the sonata." As soon as we reached his room he stormed over to the pianoforte without even taking off his hat. I sat down in a corner and he forgot me at once. For an hour or so he raged through the glorious new *finale* of the sonata. When at length he got up he was astonished to see me, and said, "I can give you no lesson to-day, I must go on with this."

A work like the "*Appassionata*" finale is like a pearl, because it represents a self-defence against something that gives its maker pain. How fortunate that he was the son and grandson of a drunkard, that he was small, pock-marked, ugly, diseased, helplessly impractical, ferociously untactful, unable to win the lasting love of women, deaf, jealous, insanely suspicious! If he had been the opposite his pearls might instead have been of the ten-cent store variety bequeathed us by his contemporaries, Hummel, Cramer, Clementi, and Weigl.

In chapter LIV, it will be seen that the *"Appassionata"* has the same germ-motive, or thematic countersign, as the *"Kreutzer"* sonata. Its chief themes are related to one another by the sign of the rising or falling interval of a second.

One misfortune was spared Beethoven at this time. He did not suffer neglect. In the nine years since the publication of opus 1, unaided by modern journalism and press agents, he had arrived. Everyone ranked him with Haydn and Mozart. He could not catch up with the orders that poured in. A friend wrote: "He demands and they pay." Publishers at home, and as far abroad as Scotland, competed eagerly for his manuscripts. In 1803 Zulehner of Mayence announced a complete uniform edition of his works for piano and strings. Two years later a Viennese publisher did him unparalleled honour in printing a complete classified catalogue of his compositions.

His concertos and sonatas had become established everywhere in the repertory of the professional pianist. The German and Austrian amateurs recklessly stormed their lesser heights. We even read in a French musical journal of the day the assertion that there are in Paris *"quelquefois des amateurs qui croient les jouer"* ("sometimes amateurs who imagine they play them").

More personal tributes were not lacking. One evening Disciple Ries called in for a lesson but found a beautiful young woman sitting on the sofa with the Master. Discreetly he made to withdraw. Beethoven held him back and urged: "Play a little." Ries had the impression that the lady was ruffled, perhaps by some too sudden initiative on the part of the Master, who was now trying to placate her. After the pupil had played Beethoven's works a long while he heard from the sofa back of him: "Ries, play some love music!" Then, after a while, "something melancholy." Then, "something passionate," and so on.

When she left Ries was astonished to hear that Beethoven did not know her name, only that she was a lover of his music who had dropped in to get acquainted. The two men rushed out into the moonlight and followed her at some distance. But suddenly she vanished.

"I must find out who she is, and you must help me, Ries!"

Long afterwards they learned that she was the sweetheart of a foreign prince.

What more could a composer ask than such public and private tributes as these? One thing more: not alone to have his works played, but to have them well played. His growing deafness was often assuredly a blessing in disguise. The sonatas were terribly difficult for the fingers of those days, and they must have been murdered wholesale.

In a Sketch Book of 1805, between fragments of *Fidelio*,

we find one of those scribbled remarks with which Bee-thoven used to ease his mind:

Finale still simpler. Piano music likewise—God knows why my piano music always makes the worst impression on me,—especially when badly played.

The same year he complained by letter of an orchestral performance of some of his music in which

all *pp, crescendo,* all *decres.* and all *forte, ff,* have been elided—at any rate, they are not played. All delight in composing departs when one hears it [one's music] played *thus!*

During September, 1805, Beethoven published a setting of Tiedge's poem, *An die Hoffnung.* Though nothing exceptional in itself, this little song *To Hope*

Ex. 56

has for us one striking point of interest. It was one of the seeds destined to flower, two decades later, in the beginning of the *Choral* symphony's Joy theme. Compare this seed with that of the *Choral* tune

Ex. 57

and the latter is seen at once to be simply a rhythmic simplification of the former.

It is appropriate that the Joy movement should have grown out of a song about hope, and that Beethoven should have written the latter at a time when the hope of his setting music free was ripening to certainty, and that the music should embody an immediate hope of the period of his most fertile fruition.

Chapter XIX

FIDELIO: ROUND PEG, SQUARE HOLE

Search for a Libretto — Bouilly's Leonora, or Conjugal Love *— The Plot — First Production, November, 1805 — Failure — Compressed to Two Acts — Second Production, 1806 — Second Revision — Third Production, 1814 — His Genius Unoperatic — Thoughts Too Deep for Words — Lack of Sympathy for Vocal Music — His "Crown of Martyrdom" —* Fidelio *Involved a Loss to Music — Beethoven an Introvert — The Opera's High Lights — Chances for Self-Expression — Fidelio's Influence — The Overtures — Leonore No. 3 Too Overpowering — Beethoven Liberates the Overture — and the Opera Composer — Catastrophe and Courage*

HAVING surpassed Mozart in the symphonic and chamber music fields Beethoven was tempted to triumph over his illustrious predecessor in opera as well. He began casting about for a suitable libretto.

For a long time it seemed as though this libretto were published at the sign of the foot of the rainbow. And Beethoven was no gullible prospector. First and last he considered and rejected, among others, these subjects:

Romeo and Juliet
Alexander the Great

Macbeth
Bradamante
Romulus and Remus
Dragomira
Faust
Alfred the Great
The Founding of Pennsylvania
Melusine
The Return of Ulysses
Bacchus
The Ruins of Babylon

He was always combing antiquity and the Dark Ages for an opera subject. Once he even threatened to write a libretto himself. It was fortunate that he never stumbled into the field of Teutonic mythology, for he probably would have done little more than take the edge off the Nibelungen Ring subjects for his doughty successor, Richard the First-and-Last.

Many versifiers offered him their services. One of them was a Dr. Helmuth Winter, who admitted that in himself "a very wild and tempestuous imagination is inborn." He felt that his librettos were bound to "cleave a way to glorious immortality for the musician. If the music of Shakespeare and Schiller inspires you, you must have been born for my poems." This admission reminds one of the American bard named Elshemus who, a few years ago, used to advertise himself extensively as, "the grandest, sweetest, vastest poet of all time." Winter was the Austrian Elshemus.

But Beethoven turned from these allurements to "*Leonora, or Conjugal Love.*" This was the only unset libretto he ever found which had genuine appeal for him. It was a fair specimen of the so-called "Rescue" drama in vogue in the late Eighteenth Century. The original French text, by Bouilly, was done into German, less for better than for worse, by Sonnleithner, and called *Fidelio.*

The plot comes to this. Leonora's husband Florestan has been unjustly imprisoned in a Spanish castle by Pizzaro, his political enemy. (Note the reappearance of the castle in Spain, and how it recalls the youthful nickname "Spangy.") Disguised as a boy the devoted wife takes service with the jailer in order to secure Florestan's release. This is finally effected by her own heroism, abetted by the timely appearance of a *deus ex machina* (the Minister of State), who hurls the murderous Pizzaro, with no little gnashing of teeth, into outer darkness; while the chorus of released prisoners (all spotlessly innocent) join the populace in chanting appropriately:

> *Wer ein holds Weib errungen*
> *Mische seine Jubel ein!*
>
> (Who has won a lovely woman,
> Let him swell our jubilation!)

—a sentiment which was to reappear in the *Choral* symphony.

Fidelio was produced in November, 1805, only to be withdrawn after three representations. Its failure is usually laid to the fact that the Viennese aristocracy had recently fled before the advance of the Napoleonic troops. These had captured the city, and these had supplied the bulk of the audience. But a study of the original three-act score of the opera, with its paralysis of action and its dramatic ineptitude, suggests a more cogent reason.

The following month some of Beethoven's devoted and intelligent friends put their heads together and conspired to achieve the impossible. Meeting in Prince Lichnowsky's palace at noon they laboured until one in the morning with the violently obstinate composer to induce him to make numerous cuts.

At first Beethoven cried, "Not one note!" He seized the score and would have fled, but Princess Lichnowsky, half kneeling, embraced him and solemnly adjured him to make *Fidelio* safe for posterity. "Beethoven, it must be. Give in! Do this as a memorial to your mother! Do this for me, for your trusted friend!" Beethoven looked long at the Princess and then cried, with a sob in his voice: "I will—I will do all—all; for you—for my mother!" He lifted the Princess to her feet and gave her his hand to seal the promise.

Vastly improved by its reduction to two acts the opera was produced again in 1806 and drew increasingly. But Beethoven, besides being unversed in business affairs, had the suspicious temper of the deaf. He went to the impresario, Baron Braun, and complained that he was being cheated. According to Roeckel, who overheard the interview, the Baron assured Beethoven that his employees were above suspicion. He explained that up till now only the first-rank stalls and pit had been occupied. Soon he hoped that revenue would come in from the upper ranks.

"I don't write for the galleries!" cried Beethoven. "No?" said the Baron. "My dear sir, even Mozart was not above writing for them."

Cutting short the argument, Beethoven sprang to his feet and shouted in a wild rage: "Give me back my score!" The Baron rang and ordered an attendant to bring it. "I am sorry about this," he said, "but I think that when you have had time for calm reflection——" But without paying the least attention to these words Beethoven snatched the huge book from the attendant's hand and rushed out.

This quarrel turned out later to have been highly fortunate. In 1806 Beethoven's eyes were too near the dramatic canvas to make a really effective revision of *Fidelio*. But for the set-to with the Baron the opera might have crystallized in that stage and never have been improved. As it happened, by laying it aside for eight years, and by writing, in the meantime, such works as the Rasoumowsky quartets, the Fifth and Seventh symphonies, the B flat trio, and the *Egmont* music, he gained so much in perspective and mastery over his materials that, after expert rewriting of the text by Treitschke, he took it in hand again and improved it immeasurably. Since the third production, in 1814, it has enjoyed a vigorous life in Germany and Austria and has never been wholly dead even to the American operatic repertory.

But in spite of the beautiful and inspiring pages liberally strewn through *Fidelio* it seems unfortunate that Beethoven ever developed dramatic ambitions. His genius was leagues from suiting the boards. He was too hopelessly out of touch with the world of action to collaborate successfully in representing action on the stage. True, he had a vivid dramatic gift. But it was only for the interior psychological drama that is alien to footlights and back-drops. If Wordsworth's thoughts were sometimes "too deep for tears," Beethoven's were usually too deep for words.

His most important states of consciousness [writes Mr. J. W. N. Sullivan], what he would have called his "thoughts," were not of the kind that can be expressed in language.[1]

This is one reason why, though he wrote many lovely things for the human voice, Beethoven was not essentially a vocal composer. Consciously or unconsciously he resented the cramping effects of the singer's limited range and the still more cramping effect of words upon the infinite art of music.

He was, moreover, too intelligent not to realize that this bad influence, like the traditional mule, works both ways. Most composers are usually absorbed too exclusively in their own art, and, not being poets, they are too ignorant of the highly perishable subtleties and delicacies of word-music to realize when their own effects are destroying those of the poet with whom they seek to collaborate. Beethoven occasionally used words with rare felicity, but he had an uncertain taste in poetry and often sinned grossly against the art. He was, however, enough of an all-around artist to

---

[1]*Beethoven: His Spiritual Development,* 1927.

feel this, though he may never have formulated it in thought. And this may have been a factor in his somewhat less than whole-hearted attitude towards vocal music.

So opera composition went against the grain. He accomplished it slowly, painfully, and spoke of winning thereby his "crown of martyrdom." The process exhausted him correspondingly. "This business of the opera," he complained during the last revision, "is the most tedious in the world. I am dissatisfied with most of it, and almost every piece in it is patched. It is a very different matter when one can give oneself up to one's own free reflections or inspiration."

Though parts of it showed Beethoven at something like his best, the completed *Fidelio* was far from justifying the precious expenditure. Let us suppose that the Master had not invested all that time and creative energy in searching for a libretto, setting it, producing it, revising it, and again producing it, with all the exasperating nervous wear-and-tear involved—only to be cruelly disappointed at each stage of the process. We might have had, instead, a few more sonatas, two or three more quartets and trios, another symphony or so, and that overture on the name of B–A–C–H which he was always planning and never managed.

Thus it is probable that the one glorious failure to adapt his gift to an æsthetic compromise—a hybrid form of art—represents a serious loss to music. Except for two of its four overtures *Fidelio* does not rank with Beethoven's supreme works. It cannot claim any such place in dramatic music as the sonatas, quartets, and symphonies take in the instrumental field.

Beethoven was of the type which the psychologist of to-day calls the "introvert." His eyes and his mind were directed inward. He was too absorbed in the drama being enacted on the subjective scene to enter with any great heartiness into the joys and sorrows and little affairs of any persons, actual or fictitious, who were not reflections of himself or his complexes.

His passionate hatred of dissipated women led him to condemn Mozart for having set such frivolous books as *Figaro* and *Don Juan*. It led him to endorse with corresponding heartiness the wifely devotion and heroic self-sacrifice of the virtuous Leonora. A factor in this heartiness may have been his own ardent longing for conjugal love, coupled with some dim recognition of the fact that any woman who became a successful Frau Beethoven must needs possess the blind devotion and selfless courage of a Leonora.

When, amid the rather commonplace wastes of the first act, the preluding high wood winds give a foretaste of the Missa's *Benedictus*, of *Lohengrin,* and of *Parsifal,* and Leonora at length has a chance for self-expression, the real Beethoven suddenly comes into action, and her resplendent aria shines out with the startling and solitary refulgence of the evening star in Tannhäuser, when it gleams through the dingy scenery of a one-night troupe. This is one of the most luscious bits in all pre-Wagnerian opera. Its tenderness, its spine-thrilling heroic quality could have been conceived by no one but the man who led the *Eroica's* Hero theme up to the two splendid climaxes of the development, and created the coda of the Funeral March.

Like the Senta and Elsa and Elizabeth of the future, and like this opera itself, Leonora is a typically German conception—Teutonic through and through. And herein lies much of *Fidelio's* stubborn vitality.

None of those parts of the work which were foreign to Beethoven's nature contain anything noteworthy. The light loves of Marcelline and Jaquino, and later of Marcelline for the supposed youth, Leonora, left Beethoven and his audience coolly unconvinced.

But the hymns of hate bellowed by that absurd stage villain Pizzaro were zestfully put to music of demoniacal convincingness by the composer to whom periodical outbursts of sheer rage—with or without adequate cause—seemed to be necessary. Rage was his safety valve. Without this relief he would have resolved himself into his elements.[2] Hence the true ring of Pizzaro's ravings.

Beethoven could also write from the heart when it came to the plaints of the dungeoned Florestan and his fellow captives. Did not this poor deaf genius, plagued by his mania of persecution, conceive himself as imprisoned in the cell of a dark, dank, sordid, uncomprehending world? —a world that would yield him only a grudging sustenance

---

[2]"Temperaments of volcanic energy, which have to be continuously collected," remarks Count Keyserling in his *Travel Diary of a Philosopher*, "require a safety-valve opened at certain intervals if they are not to burst; and the steam rushes forth from them all the more impetuously the more condensed it was."

in depreciated currency? Was he not—a more unhappy Prometheus—chained to a subterranean rock and shut away from those sounds which were to him what the sun's rays were to ordinary folk?

No wonder that the poignant horror of the introduction to the second act and Florestan's touching aria

Ex. 58

and the grave-digging duet and the quartet which decides Florestan's fate move us with an authentic emotion.

And when the trumpet of salvation is heard outside, bringing the duet and chorus of the happy ending, we are sympathetically stirred by the man who had known the deliverance of happily ending—after bitter struggle—such wonders as the D major, C sharp minor, and *"Appassionata"* sonatas, the C minor quartet, and the *Eroica*.

We may say what we please against the libretto of *Fidelio*. We may call it lacking in motivation and literary value, dramatic effectiveness, and the rest. But it had one undeniable virtue: it offered this introvert composer a number of felicitous chances for self-expression. Luckily for instrumental music, this proved to be a unique opportunity. Beethoven patiently searched the wide world for another such complaisant book. He was fortunately destined not to look upon its like again.[3]

This master of absolute music undeniably exerted a strong influence upon successive generations of opera composers. But *Fidelio* has had far less emancipatory force than most of Beethoven's instrumental compositions or than even some of his songs. His sole opera has had less influence on the development of opera than the works of his inferior contemporary, Weber.

Fidelio's supreme service to æsthetic history was done in turning Beethoven's attention to the dramatic overture, a field in which he brilliantly shone. There is more real dramatic art in the overture which was called by a printer's error "*Leonore No. 3*"—or in *No. 2*, for that matter—than in the entire bulky score of the opera for which it was designed as a prelude.

The scholars have differed earnestly about the order in which the four overtures to this opera were composed. But the balance of probability seems to be with Nottebohm and with Thayer's editor, Krehbiel, that the one known as *Leonore No. 2* was first written for the initial performance in November, 1805.

A certain difficult thirty-one measures which the wood winds massacred set Beethoven to altering the work into *Leonore No. 3* for the second production in 1806. His imagination took fire. Sternly he shortened the first part, ruthlessly crossing out one lovely passage after another.

---

[3]Brahms was luckier. He was just a little harder to suit with librettos than Beethoven, so he found not even one. If he had, the result would probably have involved almost as much waste as in the case of that giant, his predecessor.

Then he ended with a coda which remains one of the most stirring and brilliantly effective episodes in all orchestral music. It is a work of incomparable form, self-contained and satisfying, a complete psychological music-drama *in petto*. But this very completeness and lack of suspense made it even less suitable than *No. 2* had been to perform the functions of a prelude to an opera. A full programmatic appreciation of it presupposed a knowledge of the very opera which the overture was ostensibly preparing one to hear. Besides, the piece was so grand that it dwarfed what followed. It was as if a perfectly good play by Henry Arthur Jones should be prefaced by the most compelling act, on the same theme, that Shakespeare ever wrote.[4] Little by little Beethoven came to realize this fact. So the indefatigable man dashed down the broad and pleasant *Leonore No. 1*, for a projected production of his opera at Prague in 1807, afterwards abandoned. Finally, for the revision of 1814, he cynically turned out the piece now known as the *Fidelio* overture, a cheerful, breezy, graceful little thing, leagues from the sublimities of *No. 3*.

Beethoven has often been lauded for letting the fashionable enthusiasms of the day turn from him to its new idol, Rossini, without making one effort at conciliating the trashy popular taste. But the unbiassed listener to this composition and to the end of the *Egmont* overture (composed four years earlier) must recognize with regret what every-

---

[4]"What is the dramatic action of the text to the opera of *Leonora*, but an almost repulsive dilution of the drama presented in the overture, like perhaps, a tedious explanatory commentary by Gervinus upon a scene of Shakespeare's?" (Richard Wagner, *Beethoven*, 1871, p. 86.)

one can recognize in the deplorable *Battle of Vittoria* (composed in 1813)—a bid for the favour of the Rossini enthusiasts.

In the *Leonore Nos. 2 and 3* Beethoven began to liberate the overture and set it on its own feet with: *Man, help thyself!*—just as Grandpapa Bach in his suites, those ancestors of the symphony, loosed dance music from its slavery to the dance floor.

His emancipative activities went further. By successfully insisting on receiving a royalty instead of an honorarium for *Fidelio* Beethoven helped to free the operatic composer from financial subservience and to place him on a more professional basis.

After such a catastrophe as the collapse of his operatic dreams in 1806, almost anyone else would have yielded to vain regrets and the lassitude of discouragement. Not so the little giant from Bonn.

This modern Antæus leaped up from every knock-down like a god refreshed. He was the most resilient of mortals. There was never a blow so savage as to bow his head for more than a moment. It merely summoned fresh blood to the teeming brain. The man never wrote more triumphantly than on the rebound from catastrophe. And now, in 1806, he picked himself up from amid the ruins of his hopes and plunged without hesitation into one of the most astonishingly, consistently sustained and vital creative periods ever achieved by any artist since Tubal Cain.

Chapter XX

QUARTETS "FOR A LATER AGE"

"In the country I know no lovelier pleasure than quartet music."

—BEETHOVEN TO ARCHDUKE RUDOLPH.

1806, Beethoven Rebounds from Misfortune — Finds Self-Defense and Escape in Composition — Therapeutic Music — Sustained Quality of Works 1804–1809 — A Happy Period — 1806, Count Rasoumowsky Commissions Three String Quartets — 1808, Founds Schuppanzigh Organization — Lobkowitz and Rasoumowsky Quartets Contrasted — Chief Characteristics of Op. 59 — F Major Quartet — Liberates Sonata-Form — A New Kind of Scherzo — E Minor Quartet — B–A–C–H Anagram — "Hero" Quartet — Hostile Reception — Beethoven's Confidence in His Future

AMONG the all but undecipherable notes in a certain Sketch Book one comes upon these blindly scribbled words: "The great distinction of a superior man: steadfastness under grievous misfortunes." That of the most superior man, he might have added, is a quality of still higher distinction: resilience. Any ordinary talent, as we have remarked, would have been prostrated by the *Fidelio* fiasco of 1806, and would have recuperated slowly, if at all. This giant took it in his elastic stride. He turned defeat into victory by presently bringing to light such a Nibelungen-horde of sheer masterpieces as the world of art has scarcely ever known.

But the first part of this romantic search was carried out in the dark. Sunlight and sparkle were to come later. In self-defense he cached his grief and disappointment, his unsatisfied passion, his nervous irritability and despair in the stark *finale* of the *"Appassionata,"* which appeared in 1807. Then, eagerly, instinctively, he turned to another form of psychic healing—escape. On that spiritual airplane, the quartet, so long neglected, he got clean away to an enchanted and undiscovered land.

Perhaps one reason why Beethoven's music, especially at this, the height of his second period, is so successfully therapeutic for us is that it was therapeutic for him. There are few more potent vehicles of defense against, or escape from, pettiness, disappointment, disaster, and sorrows of all kinds than the first movements of the G major piano concerto, of the First Rasoumowsky quartet, the Fourth symphony, the violin concerto, and the *Pastoral* symphony; or than the slow movements of the *"Appassionata,"* the Second Rasoumowsky quartet, the violin concerto, the Fifth symphony, and the *"Emperor"* concerto.

A catalogue of his works from the *"Waldstein"* (composed in 1804) to the *"Harp"* (composed in 1809), makes astonishing reading. Let us leave out those tardily published early pieces (Op. 63–66 and Op. 71), and the uninspired Triple concerto (Op. 56), which was most likely an occasional work written to please the Archduke Rudolph, and bore to the opuses before and after it much the same qualitative relation that fourth-class travel bears to first on a European railway. Apart from these, every single opus was a masterpiece. Nothing else missed the very centre of his target. See in this succession of musical miracles how he kept up the scoring:

Opus	53	"Waldstein" sonata
Opus	54	F major sonata
Opus	55	Eroica symphony
Opus	57	"Appassionata" sonata
Opus	58	G major concerto
Opus	59	Rasoumowsky quartets
Opus	60	Fourth symphony
Opus	61	Violin concerto
Opus	62	Coriolanus overture
Opus	67	Fifth symphony
Opus	68	Pastoral symphony
Opus	69	A major violoncello sonata
Opus	70	"Geister" and E flat trios
Opus	72	Fidelio
Opus	73	"Emperor" concerto
Opus	74	"Harp" quartet

And all these glories were put on paper between early in 1804 and late in 1809. Six years of almost perfect creation! Thayer says that the last half of this period, 1807–1809, was "unquestionably the happiest in the last half of his life." The professional myth makers and purveyors of biographical crêpe, misled by the passing mood of the Heiligenstadt Testament and the eloquent epistolary lamentations of his more or less fleeting darker moments, would have us believe that he was already the morose and melancholy person of his closing years.

Far from it. At this period his naturally cheerful, buoyant temperament had not yet been sicklied o'er by a pale cast of almost total deafness. His fame was growing brilliantly. He had a delightful, devoted circle of friends. He had as much of the love of women as a man of his age and handicaps could reasonably expect.

Above all he had the continual bliss of triumphant creation. True, we know from the evidence of the Sketch Books that his process of composition was usually long, tentative, and full of painful misgivings and savage self-criticism. Yet the final results of such travail must have stood out in his consciousness all the more luminously from the dark background of their evolution.

A short time before the *Fidelio* catastrophe, by some auspicious chance, Count Rasoumowsky, the Russian Ambassador to Austria, commissioned Beethoven to write him three string quartets. The Count's half-Cossack father came, like Beethoven, from "the people" and owed his rapid rise to a love affair with the Empress Catherine II. The Ambassador married Princess Lichnowsky's elder sister and made his luxurious palace in Vienna a centre of musical life.

In 1808, two years after Beethoven had weatherproofed this nobleman's name by inscribing it upon opus 59, Count Rasoumowsky founded the famous Schuppanzigh Quartet. Weiss, his old associate of quartet days in the Lichnowsky palace, played viola. The Count himself officiated capably at second violin, while the violoncello was brilliantly handled by Linke, a slightly deformed young man whose playing Beethoven especially liked.

Czerny declares that Beethoven "pledged himself to weave a Russian melody into each of the quartets." But from what we know of the Master's savage independence in matters of outside interference with his art it would seem more likely that he introduced these tunes of his own accord, out of compliment to the Russian patron. So far as we are aware he used only two: one in the *finale* of the First and the other in the third movement of the Second quartet. How completely he Germanized and Beethovenized the latter may be judged from Moussorgsky's highly Muscovite use of this tune in the *Coronation Scene* chorus in *Boris Godounov*.

Comparing these revolutionary Rasoumowsky quartets with the half dozen dedicated in 1801 to Lobkowitz we find two epochs in vivid apposition. This contrast is as sharp as that of the Second symphony with the *Eroica;* as a periwig with real hair; as a formal garden with a naturalistic garden; in a word, as the rococo with the romantic.[1]

True, the Lobkowitz quartets here and there prophesied the ripeness, the depth of thought, and the intense emotional power of these later ones. One remembers such movements as the *Adagio* of the F major (No. 1) and the begin-

---

[1]In the matter of mere bulk as well, the contrast holds good. The Second symphony has 1,208 measures, the *Eroica* 1,851. The D major, the longest of the Lobkowitz quartets, consists of 952 measures; the First Rasoumowsky, of 1,336. Roughly, an increase of a third over all previous proportions.

ning and ending of the C minor (No. 4). But during the new century Beethoven had grown in wisdom and artistic stature through the discipline of completing music like the "*Moonlight*," E flat, and "*Appassionata*" sonatas; the "*Kreutzer*" violin sonata; the *Eroica* symphony; and the *Leonore No. 3* overture. Not until then was he ready to show the world what reserves of power lay hidden in that string quartet form invented by Papa Haydn.

The chief characteristics of these Rasoumowsky quartets are wealth and depth of ideas, a noble objectivity, such brilliant effectiveness for concert purposes as none of his chamber music had yet shown. They have such an air of inevitability that the most surprising dramatic contrasts seem to grow out of one another as by some law of nature. There is such a revolutionary mastery of form that its technic becomes invisible. One immediately notices the almost orchestral variety and power with which these pages inform the small group of fiddles; so that one is sometimes tempted to call them quartet-symphonies.

Here is a new, severely Olympian disregard of the traditional expectations and petty comforts of listener and performer. When Schuppanzigh came to him, complaining about technical difficulties, Beethoven (who always addressed "Milord" in the third person) impatiently retorted: "Does he really suppose I think of his puling little fiddle when the spirit speaks to me and I compose something?"[2]

---

[2]All the same, though perhaps unconsciously, he did think about the "puling little fiddle's" requirements. There is no passage in all his chamber music incapable of fairly effective performance. The early viola routine in the Bonn orchestra had given him a flair for what could and could not be expected of instruments.

The F major (Op. 59, No. 1) was the first string quartet to adopt the innovation of having all four of its movements in sonata-form. It was begun on May 26, 1806—the day after the shame and sorrow of his brother Karl's marriage with Johanna Reiss, an unconventional woman. Ludwig took this event sadly to heart and must have started the quartet as a means of escape from his chagrin.

A lightly wielded but overpowering force streams from almost every bar of it. Once the violoncello has opened the proceedings with the soaring flight of its broad-pinioned tune

Ex. 59

and the violins have started mellow horn music over an organ-point

Ex. 60

we are so completely under the spell of this man of might that we can endorse his angry exclamation on hearing that Napoleon had beaten the Prussians at Jena, October 14, 1806: "Too bad! If I understood the art of war as well as I do the art of music I'd crush him yet!"

This opening movement performed an epochal exploit in the liberation of sonata-form from the strait-waistcoat of the rococo. The chief weakness of this particular form[3] had always been that its highest point of interest lay in the development section. The recapitulation which followed was accordingly almost sure to produce an effect more or less anticlimactic. It was as if a naïve rustic *raconteur* should tell a good story (the exposition) to a wittier friend who struck from it a more brilliant *jeu d'esprit* (the development); and then the party of the first part should repeat his original story (the recapitulation), in true country-grocery, cracker-box-club style, vainly hoping for a second laugh equal to the first.

Heretofore such a necessity for anticlimax had always been supposed inherent in this mode of writing. But now Beethoven, by some deft stroke of magic, gave the future an example of how sonata-form may abide strictly by the unity of its architectural scheme yet go on climactically from grace to grace and from strength to strength without the least suggestion of let-down anywhere.

He did it by taking away the double bar repeat at the close of the exposition, thus suppressing its repetition, for the first time in all quartet literature. He did it still more

---

[3]For a brief definition of sonata-form, see Glossary, pp. 632–633.

by making the last section upon which custom had bestowed the dubiously honourable name of recapitulation look toward the future rather than toward the past. This apparent contravention of the essential nature of sonata-form was one of the most brilliant advantages ever gained by spirit over matter in the structural history of music.[4]

The *Allegretto vivace e sempre scherzando* which continues this pioneer work offers a bewildering profusion of paradoxes. Here is merriment laced with tears; melancholy twinkling with joy; mock poverty that pares its expenditures down to a single famous tone; a tropical luxuriance of melody such as had never before been crammed by the most prodigal hand into a single movement; pain that, like certain queer borderland sensations of illness, tiptoes on the frontier of pleasure. Here is a real *scherzo* cast surprisingly into its opposite—a first-movement—form, yet moving at a slower pace than befits either a *scherzo* or a first movement.

His smiling alchemy was never more incredible than in the famous one-tone opening theme for violoncello

Ex. 61

Allegretto vivace e sempre scherzando.

pp Violoncell

2d Viol.

---

[4]A similar progressive climactic effect was attained a little later in the Fifth symphony's opening movement by means of a recapitulation that recapitulated even less strictly than the First Rasoumowsky had. Thus Beethoven began to free music from the vain anticlimaxes of the musical cracker box.

(of which more anon) and its mischievous elfin continuation. Robert Schumann was right: "Beethoven finds his motives lying about in the street, but—he fashions them into cosmic utterances." And M. Brousson was right in referring to art as *"une chose très banale, usuelle, magnifiée, pour l'éternité, par la sensibilité d'un artiste."*[5]

The creative listener is never done exploring the possibilities of this fascinating, capricious *scherzo*. It was apparently flung upon paper with the amused ease of a veteran angler dropping a light leader full of brilliant flies exactly over the post-graduate old trout, through the overhanging alders fifty yards upstream. But if we look into the Master's Sketch Books we learn, on the contrary, what hard writings made this easy hearing. For the amateur fiddler—including the second fiddler—once he has struggled through the tangle of technical barbed wire which guards the Rasoumowskys, there are few more inexhaustible delights,[6] even after hundreds of performances. What is more, the noteweary professional finds these pages constantly renewed for him.[7]

If readers' time and book-space were more elastic, one would like to go in for the pleasure of detailed remarks about the sustained, sad loveliness of the *Adagio molto e*

---

[5]J. J. Brousson, *Itinéraire de Paris à Buenos-Ayres,* 1927, p. 67.

[6]In former books by the writer, the name of this group of quartets has taken on almost the character of a refrain. In *Fiddler's Luck,* 1920, this is explained by a footnote: "Beethoven's three string quartets (Op. 59) are usually regarded by amateur fiddlers as their extreme ideal limit of difficulty and of delight."

[7]Mr. Waldo Warner is a talented composer and plays viola in the London String Quartet. After his organization had covered most of the globe and given the complete cycle of Beethoven's sixteen quartets and Great Fugue for the twenty-eighth time, he confessed to the writer that his favourite among them all remained this First Rasoumowsky.

mesto. And about the tremendous onward drive of the *finale,* with its rhythmical subtleties. And about the other two quartets.

Instead, let us consider only a few high points, such as the majestic calm and wide sweep of the *Molto adagio* of the Second Rasoumowsky in E minor. Czerny says that the theme of this movement occurred to Beethoven one evening "as he gazed at the firmament and thought about the music of the spheres." We know that astronomy fascinated the Master. He owned a copy of Bode's *Guide to a Knowledge of the Starry Heavens.* In his copy of the Odyssey he scored the line about the Pleiades. And in one of his diaries he wrote with emphasis: "The moral law within us, and the starry sky above us—Kant."

The skyey luminosities of this movement take one back in thought to the man whom Beethoven revered as "the first parent of music." And of whom he punningly remarked: *"nicht Bach sondern Meer"* (not Bach [brook] but ocean). It is as near in mood to the spirit of the Bach *Larghetto* from the Concerto for two violins, as the mature Beethoven could be to anyone else's spirit. So that the musical anagram

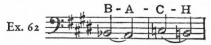

Ex. 62

(In German our B flat is B and our B natural is H)

upon which the writer recently stumbled at the point where the violoncello carries the tune near the beginning of the development (bar 63) would seem to be more than

an accident. This anagram may have originally suggested
to Beethoven the opening of the first subject,

Ex. 63

which is indeed only such an unmodulated simplification
of the B–A–C–H theme as would make it suitable for the
beginning of a Beethoven *Adagio*. This possibility seemed
more probable to the writer through a discovery which
he made in the Prussian State Library in Berlin. There, in
a manuscript volume of Beethoven's miscellaneous chamber
music sketches, he happened to notice this same anagram
standing by itself. Of course it is well known that Beethoven projected an overture on this B–A–C–H theme
and also planned to use it in his Tenth symphony. But in
the mountainous literature of this subject the anagram
seems never to have been mentioned in connection with his
chamber music, nor with any time as early as 1806.

The humour in bars 89–106 of the rondo concluding
the E minor quartet is delicately roguish. Each instrument
seems politely to stand aside, murmuring to his neighbour:
"After you!" then seize him by the arm and try to propel

him into the foray. This pleasantry occurs with even more piquancy at bars 251–74.

The C major, the third of the series, is sometimes called the *"Hero"* quartet. Its only particularly heroic portion is the tremendous *finale*, the Master's first and finest combination of the fugue with binary form.

Ex. 64

As far as mood and largeness of conception go this movement might perhaps end the *Eroica* more satisfactorily than the *Prometheus* variations have ever been able to end it. And it has an undeniably symphonic quality which cries aloud for masses of strings (by which it is often played) and for wind choirs as well. Another thing which helps to justify the name *"Hero"* is the resemblance of the germ of the first movement's opening theme

Ex. 65

to a motive in the heroic *finale* of the Fifth symphony,

Ex. 66

which at this time Beethoven may already have been carrying about in his mind.

When Beethoven's friends heard this revolutionary music many were shocked. They found the Master's new sayings too difficult for them and, like the rich young man in the Bible, "went away sorrowful," for they had great possessions in the rococo period, in the land of the Lobkowitz quartets, the septet, and the early symphonies.

Others, like the Schuppanzighs, held their sides, suspecting the practical joker whose tricks and whose manners they all had rueful cause to know.

Still others were furious. When Gyrowetz had bought and examined these novelties he growled: "Pity to waste the money!" In 1812 the Master's boyhood friend, Bernhard Romberg, was the world's leading violoncellist. His quartet read the F major at Count Soltikoff's in Moscow. When the *scherzo* began with the one-tone violoncello solo (see Ex. 61) everybody burst out laughing.

Romberg was like Tailor Böck in *Max und Moritz* when those practical jokers saluted him with *"Meck! meck! meck!"*

> *Alles konnte Böck ertragen*
> *Ohne nur ein Wort zu sagen;*
> *Aber, wenn er dies erfuhr,*
> *Ging's ihm wider die Natur.*
> (Böck could stomach any affront
> Without giving even a grunt;
> But when he heard *this* again,
> It went clean against his grain.)

The violoncellist saw red. Snatching his part from the rack, he hurled it to the floor and danced apoplectically upon it. Like Paolo and Francesca, the musicians read no more in the music book that day—nor for many years after.

When the Rasoumowsky quartets came out in London, Radicati, the Italian violinist, picked them up in a friend's house and remarked that Beethoven was music mad.

He showed them to me in manuscript and, at his request, I fingered them for him. I said to him, "You surely do not consider these works to be *music?*" and he replied, "Oh, they are not for you, but for a later age!"

The truth of this surprisingly moderate retort calls to mind that tribute which Ben Jonson paid Shakespeare:

"He was not of an age, but for all time."

Chapter XXI

PEACE, POWER, AND PLENTY

Violin Concerto, 1806 — Fondness for Rhythmic Mottos — G Major Piano Concerto, Composed 1805–1807 — Beethoven Abolishes Opening Tutti — Frees the Concerto Orchestra — Aids Evolution of Piano — Alternation of Mood in His Works — Fourth Symphony, 1806 — Echo from His Popular Minuet

A CARNIVAL of sunlight in the rain-washed atmosphere followed the tempestuous despair of the *"Appassionata" finale* and such darker moods as the poignant, grieving *Adagio molto e mesto* of the F major quartet, the sombreness of the E minor's first movement, the wistfully melancholy prophecy of Schubert's and Mendelssohn's best work that breathes from the C major quartet's strangely morbid *Andante con moto quasi Allegretto,* the blood and iron of its heroic fugue.

To lovers of pure music that form of technical display known as the concerto has always seemed of somewhat dubious musical respectability. Those concertos which had the perilous honour of following the Rasoumowsky quartets filled this precarious position less unworthily than any other concertos could have filled it.

Despite a virtuoso element which seems to our modern taste a bit too florid-for-floridity's sake, the Violin concerto in D major (Op. 61) still holds its own as the most limpidly lovely work in its class. The G major piano concerto, on its appearance in 1808, assumed a corresponding position, until somewhat overshadowed a year later by the so-called *"Emperor"* concerto in E flat (Op. 73).

Not a shadow blurs the Violin concerto. From the ingenuous opening march, that sounds like the subdued laughter of absorbed and delighted children, through the tingling serenity of the second subject,

Ex. 67

through the mystical vision of the slow movement, that makes religious ecstasy seem as easy and natural as daydreaming, through the profoundly exuberant humour of the infectiously swaying *finale*, all is young, innocent, wide eyed.

The sole suggestion of anything more sophisticated comes in the ironic insinuations of the rhythmic motive

Ex. 68

heard from the kettledrum at the start of the opening *Allegro ma non Troppo* and repeated with ever-varying context at short intervals throughout the movement.[1]

We have already remarked Beethoven's love of such rhythmic mottos in connection with designs like this of Fifth symphony fame[2] and the

[1]Brahms was fond of cryptic musical allusions. The four quarter-note F's with which he began *A German Requiem* may have been like a gesture of reverent salutation to this great work of his mighty predecessor.

[2]See pp. 153–154.

[191]

peculiar opening of the *scherzo* of the First Rasoumowsky quartet. We shall find such mottos in other places, including the *scherzo* of the B flat trio (Op. 97).[8]

The highly personal and interesting yet noncompetitive quality of the instrumentation is worth attention. While never degraded into a mere accompanist the orchestra constantly avoids blanketing the soloist and always gives him an inspiringly effective background.

In its feminine charm, its adolescent happiness, and fairy-tale atmosphere the G major piano concerto (Op. 58) is next of kin to its violin brother. By daring to give the soloist the first word alone—a justly renowned opening—

Ex. 69

---

[8]See Ex. 113, p. 293.

Beethoven freed this form from the bonds of that hoary Mede and Persian precedent, the initial orchestral *tutti*. True, Mozart had, in an early concerto, partially revolted at this convention, but without making much headway against the tyranny of custom.

Only once for a page or two is the smiling face of the work ruffled by the dramatic little *Andante con moto* where the strings, in coarse, menacing octaves, are answered by the piano in a wistful, infantile, pleading melody that goes to the heart.

Ex. 70

This folk tune finally melts the harsh opposition. Then the movement swings without pause into the *finale* and, like "the happy Princess," goes lilting over the upland meadows,

Beyond the night, beyond the day.

The G major marks a long stride in that evolution of a concerto from a mere show-off piece with a servile orchestral accompaniment, toward the fuller emancipation of the concerto orchestra by Schumann and Brahms which has led to that usual form of to-day, the symphony or symphonic poem with piano obbligato.

At this period the great emancipator was also active in helping to free piano music from its subjection to the feeble, effeminate instruments of his youth. His practical suggestions and prestige brought about a marked improvement in piano action and tone.

On February 7, 1809, Reichardt wrote:

Streicher has abandoned the soft, yielding, repercussive tone of the other Vienna instruments, and, according to Beethoven's wish and advice, given his instruments greater resonance and elasticity, so that the virtuoso who plays with strength and significance may have the instrument in better command for sustained and expressive tones. He has thereby given his instruments a larger and more varied character, so that they must give greater satisfaction than the others to all virtuosi who seek something more than mere easy brilliance in their style of playing.

Beethoven originally intended to follow the *Eroica* with what has turned out to be his most popular work. In 1805 he actually wrote large portions of the first two movements of the C minor symphony.

Then, in 1806, he interrupted this task to begin and finish the B flat symphony (Op. 60) which stands fourth in his momentous series of sonatas for orchestra.

In spite of all his misfortunes he must have been bursting

with exuberance and happiness, and he simply could not help laying aside the grandeurs and glooms of the C minor symphony for the time being, to give expression to this zest in common life. Also he must have felt that two such stupendous works as the *Eroica* and the Fifth should neither be offered the public so close together nor be created without some pause for recuperation.

In running down the list of his works given in the Appendix one feels how Beethoven needed and took the relaxation of gaiety after serious effort on a large scale. The string quartets in C minor, E minor, F minor, and C sharp minor are all sandwiched between more light-hearted companions.[4] Likewise the piano sonatas in C sharp minor, D minor, F minor, and the one for violin in C minor, show all the darker in their bright frames. But most strikingly the Fourth, *Pastoral*, and Eighth symphonies blithely separate, like sun-drenched valleys during vintage, the august cloud-capped peaks of the *Eroica*, the Fifth, the Seventh, and the *Choral*.

The chief features of the Fourth symphony are an adolescent blitheness akin to that of its contemporaries, the Violin and G major piano concertos; an exhilaration and a humour even more irresistible than anything in these works; a lyric passion and a finish of workmanship unheard before; and a unity and perfection of proportion never surpassed in his symphonic writing.

To the mind of one hearer the introduction's gropings

---

[4] The tragic A minor quartet (Op. 132) was written before the *"Scherzoso"* quartet in B flat (Op. 130) and after the happy one in E flat (Op. 127).

and stumblings in a twilit diminished-seventh chaos[5] spontaneously assume, at the irruption of that sunrise, the *Allegro Vivace,* a form as exquisitely proportioned, as airy and playful

As a silver-wrought garment that clings to and follows the firm
sweet limbs of a girl.[6]

One of the miraculous things about this symphony is the easy, convincing way in which it blends the three humorous fast movements with the passionate love song of the *Adagio,* so that they complement one another as perfectly as three irises and a scarlet rose set in a slender vase by a Japanese master of flower arrangement.

Apart from variation movements and the *Eroica* Funeral March, this scarlet rose is the greatest of Beethoven's symphonic *adagios.* Indeed, it is one of the most intense, well-sustained, and gripping non-variation slow movements in all his work. The piece is almost as poignantly lovely as the comparatively short *adagios* of the "*Harp*," the "*Scherzoso*" and the last quartets. And it is in a class with the full-length slow movements of the D major and *Hammerklavier* sonatas, of the First and Second Rasoumowsky quartets, of the First Lobkowitz quartet, and of the "*Geister*" trio.

But this praise must at once be tempered by admitting that Beethoven was never quite such a magician in the song-form slow movement as he was in his *allegros, scherzos,* variations, and the best of his late fugues. Naturally one

[5]This opening of the Fourth symphony may have been inspired by Haydn's *Creation,* produced in 1798, only eight years before. But what an improvement!

[6]Sidney Lanier, "The Marshes of Glynn."

person could not be expected to revolutionize every department of music with equal mastery. And it was left for Brahms to carry the torch of the *adagio* on into new regions.[1]

The passionate second subject of the Fourth symphony's *Adagio*

Ex. 71

is every whit as fine as the familiar first subject, and less known. Its most ardent phrase (at bars 3–5) is an echo of the second of six piano minuets (bars 2–3) which the young composer had published ten years before, without the dignity of an opus number.

Ex. 72

For convenience of comparison this example is transposed from G to B flat. Almost a century this unpretentious piece slumbered forgotten, with those "rude forefathers of the hamlet," its five fellows. Then it suddenly leaped to popularity and the invidious distinction of being familiarly known as "Beethoven's Minuet"—very much as the C minor is sometimes called "Beethoven's Symphony."

[1] As in his first two symphonies, the violoncello sonata in F, the Clarinet quintet, and the three piano quartets.

Chapter XXII

THE PRINCELY RABBLE

Takes Archduke Rudolph as Pupil, about 1805 —
Smashes a Bust of Prince Lichnowsky, 1806 — Applies
for Subsidy as Opera Composer — Loyal Support of Vien-
nese Nobility — Coriolanus, 1807 — Universalizes the
Descriptive Overture — Reconciled to Clementi, 1807 —
Count Gleichenstein Replaces Zmeskall as Factotum — The
Brothers — Mass in C Major, Finished September, 1807 —
Pioneer in the Emancipation of Church Music — Prince
Esterhazy Disappointed—Fancied Insult by Hummel

ABOUT the year 1805 Beethoven took as a pupil in piano and composition the young Archduke Rudolph, a half brother of Emperor Franz. The boy had real talent and, until the end of the Master's life, was a true and generous patron.

On his side Beethoven, though he had a genuine regard and affection for the lad, refused to be overawed by the demands of etiquette. At times he went so far as to rap his august pupil over the knuckles. And Ries relates that when the imperial functionaries undertook to "court-tutor" him forcibly in the intricacies of ceremonial he grew angry, violently made his way into the Archduke's presence,

and flatly declared that while he had the greatest reverence for his person, he could not be bothered to observe all the regulations that were daily urged upon him. The Archduke laughed good-naturedly and gave directions that Beethoven should be allowed to go his own way undisturbed. It was his nature and could not be altered.

Later on, however, as the constraints of teaching interfered with composition and rubbed on his nerves, Beethoven seems to have absorbed some of the verbiage of diplomacy. And one of the least attractive features of his collected letters is the long series of propitiatory notes of excuse for nonappearance at the imperial lessons. They brim over with transparent fibs and palpably insincere flattery.

Naturally enough, from a mere prince Beethoven resented any sort of coercion more savagely than from an Archduke, even though the prince were such a warm old friend as Lichnowsky. During the summer of 1806 he visited the latter on his Silesian estate in Troppau.

Lichnowsky begged him to play for some French officers, his fellow guests. Beethoven curtly refused. At the best of times he needed a great deal of urging. But nothing could induce him to perform for creatures to whom he had unconsciously transferred some of the hatred he felt toward their emperor, the treacherous hero whose name he had struck from the title page of the *Eroica*.

Unwisely the Prince persisted, and jokingly threatened him with "house-arrest" if he did not yield. But in that mood Beethoven was as impervious to humour as a crocodile to a small boy's catapult. Late at night, still breathing out threatenings and slaughter, he bolted from the house, stormed a mile through the dark to Troppau, and took an extra post chaise for Vienna. Arrived there, his first act was to pulverize a bust of Lichnowsky. This fit of fury lasted abnormally long. Not until 1811 did he accept another country-house invitation from his old friend.

Towards the end of 1806 the direction of the Court Theatre and the Theater an der Wien was taken over by a committee of noblemen. One of these was Prince Lobkowitz, whom Beethoven immortalized by the dedications of seven quartets and three symphonies, and whom he called a donkey in that regrettable incident of the truant bassoon. Acting on a kind but injudicious hint from this prince, he wrote to the committee, asking for the position of subsidized opera composer.

It should be borne in mind that, when it came to matters of musical business, Beethoven was usually practical; that he resented dictation; that his already profound knowledge of his own powers and limitations had been sharpened by years of unsuccessful struggle with *Fidelio*. But in this appeal he showed a wild impracticality which suggests either aberration or insincerity.

He proposed binding himself to deliver a large opera once a year. Also "an annual operetta or a *Divertissement*, choral works or occasional pieces, according to the demands and requirements of the praiseworthy Direction."

Leaving out of account Lobkowitz's original indiscretion, the praiseworthy Direction handled this matter in a manner praiseworthy indeed. They knew how impossible it would be to make the erratic genius finish even a single large-scale work by any certain day or year. They realized how unfortunately any sort of coercion reacted upon the quality of his writing, and how the irascible deaf man was bound to antagonize the singers and the orchestras at rehearsal. Perhaps they had some realization, as well, what a tragic loss to instrumental music his entire absorption in opera might entail. So they solved the difficulty by never answering his appeal. Naturally Beethoven was furious. In a note to Count Brunswick, May 11, 1807, he referred bitingly to the *"fürstliches Theatergesindel,"* "the princely theatre-rabble."

But the "rabble" did its princely best to make things up to the poor genius. In his own palace Lobkowitz gave two concerts of Beethoven's works, while Prince Esterhazy ordered a mass from him.

Even for a prince, to be Beethoven's friend was a task of heartbreaking difficulty, requiring the combined endowments of Job, Lord Chesterfield, Sancho Panza, and the Good Samaritan. After we have made all due allowances for their shortcomings the noblemen of Vienna who stood so staunchly and consistently by him deserve our sincere gratitude and consideration. They were true noble-men. However, in spite of their touching forbearance, sympathy, appreciation, and generosity, the composer's theoretical attitude towards them, noted on the margin of a Sketch Book for 1814, was no heartier than this: "Never openly show to all men the contempt they deserve; one never knows where one may need to use them."[1]

---

[1]This recalls a witticism by Brahms. He was looking over a prince's manuscript symphony with a friend, who began tearing it to pieces. "Hold hard," cried Brahms. "In criticising the compositions of the nobility, the greatest reserve should be exercised. One never knows who wrote them!"

But, though in practice he seldom lived up even to this cynical ideal, most of the Viennese aristocracy graciously swallowed his boorishness and stuck to him loyally till death did them part, philosophically putting up with affront after affront.

It would be hard to find any other genius anywhere who has been treated by his aristocratic neighbours with such kindness and clairvoyant intelligence. All honour to "the princely rabble"!

At the concerts in the Lobkowitz palace the work which made the deepest impression was the new overture to Collin's (not Shakespeare's) *Coriolanus*. The hearers, familiar with the play, were able to follow from the first the main argument of its tonal counterpart. Not an exalted form of musical appreciation, it is true, but it sufficed to start the overture on the popular road it has ever since travelled.

Here is music starkly simple as a Greek discobolus or a Tyrolean avalanche. Here is drama bereft of mask, wig, and cothurnus. And, for swifter movement, it is clad in running garb instead of flowing robes. Here is concrete tragic conflict between two particular opposing forces, suddenly and elementally transfigured to something universal as a thunderstorm. And here is skill in characterization not to be again equalled in music until the *Nibelungen Ring*.

Consider the inevitability of its two main themes: the ruthless will of Coriolanus

Ex. 73

in conflict with the fond pleading of his mother's love.

Ex. 74

But Beethoven, true to the genius of music and never content to be a mere illustrator, shattered with one fierce blow the chains which had bound the descriptive overture to the corpse of literalism. In doing so he universalized his matter so that it may stand, as you please, for the conflict of such fundamental antitheses as:

positive	*vs.*	negative
masculine	"	feminine
cruelty	"	kindness
pain	"	pleasure
good	"	evil
optimism	"	pessimism
egoism	"	altruism
love	"	hate

or almost any other of those fundamental conflicts which constitute the primordial stuff of drama.

In 1805 the celebrated composer and pianist, Muzio

Clementi, came to Vienna. As the younger, Beethoven would have gone at once to pay his respects, but his intriguing brothers felt this would be *infra dig*. Then gossip took a hand to keep Clementi from seizing the initiative. Soon there was so much bad blood that when the two masters dined at the same table in The Swan they observed a strict silence, while the attendant pupils of each, for fear of losing their lessons, glared at one another like so many stage Capulets and Montagues.

Eighteen hundred and seven saw the feud patched up. How this was done, Clementi, who was also a London publisher, informed his partner in the following English letter:

MESSRS. CLEMENTI & CO., NO. 26 CHEAPSIDE, LONDON.

Vienna, April 22d, 1807.

DEAR COLLARD:

By a little management and without committing myself, I have at last made a complete conquest of the *haughty beauty*, Beethoven, who first began at public places to grin and coquet with me, which of course I took care not to discourage; then slid into familiar chat, till meeting him by chance one day in the street—"where do you lodge?" says he; "I have not seen you this *long* while!"—Upon which I gave him my address. Two days after I found on my table his card brought by himself, from the maid's description of his lovely form. This will do, thought I. Three days after that he calls again, and finds me at home. Conceive then the mutual ecstasy of such a meeting! I took rather good care to improve it to our *house's* advantage, therefore, as soon as decency would allow, after praising very handsomely some of his compositions: "Are you engaged with any publisher in London?"—"No," says he. "Suppose, then, that you *prefer me?*"—"With all my heart." "Done. What have you ready?"—"I'll bring you a list." . . .

This list included the Rasoumowsky quartets, the Fourth symphony, the *Coriolanus* overture, the Violin and G major piano concertos. Clementi informed Collard that he had made a good bargain for the English rights at £200, cash on delivery.

The composer, too, was pleased. But only for a short time. Try as he might he could not, until three years later, extract that £200 from Clementi.

Beethoven's old factotum, Zmeskall, had lost his health. About the year 1807 he was replaced by Count Ignaz von Gleichenstein. In spite of the *burschikos* tone of his letters to Zmeskall, Beethoven had always kept him at a certain distance and regarded him in the light of 'a useful instrument on which he played.' But Gleichenstein he thee'd and thou'd and held in warm affection. Though he made him buy shirts, pens, neckcloths; though he made him draft letters in French and lend a hand with pension and love affairs, he was always ready to return such favours by helping him socially. Once he procured him an invitation to a Beethoven evening at Archduke Rudolph's. And when the factotum did not appear the Master wrote:

You lost a lot, not by missing my music, but you might have met a lovable talented prince, and—as the friend of your friend— you would certainly not have been made painfully conscious of the height of his rank. Forgive this small expression of pride. It comes more from the pleasure of knowing that those I love are instantly lent distinction, than from petty vanity.

Herr Ernest comments pithily on this letter.

An amazing vignette, doubly amazing when one recalls the social standing of a Haydn and a Mozart. The artist who benevolently takes the aristocrat under his wing and deflects to him some of the lustre of his own name!

Nearly all of his biographers have depicted Beethoven's brothers as impossible persons who treated the noble Ludwig with malignant dishonesty and base ingratitude. Thayer, however, as we have already seen, gallantly wielding the whitewash brush, left Karl and Johann rather too light of hue. The truth seems to lie, not halfway between these limits, but somewhat closer to Thayer's side.

The jealousy of the pair worked Ludwig many an injury. (But Ludwig was savagely jealous, too.) They were dishonest in business matters. (But so was Ludwig.) Like their brother, they were badly brought up in a deplorable home atmosphere and ill educated. Lacking any touch of his genius they had mentally little in common with him. Owing to that universal phenomenon, intra-family antagonism, they refused him that unquestioning obedience which the composer's imperious spirit exacted from the rest of mankind, including princes—and stopping only at archdukes. This recalcitrance was a sharp and permanent grain of sand in the inflamed eye of the genius.

On the other hand, if he was almost impossible to get along with in the world at large this senior brother must have been a grade worse inside the family. His sexual obsession prompted him to mix, with almost the hard officiousness of a monomaniac, in the private domestic affairs of his brothers. Karl's fiancée was a well-to-do and apparently a not too impossible person, but Ludwig was fiercely opposed to the match. On the manuscript of the First Rasoumowsky quartet, composed at the time of the wedding, he wrote above the tragic *Adagio molto e mesto*: "A weeping willow or acacia tree over the grave of my brother." Ever afterwards, with a very few short atoning reactions, he treated Frau Karl with the utmost offensiveness. And, as we shall see, he went so far in Johann's case as to precipitate an unfortunate marriage with his mistress by invoking the law to have the girl driven out of town.

In order to make expensive journeys in 1806 he borrowed heavily from Johann's scanty savings. The following year this brother had a chance to buy an apothecary shop in Linz, at a great bargain. Knowing that Ludwig then had plenty of cash, he asked for the return of the loan, which he desperately needed. This situation was shabbily met.

DEAR GOOD GLEICHENSTEIN:—You may tell my brother that I shall certainly not write to him again. The reason why I know. It is this: because he has lent me money and laid out some on my account he is already concerned, I know my brothers, since I cannot yet pay it back to him, and probably the other who is animated with the spirit of revenge against me and him too—the best thing is for me to collect the whole 1500 florins (from the Industrie-Comptoir) and pay him with it, then the matter will be done with—heaven keep me from being obliged to receive benefactions from my brothers—Be good to yourself.

Your BEETHOVEN.

Of all the known letters of Beethoven [comments Thayer], perhaps no one is so much to be regretted as this, written near the end of 1807, just when the contracts with the Kunst-und-Industrie-Comptoir and Simrock made his pecuniary resources abundant. doubtless increased by a handsome honorarium out of the receipts of the Liebhaber Concerts.

Note the false statement "I cannot yet pay it back to him," so characteristic of his growing avarice. Note the flat contradiction involved a line or two later in his unwilling resolve to pay the money back forthwith. Notice too the extraordinary incoherence of style and the irrelevance of the phrase dragged in about brother Karl—both indications of his obsession of persecution.

The mass in C major (Op. 86), with its backward look and flavour of the first period, is a surprising appearance between such ripe second period masterpieces as the Rasoumowsky quartets and the C minor symphony. But surprising only until one recalls Beethoven's custom of groping his way cautiously into each new form.[2] He seemed timid, anxious, fettered by its demands. His imagination did not flow with the exuberant spontaneity which was one of his chief traits.

Think of the first piano trio, the first piano sonata, the First quartet, the First symphony, the *Prometheus* overture, the B flat piano concerto, the first violin and violoncello sonatas. They all seem more or less tentative, constrained things, with one eye on precedent. True, the Mass in C has many beautiful pages. There is the whispered end of the *Kyrie*; the end of the *Crucifixus*, so gruesomely suggestive; the impressive *Sanctus* and the *Benedictus*.

In writing to Prince Esterhazy, who had ordered the Mass, the haughty composer expressed himself about it with an unusual modesty which tempts one to suspect that he not only feared the Prince's conservative taste, but that he

[2]See p. 63.

himself thought none too highly of his first essay in this form.

May I say that I will turn over the Mass to you with much misgiving, as you are used to having the inimitable masterpieces of the great Haidn performed for you.

Of course this is largely flattery of the reactionary old patron of Papa Haydn. For Beethoven realized quite well that his own work surpassed all previous masses with which he was familiar. (He had had no chance to hear Bach's B minor.) He must have realized also that its dignity and devotional spirit made it a pioneer in emancipating church music from the profane and theatrical tone which had, since Bach, invaded it, and which showed plainly in the masses of even Mozart and Haydn.[3]

At the same time one can scarcely imagine him writing in any such lowly strain to Count Oppersdorf, for whom he made the Fourth symphony, or to Lobkowitz and Rasoumowsky, whose names stand on the title page of the Fifth symphony.

The Mass in C was first performed September 13, 1807, at the Esterhazy castle in Eisenstadt. The disappointment was general. "But dear Beethoven," cried the Prince, "what's this you have done again?" Hummel, the Prince's new music director, happened to overhear these words. Their naïveté was probably too much for him. Beethoven, as Schindler relates,

saw the chapelmaster laugh, as he stood near the Prince. He thought he was being ridiculed. And nothing could keep him at

[3]See Felix Raugel, *Les Messes de Beethoven, Le Courrier Musical*, Feb. 1, 1927.

the place where his work had been so misunderstood, and where a brother in art had, as he thought, laughed at his discomfiture. He left Eisenstadt the same day.

For years he never forgave the well-meaning man whom, long before, he had once addressed as *"Herzen's Nazl."*[4]

We cannot wonder that the mature Beethoven should have been dogged thus insistently by his obsession of persecution when we recall that, as a lad, he had actually been persecuted by cruel and unusual music lessons, poverty, and a drunken father, and that he now was famous, envied, and deaf.

Fortunately, however,

A dram of sweete is worth a pound of sowre.

One of Dr. Jekyll's rarest moments, like the *Andante con moto* of the B flat trio, is enough to blind us to the most deplorable antics of Mr. Hyde. Or such an incident as was told to Felix Mendelssohn by that excellent pianist, the Baroness Dorothea von Ertmann,

when she lost her last child. Beethoven at first did not want to come to the house. At length he invited her to visit him, and when she came he sat himself down at the pianoforte, saying simply: "Now we will talk to one another in tones." More than an hour he played without stopping, and as she remarked, "he told me everything and at last brought me comfort."

Since then for how many sorrowing millions has he not performed a like service!

---

[4]See p. 48.

Chapter XXIII

WHO KNOCKS AT THE DOOR?

Fifth Symphony, Composed 1805–1807 — Compared with Eroica *— The* Per Aspera ad Astra *Pattern — Questionable Origin of "Fate Knocks at the Door" — Duping Schindler — Many Possible Interpretations of the C Minor — Beethoven and the Sea — Self-Determination for Listeners — Music's Emancipation from Literature — The Music of the C Minor — Sketch Books — Borrowings from Mozart — The Symphony and the Listener*

WE HAVE come to Beethoven's best known work—the most popular orchestral piece of its length in the world. The Fifth symphony in C minor (Op. 67) was begun in 1805, laid aside for the Fourth, finished probably late in 1807, first publicly performed December 22, 1808, and published in 1809. It could have been written only by an imagination with the *Eroica* behind it.

The Fifth surpasses the Third in concentration, clarity, directness, in the elemental climactic force of its closing portion, and, as the writer hopes presently to show, in its freedom from deliberate literary appeal.

The first movements of both are alike full of that dæmonic power which tornadoes even more irresistibly through the beginning of the *Choral* symphony. The Fifth is superior in the mysticism pulsating in the *scherzo* as if with the restless wings of earthbound spirits; above all, as

Sir George Grove happily remarks, in the consistent way
in which, all through the work, "technicality is effaced by
emotion." In this respect it represents the full maturity of
the Romantic movement. Without the fertilizing Fifth
there could scarcely have blossomed such an essentially
romantic aftermath as the Mendelssohn Violin concerto, the
Symphonic Etudes of Schumann, the Brahms Second symphony and Clarinet quintet, Tschaikowsky's *Pathétique,* or
Debussy's quartet.

That the *Eroica* as a whole seems to stand the test of
time better is due perhaps to the greater originality of its
themes, the finer subtlety of their inter-relations, and the
more human force and poignance of those two supreme
portions, the Funeral March and the development section
of the first movement. Exalted as it is, the Fifth can offer
us nothing quite comparable to these two portions—not
even the stupendous unison opening, nor the sorcerer's
bridge following the *scherzo,* nor the three conquering tonic
chords that begin the *finale*

Ex. 75

even more jubilantly than the start of the *Mastersingers* overture—those chords that made the veteran of Napoleon's Old Guard spring to his feet, oblivious of surroundings, and cry: *"C'est l'Empereur!"* Last but not least the *Eroica* has not been played so close to satiety as this, the typical symphony.

Emotionally, the Fifth is built on that old pattern which Beethoven used so originally in a considerable number of his works: *per aspera ad astra*. This struggle-to-victory scheme is apt to suggest a triumph of positive over negative forces. It is often subdivided, as in the Fifth, into I, Outer Struggle; II, Comfort or Reassurance; III, Internal Struggle; IV, Victory.

In some such broad general way, valid for everyone, it is usually possible to define the argument of a musical composition; but with no more particularity than if one were to determine beforehand about some proposed fresco merely its size, shape, and principal colour scheme. To attempt to squeeze such a sonata or symphony, dogmatically and once for all, into any narrower, more definitely concrete pigeonhole is the unpardonable sin against the holy spirit of music.

This it surely is, to decide for all time—on the strength of a phrase casually dropped by the Master and reported by one of the least trustworthy of his biographers (the man whom Bülow called a "strawhead")—that the Fifth symphony means nothing but a duel between free will and determinism.

Suppose we grant that Beethoven, many years after finishing the Fifth, actually remarked to Schindler, "Thus fate knocks at the door," when that arch-Philistine naïvely demanded the meaning of the first movement. We must bear in mind that this factotum of his was one of those half-baked people, like Wagner in the first part of *Faust*, whose literal minds and musico-literary urgencies easily roused the Master's impatient scorn or his mischievous instinct—or both. When such folk tried to put him on the witness stand he would, for peace, blurt out any fantastic thing that popped into his head. At the same time he often yielded to that love of horseplay which would not be gainsaid even in connection with so serious work as the C minor.[1]

This Schindler was a favourite victim. The Master once informed him solemnly that the naïve little "Children's Trio" in E flat which he wrote as a lad of fifteen, was "one of the loftiest experiments in the free style of composition."

In 1823 he went for a walk with his trying disciple in that country near Heiligenstadt where the *Pastoral* symphony had been written. The deaf man inquired if there were any yellowhammers to be heard in the trees.

But all was still [records Schindler]. Then he said: "Here I composed the *Scene by the Brook*, and the yellowhammers up there, the quails, nightingales, and cuckoos round about composed along with me." When I asked why he had not also put the yellowhammers into the scene, he pulled out his Sketch Book and wrote:

Ex. 76

----
[1] See chap. XVII.

"That's the composer up there," he remarked. "Hasn't she a more important rôle than the others? *They* are meant only for a joke." And he went on to explain that he had not labelled this last co-worker for fear of the critics who had accused him of undue realism in the Eroica!

Instead of greeting this fictitious collaborator with

Hail to thee, blithe spirit!
Bird thou never wert—

the gullible Schindler duly swallowed the nonsense whole, although it is notorious that no created yellowhammer ever sang anything that could possibly be tortured into the faintest resemblance to an arpeggio. Indeed, on another page this same famulus quoted Czerny as saying that Beethoven declared he had taken the opening theme of the Fifth symphony from a yellowhammer's song in the Viennese *Prater*. There is more rhyme and reason here, for the bird undeniably sings a number of short notes of the same value, followed by a long one. But this, too, may have been a *jeu d'esprit*. For the shrill pipings of such a small creature are among the first things to be lost by ears turning deaf.

Thus, when Beethoven said those words about fate knocking at the door, they may have reflected a momentary (and, let us add, well justified) poetic mood. Or they may have represented an attempt to stimulate the inadequate and prosaic orchestras of those days to give more stirring and imaginative readings of his symphony. Or they may have been a deliberate mystification trumped up to serve as a gag. For he well knew that his boring famulus was a person who would have solemnly accepted and perhaps annotated such a line as that about Prince Agib:

His stately spirit rolls in the melody of souls.

Whereon its author, W. S. Gilbert, comments under his breath:

Which is pretty but I don't know what it means.

It is as futile to demand *the* meaning of the Fifth symphony as to demand the meaning of Mont St. Michel or the Grand Canyon. Such music can mean an almost infinite number of things. It is subject to kaleidoscopic change without notice, according to mood, tense, person, gender, and number.[2]

Even if Beethoven's remark about the door were made in good faith, it should never be understood as implying that this music might not have many other interpretations equally valid. The broad-gauge composer who wrote on the manuscript of the frankly programmatic *Pastoral* symphony: "More expression of feeling than tone-painting," knew that music cannot be stereotyped, constricted, and degraded into any such petty business as a single poetic idea. Even if it conveys to the mind of Smith such a Goethean conception[3] as fate supplanting the traditional

[2]Schindler's question was as Babbitt-like as that of an old lady who once bore down upon the writer of these lines after a lecture. He was trying to catch a train, but her determined fingers detained his lapel. "I won't keep you a moment," she panted. "Please just tell me, how does one write poetry?"

[3]A passage about Shakespeare from Goethe's *Wilhelm Meister's Lehrjahre,* Book III, chap. XI, sounds strangely like the outpourings of the more naïve symphony program annotators of Beethoven concerts a century after: "These are no poems! One imagines he is standing before the monstrous open books of Fate, wherethrough sweep in wild commotion the stormwinds of agitated life." Beethoven had read Goethe's novel and may possibly have had this passage in mind when he made his famous remark to Schindler.

wolf at the door, it may quite as reasonably convey entirely different things to a group of creative listeners unbiassed by program annotations.

To Brown it may signify a fierce conflict with a sexual obsession. To Jones a desperate campaign against an inferiority complex. To Robinson, an old-fashioned pitched battle *à la* "Paradise Lost," between the forces of good and evil. To a victim of hysteria, it may depict a war between sanity and bedlam. To a neurasthenic, the struggle between those two mutually exclusive objectives: "To be, or not to be?" To an evolutionist, it may bring up the primordial conflict of fire with water, of man with beast, of civilization with savagery, of land with sea.

Perhaps the last suggestion is the best. What music, in fact, collaborates more naturally with dreams of "perilous seas" in their elemental rage—yes, and of "magic casements" too (think of the second subject!)—than the opening movement of the C minor?

If we should hear the shriek of the midocean wind issue from this music and taste its brine in our throats, let us recall that Beethoven saw the sea only once, and that was when, as a lad of eleven, he was shown the harbour of Rotterdam. Yet we can sometimes get from his pages more of the wash and shock, the kelpy fragrance, the spindrift and hammering surf of the seven seas than from those of any other composer. Geniuses need little in the way of stage setting—just to be left in comparative peace and allowed to conduct their experiments in transubstantiation.

Beethoven would have been the first to deplore our use of

any one fixed image in connection with his absolute music. This man was no intellectual despot. He once scribbled on the manuscript of his song *North and South* a direction indicating that the metronome mark should be "100 according to Maelzel, but this can apply only to the first measures, for feeling, too, has its own tempo." He who fathoms this touching and profoundly democratic remark must understand why the man who made it protested so furiously against the program-note autocrats of the poetic idea, and why he raged when some fool proposed to call his unnamed overture (Op. 115) *"La chasse."* And we shall see[4] what he said of the poetaster who wished to paste a program upon his Seventh symphony. Beethoven was one composer who stoutly upheld the rights of the smaller, less favoured fancies to self-determination.

If he had foreseen that his perhaps impatient, perhaps roguish remark to Schindler was destined to associate his most widely known work exclusively with the figure of fate, he would, before uttering those words, have bitten out large sections of his tongue. Here was the Prometheus who had already done much toward the temporary emancipation of the art from its secular servitude to literature. The process had begun late in the Fifteenth Century, with those first timorous attempts of the Italians to free music from its vocal dungeon and let it totter a step or two alone. Whatever untoward, unforeseen influence the *Pastoral* symphony may have afterwards exerted upon the history of program music it is certain that Beethoven was not the man

[4]See p. 305.

to turn around and deliberately seek to reimprison his art in the dungeon of the poetic idea.

The Fifth symphony would have lent itself more proteanly to association with a million different poetic ideas in the imaginations of a million hearers if only that luckless remark to Schindler had not standardized the million varieties into one identical factory product.

The first movement, with those cognate first movements of the Third and the Ninth symphonies, represents Beethoven's freshest, most characteristic contribution to the art—always excepting the *scherzos* of these same symphonies.

The strongly masculine motive with which it opens

Ex. 77

is surely, like many other bird calls, one of the least promising of all created tunes. When it was first played it sounded so poverty stricken that people in the audience burst out laughing.

Even so, it was scarcely original. For, whether Beethoven knew it or not, it was nearly an inversion of a theme of Legrenzi's, used by Johann Sebastian Bach for his C minor organ fugue.

Ex. 78

And it had been vigorously exploited in Haydn's third piano sonata, in E flat.

However, *"il n'est pas le ton qui fait la musique."* More intervals or tones scarcely count, but the way in which they are used. As Burns might have phrased it, the motive is but the guinea stamp, the treatment's the gowd. And when one hears this movement Legrenzi seems a continent away.

Beethoven performed such prodigies with this seemingly barren affair of three eighths and a half—made them so startlingly original—that they became the most famous four notes in existence. The most unmistakable sign of Beethoven's genius, according to Wagner, was "his miraculous faculty for creating worlds out of nothingness."[5]

Just as the rhythm of the yellowhammer source-motive is to be found in many of his works,[6] it threads its old but ever varied refrain as a germ-motive through each division of the C minor.[7]

There is no weak movement in the symphony. The *Andante con moto* is the least powerful of the four. Yet the last time the writer heard Signor Toscanini give it— distorted though it was by the bad acoustics of the top gallery of the Metropolitan Opera House—half the humble music lovers up there paid it the tribute of tears.

In 1803 Goethe wrote to Zelter:

One does not learn to know nature and works of art if they are finished; in order to comprehend them somewhat one must surprise them while they are still being formed.

[5]T. de Wyzewa, *Beethoven et Wagner,* p. 130.

[6]See pp. 153-154.

[7]See p. 540.

The study of such Note Books as Beethoven's and Shelley's is a most illuminating experience. One sees how they toiled over the raw material, gradually shaping it from commonplaceness to the most highly individualized product of genius. One sees how vastly more important was the recasting than the original writing, and that the labour usually made the difference between mediocrity and immortality.

Few things are more inspiring to the creative artist than a study of the Sketches for the *Andante con moto* of the C minor. From the banality of this unpromising first thought—

Ex. 79

Beethoven finally forged out by sheer industry this well-rounded and distinguished theme for his variations.

Ex. 80

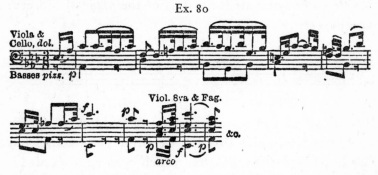

Notice how the Master's irrepressible waggery winks out for a moment at the 134th bar. This bit might be nicknamed the Mouth-organ Passage, from the Procrustean way in which the harmony is forced to fit the exigencies of two progressions of thirds working in contrary motion —a purely musical joke.

It is curious to find that a work which sounds as original as the C minor symphony achieved two triumphant and masterly plagiarisms from Mozart. Nottebohm[8] pointed out that the beginning of the *scherzo*,

Ex. 81

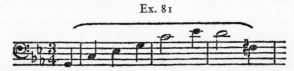

like the opening of the F minor piano sonata (Op. 2, No. 1),

Ex. 82

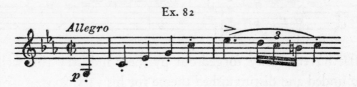

has the same intervals as the start of the *finale* of Mozart's G minor symphony.

Ex. 83

(Both of the latter examples are transposed to C minor for comparison.) Notice that Ex. 81 is far more completely Beethovenized than Ex. 82, which was appropriated a dozen years earlier. That Beethoven's borrowing was de-

[8]*Zweite Beethoveniana*, p. 531.

liberate in the C minor is shown by his having copied out twenty-nine bars of the Mozart symphony's *finale* on the next page of the Sketch Book.

Not content, however, with this, the second part of the first subject of the C minor's *finale*

Ex. 84

has the same intervals, and very much the same movement, as the first subject of the *Andante* in Mozart's *"Jupiter"* symphony.

Ex. 85

Conscious of his power, Beethoven began to use the material of his forerunners more audaciously than he had in the young days when he was an avowed Haydn-Mozart imitator. For he knew he might now quote their tunes— as he quoted the Russian airs in the Rasoumowsky quartets —almost note for note and still saturate them so wholly with his personality as to follow Goethe's injunction:

> *Was du ererbt von deinen Vätern hast,*
> *Erwirb es, um es zu besitzen.*

> (That which your fathers have bequeathed to you,
> Earn it in order to possess it.) [9]

[9]*Faust*, Pt. I, Sc. I.

And what creative listener to this music can deny that the man who made it had come into full possession of the power of his prime? One means the sort of listener who, at some inspired performance, is overwhelmed by the emotional impetus and structural wonder of the first movement; charmed by the contrast of wistful loveliness and heroic strength in the variations; spellbound—almost awestruck—under the hypnotic mystery of the *scherzo;* held in an almost unendurable passion of suspense by its throbbing *ppp* close and the *crescendo* culminating in the fiery magnificences of that triumphal dawn, the *finale,* which fills him with the exultation of one who scorns to change his state with tone-deaf kings.

Chapter XXIV

FATE FUMBLES AT THE BOX OFFICE

1808, Threatened Loss of Finger — Honours Haydn — Material Sources of Inspiration — In Questa Tomba — 1808, "Ghost" and E Flat Trios, Op. 70 — First and Second Period Compared — Were These Trios Begun as Piano Sonatas? — Friendship with Countess Erdödy — A Major Violoncello Sonata, 1808 — "Inter Lachrymas et Luctum" — Bombardment of Vienna — G Minor Phantasie — Improvisation on a Second Violin Part — Memorable Beethoven Concert, December 22, 1808 — Criticisms of Fifth Symphony's Début — Meagre Receipts — Performance Botched — Choral Fantasia, Op. 80 — Beethoven Humiliates the Orchestra

A FEW words of petty chronicle.

In the spring of 1808 Beethoven suffered from a felon and nearly lost one of his fingers. Fate seemed to be doing its best to hasten the end of his career as pianist.

After all the unpleasantness with Papa Haydn it is good to know that his better self came forward on the occasion of the old master's seventy-sixth birthday. In company with other leading citizens of Vienna Beethoven showed him public honour at a gala performance of *The Creation*.

He often drew inspiration from sources even more unlikely than the fateful yellowhammer. Late one night the persistent knocking of a belated traveller on a near-by door suggested to his imagination the four quarter notes[1] which were to play such an interesting rôle in the first movement of the Violin concerto. The characteristic clatter of a horse's hoofs galloping past his window in Heiligenstadt tapped out in his mind the first theme of the *finale* of the *"Recitative"* piano sonata.

Ex. 86

A bit of artistic fooling originated one of his best known songs. Countess Rzewiska improvised a tune at the piano. Not to be outdone, the poet Carpani improvised a text for it. The resulting song, *In Questa Tomba* was made the basis of a competition among a number of well-known composers. A book of sixty-three settings of it was published. Beethoven's, the sixty-third, though never very highly regarded, is to-day the sole survivor.

In 1808 Beethoven returned to a form which he had for ten years neglected. If one may judge from internal evidence he began composing the two trios for piano, violin, and violoncello, in D and E flat major (Op. 70), with almost as much enthusiasm as he had shown for the Rasoumowskys after six years of abstinence from string quartets. The eerie quality of the D major's *Largo assai* originated the nickname the *"Geister,"* or *"Ghost"* trio.

Significantly enough, sketches for this weird movement occur in a Sketch Book immediately after some notes of a

---

[1]See Ex. 68, p. 191.

Witches' chorus for an uncompleted opera on Macbeth.[2] It is not known whether the spectral character of the play found its way into the trio or whether the supernatural atmosphere of the *Largo assai* turned Beethoven's thoughts toward that brother artist who had created the ghosts of Banquo and of Hamlet's father.

The writer cannot follow Herr Paul Bekker in finding much resemblance between the D major trio (Op. 70, No. 1) and the D major violoncello sonata (Op. 102, No. 2). On the contrary the trio seems to turn its face firmly toward the past. Its opening strain

Ex. 87

follows virtually the same intervals as the fourth theme of the Fifth symphony's *finale*, if one discounts the repetitive third and fourth measures (which are here indicated only by repeat marks).

Ex. 88

---

[2]An adaptation of Shakespeare's play was begun by Collin, the author of *Coriolanus*, but abandoned in the middle of the second act "because it bade fair to be too gloomy."

In many more subtle and striking ways the D major trio reminds one, rather, of the early piano sonata in the same key (Op. 10, No. 3). In fact, when closely studied, the *"Ghost"* trio sounds like a sort of abridged edition *de luxe*, a second-period *revenant*, of the sonata. Details of this relationship will be found in chapter LIII, pp. 517–519.

The somewhat similar use of cognate material in these two masterpieces, which were created at about the same level of inspiration, gives an unusual opportunity for comparing Beethoven's first period with his second, a decade later.

In the two trios (Op. 70) one sees him ripened, mellowed, in easier, more powerful command of a richer, profounder material. Notice in these examples

Ex. 89

Ex. 90

how the former (the sonata) theme shows his economical, Mozartian first-period method of harmonizing melodies by suspensions, while the trio example is characterized by his second-period way of giving each successive note a new harmony.[3]

Incidentally, in the *"Ghost" Largo,* as in the *scherzo* of the Fifth symphony, there is already foreshadowed the mysticism of the third period which broods over such *adagios* as those of the *Hammerklavier* sonata and A minor quartet, and over the *Incarnatus* of the *Missa Solemnis.*

A study of certain letters which Beethoven wrote to Breitkopf and Härtel at this time suggests that he had probably planned these trios, in the first instance, as piano sonatas. If this be true he may have changed them to trios, partly because there was a dearth of trios, but chiefly because he noticed too great a similarity between the D major trio (Op. 70, No. 1) and the D major sonata (Op. 10, No. 3).

Probably he also realized what Herr Bekker points out, that the other trio (Op. 70, No. 2) has several features in common with another sonata (Op. 31, No. 3), viz.: the key of E flat, four movements, the absence of an *adagio*, etc. The reader is again referred for details to pp. 519–520.

These trios (Op. 70) were dedicated to the Hungarian Countess Erdödy. Although an invalid, she was an able pianist and interpreter of Beethoven's works. Their friend-

---

[3]For a fuller discussion of this point see an article by Dr. Hans Gál, *"Die Stileigenthümlichkeiten des jungen Beethoven,"* in the *Studien zur Musikwissenschaft,* issued in conjunction with the *Denkmäler der Tonkunst in Oesterreich (Viertes Heft,* 1916). Cf. also Ernest Newman, *The Unconscious Beethoven,* pp. 107–109.

ship had begun some years earlier. It lasted valiantly through the ups and downs inevitable in any intimacy with the volcanic Master. Finally, in 1820, the lady was sentenced to life banishment from the Empire. She seems to have been under suspicion of having conspired with her old friend Magister Brauchle to do away with her only son August, who had died suddenly on an estate in Croatia.[4] But there is no convincing evidence of their guilt.

While writing the trios Beethoven lived in Countess Erdödy's house. Shortly after this visit he quarrelled with her and asked his publisher to change the dedication. But it was too late, and Beethoven came to be glad of it. For he soon saw his error and wrote her a fully orchestrated apology.

MY DEAR COUNTESS, I have been in the wrong, that is true, forgive me, it was certainly not deliberate malice on my part if I pained you—only since last evening have I known how all stands, and I am very sorry that I acted as I did—read your note in cold blood and judge for yourself if I deserve all that, and if it did not pay me back six times over. Since I offended you without meaning to, do send me my note back to-day, and write me only one word that you are again my friend, I shall suffer no end if you do not, I can do nothing if things are to continue this way—I await your forgiveness.

The A major sonata (Op. 69) for violoncello and piano was written in 1808. It holds the same position among Beethoven's violoncello sonatas that the *"Kreutzer"* has among those for violin. Though not written so gratefully for the instruments it is musically a finer work. Standing midway

---

[4]Frimmel, *Beethoven Handbuch*, 1926, Vol. I, p. 124.

between the first two violoncello sonatas (Op. 5) and the last two (Op. 102), it has the grace and buoyancy of the former pair without their rococo flavour of superficiality. It possesses much of the depth of the latter pair without their undeniable crabbedness.

The sonata begins with a strain which may well stand as the ideal Beethoven melody of the second period.

Ex. 91

One admires the subtlety with which the rhythmic pattern of each measure differs from, yet balances, that of every other measure. This is an art which few later composers have ever mastered. Rhythmically speaking, Ex. 91 might be called the perfect tune.

In the tiny introduction to the *finale* no use is made of material rich enough to have tempted almost anyone else to develop a long *adagio*. Which shows what boundless resources the spendthrift Master felt within himself at this period. The *finale* opens with one of those patterns which pursued Beethoven with the insistence of *The Hound of Heaven,* "down the nights and down the days," and which we have called source-motives. The influence of its rhythmical scheme—

Ex. 92

four quarter notes with suspension in the tonic, followed by a dotted half—was to be felt through the years.[5]

In spite of certain technical awkwardness which seldom, in performance, allow its blithe mellowness to come through, this sonata still stands, with the two by Brahms and the authorized violoncello version of the Franck, at the head of the sonata literature for this difficult and elusive instrument.

Beethoven dedicated the work to Gleichenstein, and, March 4, 1809, scrawled upon the manuscript these words: "*Inter Lachrymas et Luctum*" (Amid Tears and Distress). This was doubtless a reference to the victorious advance of the French troops who, the following August, bombarded and took Vienna while Beethoven lay in a cellar with pillows over his suffering ears to shut out the noise of the artillery.

The *Allegretto* theme of the G minor Phantasie for piano (Op. 77) is the highly Beethovenian heart of a composition which seems like an almost literal transcript of what used to happen when Beethoven was caught at the piano in one of his moods of inspiration, or what he called "raptus." Together with the two fantasia sonatas (Op. 27) it is the only musical report we have of his genius for improvisation, such as Czerny described in words.

Ignatz Pleyel, who was just then the most widely known and popular living instrumental composer except Bee-

---

[5]See pp. 570–571.

thoven, had come from Paris, bringing with him his last new quartets,

which were performed before a large and aristocratic society at the house of Prince Lobokowitz.

At the close, Beethoven, who was also present, was asked to play something. As usual, he let himself be urged for an infinitely long time, and at last was almost dragged by two ladies to the pianoforte. In an ill humour he grabs a second violin part of the Pleyel quartet from a music desk, throws it on the rack of the pianoforte and begins to improvise. He had never been heard to improvise more brilliantly, with more originality and splendour than on this evening! But through the entire improvisation there ran through the middle voices like a thread or *cantus firmus* the notes, in themselves utterly insignificant, which he found on the accidentally opened page of the quartet, upon which he built up the most daring melodies and harmonies in the most brilliant concerto style. Old Pleyel could show his amazement only by kissing his hands. After such improvisations Beethoven used to break out into a ringing peal of amused laughter.

On December 17, 1808, the following notice appeared in the *Wiener Zeitung:*

MUSICAL ACADEMY

On Thursday the 22d of December Ludwig van Beethoven will have the honour to give a musical academy in the R. I. Priv. Theatre An der Wien. All the pieces are of his composition, are entirely new, and not yet heard in public. . . . First Part. 1. A symphony entitled: "A Recollection of Country Life," in F major (No. 5). 2. Aria. 3. Hymn with Latin text, composed in the Church style with chorus and solos. 4. Pianoforte Concerto played by himself.

Second Part. 1. Grand Symphony in C minor (No. 6). 2. Holy, with Latin text, composed in the Church style with chorus and solos. 3. Fantasia for pianoforte which culminates in the gradual entrance of the whole orchestra and at the end with the introduction of choruses as a finale.

Boxes and reserved seats may be had in the Krugerstrasse No. 1074, first floor,—beginning at half past six o'clock.

How many of that audience suspected for a moment that they were privileged beings, treading on hallowed ground? It is doubtful if anyone had the slightest idea that these new symphonies (with their numbers transposed) were to hold a commanding position in history, or that Beethoven was to close his career then and there as a piano virtuoso.

Johann Friedrich Reichardt was one of the leading music critics and composers of his time. He reported the C minor as a "big symphony, much worked out and very long." The feature of this composition that most forcibly struck a gentleman sitting near by was that the violoncello part alone had "lots of business in it." It consisted, as he had noticed at the rehearsal, of thirty-four double sheets of manuscript.

How human! An overwhelming number of people cannot see the Forest of Arden for the trees. Often they cannot see the trees for the leaves of the scholarly editions with footnotes.

Imagine not appreciating the chance to hear the *première* of the G major concerto, the *Pastoral*, and the C minor! In after years those listeners must have had a sinking sensation when they learned to what they had been deaf that night.

The concert was far from successful. The box office returns were dismaying and cast Beethoven into deep gloom. A Russian count named Vielhorsky told Hiller he had sat in the orchestra stalls enjoying such conspicuous solitude that once, in acknowledging applause, Beethoven made him "a so-to-speak personal little bow, half friendly, half ironic."

As usual the orchestra and chorus were poor. Actually they had not gone through a single full rehearsal. And even during the partial rehearsals the players were so angry at Beethoven that they banished him from the hall. The place was bitterly cold; the program, more than twice too long.

Frau Milder, the famous singer, had promised to give "*Ah, perfido!*" but the Master, once more at fault, quarrelled with her as well. Her place was taken by a young girl who was at first so frightened that she could not utter a note. Then she took a stimulant. This worked only too well, so that she made hash of the aria. To add to the disaster the numbers from the C major Mass were botched. And the final piece, the *Choral Fantasia* in C minor for piano, orchestra, and chorus (Op. 80), was done to death. In the first place, Beethoven, who played the piano part, absent-mindedly made a repeat which he had agreed to suppress. And then the clarinets were guilty of a false entrance. When that happened the Master jumped from his seat, calling out loudly and angrily: "Stop, stop! That will not do! Badly played! Again! Again! Again!"

The musicians were so indignant at this that several wished to leave the hall. But the unhappy concert was somehow muddled through. Afterwards, when Beethoven had been made to understand how he had humiliated the men, he handsomely begged their pardon.

The idea of this *Choral Fantasia* had occurred to him eight years before. But he worked it out in haste at the last moment, in order to provide, as he vainly trusted, a brilliant end for his concert. It was founded on his song *Gegenliebe*.[6]

Its chief interest for us lies in its being, in a superficial sense, a sort of miniature prototype of the somewhat less unfortunate choral *finale* of the Ninth symphony.

---

[6]See Ex. 280, p. 572.

Chapter XXV

"THE PRINCELY RABBLE"
IS PRINCELY

Growing Obsession of Persecution — Vienna an Appropriate Home for Beethoven — Offer from Court of Cassel, before November 1, 1808 — Annuity from Viennese Nobility, February 26, 1809 — Irregular Payments and Depreciation — Ries in Trouble — F Sharp Major Sonata, October, 1809 — "Adieu, Absence, and Reunion" Sonata, 1809–1810 — "Emperor" Concerto, 1809 — "Harp" Quartet, 1809 — Beethoven Repels the Old, Attracts the Young

THE lean receipts from the academy, and the coolness of the first press notices, strengthened Beethoven's obsession of persecution. He brooded over his lack of official recognition and the appointment of lesser men like Gyrowetz, Salieri, and Eybler as imperial chapelmasters. He never realized how much more comfortable he might have been at that moment if only he had had some idea of economy, arithmetic, and the value of money, and had been content with one or two apartments at a time instead of three or four.

As a matter of fact, in spite of his constant and violent denunciation of Vienna and the Viennese, and his romantic idealization of England as the earthly paradise, he was probably better off where he was than he would have been anywhere else. For musical enthusiasm, culture, and knowledge extended farther down in the social scale there than in any other city in the world. What other metropolis would even to-day give a musician—as Vienna gave Beethoven—the freedom of the city? Imagine London conferring its keys upon M. Ravel, or New York upon M. Stravinsky. And supposing that the latter, in the throes of some new *Sacre du Printemps,* should so far neglect his clothing and demeanour as to be jailed for disorderly conduct,[1] can we picture a Tammany mayor rushing to the Tombs in the dead of night to apologize and send M. Stravinsky home in a municipal Rolls-Royce?

It never occurred to Beethoven that his irascible temper, his erratic habits of life, and his ailments would have prevented his holding any chapelmaster's position a week. In spite of all his adorers, self-sacrificing friends, and disciples he felt himself a cruelly misused, neglected, and misunderstood being, alone against a hostile world.

Not long after the Fifth symphony's distressful début he wrote brother Johann:

May God only give that gentleman, my other brother, instead of his heartlessness—heart. It causes me no end of suffering. With my bad hearing, you see, I always need somebody, and whom shall I trust?

At a truly psychological moment some time before November 1, 1808, he received an offer from King Jerome Bonaparte, the wild new King of Westphalia. Beethoven should have 600 gold ducats a year as chapelmaster of the

---

[1]See p. 376.

Court of Cassel, and "nothing to do but play occasionally for the King and conduct his chamber concerts."

The Master was about to plunge himself into far worse troubles by accepting this offer. But Countess Erdödy got wind of the matter and persuaded Archduke Rudolph, Prince Lobkowitz, and Prince Kinsky to save Vienna's good name by offering Beethoven, on February 26, 1809, a subsidy of 4,000 florins, payable yearly until he should receive an appointment; otherwise for life.

The Master accepted with enthusiasm. But this emotion was short-lived. It was not long before Lobkowitz's property went into the hands of a receiver. And Kinsky was soon killed by falling from a horse. When Beethoven managed, by process of law, to reëstablish regular payments, an inflation had depreciated the subsidy's real value to less than half of the original amount.

Ferdinand Ries tells of an unfortunate effect which this business had upon himself.

Kapellmeister Reichardt came to me and said "Beethoven will positively refuse the Cassel position, would I as Beethoven's only pupil like to go over for a smaller salary?" At first I did not believe it and went straight to Beethoven to find out the truth of this remark and ask him for advice. For three weeks I was turned away and even my letters on this subject remained unanswered. Finally I found Beethoven on the redoubt. I went straight up to him and informed him of the reason for my visits. He answered in a cutting tone: *"So—do you suppose that you could fill a position which had been offered to me?"*—Having said this he remained cold and repellent.

The next morning I went to his house to have an understanding with him. His servant told me in a rough voice: "My master is not at home," although I heard him playing and singing in the adjoining room. So, as the servant positively refused to announce me, I started to go directly in. But he leaped to the door and hurled me back. This made me furious. I caught him by the throat and threw him violently to the floor. The tumult aroused Beethoven's attention. He rushed out, found the servant still on the floor and me pale as a corpse. In my terribly excited state I overwhelmed him with such reproaches that he was dumb with astonishment and stood stock still. When the matter was cleared up Beethoven said "I did not understand it that way. I was told that you tried to secure the position behind my back." On my assurance that I had not yet given my answer he went out with me immediately to make his mistake good. But it was too late. I did not get the position, although at that time it would have meant for me a very important bit of good fortune.

Money troubles, together with the siege of Vienna, hurt the Master's work in quantity. But, by some miracle of psychic resistance, they could not harm its quality. This ugly time of *Sturm und Drang* yielded the F sharp major piano sonata (Op. 78). In much the sense that Shelley is the poet's poet and Velasquez the painter's painter this is the absolute musician's sonata. It is seldom played because, foreshadowing the style of the third period, Beethoven took no care to make it grateful or effective for the performer or easy for the audience. But what the composer himself thought of it appears in his remark to Czerny:

> People are forever talking about the C sharp minor sonata; but really I have written better things. The F sharp major sonata (Op. 78) for example is quite a different affair.

Here we can see Beethoven concerned with sheer music for its own sake and see the rapid dwindling of his interest in the pianoforte as the virtuoso instrument of the *"Moon-light,"* the *"Waldstein,"* and the *"Appassionata."* The end had begun to oppose the means and to force them from the field.

For the writer the F sharp major is lit with the same autumnal glow that suffuses the *"Harp"* quartet. And it is interesting to find the sonata's opening *Allegro*

Ex. 93

beginning with an almost direct quotation of that quartet's introduction.

A programmatic sonata in E flat (Op. 81) was inscribed by Beethoven: *"das Lebewohl, die Abwesenheit, das Wieder-seh'n"* (Adieu, Absence, and Reunion). It suffered more ill effects from the internal and external war than the other works of this period. Begun in falsification of Beethoven's true instincts, the sonata was written as a courtier's compliment to Archduke Rudolph on his being driven from Vienna by the French and on his return. The blight of outer compulsion and lack of spontaneity lies here and there on the two first movements. By the third, Beethoven had evidently found inspiration and momentum. He was probably thinking of some lady rather than of the imperial friend and pupil whose regular lessons caused him so many sincere but smothered imprecations, and extorted from him so many letters filled with insincere excuses.

A glance at the music will show with what ingenuity he constructed nearly the whole first movement out of three notes which he set to the programmatic motto,

and which are usually associated in the minds of English speaking folk with the start of the popular round, *Three Blind Mice*. The necessary lack of contrast between the first and second subjects, involved in such a scheme, represented another step towards freeing sonata-form from the "rules" of such pedants as Albrechtsberger.

The name *"Emperor"* as applied to the E flat piano concerto (Op. 73) is meaningless unless it suggests that the work holds a commanding position in its own realm similar to that held in theirs by the Violin concerto, the *Leonore No. 3* overture, and the *Eroica* symphony. This mas-

culine counterpart of the feminine G major concerto
was composed in 1809. Its opening transformed the traditional cadenza into an impressive proclamation far above
any suggestion of mere display.

The motive underlying the first subject,

when pared down to sheer essentials, looks back five years
to the germ-motive of the *Eroica* symphony (see Ex. 25,
p. 127), and forward seventy years to the opening of the
Brahms violin concerto.

(Transposed here for comparison)

Although it abounds in driving power and infectious
vitality, the balance of this movement carries on at a lower
level than the two works just mentioned.

But the *Adagio un poco mosso* is the purest example of
mystical ecstasy to be found thus far in the Master's work.
It is such a song as St. Theresa or St. Francis in their rapt
hours might have overheard.

Ex. 98

Adagio un poco mosso.

And then, in the half-ashamed way characteristic of Beethoven when suddenly made conscious how far music had led him beyond the sphere of ordinary life, he leaps without pause into a rondo that sparkles and shouts and laughs and capers with even more hilarious abandon than the good gray poet showed when he let himself go in "The Song of Joys."

Most of the Master's works written before 1809 are not hard for the modern listener to appreciate at a first or second hearing. But in the *"Harp"* quartet in E flat (Op. 74), especially in the first movement with its subtle introduction, and in the *scherzo*, we find a slight premonition of those mysterious treasure-filled depths which make the last sonatas and quartets so difficult of approach but also such inexhaustible lodes of delighted surprise for those who are unafraid of the dark and are equipped with safety lamps and adequate equipment for digging.

At the fourth or fifth hearing the first movement of this Tenth quartet leads us back into the sunlight and begins to take on the October mellowness of old wine, of good tobacco, russet apples, burning leaves, and hillsides of ripe-fruited beeches turning a dull gold. The name *"Harp"* is fetched somewhat far—from the arpeggios which start upward in the violoncello part at the end of the development, and again toward the beginning of the coda.

Ex. 99

But the whole work is really a strange harp of four strings or movements, each of which, when plucked, gives forth an entirely different tone quality. For this quartet has small unity. If one takes the introduction and its sequel as one, the four movements have none too much in common.

The *Adagio*, like that of the *"Emperor"* concerto before it and of the B flat trio to follow, is a faint foretaste of that uniquely inspired and wholly celestial music which, years after, Beethoven was destined to overhear on the lonely Patmos of his deafness.

Both thematically and emotionally the *Presto* (not marked *scherzo*) is an exciting recapture of that battle atmosphere into which one is hurled by the first four notes of the C minor symphony,[2] whose variant here is Ex. 99.

The suave and agreeable variations that finish the work give this hearer, at least, somewhat the same disappointed feeling of anticlimax exquisitely tempered by beauty that has been mentioned in connection with the *finales* of the *Eroica*, the B flat trio, and the *Choral* symphony. Incidentally their theme was borrowed from the *Adagio* of Haydn's C major symphony (Breitkopf & Härtel, No. 97).

Though he was that rarest phenomenon, a successful fusion of romanticist and classicist, Beethoven was often a sore trial to the older generation. As we have already seen, many of his pages caused the elders to sit up with a start and mutter words about degeneracy. These men remind one of Koninck's painting, in the Alte Pinakothek in Munich, of young Jesus in the Temple talking to the scandalized doctors, some of whom are sticking their gray beards into musty books in the attempt to confute him.

But the young were enthusiastic Beethovenites. The young of every age consider the new music the greatest ever

[2] See Ex. 77, p. 219.

written. In their teens, those readers of this book who are now middle-aged were of much the same opinion about Richard Strauss's *Also Sprach Zarathustra* and *Ein Helden-leben* when those ultra -modern portents crashed into an astonished world. Likewise the adolescents of the early Nineteenth Century thought that very thing of the Rasoumowsky quartets, the Violin concerto and the Third and Fifth symphonies. They differed from us in being, for once in a way, right.

Chapter XXVI

WHAT FICTION DOES TO MUSIC

The Goriest Battlefield in Æsthetics — Music and Meaning — A Test of Music's Infinitude — Caging the Phœnix — Fiction the Popularizer — Effects of Music and Poetry on One Another — Music the Last Art to Discard Fiction — Story of Program Music — The Epoch-Making Pastoral Symphony, 1808

WE HAVE come to the *Pastoral* symphony and to the subtle and fascinating problem of program music with which that work confronted the year 1808.

During the dozen decades since then, the relation of music to literature has constituted the goriest battlefield to be found in the whole realm of æsthetics. In that conflict quarter is never asked or given. Each side makes its position clear with the blunt force and uncompromising directness of a machine-gun company.

Company, attention! Fire at will!

Program music is absolute music belittled by a single fiction. Absolute music is program music with ten million unwritten arguments, *ad libitum.*

Good music is never exclusively "about" any one particular subject, *even though the composer himself may suppose so.* It is no fatal objection to point out such a title as the *Pastoral* symphony, or even some poem which music ostensibly "sets" or illustrates. The composer's conscious mind is mistaken—that is all. As Mr. Grace[1] has well said:

> No music worth the hearing can be "explained," as you can explain a picture or a poem; it gives us the essence of both, sublimated beyond analysis.

Come fresh to these measures, unaware that any title, argument, or text has been associated with them. The chances are ten thousand to one that they will suggest to your mind some idea emotionally akin, but in detail totally alien, to the officially accepted one. And, fortunately, your idea will be as valid as anyone else's—even the composer's!

Suppose you test this. Select as audience some sensitively musical persons, ignorant of Beethoven and his nomenclature. Try playing for them, without a word of comment or of song, the first movement of the *Eroica,* the *scherzo* of the *Pastoral,* the prelude of the *Benedictus* from the *Missa, Adelaide, The Praise of God in Nature,* and Leonora's *"Last Star"* aria from *Fidelio.* Note the reactions. Then give thanks that music, the immeasurable language, begins "where speech ends"—that at least one of the fine arts is vast enough to be all things to all men!

M. Alfred Cortot[2] has wisely remarked that true interpretation means: "to dream the work anew beyond the man." This holds good even of that somewhat inferior species, program music. Such a work as Beethoven's Sixth symphony can be most adequately interpreted by a conductor who opens his imagination, not alone to the com-

---

[1] Harvey Grace, *Beethoven,* 1927, p. 269.
[2] Behrend, *Ludwig van Beethoven's Pianoforte Sonatas,* 1927, Introduction, p. vi.

poser's literary suggestions, but also to the many other alternative poetic schemes which might as reasonably apply to this score.

No one has been invested with divine authority to cage the Phœnix of music and fasten a label across the bars. But beginners in the appreciation of music, or, in fact, of any art, naturally like things made easier and more palatable by having the bread of absolute beauty smeared with the marmalade of fiction. For this reason story-pictures, story-statues, and story-poems are so popular. This is why song, the opera, and the symphonic poem have an audience so much larger, and less intelligent, than the symphony and the string quartet. Though one will not be thanked for saying so, there are as yet comparatively few adults in the æsthetic world.[3]

As a rule the union of music and poetry takes much from both. The music slows up, distorts, disguises, and suffocates the delicate word-music; the concrete argument of the poetry takes away the most precious characteristic of the infinite art of music—its infinitude. One cannot make a perfect whole out of two imperfect halves.

It is time for those who sincerely care for music to decry this childish demand for stories everywhere. Here the other arts are well in advance. For almost a generation now, intel-

---

[3] In *Wilhelm Meister's Lehrjahre* (Book VIII, chap. VII) Goethe made Jarno shrewdly remark that in order to enjoy the greatest and the best which can be brought to them by an artist, ordinary people "must first imaginatively diminish it as much as possible, in order to bring it somewhat into relation with their own straitened mental and spiritual circumstances." The composer of music often saves such people this trouble by himself attaching a poem or a story to his piece. For literature diminishes every other art it touches. But, happily, the audiences of to-day contain fewer of such "ordinary" listeners than those which attended Beethoven's "Academies."

ligent lovers of painting and sculpture have discarded the fiction element as juvenile. They have laughed at the literalism of Watts, Landseer, and the Rogers groups.[4] Why, the story has even begun to disappear from fiction itself. Witness Marcel Proust and James Joyce. But here is the lover of the most abstract of all the arts, still almost as childish and keen as ever, to have a tale plastered for him upon every tune.

When listeners begin to prefer their Wagner in a symphony concert, undistracted by plot, lines, acting, or scenery—no matter how beautiful these in themselves may be; when they outgrow their present unimaginative passivity and become sufficiently mature to make up their own arguments for Beethoven's Sixth symphony and Strauss's *Till Eulenspiegel,* they may feel that musically they have come of age.[5]

The history of music has been a fluctuating struggle to outgrow the crude ideals of its programmatic infancy. It has been a slow evolution out of the concrete towards the abstract.

In the Sixth Century B. C., a Greek composer named

---

[4]As "Saki" laughed at Egbert and Lady Anne: "They leaned towards the honest and explicit in art, a picture, for instance, that told its own story, with generous assistance from its title. A riderless war-horse with harness in obvious disarray, staggering into a courtyard full of pale swooning women, and marginally noted 'Bad News,' suggested to their minds a distinct interpretation of some military catastrophe. They could see what it was meant to convey, and explain it to friends of duller intelligence." (*Reginald in Russia,* 1928, p. 94.)

[5]"Let us . . . in simple, reverential honesty, accept the great music as we find it, and decline to listen to those latter-day prophets who (in flat disregard of everything that their supposed leader, Wagner, said on the subject) would degrade instrumental music from her . . . proudly independent sovereignty to the position of an importunate beggar woman at the doors of the painter and the novelist." (Ernest Walker, *Beethoven,* 1920, p. 183.)

Sakadas won a victory in the Pythian games at Delphi with a piece of program music describing Apollo's fight with the dragon Python. Two millenia later, when instrumental music began to struggle free of vocal bondage toward a modest independence of fiction, we at once find the same crass, materialistic sort of program music. Jannequin, in 1545, wrote *La Bataille*; Frohberger composed a piano suite portraying an adventurous Rhine journey of the early Seventeenth Century. As an incident of the trip one of the party, while passing the boatman his sword, falls into the water with a loud splash. In 1700 Kuhnau published six Bible-story sonatas. Among other matters they illustrated Jacob swindling Laban, and David registering accurately with a pebble upon Goliath's forehead. Vivaldi composed a series of four concertos, *The Seasons*. According to Sir John Hawkins[6] they are "a pretended paraphrase in musical notes of so many sonnets on the four seasons, wherein the author [meaning the composer] endeavours, by the force of harmony and particular modifications of air and measure, to excite ideas correspondent with the sentiments of the several poems."

Even Johann Sebastian Bach deigned to write a "Capriccio on the departure of his dear brother" with a "representation of the diverse accidents that might happen to him abroad."

That the *Pastoral* symphony was the first fairly good piece of this class was due to Beethoven's musical genius, to his penetrative wisdom in avoiding many of the mistakes

---

[6]*History*, 1789, Vol. II, p. 561.

of his predecessors, and to his whole-hearted enthusiasm for the subject.

Almost word for word, he used the program of *"The Musical Portrait of Nature,"* a "grand symphony," published in 1783 by Justin Knecht. We know that this program had been familiar to Beethoven for a quarter of a century, because it had been advertised on the cover of the three piano sonatas which he published as a lad of twelve.

The Master studied such crude old descriptive music as Knecht's. He reflected deeply about it and decided that it was on the wrong track. It attempted the impossible. It set out to convert a cart horse into Pegasus; but it succeeded only in making an ass of the creature. It tried to make music do unmusical things. Beethoven's Sketch Books of this period are filled with random reflections on the problem of program music:

Sinfonia caracteristica, or a recollection of country life.
The hearers should be allowed to discover the situations.
People will not require titles to recognize the general intention to be more a matter of feeling than of painting in sounds.
Pastoral symphony: no picture, but something in which the emotions are expressed which are aroused in men by the pleasure of the country.
All painting in instrumental music, if pushed too far, is a failure.

These, then, were his principles. If he had stuck steadfastly to them we might have had, in the Sixth symphony, a somewhat less original, less epoch-making work. But it would probably have been a better piece of music. We should have missed an influence which has fathered many of the most interesting and suggestive tone-poems of the last century and more, but which has, on the other hand, misled many a talent into bypaths; and has on the whole exercised a constantly constricting, if not degenerating, effect on the art. For program music is dramatic music. And dramatic music, as the composer Henri Duparc justly observed, "is an inferior species, which does not allow the artist to express himself directly, to reveal freely the beautiful soul."

Let us turn, however, from æsthetic theory to the *Pastoral* itself.

Chapter XXVII

PROGRAM MUSIC AND THE *PASTORAL*

Pastoral Symphony Published 1809 — "More Expression of Feeling than Tone-Painting" — Beethoven Struggles Against Realism — Love of Nature — Fondness for Water — And Animals — Making Nature Natural — Heiligenstadt — First Movement — Scene by the Brook — The Bird Joke — Enter Mr. Hyde — A Daring Harmonic Effect — Beethoven Relishes Bad Music — Makes Friends with Tavern Orchestra — Jovial Origin and Humour of "Peasants' Merry-Making" — Beethoven's Theory of Program Music Summarized — Overtures, His Best Program Music — All Music is Program Music — Literature : Music :: the Conscious : the Unconscious — "My Realm Is in the Air"

THE Sketch Books bear witness that when Beethoven wrote music his last thoughts were almost invariably his best. But as an æsthetic thinker his first thoughts were best. The memoranda given in the previous chapter show that in writing the new symphony he intended rigorously to subordinate the program element and let the creative listener do his part. We shall see how consistently he adhered to this admirable intention.

When the *Pastoral* symphony (Op. 68) was published, in 1809, it bore these legends:

Pastorale-symphony or Recollections of rural life (more expression of feeling than tone-painting). 1. *Allegro ma non molto.*

Awakening of cheerful emotions on arriving in the country.—
2. *Andante con moto.* Scene by the brook.—3. *Allegro.* Peasants'
merry-making.—4. *Allegro.* Thunderstorm. Tempest.—5. *Allegretto.*—Shepherd's Hymn. Happy and thankful feelings after
the storm.

In view of the popular realism of his famous predecessors
it was a triumph of just and sympathetic perception to
declare that "all painting in instrumental music, if pushed
too far, is a failure."[1] Consider the mosquitoes, the frogs,
and the hailstorm in *Israel in Egypt,* by Handel, the man
whom Beethoven to the end of his days considered the chief
of all composers. Think of the lion's roar, the whinnying
horse, the stag's branching horns, the galumphings of heavy-
footed beasts, and the ophidian sinuosities which won universal suffrage in Haydn's *Creation.* Then see with what
sure critical insight and fragrant brevity Beethoven
sketched in those six words on the title page, the wisest
possible constitution and codex of law for composers who
feel irresistibly impelled toward the domain of program
music.

"Mehr Ausdruck der Empfindung als Mahlerey" (More
expression of feeling than tone-painting): it is as simple,
direct, and completely expressive as a New Testament
parable.

Beethoven did not go into any details of his program because (as he noted): "any one who has the least understanding of the countryside will know at once what the author
wishes to express."

---

[1]See p. 253.

It was not the material, but the broadly emotional meaning that the composer felt sure his hearer would understand. He knew that a wordy description of any concrete poetic image that happened to be in his own mind would only weaken and interfere with the necessary creative response of the listener.

As may be concluded from the evidence of his various utterances, this was Beethoven's well-judged position on the subject. But the fact is not important. Even if he had held the contrary opinion such a heresy would scarcely affect his value. Fortunately the worth of a creative artist is not wholly dependent on his stature as an æsthetic thinker.

Suppose the Master had crassly insisted that the functions of composer and poet were really interchangeable. Or suppose he had issued detailed ukases as to exactly what stories his audiences were to imagine and not to imagine during each movement of each of his works. This would probably have made slight difference in the quality of the music itself, and, in time, the ukases would laughingly have been banished to the inevitable dust bin, and the creative listener would have continued, as before, on his independent way, and

Ever let the fancy roam.

In hampering himself with a fictional scheme, Beethoven was unfortunate in taking one ready made from Knecht. Such a proceeding is a handicap to any artist—most of all to such a fanatical lover of independence as Beethoven.

But, on the other hand, he was fortunate in choosing a subject he knew and loved well: the idyllic atmosphere of semi-wild woods and meadows. Charles Neate, his close companion, testified that "nature was almost meat and drink to him; he seemed positively to exist upon it." In fact no small part of the candour, simplicity, and direct force of Beethoven's hundreds of compositions may be traced to the fact that his first inspiration usually came to him out of doors.

"I think," confides Walt Whitman in his "Song of the Open Road":

I think heroic deeds were all conceiv'd in the open air, and all free poems also.

Surely most of Beethoven's music may be classed—for all its loyalty to form—under the head of free tone-poems.[2]

Schindler, indeed, confessed that the Master taught him even more about nature than he did about music. When Beethoven wrote or talked on this subject his naturally halting, crabbed utterance foamed over the weir of language into a sort of prose poetry. His words look more natural in the form of free verse.

---

[2] *Nous faisons en ce temps-ci de bibliothèques et de musées. Nos pères s'embarrassaient de moins de choses et sentaient mieux la nature. M. de Bismarck a coutume de dire pour faire valoir ses arguments: 'Messieurs, je vous apporte des considérations inspirées non par le tapis vert, mais bien par la verte campagne.' Cette image, un peu étrange et barbare, est pleine de force et de saveur. Pour ma part, je la goûte infiniment. Les bonnes raisons sont celles qu'inspire la vivante nature. Il est bon de faire des collections: il est meilleur de faire des promenades.* (Anatole France, *La Vie Littéraire*, 1921, Vol. II, p. 73.)

My bad hearing
Does not trouble me here.
In the country
Every tree
Seems to talk to me,
Saying: "Holy! Holy!"
In the forest
Is enchantment
Which expresses all things—
Sweet peace of the forest!

Almighty, I am happy
In the woods,
Blessed
In the woods,
Every tree has a voice
Through Thee.

O God, what glory
In such a woodland place!
On the heights is peace—
Peace to serve Thee—

How glad am I
Once again
To be able to wander
In forest and thicket
Among the trees,
The green things and the rocks
No mortal can love
The country as I do;
For woods and trees and rocks
Return the echo
A man desires.

Like many another genius he was also passionately fond
of water. In the city he often recaptured inspiration by
playing with a ewerful of it, pouring it over his hands
and head. Indeed, this habit may have hastened his deafness,
for he often carried it to such dangerous lengths that cas-
cades ran through the floor into the rooms of the indignant
neighbours beneath, while the absent-minded Master sat
obliviously scoring, soaked to the skin. One day a heavy
shower caught him writing out of doors. He never noticed
what was going on until the paper grew too wet for his
pencil. In one of the doubtful letters to Bettina he says that
"the delicious May rain" had been "wholly fruitful" for
himself as well as for the earth. What might a fascinating
seacoast not have done for him? No doubt, while brooding
over the *Pastoral,* he sat hour after hour letting that small
Heiligenstadt brook gurgle through his fingers.

He loved animals, too, and prided himself on their affection.

You are wrong [he wrote Gleichenstein, in 1810, about Dr.
Malfatti's dog] if you suppose that Gigons looks for you alone;
no, I too have had the joy of seeing him stick near to my side,
he ate his supper close by me at night, what's more, he saw me
home, in a word, he entertained me very well.

In his love of outdoors, as well as in music, Beethoven was
far ahead of his day. The neo-classical artificiality of the
early Nineteenth Century looked at nature more as a setting for made-to-order Greek temples, broken columns,
lyres, nymphs, gods, and satyrs than as something to be
enjoyed for its own wild sake. The natural Beethoven dis-

liked this sort of thing so much that one wonders why he allowed the artist Maehler to introduce it into the background of his own portrait.[3]

The Master once remarked that a clipped avenue in the park at Schoenbrunn was trimmed up "like an old-fashioned crinoline," and confessed that he was "only happy in the midst of untouched nature." In the field of program music, with the remote means at his legitimate disposal, he was the pioneer in freeing landscape of artifice—in making nature natural. The opening part of the *Pastoral* symphony was the first music frankly to reflect impressions of a landscape unsophisticated by art, literature, mythology, or fashion.

The half-wild woods and fields among which he spent the summer of 1808 exactly rhymed with his inclinations. Literally translated, Heiligenstadt means "The Town of the Holy Ones." Surely an apposite name for the place whose beauty played a part, at various times, in the creation of things that are to music lovers as sacred as the sonatas in G major and D minor, the Second, Fifth, and *Pastoral* symphonies, and the two Masses.

If a literary program must be tacked upon a piece of music, by all means let it pattern after the motto of the first movement of the *Pastoral* and lean away from clear-cut detail, toward the unspecific generality and breadth of music itself. "The awakening of cheerful feelings on reaching the country" contains a million possible specific programs. It is almost as wide as the realm of nature itself.

---

[3]See plate facing p. 267.

Whereas such a program as that of Strauss's *Alpine* symphony—a feeble derivative of the *Pastoral*—narrows music down intolerably.

The opening *Allegro ma non troppo* begins with a subject as simple, unmonotonously monotonous, and peaceful as a grass blade or an oak twig. Like them it holds out the promise of entire countrysides of meadow and forest.

Ex. 100

For in these measures the whole first movement is implicit.

Simplicity, unmonotonous monotony, and peace. See how perfectly they suffuse the closing portion of the second subject, as well.

Ex. 101

This whole movement and the *Brook Scene* are redolent of these things.

In almost every bar the composer took extraordinary precautions against realism.[4] He went the length of giving bird-like figures to the unbird-like strings. He had carefully ascertained that the brook near which he composed gave forth as its two principal notes a bass F and a middle C. Here is an extract from a Sketch Book of 1803:

Ex. 102

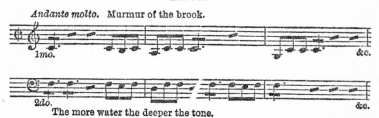

So he deliberately changed the figure which represented running water to a key in which these two notes were not so prominent.

Herr Ernest has a happy explanation of why, despite such precautions, the nature illusion is as convincing as it is.

By a wholly natural process it comes about that, as in the Master's case sights transformed themselves into feelings, and these feelings in turn into tones, so in the hearer's case, the tones transform themselves into feelings and these in turn into sights.

This sounds remarkably like the two reciprocal processes involved in phonographic recording and reproduction.

---

[4]Amiel says that art works through " 'that poetical and artistic illusion which does not aim at being confounded with reality itself.' But 'the groundwork of the real' must somehow underlie it, or the spell fails to hold." (*Journal Intime,* November 7, 1878. Mrs. Humphry Ward's translation, 1889, p. 252.) Quoted in Lowes, *The Road to Xanadu,* p. 298.

Only, Mr. Edison's invention stands to such a phonograph apparatus in much the same relation that a watchmaker's monocle stands to the Mount Wilson telescope.

This long slow ruminative *Scene by the Brook* flowed on quietly, endlessly, to water the musical woods and meadows of the future. Without it there would have been no *Wald-weben* and no *Après-midi*. Almost up to its end Beethoven was consistently true to the principles he had laid down. He was superb so long as he concentrated far more on the expression of feeling than on that tone-painting, which, as he had noted, "is a failure if pushed too far." Then, however, he allowed himself to become so enmeshed in his ready-made program as almost to spoil the symphony. In the bird episode which ends the *Scene by the Brook*, and in the *Storm* and Thanksgiving movements he forgot himself and con-descended to realistic *"Mahlerey."* And at once the music degenerated into measures unworthy of a place in the nine symphonies. They became an unheeded warning to the Strausses and Respighis of the future.

In chatting with Schindler toward the end of his life the Master sought to excuse the nightingale-cuckoo-quail episode as a joke. But, if it was a joke, it was a bad one, such as he often cracked, to the general annoyance, in connec-tion with his loveliest inspirations. And some of his musical heirs, not scenting the mischief, took it seriously, to their own undoing.[5]

[5]Signor Respighi, indeed, went so far as to introduce into his *Pini di Roma*, not a realistic imitation, but the gramophone record of an actual nightingale. Whereupon Mr. Lawrence Gilman justly remarked that this proceeding had exactly as much to do with art as if a landscape painter should cut leaves from an actual tree and pin them upon his canvas.

As we go on in the *Pastoral*, shock follows shock. The humour, almost farce, of the *scherzo*, though deliciously infectious, is on a somewhat lower plane. Then the melodramatic *Storm*, the bathetic shepherd's pipe and Thanksgiving hymn that follow suddenly reveal a degenerate Beethoven, almost on the abject plane of that *"Battle"* symphony which he was presently to concoct for Malzel's Panharmonicon.

When one turns the pages of opus 68 it is as though Dr. Jekyll had begun it. But the brook turned out to be composed of the fatal elixir, and it seems that, the good doctor having sipped of it, Mr. Hyde suddenly obscured the issue with an unseemly joke. Then he gradually took over and finished the score alone.

Even at his worst, however, Beethoven is nearly always interesting, suggestive, and liberating. Before dismissing the *finale* with a gesture of superiority, notice for a moment the harmonies at the fifth measure.

Ex. 103

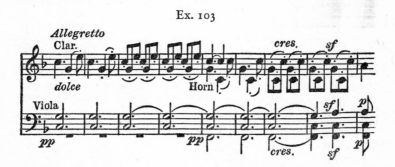

This simultaneous tonic and dominant of the triple pedal F–C–G is a commonplace of to-day, but in 1809 it was a revolutionary manifesto against the "rules" of the pedantic theorists. It was in a class with that other tonic horn solo in the *Eroica*,[6] accompanied by dominant fiddles. Coming abruptly in this apparently reactionary[7] work, it fluttered the conservative breast. It was a proceeding symbolically suitable for a *finale*—this fusing of the two chief chords in music. Here was the harmonic snake swallowing its own tail. Here was Alpha coasting down the last hill upon the shoulders of Omega.

The origin of the *"Peasants' Merrymaking" scherzo* shows the composer in almost as admirable a light as the episode of Dorothea von Ertmann's bereavement when he laid his healing hands upon the piano and her poor heart.[8] Beethoven derived immense enjoyment from naïvely bad music.[9] And he often went with zest to the Sign of the Three Ravens, a tavern near Mödling on the outskirts of Vienna. There an orchestra of seven wholly unsophisticated peasants held forth. They were quite unconscious of their privilege in being the first to introduce Beethoven to the

---

[6]See p. 147.

[7]In most artistic ways the *Pastoral* is a reaction from the C minor symphony. Even structurally, it marks the reappearance of the bridge-passage—that old-fashioned device which had been apparently scrapped after the Second symphony.

[8]See p. 210.

[9]And often profit. An effective figure in the *Credo* of the C major Mass came to him while laughing at an awkward violoncellist who, impotently fumbling for a C major arpeggio, produced something like this:

Ex. 104

Other composers have followed suit in capitalizing naïve and unskilful playing. One need only recall Beckmesser's *Serenade*, Stravinski's *Valse* from the Second *Suite for Small Orchestra*, and the fun in *Petrouchka* shortly before the *Dance of the Moujiks*.

unadulterated Austrian folk music which was to prove so fertilizing to him and his successors, Schubert and Brahms.

The Master made friends with these humble colleagues. There is something extremely engaging in the fact that more than once he composed dances for them, adapting the easy notes with laughing sympathy to the curious habits of these children of nature. No other rural orchestra has ever been so honoured. The chances are that none ever will be.

Schindler recorded that in 1819 Beethoven

again complied with the wishes of the band. I was present when the new opus was handed to the leader of the company. The Master in high good humour remarked that he had so arranged the dances that one musician after the other might put down his instrument at intervals and take a rest, or even a nap. After the leader had gone away full of joy . . . Beethoven asked me if I had not noticed how village musicians often played in their sleep, occasionally letting their instruments fall and keeping quite still, then waking up with a start, getting in a few vigorous blows or strokes at a venture, although usually in the right key, and then dropping to sleep again. He had tried to hit off these poor people in his "Pastoral" symphony. Now, reader, take up the score . . . Note the stereotyped accompaniment figure of the two violins (bar. 87); note the sleep-drunken second bassoon (bar 95) with his repetition of a few tones, while contrabass, violoncello and viola keep quiet. (At bar 127) we see the viola wake up and apparently awaken the violoncello—and the second horn also sounds those notes (bar 131), but at once sinks into silence again. At length contrabass (bar 149) and the two bassoons (bar. 154) pull themselves together for a new effort and the clarinet has time to take a rest.

Schindler might also have pointed out how the oboe apparently comes to his wits too late for his solo in the 91st measure, starts with a false accent, and takes four bars to catch up with the procession.

The rough but tender humour of this strictly musical farce was something quite novel in music, and one must admit that this sort of tenderness is not very often to be found elsewhere in the Master's compositions or in his life.[10] Here he enriched music with a new kind of laughter.

The chief value of Beethoven's labours in connection with the *Pastoral* lay not so much in the symphony itself as in the admirable working theory of program music which he formulated—without consistently following. This theory may be summarized as follows: Program music should be more the expression of feeling than tone-painting. The latter loses when it becomes too realistic. The nearer to photography, the farther from art.

Beethoven composed far greater program music than the Sixth symphony. In the overtures, *Coriolanus, Leonore, Nos. 2 and 3,* and *Egmont,* and in the *Eroica* symphony, he created a newer, freer, more musical program music. These tone-poems of psychological conflict are superior even to the finest parts of the *Pastoral* in being expressions of almost pure *"Empfindung"* rather than, as in opus 68, the expression of *"Empfindung"* alloyed by *"Mahlerey,"* or, as in the *"Battle"* symphony and its old-fashioned precursors, simply materialistic and superficial description. This last is

---

[10]But there is a charming instance of it in a letter written in 1816 to his nephew's schoolmaster, Del Rio: "As regards my indebtedness for the quarter, I must ask you to be so kind as to come and collect it in person, as the bearer of this has been blessed by God in being somewhat simple, a trait which one doesn't begrudge him as long as others do not suffer thereby."

the worst kind of music, because it seeks to usurp the natural functions of some other art in striving to express concrete, and therefore unmusical, things.

The best sort, like *Coriolanus,* leaves the listener free to make up his own program afresh at each hearing. It leaves him less foiled by the irrelevant question: "What poetic idea did the composer happen to associate with these pages when he wrote them?" In truth the chances are that this imaginative composer associated them, on various occasions, after their first conception, with a variety of mental pictures.

To a vividly creative listener all music is program music; and the less argument accompanies it in the form of title, poetic synopsis, speech, song, or action, the more vitally, variedly, and creatively may the listener respond to it.

The narrow definiteness of conscious mental imagery has an appropriate vehicle in literature. The inclusive indefiniteness of the imagery of the unconscious has an equally appropriate vehicle in music. And music is as much more suggestive, rich, and endless than literature, as the unconscious mind is more suggestive, rich, and endless than the conscious.

"My realm is in the air," Beethoven once exclaimed. These words might apply to the art of music. Free of rigid formulas, it roves the universal ether, far swifter and freer than thought. But programs cage the eagle and crash the plane.

Chapter XXVIII

THE IMMORAL, IMMORTAL BETTINA

Extraordinary Productiveness 1800–1810 — Sterility 1810–1820 — The Climacteric Theory — Woos Therese Malfatti, 1810 — Enter Bettina Brentano, May 1, 1810 — She Takes Him to Dinner — First to Express His True Greatness — Was She Reliable? — Her Letter to Goethe, May 28, 1810 — "Music Is a Higher Revelation than all Wisdom and Philosophy" — Effect of Goethe's Poetry on Beethoven's Creative Faculty — The Essence of Music — "I Had a Raptus" — Automatisms — Goethe's Reply — Controversy about Beethoven's Letters to Bettina — He Slights Bettina — Heals Her Sister-in-Law with the Music Cure

ON NEW YEAR'S DAY, 1810, Beethoven rounded off one of the most superbly fertile decades, as regards quantity, quality, and variety, which any creative artist ever enjoyed. These ten years began with the *Lobkowitz* quartets and ended with the F sharp major piano sonata. They gave the world, among many other compositions, a half dozen symphonies, fifteen piano sonatas, a septet, a quintet, ten quartets, two trios, seven duet sonatas, five concertos, six overtures, an oratorio, a ballet, an opera, and a Mass.

Suddenly, mysteriously, the luxuriance came to an end. In the following decade, between 1810 and 1820, the only fairly productive year was 1812, when the Seventh and Eighth symphonies and the G major violin sonata (Op. 96) were written.

The leanness of this period can scarcely be explained by financial troubles or friction with his fellow creatures; for the irresponsible and irascible genius was already abundantly used to these things. Nor by the period of greater affluence which began in 1814; for he had been in pocket before, without suffering in productivity. Nor by ill health or age; because his health was quite as bad and his age worse during the glorious days after 1820 which produced the three last sonatas, the *Choral* symphony, and the final quartets. Nor by the process of fermentation and clarification which ushered in his third creative period. True, all these factors decreased his fertility, but even the sum of them can scarcely account for the dismaying sterility of this decade.

In a curious recent work called *Auf der Fährte des Genius*, a German physician, Dr. Richard von Waldvogel, develops the interesting theory that men, especially men of genius, are subject to a sort of mental and spiritual climacteric for some years in their forties. He thinks that this was the trouble with Beethoven between forty and fifty. The idea sounds fantastic, but it is flanked by a considerable array of biographical evidence.

Thayer suggested another reason for the unproductiveness of the first part of this period. The depreciation of the currency which resulted from the Napoleonic Wars had made most people too poor to attend concerts and buy music. And

> Beethoven was not the man to hasten his works to completion when there was no prospect of making either in public or in private any present use of them.[1]

In the summer of 1810 his creativeness was temporarily paralyzed by a bitter disappointment. This deaf, irascible invalid of thirty-nine had recently fallen in love with Fräulein Therese Malfatti, the pretty, fifteen-year-old niece of his physician.

At once all was activity in the haberdashery department. He sent Gleichenstein incredible sums to buy him shirt cloth and cravats. He broke his mirror prinking, borrowed Zmeskall's, sent the "music-count" scuttling for another, and pictured himself as a new Hercules at the feet of a latter-day Omphale.

With emphatic urgency he wrote to his boyhood friend Dr. Wegeler for his own birth certificate, a document essential for marriage, and said that he would, if necessary, pay for a special journey from Coblenz to Bonn in order to get it.

To Gleichenstein, who was soon to marry Therese's sister, he wrote:

> I have slept little, but I prefer such an awakening to all sleep.

Of the Malfattis:

> I have such a wonderful feeling when with them all, it seems as if the wounds with which wicked men have lacerated my

---
[1]Thayer, Vol. II, p. 209.

soul [the mania of persecution again!] might be healed by them.
. . . Greet all that are dear to you and me, how gladly would I
add *and to whom we are dear????* . . . Farewell, be happy—
I am not.

When Gleichenstein, who was in the Malfattis' confidence, tried to prepare his friend by delicate and gradual diplomacy for disappointment, the Master was suddenly overcome by the horror of his position.

No, friendship and like emotions have nothing but wounds for me! Well, so be it, for thee poor Beethoven there is no happiness from without, thou must create it all within thyself, only in the ideal world findest thou friends.

And to Wegeler a few weeks later:

Oh, life is so lovely, but mine is poisoned forever.

Then, rebounding from these depths, even as the *finale* of the "*Geister*" trio rebounds from the ghostly *Largo,* he sent a written application for Therese's hand.

The good doctor, her uncle, threw his influence against such a project. And perhaps the recording angel was spared a dark entry and rejoiced over one more danger averted from Beethoven's third period just ahead. In fact, had this marriage taken place, not only might a girl's life have been wrecked, but the Master, torn between his art, his illness, his manias, and the demands of a young wife, would very likely have never reached the last sonatas and quartets. And he might even have stopped short of the three last symphonies. So a double bar was ruled with a tear-laden goose quill at the bottom of "love's sweet-scented manuscript," and Beethoven fell into the sombre mood which was shortly to find echo and be immortalized in the grimly melancholy opening strains of the *Quartett Serioso* (Op. 95).

At this psychological moment there danced into his room on fairy feet one of the most enlivening, sympathetic, and altogether tonic adventures that ever befell a composer.

It was a May day in 1810. Beethoven had just finished composing a Goethe song about Italy, that land which he was forever planning to visit but which was to remain the inaccessible Carcassonne of his dreams. He felt two small hands on his shoulders, and turning with an angry word poised was struck dumb by the impish eyes of a lovely young girl.

"My name is Brentano," she said, and needed no further credentials. For Beethoven was a close friend of her married brother Franz, whom she had come from Frankfort to visit.

Without stirring he smiled—according to her own report—took her hand, and murmured:

"Look, I have just written you a beautiful song. Want to hear it?"

In a voice vibrating with passion he sang *"Kennst du das Land."* Seeing her cheeks and her eyes burning, he exclaimed: "Beautiful, isn't it?—marvellously beautiful. I'll sing it again." After which he turned around triumphantly, pleased by her fiery approval, and told her that as a listener she was the sort of artist sorely needed by musicians.

Ex. 105

Instantly the two made friends. After considerable coaxing Bettina persuaded the Master to don his best coat and go home with her. She took him by the hand. They threaded their way past the trunks that held the pell-mell mass of his wardrobe, the sack of straw on which he slept, the wash basin on the inundated pine table, the night clothes strewn over the floor, and two or three legless pianos, prone like the ruins of Greek temples in Sicily.

At first walking with him took all her courage, for, in talking about music, he would suddenly stand still and begin to thunder, gesticulating eloquently. Here is a sample of his thundering as reported by her:

Music is the climate of my soul; there it blooms and does not run merely to weeds like the thoughts of others who call themselves composers. But few understand what a throne of passion every single movement of music is—and few know that passion itself is the throne of music.

Presently, in her astonishment at the man's greatness, she too forgot the outside world.

She wrote Prince Pückler-Muskau that on this walk he spoke to her as if she "had been for years his trusted friend." And continuing:

There was surprise when, hand in hand with Beethoven, I entered a gathering of more than forty people who sat at table. Without ado he seated himself, and said little (doubtless because he was deaf). Twice he took his writing tablet out of his pocket and made a few marks in it. After dinner the whole company went up to the tower of the house to look at the view. When they had gone down again and he and I were alone, he drew out his tablet, looked at it, wrote and elided, then said: "My song is finished." He leaned against the window frame and sang it out upon the air. Then he said: "That *sounds*, doesn't it? It belongs to you if you like it. I made it for you. You inspired it. I read it in your eyes just as it was written."

On going down, without being urged, he walked straight to the piano and played long and gloriously.

There was [wrote Bettina to Goethe] a simultaneous fermentation of his pride and of his genius. When he is in such a state of exaltation his spirit begets the incomprehensible and his fingers accomplish the impossible.

This strange young girl was the first person to discover and express on paper the true greatness of the Beethoven we know to-day. That she was the Balboa of this musical ocean is proved by the date of her long letter to Goethe.

Further extracts from it will presently follow. It was written five weeks before E. T. A. Hoffman's epoch-making essay on the Fifth symphony, which inaugurated the enlightened criticism of Beethoven's works.

To this dainty young Bettina, with the charm of a child, the intellect of a philosopher, the intuition of a prophetess, and, we must add, the dubious honesty of a coquette "on the make," it was given to enjoy a deeper intimacy with the mind of Beethoven than ever fell to the lot of his other contemporaries. And she was to transmit to us the most interesting account we have of this mind.

One must not demand too much of her. She was no shorthand reporter. She put down the Master's words more or less as she recalled them, unavoidably saturating them and colouring them with her vivid personality. Indeed, Beethoven's own self-expression, even as it formed in his brain, must have been appreciably tinged by the spell of the youth, beauty, intelligence, and clairvoyant comprehension of this Nineteenth Century combination of Hebe, Psyche, and the Delphian Sibyl.

From Vienna, on May 28, 1810, Bettina wrote to Goethe:

When I saw him of whom I shall now speak to you, I forgot the whole world, as the world still vanishes when the memory grips me,—yes it vanishes . . . It is Beethoven of whom I now wish to tell you, and in whose presence I forgot the world and you. I am not yet of age, it is true, but I am not mistaken when I say—what no one, perhaps, now understands and believes—he strides far ahead of the culture of all humanity. And shall we ever overtake him?—I doubt it. But if he only lives until the puissant and sublime enigma that lies in his soul has attained its fullest fruition,—if he only reaches his loftiest goal, then surely he will lay in our hands the key to a divine knowledge which will bring true blessedness a step nearer to us.

To you I may surely confess that I believe in a godlike magic which is the natural element of the spiritual life. This magic Beethoven practices in his art. Everything about which he can teach you is sheer magic . . . and so Beethoven feels himself the founder of a new sensuous basis of the spiritual life. . . . Who could replace this spirit of his for us? From whom could we expect the like?—The sum of human activity seethes around him like so much mechanism; he alone begets independently out of himself the unsuspected, the uncreated. What should contact with the world mean to him who is at his sacred daily task before sunup, who after sundown scarcely looks about him, who forgets sustenance for his body, and who is hurled by the current of his enthusiasm past the flat shores of the work-a-day world?

He himself said, "when I open my eyes I must sigh, for what I see runs contrary to my religion, and I must despise the world which does not divine that music is a higher revelation than all wisdom and philosophy. It is the wine which inspires to new acts of creation; and I am the Bacchus who presses out for men this glorious wine and intoxicates their souls. Then when once more they are sober, they find they have fished all sorts of things out of the sea of tone and brought them along to the shore. . . . I have no anxiety whatever about my music; it can have no evil fate. He who truly understands it must thereby go free of all the misery which others bear about with them.

[Beethoven is speaking of the inspiring power of Goethe's poems:] ". . . I am put in tune and stimulated to composition by this language which builds itself up into higher orders as if through the work of spirits, and already bears within itself the secret of its harmonies. Then, from the focus of enthusiasm I must needs discharge melody in all directions; I pursue it, passionately overtake it; I see it flying away and losing itself in the mass of varied agitations; now I seize upon it again with renewed passion; I cannot tear myself from it; with sudden ecstasy I am impelled to multiply it with all possible modulations; and in the final instant there I stand triumphant over the first musical ideas: —behold, a symphony! Yes, music is indeed the mediator between the life of the spirit and that of the senses. . . .

"Speak to Goethe about me. Tell him to hear my symphonies. And he will agree with me that music is the sole incorporeal entrance into the higher world of knowledge, which comprehends mankind, but which mankind may not comprehend. . . .

"A certain rhythm of the spirit is needed in order to grasp the essence of music which gives prophetic vision, and the inspiration of heavenly wisdoms. What the spirit feels therefrom through the senses, is the incarnation of spiritual perception.

"Although the spirit exists on music as we exist on the air we breathe, it is a very different thing to grasp music with one's spirit. But the more the soul draws its sensuous nourishment therefrom, the riper will the spirit be for a happy mutual understanding with it. . . .

"Every art, all genuine feeling is a moral progress. . . .

"What we conquer for ourselves through art is from God, divine inspiration, which gives human possibilities a goal that they can reach. . . .

"Every genuine creation of art is independent, mightier than the artist himself, and, through its manifestation, returns to the divine. With man it has only this in common: that it bears testimony to the mediation of the divine in him."[2]

Some critics have felt that all this was nothing but a tissue of inventions by the imaginative Bettina, and that Beethoven could not have said these things because they do not sound like his everyday utterances. On the other hand, certain hard-headed specialists like Thayer and Herr Bekker are satisfied that, in this letter to Goethe, she reported the Master's words in good faith and as literally

---

[2]Cf. the fuller extracts given in Thayer, Vol. II, pp. 187–189.

as she could manage to remember. With these two critics the present writer agrees.

The point is that these were very far from "everyday" utterances. By some happy chance, "the time and the place" and the unique creative listener had all come together. The spirit of enthusiastic reverence in which she wrote this report breathes from an exclamation near the close:

> If I understood him as I feel him, then I would know everything!

When, next morning, Bettina read him her letter, he himself was surprised and answered:[3] "Did I say that? Well, then, I had a raptus!" He read it through again attentively, crossed out certain things, and wrote between the lines. Now, "raptus" was one of Beethoven's own particular words. From his use of it ever since his boyhood it would seem to indicate a rare state of mind by which he was taken in charge by his unconscious mind, a condition in which creation became more or less automatic. It is well known that automatic writers or speakers are often oblivious of what they have just written or spoken and ordinarily refer to these products in much the same detached, impersonal, surprised language that Beethoven then used.

Many utterances in this letter are exactly the sort of thing one would expect from the creator of the *Eroica*, the B flat trio, and the C sharp minor quartet, if some degree of trance had loosed his tongue from thralldom to his ugly,

---

[3] According to her letter to Goethe.

pock-marked, diseased little body, and from the self-consciousness of his poorly educated objective mind. The accounts of some of his improvisations sound as though they might have been automatic playing. Automatisms notoriously often manifest themselves in more than one way through the same person.[4]

Indeed, it is perhaps no coincidence that in the same letter Bettina should have referred to Beethoven's "state of exaltation" when "his spirit begets the incomprehensible and his fingers accomplish the impossible,"—and have reported his remark that the writings of Goethe seemed done "as if through the work of spirits,"—and have described how he himself was "impelled" as though by some external force to create "the one incorporeal entrance into the higher world of knowledge,"—and "the incarnation of spiritual perception."

On the other hand, we must confront this automatic hypothesis with the evidence of the Sketch Books that most of Beethoven's written compositions were laboriously conscious and far from automatic; and with his assertion that he could accurately reproduce his improvisations.

Goethe was delighted with Bettina's letter, and the two celebrities began making plans to meet. In his reply he wrote of Beethoven's "truly great spirit."

Before that which is uttered by one possessed of such a dæmon, an ordinary layman must stand in reverence. . . . Here the gods are at work strewing seeds for future discernment. . . . To think

---

[4]This curious word "raptus," meaning "caught up" suggests the passage of Scripture (II Cor. 2, 3) where St. Paul tells of a man he knew who had been "caught up to the third heaven."

of teaching him would be an insolence even in one with greater insight than mine, since he has the guiding light of his genius which often illumines his mind like a stroke of lightning while we sit in darkness and scarcely suspect the region from which daylight will break upon us.

Bettina soon left Vienna. In the three letters she claimed to have received from him Beethoven did not throw out any more of such fireworks as her charming presence had kindled. The original of only the second of these letters has been found. And Bettina has been freely accused of everything from slightly revising the other two to fabricating them outright. A bitter controversy still rages about the problem.

Personally the writer is inclined to think that these two letters were probably written by Beethoven and were afterwards dressed up by Bettina in order to flatter the vanity of the minx who had turned the two most creative heads of the age and collected their revered "scalps." She overreached herself in the first letter, for example, by making Beethoven write on August 11, 1810:

I have saved all the little slips, containing your brilliant, dear, dearest answers.

Unfortunatly she overlooked the fact of having, the previous May, written to Goethe that she had talked with the Master without the need of writing. And from no other source do we hear of any necessity for scribbled conversation with him before 1818.

But when we strip from the doubtful letters the husk

of Bettina's vanity, the *bona fide* Beethoven emerges. Here are some lines from all three:

FROM THE FIRST LETTER, VIENNA, AUGUST 11, 1810

In society I am like a fish on the sand, that flops and flops and cannot get away, until some good-hearted Galatea pops him back into the mighty ocean.

.   .   .   .   .

Your ears know how to flatter when they listen.

.   .   .   .   .

Hope nourishes me; it nourishes half the world.

FROM THE AUTOGRAPH LETTER, VIENNA, FEBRUARY 10, 1811

When you write Goethe about me, seek out all the words that may express to him my deepest reverence and admiration. I am myself just writing him about *Egmont* which I have set to music, and indeed simply out of love for his poems, which make me happy; but who can sufficiently thank a great poet,—the most precious treasure of a nation!

FROM THE THIRD LETTER, TEPLITZ, AUGUST, 1812

Kings and princes may be able to create professors and privy counsellors, and bandy about titles and decorations, but they cannot create great men.

.   .   .   .   .

A musician is also a poet, and he can feel himself suddenly transported by a pair of eyes into a lovelier world where greater spirits amuse themselves with him and set him right suitable tasks. —The things that came into my mind as I was getting acquainted with you in the little observatory during the delicious rain of May, which was wholly fruitful for me too! That evening the most beautiful themes slipped out of your glances into my heart;

themes that will one day delight the world when Beethoven conducts no more.

· · · ·

One must be something if he would appear something.

· · · ·

Your last letter lay a whole night upon my heart and refreshed me there, musicians allow themselves everything.

God, how I love you! Your most loyal friend and deaf brother
                                                        BEETHOVEN.

Throughout this Bettina episode Dr. Jekyll has been touchingly in evidence. Now, for a moment do we catch a glimpse of Mr. Hyde? After all these protests of loyalty and affection; after experiencing the thrill of dedication-at-first-sight, when Bettina put her hands on his shoulders and he told her (if he really did), "I have just made a beautiful song for you"—did he dedicate "*Kennst Du das Land*" to her after all? He did not. He inscribed it instead to the widow of his patron, Prince Kinsky. And one can find no evidence that he ever substituted anything else for it.[5]

Unless these words of his, with their implicit pledge, were only figments of Bettina's warm imagination, such a miscarriage of justice must have convinced the little person, after meeting Beethoven, that Goethe was right in calling him "a totally uncurbed personality." Especially as the slight was afterwards underlined by his dedication of the tremendous *Diabelli Variations* to her sister-in-law Antonie Brentano, and of a trio and the E major sonata (Op. 109)

---

[5]Though the imaginative M. D'Indy states (p. 52)—one wonders why—that "the illustrious, flighty Bettina received the dedication of only an unimportant *Lied*."

to her niece Maximiliane. Truly, as the Master admitted, "musicians allow themselves everything."

Against his thoughtlessness towards Bettina, however, one may balance his delicate kindness to her sister-in-law. At this time Madame Antonie was often so ill that she had to keep to her room and refuse all visitors. But Beethoven had discovered the science of musical therapy a century or so before it received more general recognition. He used to call regularly on the invalid, go without a word to an adjoining room, open the piano and improvise—then leave the house as silently as he had come. Just as he once did for Dorothea von Ertmann, he accomplished far more for his privileged patient than all the drugs and all the doctors.

Chapter XXIX

EGMONT, THE SERIOSO AND THE "ARCHDUKE"

Egmont, *1810* — *Growing Fame* — Quartett Serioso, *1810* — *Celestial Music* — "Archduke" *Trio, 1811* — *At Teplitz, 1811* — *A Circle of Poets* — *Amalie Sebald*

ALL art is autobiography. Whatever the artist may ostensibly express he really expresses his own experiences, thoughts, emotions—in a word, himself.

Beethoven was so enamoured of Goethe's *Egmont* that in 1810 he refused any payment from the theatre for writing incidental music to it. One reason for this enthusiasm was that he felt the situation of *Egmont* was largely his own: a misunderstood but self-reliant hero gloriously struggling with a relentlessly persecuting fate and filled with tragic longing for a pure and ideal love.

Now, the man who freed music strikingly combined in one personality those unusual companions, a mania of persecution and lofty courage. The combination is exemplified in a letter to Zmeskall:

I shall not long keep on living here in this outrageous fashion, Art, the persecuted one, finds an asylum everywhere; why, Dædalus, shut within the Labyrinth, invented wings which bore him forth into the air, Oh I too will find them, these wings!

This imagined situation of Egmont-Beethoven inspired the Master to write an overture as terse, strong, and dramatically moving as his curtain raiser to Collin's *Corio-*

lanus. It was richer and subtler, as well. The two were companion masterpieces and counterparts.

No such puissant characterization of a hero had ever before been known in dramatic music as the opening theme of the *Egmont* overture, both as it appeared in the slow introductory movement

Ex. 106

and, electrified, in the *Allegro.*

All of the *Egmont* music bears the stamp of greatness, especially Clärchen's two songs, "*Die Trommel gerühret*" and "*Freudvoll und leidvoll,*" not forgetting the exquisite *Larghetto,* where the heroine's breath flickers out with the dying lamp.

Beethoven spent the summer of 1810 partly in Vienna, partly in the near-by village of Baden. But even to that obscure corner the world tracked him and beat a path to his door. He was growing too famous for comfort.

Every day [he wrote Zmeskall, July 9, 1810] there come new inquiries from strangers, new acquaintanceships . . . sometimes I feel I could soon go mad over my unearned fame, fortune seeks me out and just because of that I must fear some new misfortune.

Toward the end of the summer he wrote what he called the *"Quartett Serioso"* (in F minor, Op. 95). It is shorter than any of his quartets except the early one in B flat. By ruthlessly paring it to the quick, lopping off every non-essential, and establishing such a community of thematic material between the movements, as we have already noticed in the *Eroica* and the *Pathétique,* he lent this composition more concentration and unity than is found in any of his other chamber music.

Unlike the Rasoumowskys, it has no symphonic quality. This music is unthinkable as played by anything but two violins, a viola, and a violoncello. Particularly in the slow movement its pages show Beethoven in transition from his second to his third style. He still held to the clear formal structure of the middle period, but already we catch certain turns of phrase and modulation which point forward to the greater days. Among these are the newly characteristic passages of celestial song (like bars 91 to 102 of the first movement), the main theme of the slow movement, with the Beethovenesque shimmer of its persistent fluctuation between major and minor,

Ex. 107

the free, poetically fugato-ed style of the slow movement's
second subject,

Ex. 108

and the chorale of the third movement:

Ex. 109

Notice the marked family resemblance between examples
107 and 109. These two are the harbingers of such
"heavenly" music as the *Andante* of the B flat trio, the
Variation theme of the E major sonata (Op. 109), the
Arietta of the last sonata, the prelude of the *Benedictus*
of the *Missa*, the *Adagio* of the *Choral* symphony, the
Cavatina of the B flat quartet, and the *Dankgesang* of the
A minor quartet.

These passages became the prototypes of all the "celestial" pieces from their day to ours—from the *Lohengrin* prelude and the *Grail* music, through the *adagios* of Brahms's first trio, his second quartet and violoncello sonata, to *Death and Transfiguration* and the *Poème de l'Extase*.

The first movement is one of the sternest, grandest, most virile in chamber music. It begins with this grimly passionate subject in unison:

Ex. 110

A psychological conflict of a tragic kind is subtly indicated by the way in which the ascending naturals at the end of this theme undo the work of the descending flats in the middle. Roughly speaking, the Fifth symphony is largely built out of the germ-motive G–G–G–E flat[1]— its own first four notes. Speaking somewhat less roughly we may say that the *Serioso* is built out of the eleven notes just quoted.[2]

In three crowded weeks of glorious living, during March, 1811, the B flat trio for piano, violin, and violoncello (Op. 97) was created. Familiarly known among chamber musi-

---

[1]See pp. 219–220 and 540.

[2]Those who are interested in an analysis of this feat may find it on pp. 541–544.

cians as the *"Archduke,"* it is one of the proudest items in
the series of masterpieces, dedicated to Beethoven's imperial pupil Rudolph.

This is a broadly modelled, radiantly happy work. At
the end of the slow movement it reaches a pinnacle of mystic
rapture as exalted as any that art has attained. It is easily
Beethoven's foremost composition of its kind. While no
more beautiful than Brahms's revision of his trio in B major,
and at the end less consistently sustained, the *"Archduke"*
must yet claim the first place in trio literature. For it is
the archetypal work without which the production of its
successors would have been impossible.

There are few pages in music of a more blithe and lucid
nobility than the first movement, with its broad, all-
Beethoven opening subject.

Ex. III

The *scherzo* is one of the Master's foremost contributions to this form of his invention—the form in which the lion of wit was first successfully made to lie down with the lamb of melody (with the lamb outside but a smile none the less on the face of the lion).

It is that shaggy, primevally innocent sort of wit which no musician before Beethoven had dared attempt. Suddenly, with the Trio, its good humour is overcast. A sinister theme

Ex. 112

comes crawling and writing along like a serpent through the garden—or like an atheistical Uriah Heep insinuating himself into a Monday-noon luncheon of witty parsons, or like what you will, provided it is grovelling, slimy, and villainous enough. And then a merry heel is set firmly on that ophidian head, and the fun begins again, though it nowhere reaches the "unbuttoned"[3] recklessness of the *scherzos* in the *Eroica*, *Pastoral*, or Seventh symphonies, or the *finales* of the Seventh and Eighth symphonies.

This movement commences, like the *scherzo* of the First Rasoumowsky quartet, with the violoncello giving out, unsupported, a strongly rhythmical figure

---

[3] *"Aufgeknöpft"* was one of Beethoven's favourite words.

Ex. 113

something like that of the quartet's famous one-note solo which made Violoncellist Romberg dance in fury upon his part.[4]

To the writer's mind the *Andante cantabile ma però con moto*—a theme with variations—casts the dust more completely aside and nakedly rides the air of a more astral region than any other music whatever—unless it be the *Cavatina* of the B flat quartet (Op. 130). This is especially true in the deep organ harmonies of the theme

Ex. 114

Andante cantabile

[4]See pp. 183 and 188.

that reaches out to comfort mortals like the "everlasting arms," and in the pure unearthly ecstasy of the recitative-like coda that bows prostrate before the refulgence of the ultimate mystery,

> With stammering lips and insufficient sound.

Once when Mendelssohn was playing this coda to the aged Baroness von Ertmann she exclaimed: "This is so expressive one simply cannot play it!" And Mendelssohn ageed with her.

Here is music fit for any great exultation or exaltation. It is so vast that it may perform almost any function in the spheres of religion, of joy, or of love.

In one of the Conversation Books, dating from the month before the Master's death, there have come down to us fragments of a talk with Schindler about this trio. Schindler wrote:

> I hold the *Andante* to be the most beautiful ideal of holiness and divinity. . . . Words can be of no avail here; they are poor servants of the divine word delivered by the music.

The dying Master's spoken reply is not recorded. But one imagines he was pleased with the unwonted perception shown by his bromidic famulus. Although we soon find this significant entry in Schindler's hand:

> Do you feel sleepy? . . . Well, then, good-night.

The *Andante con moto* leads uninterruptedly, but with a painful shock, into the bright, hard, brilliant, rondo-*finale*.

Ex. 115

It is almost as though a gay band of Scotch bagpipers should burst without warning into the holiest of holies. Beethoven, indeed, often used to deal thus with his actual audiences. Having melted them to tears by some subliminal improvisation he would suddenly give way to reaction as if ashamed of himself and them and drum the flat of his hand hideously upon the keys, roaring derisively over their consternation and outrage.

The *finale*[6] of the B flat trio is a worse misfit than the frivolous rondo of the G minor, or the harsh fugue of the D major violoncello sonatas, or the *finale* of the *Eroica*. It is as cruel a thorn in the flesh of the sensitive music lover as the ill-advised choral feature of the *Choral* symphony, or as even the deplorable end of the *Pastoral*. For, though it is better music than the last named, it plays the iconoclast in a temple.

However, when one passes all Beethoven's work in review, it is remarkable how seldom he failed in that hardest problem of the composer, the *finale*. Among his successors his only peers in the ending of compositions have been Brahms, Wagner, and Franck.

Opus 97 shows a widening harmonic range characteristic

[6]See p. 138.

of the third period. It allows such remote keys as D, D flat, and G major to function with astonishing importance and intense dramatic contrast, in a work whose main key is B flat.

This trio also possesses a thematic unity,[7] so subtle yet so convincing that for three decades the writer unsuspectingly played its violoncello part before his ears were opened. Then he felt like a suddenly converted traveller on the road to a musical Damascus.

In the summer of 1811 Dr. Malfatti sent Beethoven to see if the baths of Teplitz could help his headaches and that persistent old enemy, colic. At Teplitz he found his friend Varena, the philosopher Fichte, and a congenial circle of adoring poets. Tiedge and Countess Elise von der Recke, Varnhagen von Ense and Rahel met him cordially, and he began an agreeable flirtation with a charming girl named Amalie Sebald. This young lady may have been at least as cordial as the poets, if we may judge from Beethoven's letter written the following September to Tiedge, in which he confounds the first and second person in a wholly original manner:

"Give Amalie a right fiery kiss for me when no one oversees us."

This girl followed in Bettina's footsteps as a collector of the hearts of geniuses, for she also captured the fancy of Carl Maria von Weber. To her Beethoven wrote his only

[7]See pp. 544–546.

attempt at rhymed verse. He called, found her not at home, and scribbled on a bit of paper:

> *Ludwig van Beethoven,*
> *den Sie, wenn Sie auch wollten,*
> *Doch nicht vergessen sollten.*

> (Ludwig van Beethoven
> Whom, even if you sought to
> Forget, you never ought to.)

Perhaps this effusion was the result of reading a book which was found in his library after his death: Fergar's *Small Poetic Hand-Apparatus* (or *The Art of Becoming a Poet in Two Hours*). This was, however, more probably cherished as a volume of humour.

And now there comes disturbingly into the story one of the most beautiful, touching, and mysterious love letters ever written by a genius.

Chapter XXX

BEETHOVEN'S ISOLDE

Letter to the "Immortal Beloved" — Controversies about Her Identity — Various Names Championed — Sonneck's List of Requirements — Was Beethoven in Love with Two Women at Once? — An Unsolved but Unimportant Mystery — The Rôle of Love in Beethoven's Life

On the 6th of July, in the morning.

MY ANGEL, my all, my very self.—A few words to-day, only, and in pencil (your pencil). . . . Why this profound sadness where necessity speaks? can our love exist otherwise than through sacrifice—through demanding less than all—can you help it that you are not wholly mine, and that I am not wholly yours?—Oh, God! gaze into the loveliness of nature and solace your heart with a sense of the inevitable;—love demands everything and love is wholly right, *thus it is for me with you, and for you with me*— only, you are so prone to forget that I must live for myself and for you as well;—were we wholly united you would feel the pain of it as little as I. . . . We shall, I fancy, see one another soon, besides, I cannot this morning share with you all that has passed through my mind during the last few days about my life.—Were our hearts always close to one another I would have no thoughts of this kind. My heart is full,—to tell you much;—ah—there are moments when I feel that speech is nothing after all—be of good cheer—remain my true, my only treasure, my all, as I am yours; the gods must send us the rest, that which must be for us and shall be.

Your faithful LUDWIG.

Evening, Monday, July 6

You are suffering, you my dearest creature.—Only now have I learned that letters must be posted very early in the morning.

Mondays—Thursdays—the only days when the post goes from here to K.—You are suffering.—Ah, wherever I am, you are there with me . . . I hold converse with myself and you, I arrange things so that I may live with you, what a life!!!! thus!!!! without you—pursued hither and yon by the kindness of humanity, which in my opinion—I little deserve and as little care to deserve.— The humility of men to men—it pains me—and when I consider myself in connection with the universe, what am I and what is he —whom one calls the greatest [?]—and yet—herein again the divine is immanent in the human—

I weep when I think that you probably will not have the first news from me until Saturday evening—much as you love me— my love for you is stronger—but do not ever hide your real self from me—Good night—as I am taking the baths I must go to sleep—[two long words scratched out] Oh God—so near! so far! is not our love a truly celestial abode—but also immovable as the firmament!

Good morning, on July 7—

Even from bed my thoughts press out to you, my immortal Beloved, from time to time joyfully, then again sadly, waiting to learn whether fate will lend ear to us—Life is possible for me either wholly with you or not at all—yes, yes I have resolved to wander far from you until I can fly to your arms and say that there I am truly at home, can send my soul enfolded by you into the realm of spirits.—Yes, unhappily it must be so.—You will be courageous, the more so because you know my fidelity to you, never can another possess my heart, never—never!—O God, why must one part from what one so loves; and yet my present life in V. [Vienna] is a grievous life.—your love makes me at once the happiest and the unhappiest of men—at my age I now need a certain uniformity and regularity of life—are these compatible with our relations?—

Angel, I have just learned, that the post goes every day, and so I must close that you may receive the L. at once.—Be calm, only by a calm consideration of our existence can we attain our pur- pose of living together—be calm—love me—to-day—yesterday

—what tearful yearnings for you—you—you—my life—my all
—farewell—Oh, keep on loving me—never misjudge the faithful heart

of your beloved
L.

ever yours
ever mine
ever for one another

This touching letter was, as we shall see, found by chance,
soon after the writer's death, in a secret drawer. No one
knows whether the "Immortal Beloved" ever received it.
For decades now the specialists have fought bitterly about
this lady's identity. They have quarrelled about the year in
which the letter was written and about the place which the
Master, without the slightest regard for the convenience of
students yet unborn, so thoughtlessly designated as "K."

Thayer, Krehbiel, and Herr Ernest entered the lists pro-
claiming Countess Therese Brunswick as the Immortal Beloved; Schindler, Nohl, Kalischer, and M. de Hevesy championed Countess Giulietta Guicciardi; La Mara backed
Countess Josephine Deym; Herr von Frimmel was on the
side of Magdelena Willmann; Herr San-Galli had an eye
single to Amalie Sebald. While Unger and Riemann, less
downright, contended that Therese Malfatti and Bettina
von Arnin had rights to consideration fully as valid as some
of the others.

Each camp has been able to prove triumphantly that all
the other camps are wrong. Their arguments, like the embattled cats of Kilkenny, have devoured each other down
to the tails.

In a recent monograph the late Oscar G. Sonneck,[1] with a trenchant logic worthy of a Supreme Court justice, conclusively showed that none of these champions can possibly be right; that the letter must have been written in 1812; that we do not know who the Immortal Beloved was; but that there still remains a chance of fresh documents being unearthed to solve the riddle.

Sonneck thought, and the writer agrees with his view, that in 1812 Beethoven was probably in love with two women at the same time: with Amalie Sebald and with the great unknown. In order to qualify as the Immortal Beloved Sonneck confronted any candidate with the following requirements: She must be

a woman other than Amalie Sebald with the initial A in her name, to whom all circumstantial evidence, whether of a chronological, topographical or psychological nature would apply. She would have to be a woman who probably lived, as did Beethoven, in Vienna, who was in *K.* during the same weeks that Beethoven wrote his "Immortal Beloved" letter at Teplitz on July 6–7, 1812, whom he perhaps met between July 2–4, 1812, at Prague and whom he expected to see again, probably at Teplitz.

This idea of Beethoven's being under the spell of two girls at once is encouraged by Ries's testimony about his Master's frequence and fickleness in love.[2]

He was very often in love, but generally only for a short time. When I once teased him with the conquest of a beautiful lady he confessed that she had captivated him most and longest—fully seven months.

[1] *The Riddle of the Immortal Beloved*, 1927.
[2] See p. 100.

Until new proof turns up, then, this question will have to join the origin of the Irish Giant and the identity of the Man in the Iron Mask, in the limbo of unsolved but unimportant mysteries.

The significant thing about Beethoven is his music. And the significant thing about this letter is the fact that, in spite of all its awkward struggling with the recalcitrant medium of words, his passion rises here to the same uplands from which the *Adagio* of the Fourth symphony was heard and the ineffable *Andante con moto* of the B flat trio.

In reality love played in Beethoven's life a part not much more important than the brief, luscious second subject plays in the first movement of the *Eroica*.[3] Its development gets along heroically without touching this subject and is all the better for that renunciation, just as the Master's life work was probably the better for renouncing the wife of his ardent dreams and drawing inspiration only from brief love episodes here and there.

But we cannot help a wistful regret at the unsolved mystery of the immortal Isolde who shared with him his crowning passion.

---

[3]See Ex. 36, p. 132.

Chapter XXXI

DRUNK WITH GENIUS

1811, King Stephen — The Ruins of Athens — *Beethoven
Overreaches the London Philharmonic* — *Seventh Sym-
phony, 1811–1812* — *Poetic Programs* — *Repudiated by
Composer* — *The "Unproblematic" Symphony* — *Devel-
opment of Introduction and Coda Forms* — *The Music of
the Seventh* — *Beethoven's First Musical Expression of
Boisterous Humour* — *His Rough Wit in Daily Life* — *The
Seventh's Illusion of Vastness*

THE next compositions show an even more lamentable
decline from the level of the B flat trio than the *finale* of
that masterpiece showed in comparison with what pre-
ceded it.

In 1811, commissioned by a newly built theatre in Buda-
Pesth, Beethoven dashed off incidental music to *King
Stephen* and *The Ruins of Athens*. This music is in every
sense incidental. It may be classed with the Triple concerto
and the *Polonaise* (Op. 89) dedicated to the Empress of
Russia, among the Master's least masterly productions.

Five years later the overtures to these plays were to figure
in an affair which sadly lowered Beethoven's credit across
the English Channel. The London Philharmonic Society,
fresh from the Fifth symphony, and moved by reverent
enthusiasm for its creator, commissioned him for seventy-
five guineas to write three overtures especially for them.

Pocketing the money, he fobbed off on them the *King Stephen, The Ruins of Athens,* and an overture in C major (Op. 115), not vastly better.

The Philharmonic musicians tried over these old pot-boilers with grievous disappointment, resentfully laid them aside as unworthy of Beethoven, and felt that he had not only cheated but also insulted them. Word flew around the Britishers publishers: "For God's sake, don't buy anything of Beethoven!" One of them, named Birchall, when urged by Neate to buy these overtures, replied: "I would not print them if you would give me them gratis."[1] Viewed in a reasonable perspective, however, such incidents are mere fly specks on the vast field map of the Master's career.

From the proper distance one may see at a glance the large lines of his psychological progress from the grim seriousness of the F minor quartet, with a single wan half smile on the last page—through the restrained cheer and mystical ecstasy of the B flat trio, to the exuberant blitheness of the Seventh symphony and that rich, sly, delicious compendium of purely musical wit, humour, and buffoonery, the Eighth.

After his bitter humiliation at the hands of the *Backfisch*, Therese Malfatti, he had to write one great composition in order to hold up his head; another to smile; a third to dance; and a fourth to laugh.

The Seventh symphony (Op. 92) was probably begun

---

[1]Here are the words of a French lady on the moral sense of genius. She who made Anatole France famous is speaking of him to his ex-secretary: *"Il a agi envers vous avec une cruauté et une ingratitude inouïes, Eh bien, et envers moi? Que voulez-vous? C'est un grand homme. Les grands hommes, ça n'a rien d'humain."* (Jean-Jacqu : Brousson, *Itinéraire de Paris à Buenos-Ayres,* 1927, p. 320.)

in 1811.[2] It was finished in a violent outburst of exuberant joy, May, 1812—the fateful month when war was declared on Russia by the hero whose name Beethoven had scratched from the *Eroica's* title page for the offense of turning tyrant. No such shout of jubilation had yet been heard in music.

Encouraged by Beethoven's recent condescension in pasting a program upon the Sixth symphony, certain poetic souls needed little encouragement to sharpen their goose quills for the Seventh. A young poetaster named Dr. Iken composed an essay to show that this work portrayed a political revolution. Whereupon the irate Beethoven pointed out the error of his ways. He said that such expositions, if necessary, should be confined to characterizing the composition in general terms, which could easily and correctly be done by any educated musician.

But this attitude was not destined to discourage Marx from interpreting the Seventh as a story of Moorish knighthood, nor Oulibischeff from seeing it as a masquerade, nor Bischoff and M. D'Indy from tagging it as another *Pastoral* symphony.

Even such a level-headed critic as Robert Schumann found a rustic wedding in the famous *Allegretto*. Ortigue saw there a procession in the catacombs; Dürenberg, "the love dream of a sumptuous odalisque." And in our own day Herr Emil Ludwig has described the symphony with great luxuriance of language as, I: A meadow and woodland

---

[2]Between it and the *Pastoral* there was a gap of four years, twice the interval which had thus far elapsed between any two of his symphonies.

festival; II: A priest's march with dance ceremonies about
a temple; III and IV: A bacchanale.

Such calisthenics for the roving fancy are, of course,
quite innocent if confined to the first person singular. The
trouble with most of these commentators is that they try
to clothe their whimsies with universal validity and to im-
pose them on others.

The Seventh symphony needs interpretation by poet
or draftsman no more than does the fragrance of a
cluster of wild-grape blooms. To the ear it is as obvious and
direct a blessing as a roast pheasant is to the palate, or a
longed-for hand to the touch, or to the eye a beautiful
young girl poised for a plunge into the waters of Capri.

Herr Bekker remarks that the Seventh and Eighth symphonies are "representative of a hitherto unknown musical
species—the unproblematic symphony, unproblematic because it stands above, not below, all problems." He does
not see that the Third, Fourth, and Fifth symphonies also
stand far above all problems. The mere fact that Beethoven
may have had in mind Napoleon, or a certain private love
affair, or possibly the wolf of fate at the door, when he
wrote three or four movements out of the twelve, can no
more make problem symphonies of them than the episode
of Griffolino or of Paolo and Francesca or of Ulysses can
make of Dante's *Inferno* a treatise on aviation, or a triangle
drama, or a sea yarn.

What the Master once wrote to Amalie Sebald about
music's independence of people applies equally to its independence of stereotyped programs:

The good, the beautiful needs no people. Without any help from others there it stands. ("*Es ist ohne alle andere Behilfe da.*")

The beginning and the end of the Seventh show characteristic examples of two structural features, the introduction and the coda, which Beethoven took in a simpler form from his predecessors and developed. In doing so he helped to unify the symphony and free it from binding conventions.

The opening *Poco sostenuto* is almost a movement in itself. Without it we should never have had the lordliest of all symphonic introductions—that of the C minor of Brahms, to whom as a youth Schumann said: "Remember the beginnings of Beethoven's symphonies and try to do something like them." This introduction of the Seventh is the longest in any of the nine, and it contains one of the most poignantly sweet little tunes he ever wrote.

Ex. 116

The first movement (*Vivace*) is a young thing of extraordinary resilient vitality. From beginning to end it scarcely stops skipping and bounding along in the rhythm of either ♩ ♪ or ♩. ♪♪ —except for the twenty-two measures of pedal-point in the coda, which caused the good-natured Weber to remark that their composer had qualified for the madhouse. The movement is written in a more popular style than most of its symphonic companions. It is sweeter and prettier. It comes more than halfway to meet one. For that reason, perhaps, it does not wear quite so well as many of its deeper and more reserved fellows.

The characteristic rhythm of the *Allegretto*

is fully as insistent as the skipping figure of the *Vivace*. This remarkable movement opens in dusky chords on the lower strings,[3] with one of the simplest tunes imaginable, more harmony than melody.

Ex. 117

This tune turns out to be like a beautiful mask by Benda, which conceals even fairer features. Beethoven was a master of such hidden meanings. We have seen how, as a lad of seventeen, when Mozart set him a theme for improvisation containing a "joker" in the form of a concealed counter subject, he saw through it in a flash.[4] And here his detective genius performed a brilliant *coup* and gave us beneath the mask of example 117 the loveliness of this:

Ex. 118

[3]These chords have an opulent mystery all their own, which was later to be exploited by Tschaikowsky in the beginning of the *1812* overture and by Brahms at the start of his youthful B flat sextet.

[4]See p. 18.

The *Allegretto* has a distinct elegiac quality. It is not a "Funeral March on the Death of a Hero" as he had labelled the A flat sonata movement; nor a funeral march for all humanity, as the slow movement of the *Eroica* often seems; nor a dirge for his doomed hearing, which one might imagine the *Largo e mesto* of the D major sonata to be. In the emotional colouring of this *Allegretto* there is something strangely mournful yet "afar from the sphere of our sorrow."

In the middle of this movement there is a sudden touching turn to the major, carrying a veiled, musician's allusion to the Trio of the *Eroica* Funeral March, such as Beethoven was fond of making. It begins with the three notes of the descending tonic triad.

Ex. 119

This is the exact counterpart of the ascending tonic triad with which the *Eroica* passage opens.

Ex. 120

Both are in the relative major and have similar fiddle accompaniments.

Beethoven was so subtle that he was conceivably capable of viewing the opposed motion of these two tonic chords as a concealed allusion for initiates only (concealed like the *Allegretto's* second theme under its first)—to the personal character of the later movement as opposed to the universality of the earlier.

Without stressing any concrete interpretation of the haunting sadness of the *Allegretto* let us not quite forget that Beethoven was almost at the end of his tether as a performer and was before very long to touch the keys in public for the last time.

The Master was evidently so pleased by the reminiscence of his favourite symphony given in Ex. 119, that, as Grove suggests,[5] he presently indulged in another allusion to the *Eroica.* For the first five measures of the next movement of the Seventh are simply the first two measures of example 120, rewritten.

This strong, fiery, exultant *scherzo* has a mellow Trio for horns, as have the *scherzos* of the Third, Fourth, and Eighth symphonies. This was taken from an old Austrian pilgrim's hymn and looks back to the chorale-like Trio of the F minor quartet and the hymn-like *Andante con moto* theme of the B flat trio. It looks forward, as well, to the prayer music so characteristic of the third period. The return to the *scherzo* proper is one of the most "romantic" pages in symphonic literature.

[5]*Symphonies*, p. 72.

Ex. 121

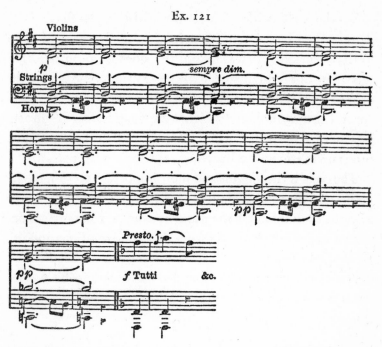

The *finale, Allegro con brio,* differs as much in kind from the light, bounding, resiliently gay *Vivace* as the angular cross-hatching of lines on the back of one's hand differs from the gracefully curving, light arabesque of markings on the palm. And yet each pair of designs seems to belong with equal inevitability to the same organism.

There is a mad, czardas-like quality of ferment in this *finale* which brings to many minds fancies of "Dionysus and his crew." It recalls the Master's recent words as reported by Bettina:

I am the Bacchus who presses out for men this glorious wine and intoxicates their souls.

To the early critic who complained that Beethoven was drunk when he wrote this movement, M. Romain Rolland neatly retorted: "It was indeed the work of an intoxicated man, but one intoxicated with poetry and genius." In the grip of this frantic *kermesse* one is reminded of the sketches for a Tenth symphony which were found after his death. The never completed work was intended to be a piece of program music where Bacchus was to appear in person.

The coda is the longest and most important section of the *finale*, and the mighty double organ-point on E and D sharp is one of the noblest terminations he ever gave a composition.

In the three fast movements of the Seventh symphony that rough boisterousness so characteristic of Beethoven's private life first came to extended expression in his works. Such pranks as the outrageous D's in the third bar of the *finale*

Ex. 122

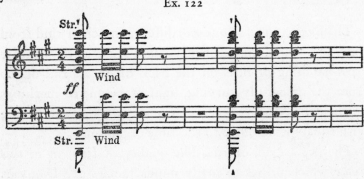

show the hand which indited the *burschikos* skits to Zmeskall. Behind them one discovers the man who, as we shall presently see, brutally insulted the imperial court in order to play a practical joke on the courtier Goethe; the man who would spit out of a front window, use the candle snuffers as toothpicks, hurl eggs that were not to his taste at the housekeeper, the waiter, or his fellow diners in the Prater,[6] and shake off the water from his soaked hat upon the hosts with whom he had come to dine. Here we find, transcribed upon lines and spaces, that famous reply to the pompous brother who left a card on him:

| JOHANN van BEETHOVEN |
| Landed Proprietor |

The Master neatly parried with another card:

| LUDWIG van BEETHOVEN |
| Brain Proprietor |

We shall see more of this sort of thing in the Eighth symphony.

The romantic Seventh somehow gives the illusion of vaster size than any of the nine, except the *Choral*, while in reality it is shorter than the *Eroica*. By some feat of legerdemain it produces the impression of instrumental sumptuousness, in spite of the Master's amazing economy in going back to the poverty-stricken small orchestra of the first two symphonies.

Although Beethoven rarely expressed any appraisal of his own compositions he twice wrote of this as one of his best works. But that was when the third period had as yet scarcely begun.

---

[6]See Frimmel, *Beethoven Handbuch*, Vol. I, p. 237.

Chapter XXXII

"WHEN TWO STRONG MEN——"

Returns to Teplitz, 1812 — Meets Goethe — Insults Imperial Court — Friction with Goethe — Scolds Him for Not Applauding — Goethe Resents Beethoven's Power — Charming Letter to Little Emily — Largeness of Outlook — Priggishness in Letters — Inconsistency of His Acts

BECAUSE Beethoven had enjoyed his stay in Teplitz he returned there in the summer of 1812. An added attraction was the presence of Goethe and Bettina. To his wife Goethe wrote a first impression of the man.

A more self-contained, energetic, sincere artist I've never seen. I can understand right well how singular his attitude towards the world must be.

But soon he was to speak in a different strain.

One day when the two great men were walking arm in arm they saw the Empress coming and all the court.

"Keep as you are," muttered Beethoven. "They must give way to us, not we to them."

Deeply shocked, the courtier Goethe broke loose and reverentially stood aside, hat in hand. Beethoven, always punctilious in receiving rather than in according respect, rammed his own hat lower upon his head, put his hands down, and went his surly way. But the imperial party courteously divided for him like the waters of the Red Sea for that insurgent Moses.

[314]

Then he paused, and when Goethe rejoined him said: "Well, I've waited for you because I honour and respect you as you deserve. But you did those yonder too much honour." Then he hauled the old poet over the coals; or, as he phrased it,—"thoroughly washed his head."

Though Bettina may have dressed this story up, in Beethoven's alleged third letter to her, Thayer seems to have been justified in accepting the incident itself as authentic. The worldly impression which Goethe, the courtier, made upon Beethoven, is recorded in the composer's words:

One cannot laugh much at the ridiculous things *virtuosi* do, when poets, who ought to be looked upon as the principal teachers of the nation, forget everything else amid this glitter.

Other incidents served to chill the relations between the geniuses. A persistent legend relates that when Goethe complained of everybody bowing to him Beethoven remarked with his usual tact: "Never mind, perhaps after all it's me they're saluting."

Beethoven played for Goethe, who seemed greatly moved and was silent. The former took this tribute in bad part. He scolded the poet for not clapping his hands.

Such a raw and superficial attitude seems hard to reconcile with an artist of Beethoven's calibre. But it must be remembered that childish impressions are strong. He had been brought up among rough, crude, lower-class professional musicians. Ever since he could talk it had been instilled into him that the only honourable applause consisted of a loud hideous noise made by striking the palms of the hands together. Then, too, he was so fundamentally shy that, except with his few very intimate friends, he shrank from nonmusical manifestations of strong and sacred emotion.

Lastly, he must in this case have felt, by means of those infallible psychic antennæ stretching out from performer to hearer, that the famous poet's strong emotion was not all based on enthusiastic comprehension and intelligent sympathy. But half of it was a conservative revulsion from anything so new and revolutionary as this music. And a good part of the remainder was jealous resentment at finding such dæmonic power in any other artist than himself.[1]

So the promising acquaintanceship was ended. A sadder and wiser Goethe broke off all further relations and wrote about Beethoven's "utterly untamed personality." The other noted:

> Goethe is too fond of the atmosphere of courts, more so than is becoming to a poet.

From Teplitz Beethoven wrote to an unknown admirer, little Emily, aged ten, who had embroidered him a stationery case and sent it with an enthusiastic epistle, placing him above all the old masters. His answer gives us pleasure by its unusual modesty and great-heartedness, which are in

---

[1]The indirect tribute of this sort of jealousy was also paid him by Tolstoi. "We have seen with what animosity Tolstoi expresses himself in *What Is Art?* on the subject of the 'pathological works of the deaf Beethoven.' . . . *The Kreutzer Sonata* allows us a glimpse into the depths of this passionate intensity. With what does Tolstoi reproach Beethoven? His power. He is like Goethe, listening to the Symphony in C minor, and, knocked off his feet by it, reacting with anger against the imperious master who has conquered him by the force of his own will." (Romain Rolland, *Vie de Tolstoi.*)

striking contrast to the swank of his rudeness towards Goethe and the princes.

. . . Do not snatch from Handel, Haydn and Mozart their laurel wreaths; these belong to them, not yet to me. . . . Art and learning alone raise men to the divine level. If you ever want anything, my dear Emily, write confidently to me. The true artist has no pride, unfortunately he sees that his art has no limits, he feels obscurely how far he is from the goal, and while he is perhaps being admired by others, he mourns that he has not yet reached the point where his better genius like a distant sun, beckons him on.

These words recall his exclamation at the end of his career:

It seems to me as though I had just begun to write!

In this letter we find the same largeness of outlook which caused Napoleon, who in his twenties had already made a brilliant start at subjugating Europe, to define that continent as a molehill, while he dreamed of outdoing the young man who had sighed for more worlds to conquer.

But the letter to little Emily is not an unmixed treat for lovers of the Master. It offers a painful glimpse of a less agreeable aspect.

I know no other superiorities of man, than those which enroll him among the better men; where I find these, there is my home.

Scattered through his letters are many such evidences of naïve priggishness.

To the Bigots:

Never, never will you find me lacking in nobility, from childhood on I learned to love virtue.

(This was written in 1808 shortly before he cheated Count Oppersdorf in the matter of an ordered symphony.)

Following a period of extravagance, he wrote Varena (1813) about taking pay for a charity concert:

If I were in my usual position I would say straight out: "Beethoven never accepts anything when the good of mankind is in question,"—but now, through my great benevolence I have been placed in a position . . .

In 1817, when, despite Mr. Hyde, he had a large number of self-sacrificing friends, and was savagely persecuting Karl's mother, he noted in a Sketch Book:

God, help! Thou seest me abandoned by all humanity, for I will not perpetrate unrighteousness.

On July 7th of this year he wrote Frau Nanette Streicher, a woman whom he was overloading with all sorts of onerous tasks:

It goes very much against my grain to be burdensome to anybody, as I am accustomed to do things for others rather than to let them do things for me.

In the same year he wrote about his "love of honour," to Ries who represented the London Philharmonic Society, which he had cheated a few months before in the matter of the three ordered overtures—and was to cheat again. In 1824, writing to Schindler (about the time he was promising to four or more different publishers the *Missa*, which he finally gave to still another), he referred to "the spotlessness of my character." (See pp. 391–392.)

September 9, 1823, he wrote vaingloriously to the poet Nägeli:

I am free of all petty vanity. . . . From childhood up my greatest joy and pleasure has been to be able to help others.

This was shortly after the disgraceful scene at supper which followed the first performance of the Ninth symphony, when his insults drove his unselfish guests and benefactors, Schuppanzigh and Schindler, from the untouched table.

The same year he wrote poor Tobias Haslinger, on whom he was to publish a cruel and disgraceful satire:

I have never revenged myself, even upon my fiercest foes.

To the publisher Schott (December 12, 1824) he simply and flatly declared in six words his perfection of character:

I have never done anything bad.

Mr. Lawrence Gilman feels that this priggishness is reflected in some of Beethoven's earlier slow movements. But here it is hard to follow this brilliant critic. His discovery seems as fantastic as if he were to find snobbishness leering from the fugues, or a hopeless passion for following the hounds feeding like a canker on the Trios of the *scherzos*. The writer can discover in Beethoven's music no more signs of his priggishness than of his hatred of light women or his mania of persecution.

Chapter XXXIII

THE HUMOROUS SYMPHONY

Meddles in Brother's Love Affair — Eighth Symphony, 1812 — "Sinfonia Giocosa" — Plays Fast and Loose with the Pedants — A Genial Conjuror — Allegretto Inspires Rossini? — It Originates in Canon to Maelzel — Minuet — Finale — Variety in Inter-Movement Unity

THE year of Napoleon's retreat from Moscow found Beethoven so full of symphony that composing the Seventh did not suffice to relieve him and, four months later, he finished the Eighth (in F major, Op. 93). It was signed *"Lintz, im Monath Oktober, 1812."* Though the Master misspelled Linz in this inscription he put the place "on the map" forever. He had inexcusably gone there in order to meddle in his brother Johann's most intimate concerns and drive from town Fräulein Therese Obermeyer, the mistress of that successful druggist. He succeeded only in coming to blows with Johann and involuntarily forcing him into an unhappy marriage with the girl. But these sordid alarums and excursions appear, surprisingly enough, to have had no effect on the gay wit of the Eighth symphony, except to take form in a grim outburst of musical wrath after the exposition in the first movement.

This work is the *Comédie Humaine* of music. Since starting the F minor quartet the composer had evidently progressed a long way toward happiness. That quartet and the Eighth symphony are as complementary to one another as Milton's *Il Penseroso* and *L'Allegro*. The F minor was fittingly named by its creator: *Quartett Serioso*. The symphony might as fittingly have been named "*Sinfonia Giocosa*."[1]

In this delectable composition the Master had his subtle and purely musical fun with the whole tribe of dry-as-dust academic critics. These gentlemen had, like Weber, always complained that his first movements were: "incomprehensible, diffuse, over-complicated." They had, like Spohr, found the slow ones "too long-drawn-out." They had condemned him for replacing the dear old minuet by the mad, capricious *scherzo*.

This new symphony seems at first blush like a contrite admission of past guilt and a return to the strictly regular fold of Albrechtsberger and the other academic rule makers and curators of plaster casts. With the old-fashioned start

Ex. 123

the mossbacks feel that the prodigal has come back from the husks and the *Schweinerei*. They are comfortably prepared

[1] If Beethoven's works are to be baptized, surely it would be preferable to proceed on strictly musical grounds, and choose names inherently suitable, rather than to go on inventing such arbitrary labels as "*Emperor*," "*Moonlight*," "*Spring*," or "*Appassionata*." For these merely record some one listener's reaction under certain accidental circumstances which may have had more to do with the name than Beethoven's music had.

to appreciate the conventional modulation from F to C for the second subject. Then suddenly the impish Master makes them sit up with a cruel jerk

Ex. 124

by threatening for nine bars to lapse into sinful E flat. Abruptly he slumps into the outrageous key of D, only to end up after all in orthodox C major.

The movement is double-faced—the apparently good boy in church, making ribald grimaces at the girls behind his hymn book, wherein he has concealed *Roughhouse Rosie or The Seven Buckets of Blood*. More subtly—though perhaps without malice or even conscious intention—Beethoven does here what Richard Strauss was to attempt later with less art, and more venom, in the "critic" section of *Ein Heldenleben*.

During the recapitulation he continues to shake powder out of the pedants' wigs[2] by springing a surprise even more

<hr />

[2]His zest in this occupation was similar to that of a late President of the United States. "Every day or two," remarked the Detroit *News* of Theodore Roosevelt, soon after he became head of the nation, "he rattles the dry bones of precedent and causes sedate Senators and heads of departments to look over their spectacles in consternation." (Mark Sullivan, *Our Times*, 1927, Vol. II, p. 394.)

shattering to the classicist's mind than the E minor episode
had been in the development of the *Eroica*.

At the start of the movement we have seen how, turning
back his sleeves like a genial conjuror to show that he has
nothing up them, Beethoven pulls amazing things out of the
borrowed high hat (exposition). He juggles with these in
a breath-taking manner (development). He puts them
back, then begins to pull them all out again (recapitulation). But when he comes to the traditional white rabbit he
stops, still holding it by the ears, blinks at it with a look
of feigned surprise, murmurs, "Pardon me, ladies and
gentlemen, but here we have an item I had overlooked"—
and produces out of its mouth something quite novel in
the way of a tune. It is a dainty melody,

Ex. 125

hidden until now in that prolongation of the first subject
which here growls along in the bass. The thing is the musical

equivalent of a chariot of spun sugar drawn by genuine white mice.

And in the coda of the *finale*, with unabated impudence he again flaunts the academicians by bringing to light a tune of a wholly unauthorized novelty,

Ex. 126

lashed along by the triplets of the first subject.

Oulibischeff had much the same sort of mind as the pedantic crew who were scandalized and ridiculed by this symphony. Whenever one finds a statement of his about Beethoven's music one usually feels that the safest course is to multiply it by minus one and abide by the result. Nor does this rule fail to work when he contends that the tiny *Allegretto scherzando* of the Eighth symphony

Ex. 127

was a deliberate parody of Rossini, that god of the groundlings of 1812. For, on the contrary, it is possible that Rossini, four years later, was himself inspired by the daintiness of this movement, its roguish tripping rhythm, and its general melodic outlines in the famous *"Zitti, Zitti"* of *The Barber of Seville.*

Ex. 128

And this, although the first six measures of Rossini's tune imitated at the same time that popular melody "Simon's Air" in Haydn's *Seasons:*

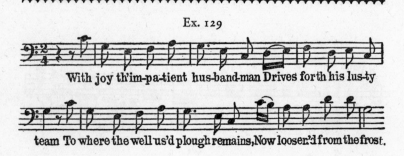

Ex. 129

With joy th'im-pa-tient hus-band-man Drives forth his lus-ty

team To where the well us'd plough remains, Now loosen'd from the frost.

The first theme of the *Allegretto scherzando* was originally improvised and sung at a convivial round table, as a
canon to Johann Nepomuk Maelzel,

Ex. 130

Vierstimmiger Canon.

ta ta ta ta ta ta ta ta ta ta ta ta ta ta ta ta lie-ber, lie-ber Mäl-zel.

ta ta ta ta ta ta ta ta la,— le-ben Sie wohl; sehr wohl.

and the ticking accompaniment referred to the Chronometer, the ancestor of the metronome, invented by that ingenious gentleman.

This exquisite elf of a piece was destined to be the
progenitor of the entire race of music devoted to elves, fays,
nixies, trolls, and fairies, from Weber and Mendelssohn to
Ravel's *Mother Goose*.

And now the dry-as-dusts—who have been sorely shaken
up by the first movement and do not know whether the
saucy little second one was intended for a *scherzo* or what

—settle themselves for a regulation *adagio*. Again they are surprised by getting instead a real old-time minuet,

Ex. 131

one of the very few Beethoven ever wrote. This appears to out-Dittersdorf Dittersdorf in old-fashionedness, yet all the while chuckles in its sleeve with the pleasure of conscious parody.

The *finale* is one of the notable movements of the nine symphonies. It opens with a careless scrap of tune, like an absent-minded bird's song.[3]

Ex. 132

—

[3]When we come to examine it, however, the bird's song appears to be a development of the *finale* of Haydn's Thirteenth symphony in G major.

This scrap meets with as superb a treatment as almost any of the Master's supreme ideas ever met with in the Sketch Books, between the banality of their first notation and the glory of their ultimate form.

For those readers who care to glance inside the studio of a genius, some cleverly unobtrusive inter-movement liaison work, which has apparently escaped the attention of Beethoven research, is discussed in Part II, pp. 546–553. Here, even more closely, literally and simply than in the case of the *Eroica*, the opening subject binds the whole symphony together.

BEETHOVEN

THE MAN WHO FREED MUSIC

Chapter XXXIV

WHEN BEETHOVEN LAUGHED

Humour in Beethoven's Music — Becomes a Creative Force — Musical Slaps on the Back — False-Start Passages — Practical Jokes on Players — Baulked Expectations — Musical Puns — Elfin Fun — Infectious Verbal Felicity — Violoncello Humour — Pun Habit — "Ears on His Feet" — Fantastic Threats — Pun in C Sharp Minor — Horseplay with the Abbé Stadler — Laughs at Himself — Irony

THE passage in the great coda of the Eighth symphony's *finale* (at bar 372), where the huge D flat ruthlessly breaks up the blameless fun, through the Gargantuan shoutings and roarings of the ensuing tumult in F sharp where the boisterous horns and trumpets strike in with F natural and herd the mob unceremoniously into the key of F, is like the unbridled wit of some Bernard Shaw born out of due time and setting a classical world agog.

This passage is characteristic of much of the laughter scattered through the Eighth and the *finale* of the Seventh symphony. To the musical humour of the past it stands in somewhat the relation of a freakish cyclone to a refined simper.

Humour had heretofore been occasionally and sparingly used in music as a kind of sauce consciously and skilfully applied to a veal cutlet. Now, for the first time on a large scale, this son of the laughing Rhineland made it one of the elemental inexhaustible forces of unconscious artistic creation. It held in solution all human emotion and lay deep as tears or wisdom.

In his able biography[1] Mr. Harvey Grace contends that "the chief ingredient" of Beethoven's humour consists of dynamic surprise—a sort of musical "slap on the back. . . . It seems a slender foundation on which to build a reputation as a humourist."

But to the mind of the present writer the obvious *Surprise* symphony kind of horseplay which he inherited from Papa Haydn seems a distinctly secondary feature of his repertory of laughs. Beethoven's choicest fun lies rather more in the roguery of *After-you!* false-start passages such as close the introduction of the First symphony's *finale;* such as grimace at bars 89 and 251 of the last movement of the E minor quartet[2] (Op. 59, No. 2), and delight us at the *listesso tempo* of the little *scherzo* in the B flat quartet (Op. 130).

It is found in such practical jokes as he played on his favourite butt, Zmeskall's instrument the violoncello. Think of the start of the *scherzo* in the First Rasoumowsky quartet (Op. 59, No. 1),[3] or of bar 147 in the first movement of the E minor quartet where, after a unison passage with the first violin, he makes the big fiddle seem to come half a measure tardy with his descending run. As we have

[1]*Beethoven,* 1927, p. 273 ff.
[2]See pp. 186–187.
[3]See Ex. 61, p. 183.

[330]

already mentioned, it is seen during the Trio of the Fifth symphony's *scherzo,* in the ludicrous apoplectic red dyeing the cheeks of the contra-bassists as they toil frantically at the musical washboard. It is seen in the kettledrum joke at bar 208 of the *Choral* symphony's *scherzo.*[4] It is found in the kindly caricature of peasant musicians in the *scherzo* of the *Pastoral;*[5] in the grotesquely contorted rhythms of the *scherzos* of the sixth quartet (Op. 18, No. 6)[6] and the G major sonata (Op. 14, No. 2).

We hear it in the development section of the Eighth symphony's opening movement, where the first subject is shooed away whenever it shows its face. And in the exasperating fashion in which a hasty Italian cadence hustles the little *Allegretto* out of doors just as the hearer is preparing to enjoy the longed-for repeat.

It is found, as Mr. Grace himself neatly brings out,[7] in the purely musical punning of enharmonic change. This is the sudden revelation of much in common between two apparently incongruous things, whereby a chord is taken in one relation and left in another. An excellent example of such a manœuvre occurs in the *finale* of this same Eighth symphony. The portentous, brazenly interrupting big C sharp[8] is taken as the leading tone of D minor. But as the movement is at once resumed in its normal key of F major, the C sharp changes in the listener's ear to D flat, the dominant

[4]See pp. 408–409.
[5]See pp. 266–268.
[6]See pp. 69–70.
[7]See p. 278.
[8]In the seventeenth measure. See last two bars of Ex. 132, p. 327.

minor ninth of F. These C sharp and D flat witticisms are more jokes of incongruous and punning tonalities than of startling dynamics. They represent the sort of humour that came, like Walt Whitman,

. . . to spread a new gladness and a new roughness among men.

Later on, at bar 372, in the passage mentioned at the beginning of this chapter, the same sort of interruption is put down as D flat, the tonic of that key—carried on as C sharp, the tonic of C sharp minor, and, by a surprising and amusing juggling feat, left as the dominant of F sharp minor.

Some highly characteristic humour is found in the tender, infectious tonal skylarking that fills the *scherzos* of the F major violin sonata (Op. 24) and of the First Rasoumowsky quartet (Op. 59, No. 1). It is found in the elfin fun that sparkles all through the first part of the *scherzo* of the B flat quartet (Op. 130). Here is something that cannot be translated into words. It is heavens removed from the obvious slap-on-the-back drum crash of the *Surprise* symphony.

This new force of humour which Beethoven set free for the enrichment of his art was very much the sort to which he had always given play in word and deed and letter. The truth is that, notwithstanding his distaste for writing words, —he once declared to Simrock that he had "rather write 10,000 notes than one letter of the alphabet,"—he was capable of a more infectious kind of verbal felicity than is generally realized. A passage in his letter to Amenda, 1801, has often been cited as an instance of his absent-mindedness. But to the writer it seems a deliberate verbal parallel to the C sharp joke in the Eighth:

Of the two persons who possessed my entire love, and of whom one still lives, you are the third.

The epistles to his factotum Zmeskall, "The Music Count," are full of solemn Eighth symphony fooling—and often in connection with his henchman's instrument, the violoncello.

Presently I will forward to you my treatise on the four violoncello strings, very fundamentally written, first chapter on gut in general—second chapter on strings composed of gut—etc.

This gibe at the glacial agility of Teutonic scholarship might have been written by Mark Twain or Mr. Stephen Leacock.

The Master depended on Zmeskall to cut his goose-quill pens, and was never weary of varying the following formula.

Damned (former) music Countlet, where is the devil concealing you? . . . We entreat you to endow us with a few feathers, we will shortly send you a whole packet so that you need not pluck out your own.—It may well be that you will yet receive the great decoration of the order of the violoncello.

This half promise was apparently fulfilled. For these words to the same friend are dated two years later. "Most well-born one, eke Violoncellistic Greatcross" (*Violoncellität Grosskreuz*).

Even in other hands than Zmeskall's the "bull-fiddle" remained Beethoven's butt. When Countess Erdödy had an ensemble house party at her country place Beethoven wrote:

The violoncello is ordered to betake himself to the left bank of the Danube and to keep on playing until everybody has crossed over from the right bank of the Danube. In this wise would your population soon increase.

One wonders whether this could have been a subtle allusion to that excess of brawn notoriously prevalent among amateur violoncellists.

Consider this note to Brauchle:

For the violoncellist let a *Guglhupfen* be baked in the form of a violoncello, that upon it he may practise, if not his fingers, at least his belly and his muzzle.

A *Guglhupfen,* be it remarked, is a Viennese raisin cake.

Beethoven's puns were most appreciated by himself. His supreme efforts in this minor department of fun were references to the *"Musikfreunde"* (Friends of Music) as *"Musikfeinde"* (Foes of Music) ; and to the *"Gelehrten"* (learnèd) as the *"Geleerten"* (emptied). But his verbal aptness was sometimes conspicuous; as when he called pay "metallic recognition."

Often he struck out compact characterizations, like this for inattention: "For me everywhere one has ears on his feet." Or this for a haughty valet: "To-day arrives the Duke who will be my servant." Or this for Zmeskall, who was striving to forestall Maelzel's Chronometer by inventing an armless metronome: "Extraordinary first oscillator of the world, and that without lever!!!!" About this contrivance he let the fancy roam in an Einsteinian manner and wondered whether the machine could not be turned to vaster uses in measuring from time to eternity.

He signed a letter to Schindler:

From low C sharp to high F,

BEETHOVEN

Composers normally feel that their publishers are not all they should be. Beethoven's persecution mania and his vivid imagination resulted in some crisp lines to his own. He warned Steiner to let him know when to expect proofs— "otherwise he will have only himself to blame for all the misery which, seething like melted sealing-wax, will trickle down upon the evildoer."

To his publisher Haslinger he wrote that if a musical paper did not retract certain lies,

I will cause the editor, with his consumptive managing editor, to be harpooned in northern waters along with the whales.

To the same:

By virtue of my exclusive prerogatives, I decree that the gentleman who bears this is to tweak, shake etc. you, first by the right ear *cresc.* . . . then by the left ear *ff mo.* . . . From the post of janitor which I had for some time considered for you, you are now again promoted to be a manufacturer of *appoggiaturas.*

To the head of Breitkopf and Härtel:

It seems to me there is a whisper that you are looking out for a new wife. . . . I wish you a Xantippe such as fell to the lot of the holy Greek Socrates, so that I might see a German *Verleger,* which is saying a lot, *verlegen, ja, recht in Verlegenheit.*

This pun was one of Beethoven's stock favourites. *Verleger* means publisher, *verlegen*, to publish—also, embarrassed.

Beethoven sent his C sharp minor quartet (Op. 131) to the publisher Schott's Sons with an enigmatical phrase which has somewhat troubled the learned: "Do not be horror-stricken at the four crosses" (*vier Kreuze*). The learned realized, of course, that the *vier Kreuze* meant the four sharps of the key signature. But why should Beethoven placate Schott on account of four sharps? The difficulties presented by the key were as nothing compared with the difficulties of the music itself. We do not find the Master apologizing for the equally awkward four flats of the F minor quartet, nor for the pages in three consecutive movements of the great B flat quartet written in five or six flats. The commentators did not see that the word *Kreuze* which means crosses as well as sharps, may have been one of Beethoven's elaborate puns. In the traditional way of an artist with a publisher he may have been making a heavy-footed allusion to the three crosses of Christ and of the two thieves, and a spare cross ready for the thievish publisher.

This possibility of a bad joke is strengthened by Beethoven's letter to the quartet player Holz (a name which signifies "wood"), in which he threatened him with transformation into a block of real wood and being nailed upon another wood (*"Auf ein anderes Holz Genagelt"*). Sometimes he addressed this youth as "Best *lignum crucis*" or "Best splinter from the Cross of Christ." In a letter to

Nanette Streicher there occurs a similar reference, about
a kitchenmaid who

> pulled a rather crooked face as she carried wood; but I trust she
> will recall that our Saviour carried his cross on Golgotha.

And the Master's low opinion of the genus publisher may
be inferred from his contemporary letter to Holz:

> It is immaterial which hell-hound licks and gnaws my brains
> . . . he will soon be plucked by the ears by Beelzebub, the chief
> of devils.

Ex. 133

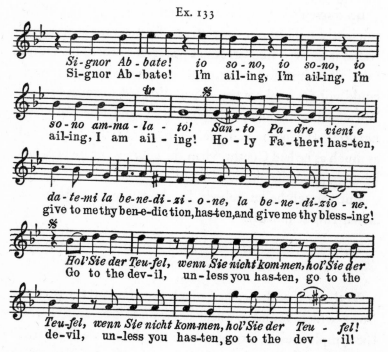

Si - gnor Ab - bate! io so - no, io so-no, io
so - no am-ma - la - to! San - to Pa - dre vieni e
da - te-mi la be-ne-di - zi - o -ne, la be - ne - di-zio - ne.

Si-gnor Ab - bate! I'm ail-ing, I'm ail-ing, I'm
ail-ing, I am ail - ing! Ho - ly Fa - ther! has-ten,
give to me thy ben-e-dic tion, has-ten, and give me thy bless-ing!

Hol'Sie der Teu-fel, wenn Sie nicht kom-men, hol'Sie der
Teu-fel, wenn Sie nicht kom-men, hol'Sie der Teu - fel!

Go to the dev-il, un-less you has-ten, go to the
de-vil, un-less you has-ten, go to the dev - il!

The Master's love of somewhat blasphemous horseplay
is illustrated in this anecdote from the memoirs of Castelli.

In a piano store Beethoven once ran across his good friend
the old Abbé Stadler. He knelt down and said: "Reverend
Sir, your blessing!" Quite unembarrassed, Stadler made
the sign of the cross over the suppliant and in Austrian
dialect mumbled the semblance of a prayer: "*Hilft's nix,
schadt's nix*" (If 'twon't help, 'twon't hurt). Then Beethoven kissed his hand and everybody roared with laughter. The canon (Ex. 133) was dashed off, if not for this, at
least for a similar occasion.

Beethoven's strong love of practical joking was like an
efficiently policed one-way street. By tolerating no return
traffic it insured unobstructed progress towards his victim.
Like Wilhelm II, he *verstand keinen Spass*. That is: he
could not see a joke when it was directed towards himself.
Witness the incident of poor Ries and the "*Andante
Favori.*"[8] If Goethe had ever embarrassed the Master half
as much as he had Goethe when the court went by he would
have snapped the old poet's head off.

But though he let nobody laugh at him he poked occasional fun at himself.

Yesterday [he wrote Zmeskall] I took a letter to the post-
office, and they asked me where it was supposed to go.

Verbally the Master had much the same pretty turn for
irony which found musical expression here and there in
the symphonies. A stranger once sent him a weak arrangement for quintet, of the C minor trio (Op. 1, No. 3). In

---

[8] See p. 150.

self-defense Beethoven arranged it himself and affixed the following inscription:

Trio transcribed into a four-voiced quintet by Mr. Goodwill, and out of the illusion of five voices brought to the light of day with five real voices, as well as raised from the utmost miserability to a certain prestige by Mr. Benevolence. . . . N. B. The original three-voiced quintet score has been rendered as a solemn burnt-offering to the gods of the underworld.

Chapter XXXV

THE BEETHOVENATE SYMPHONY

"Cockcrow" Sonata, Finished 1812 — Shows Considera-
tion for Rode — 1813, a Bad Year — Poverty — Maelzel's
Panharmonicon — Battle Pieces in Fashion — The "Battle"
Symphony — First Performance, December 8, 1813 —
Celebrities in the Orchestra — Popular Success — Defrauds
Maelzel — Repents of His Folly — His Forward-looking
Mind — Interest in Invention: Fountain Pens, Aviation,
Steam Cannons, Steamboats, Lifts — The Glorious Mo-
ment — Polonaise, Op. 89 — E Minor Piano Sonata, Op. 90
— Its Program — Last Revision of Fidelio, *1814 — The*
Germ-Motive — The Source-Motive — Marginalia — "The
Mad Musician" — "Man, Help Thyself!"

LATE in 1812 the G major violin sonata (Op. 96) was finished. This work has been nicknamed *"The Cockcrow."*
It was written for the famous visiting violinist Rode, then
in the decline of his powers. The *Adagio* is one of the most
comely and satisfying among the slow movements. But the
three fast ones show a compromise Beethoven, trying to
adapt a second-period technic to third-period thoughts, and
—with unheard-of consideration—to Rode's somewhat
shaky execution.

In composing it [he wrote the Archduke, to whom it was
dedicated] I had to consider the playing of Rode; in our *finales*
we are fond of tempestuous passages, but these do not suit Rode
and this—embarrassed me somewhat.

A surprising remark. Were advancing years making Beethoven less uncompromising? Was this the same man who had snapped Schuppanzigh up about his "puling little fiddle" when "Milord" had expostulated over certain difficulties in a quartet?[1]

Eighteen thirteen was a bad year for the composer. Little of value was added to his list. Material troubles preoccupied him. He sued Prince Lobkowitz and the widow of Prince Kinsky for arrears of his pension. And, influenced in part by his obsession against light women, he brought brother Karl's wife into court for the return of a loan of 1,500 gulden.

True, he needed the money. Nanette Streicher reported that he had no good coat and not a single whole shirt. To Spohr, who had missed him at the tavern for days, he confessed that he had suffered "house-arrest" on account of the failure of his only pair of shoes.

Poverty made him amenable to a far worse compromise than the G major violin sonata. At this psychological moment the devil, in the person of Maelzel the inventor, came and whispered, or rather shouted, into his ear. He promised to show him the kingdoms of the earth (i. e. France and England) and to fill his pockets with red gold if the Master would only write a certain piece of program music for an ingenious instrument of Maelzel's own invention.

The occasion was the Duke of Wellington's recent victory over the Napoleonic forces at Vittoria in Spain. The instrument was called the "Panharmonicon." This ancestor

---

[1] See p. 180.

of the automatic organ and piano was a sort of glorified music-box. According to Thayer it

combined the common instruments then employed in military bands, with a powerful bellows—the whole being enclosed in a case. The motive power was automatic and the keys were touched by pins affixed in a revolving cylinder.

We must bear in mind that in those days a proposal to write such compositions sounded more respectable than it would to-day. Battle pieces had long been popular. Koczwara's *Battle of Prague* was just then all the rage in Europe and America. Many suppose that the famous "grand battle piece for two flutes" was a mythical *reductio ad absurdum* of this idea. Not at all! It was actually published, as an arrangement of Fuch's *Battle of Jena*. And who can doubt its effectiveness in routing any possible enemy? Beethoven probably knew that Mozart had written an Eighteenth Century anticipation of the *Victory Ball* for Count Deym; and that Cherubini had concocted a tonal fight for Maelzel himself. With this branch of composition thus legitimized Beethoven gave ear to the tempter.

Money was needed for the proposed trip to London, where he was sure he could make tons of it. For the first time in his life he decided deliberately to prostitute his art. The result was a piece of startling crudity. Before *Wellington's Victory* was quite finished for Maelzel's machine, Beethoven arranged it, at the latter's suggestion, for orchestra. In this form it is known as the *"Battle"* symphony (Op. 91).

Among the immortal nine this so-called symphony cuts much the same figure that the *chef d'œuvre* of a sidewalk artist would cut in the main hall of the National Gallery. It consists of brisk business for drums and trumpets, with brilliant changes rung on "Rule, Britannia" and "Malbrook," the tune known to Americans as "We Won't Go Home Till Morning." The climax of this preposterous phantasmagoria is actually "God Save the King," tortured into a fast fugato,[2] with ingenious effects representing the huzzas of the populace.

Beethoven wrote this Beethovenate music in order to smite the groundlings upon the side of the head. He did. What an ironic commentary on mankind's present infinitesimal distance from the tree ape that such a man should have succumbed thus, and that his trashiest composition should have won his first overwhelming triumph!

On December 8 and 12, 1813, the Seventh symphony and the *"Battle"* symphony were performed upon the same program for charity. Still more horrible to relate, these numbers were separated by marches of Pleyel and Dussek, emanating from Maelzel's Mechanical Trumpeter.

The leading musicians gave their services and regarded the event as a huge professional joke. Spohr, Mayseder, and Dragonetti fiddled. Moscheles crashed the cymbals. Salieri conducted the battery from off stage. Hummel smote the big drum, in company with a young fellow of twenty-two named Beer, who pounded without the courage of his con-

[2] It is interesting to remember that when Brahms came to write his own essay at a celebration of victory, the *Triumphlied,* he also used "God Save the King." But, oh! the difference to us!

victions and got himself disgracefully scolded by the Master. This young fellow, owing to the terms of a legacy, changed his name to Meyerbeer and proved that a poor drummer might become a rich composer. The antics of these celebrities must have presented an amusing spectacle. But it would have been wise to do as all the prudent do who go to-day to see *Turandot*, and attend this show equipped with opera glasses—and ear muffs.

The popular success of the *"Battle"* symphony completely threw the Seventh into the shade. Its *éclat* was so shattering that, on January 2 and February 27, 1814, Beethoven gave the thing again, with the Seventh and Eighth symphonies, for his own exclusive benefit. Fate smiled upon the box office. With cash in hand he decided not to visit England after all.

Thus he defrauded Maelzel of his just profits. When the desperate inventor managed to collect the music, part by part, for his own eventual use, Beethoven called him a thief. "You're another," retorted Maelzel. And they went to court. Three years later the case was amicably settled.

The *"Battle"* symphony made Beethoven for the first time popular among the people. He was immensely pleased when, walking one day on the Kahlenberg, he was given some cherries by a couple of girls. They would take nothing in return and said adoringly: "We saw you in the Ridotto Room when we heard your lovely music."

Beethoven was now in cash and the man of the hour. But soon he came to realize that he had sold part of his birthright for a mess of pottage and gone back on the sound æsthetic principles which he had proclaimed with the *Pastoral* symphony. *"Wellington's Victory* was a piece of folly," he declared. "It was dear to my heart only because with it I gave the Viennese a sound drubbing."

His successful championship of the metronome shows one characteristic of the man who freed music. He was not a red revolutionary. Great creators seldom are. But he had a decidedly forward-looking mind. It was interested in the march of the world and in invention. He carefully noted the address of a goldsmith who made "fillable pens which may be transported"—ancestors of our fountain pen. Like Leonardo da Vinci, he was fascinated by the problem of human flight. Some of the first attempts at aviation, by the Viennese clock maker Jacob Degen, roused his lively interest. Degen used to try soaring near Baden, the scene of some of the Master's own loftiest flights above this work-aday world.

The approach of the mechanical era thrilled him.

Let us thank God for the promised steam cannons and for the already realized steam navigation. What far swimmers shall we presently have, to bring us air and freedom?!

In a day when Austria was even less equipped with elevators than at present he dreamed of an engine for lifting the Falstaffian Schuppanzigh, "because the thick one mounts badly." In a letter floridly superscribed: *"Al Signore Milord stimatissimo nominato Scuppanzig* [note the Master's humorous realization of how an Italian would pronounce the fiddler's name] *granduomo della citta da Vienna,"* we read:

As soon as my machine is finished, whereby you can be transported with perfect ease up here to me on the fourth floor, I'll let you know.

Beethoven's worldly and cynical activities in connection with the Peace Congress of Vienna were many. Besides the *"Battle"* symphony there was *The Glorious Moment*, a deplorable potboiler cantata written as a timely act of homage to the rulers of Austria, Germany, and Russia. And there was the trashy Polonaise for piano (Op. 89) dedicated to the Empress Elizabeth Alexievna of Russia. Like nearly all of the compositions which did not come from inner impulse these things were quite unworthy of Beethoven's pen. But the crowned heads, and the many-headed crowd, came in such numbers as to provide the Master a snug nest egg. We shall see how tenaciously he clung to it.

The E minor piano sonata (Op. 90), with its tender intimacy, its brooding loveliness, and its lack of appeal to the virtuoso or to the standard concert audience, seemed to arrive as a token that the Master had done dallying with the brilliant world and come to himself. This quiet revelation of one of the most hidden and alluring chambers in the mansion called Beethoven seemed to indicate that he had turned from the crowned heads in order to crown his own head with the last sonatas and quartets.

The E minor was dedicated to his good friend Count Moritz Lichnowsky, who had been divorced and, after sur-

From the painting by Stieler, 1819

BEETHOVEN'S LIFE MASK (1812)
From a painting by Stanislav Rembski

BEETHOVEN IN 1812
After the bust by Klein

BEETHOVEN IN 1814
Engraved by Höfel after a crayon sketch by Letronne

BEETHOVEN

Two pen sketches of Beethoven, about seven years before his death,
by Boehm

BEETHOVEN
From a crayon portrait by Kloeber, 1817 or 1818

BEETHOVEN'S FACTOTUM
ANTON SCHINDLER

BEETHOVEN IN 1823
After the painting by Waldmüller

PRINCE VON LICHNOWSKY
One of Beethoven's earliest and most generous patrons.
Painter unknown

I

II

Ferdinand Fürst Kinsky

III

IV

BEETHOVEN'S CHIEF PATRONS

I County Andreas Rasoumowsky   II Prince Josef Lobkowitz
III Prince Ferdinand Kinsky   IV Archduke Rudolph

BEETHOVEN'S NEPHEW KARL
Photograph taken in later life

GERHARD VON BREUNING

Nicknamed "Ariel" and "Hosenknopf"
("Trouser-button," the latter because
he stuck so close to father)

BEETHOVEN'S FIRST GRAVE,
IN THE CEMETERY AT WÄHRING

BEETHOVEN AT THE POINT OF DEATH

From drawings by Teltscher before he was driven from
the death chamber by Stephan von Breuning

mounting various difficulties, had recently married a beautiful young dancer. When the Count stupidly asked him the meaning of the music (*mille fois hélas!* as M. Arsène Alexandre exclaimed about an equally asinine question by Schindler), Beethoven, "with a boisterous laugh" gave him the stupid answer he deserved:

First movement: "a struggle between the head and heart."

Last movement: "a conversation with the beloved."

A composer with the authority of a Beethoven is like an Indian magician performing the legendary rope trick. He can hypnotize us into seeing anything he wishes us to see. He can tell us a sonata is a lovers' dialogue, or a leviathan swallowing its tail. This will force most of us to hear that, and that only, in music capable of a million equally plausible interpretations. And—another *mille fois hélas!*—sometimes as here, we take him literally when he is only trying to make a bad joke.

Late in 1814 Beethoven gave three more concerts, consisting of *The Glorious Moment* sandwiched between the Seventh and the *"Battle"* symphonies. They were liberally patronized by royalty.

But material success did not obscure his sense of values.

Of our monarchs etc., their realms etc., [he wrote Dr. Kanka] I write you nothing. . . . I prefer the spiritual realm and Him who stands above all spiritual and celestial monarchs.

This year Beethoven rebuilt, as he phrased it, "the devastated ruins of an old castle." In other words, building upon Treitschke's revision of the *Fidelio* libretto, he gave the opera its final form. It was produced with conspicuous success before the assembled potentates.

There is nothing of the Wagnerian leitmotif to be found in *Fidelio*. But the Master was hot on its trail. His ingenious idea of tying together his sonatas and symphonies by letting some germ-motive[3] appear at intervals throughout a work, either disguised or openly, gave a quite novel unity to such compositions as the *Pathétique*, the "*Appassionata*" and *Hammerklavier* sonatas, the C major violoncello and "*Kreutzer*" sonatas, the last quartets and the Third, Fifth, Eighth, and Ninth symphonies.

Indeed, in 1815 Beethoven almost anticipated the music dramatists of the future. In his notes for an afterwards abandoned music drama, *Bacchus*, one may read, under a motive for the words "*Gütiger Pan*": "It must be derived from the Bacchus-motif." In chapter LVI we shall see how one favourite source-motive recurs in the principal themes of his chief works.

Certain marginalia in the Sketch Books of 1814–1815 throw brief flashes of light on the Master's character:

Much to be done on this earth, do it soon!

. . . . . .

No time rolls more quickly by than that in which we busy ourselves with our spirits or I with my muse.

Another entry hints at Beethoven's tremendous vitality.

Let everything that has life ("*Alles, was Leben heisst!*") be sacrificed to the sublime, and sacred to art. Let me live, even with artificial helps, if these can only be found.

---

[3]His use of the germ-motive will be studied in detail in chap. **LIV.**

And here is the Master's dream for his old age—his equivalent of

> The hairy gown, the mossy cell

of "Il Penseroso":

A little court—a little orchestra, its song written there by me, performed to the honour of the Almighty, the Eternal, the Unending. So may the last days flow by. . . . The portraits of Handel, Bach, Gluck, Mozart, Haidn in my room—they might help me to lay claim to submission.

. . . . .

A peasant property, then will you escape your wretchedness.

Part of this wretchedness lay, no doubt, in being misunderstood by his fellow citizens. For about this time the Viennese began calling Beethoven *"der närrische Musiker"* (the mad musician).

It was then that he threw off what was destined to be his most famous *mot*. Young Ignaz Moscheles arranged the piano version of *Fidelio*. At the bottom of the manuscript he wrote: "Finished with God's help." The Master's instant reaction was to scrawl upon the page, "Man, help thyself!"

Chapter XXXVI

"AS GOOD AS LOST"

Last Public Appearance as Pianist, 1814 — Growing Avarice — Kindness to Brother — Karl Dies, November 16, 1815 — Beethoven Joint Guardian of Nephew — Litigation with Sister-in-Law — Fervid Love for Nephew — The "van" in His Name — A Purely Musical Witticism — Receives Freedom of City, about December 1, 1815 — Violoncello Sonatas, C Major and D Major, 1815 — Tentative Beginning of Third Period *— Its Characteristics — A Major Sonata, Op.* 101 *— Song Cycle,* To the Distant Beloved, *1816 — A Milestone in Musical History — Marginalia, 1816–1817 — Fish Suppers at Nussdorf — His Favourite Symphony — Despair — Offer from London Philharmonic — Hammerklavier Sonata, 1818–1819*

BEFORE letting the world hear the great *"Archduke"* trio Beethoven had waited three years. In the spring of 1814 he himself performed its piano part at two concerts. Then he renounced public playing forever.

It was a distressing dénouement. Spohr, who was present at one of the rehearsals, has told us how Beethoven's mastery of his instrument had failed through deafness and lack of practice.

In *forte* passages the poor deaf man pounded on the keys until the strings jangled, and in *piano* he played so softly that whole groups of tones were omitted.

Perhaps the jealous Spohr exaggerated somewhat. In any case, the Master's public career as a pianist lamentably ended with the unresolved discord of an inadequate performance of the least adequate *finale* in all his chamber music.

Beethoven's avarice grew with his fortunes. During the years after he had put by the first considerable nest egg he slipped more and more into the way of misrepresenting his resources. To Ries he wrote about his chief benefactor and closest friend Rudolph: "My unlucky connection with the Archduke has brought me almost down to the beggar's staff."[1]

In 1814 he complained to Kanka, "The table of Zeus is no more where one might propose oneself for ambrosia." In a letter to Neate, May 18, 1816, he referred to "my almost indigent life."

There is a striking incongruity [says Thayer] between Beethoven's pleas of poverty in his letters to correspondents in England at this period and the facts drawn from official and other authentic sources.

But when we consider his kindness to his dying brother, presto change! Exit Hyde; enter Jekyll. He begged Brauchle to take a journey after a horse for Karl.

Stop at no expense, I'll gladly meet it. It is not worth while to let anyone suffer for the sake of a few miserable gulden.

---

[1]Beethoven's occasional designations of such kind friends remind one of Richard Wagner's *My Life*, with its unworthy remarks about avoiding his "skulking creditors"; and about Franz Liszt, his much abused benefactor, his warmest friend, and his father-in-law, with whom this great master singer confessed that he "never actually came to blows."

He actually went so far as to ask a society woman, Antonie von Brentano, to peddle about Karl's old pipe-head among her friends: price: 10 louis d'or.[2] But, eight years after, he was royally to repay this favour by dedicating to her the *Diabelli Variations*.

Brother Karl died of tuberculosis November 16, 1815. The habit of suspicion had so grown upon Ludwig that he was sure the death had been caused by poison and would not be appeased until Dr. Bertolini had performed a postmortem. Karl left his nine-year-old son of the same name under the joint guardianship of the widow and brother Ludwig. In a codicil to his will he enjoined upon the former of these ill-assorted guardians compliance, and upon the latter, moderation.

Appreciable amounts of neither compliance nor moderation were ever shown by either guardian. Driven by his hatred of the "Queen of the Night," as he called his sister-in-law, Beethoven took her into court and fought her for five years. At the end of this time he obtained full custody of the lad.

The long, tedious, sordid story need not be gone into. It is enough to say that Beethoven's own physical and temperamental limitations made him a preposterous guardian for any child; and all the worse for a lad who had inherited most of the weaknesses of the Beethovens with few of their stronger traits. The quarrels, lawsuits, anxieties, and annoyances of this affair cast a shadow, deepening

---

[2] "Never in my life," wrote Dr. Weissenbach, who knew Beethoven at this time, "have I met a more childlike nature paired with so powerful and defiant a will."

to tragedy, over the rest of the Master's life, and sadly hampered his creative work. But even so, his natural kindness of heart often showed itself toward that "Queen of the Night," upon whom he looked as the chief cause of his woes. After he had decreed that she should never see her boy again he broke out: "Mother—even a bad one still remains a mother." He relented, let her see the boy, sent her money, paid her debts. This side of him moved Dr. Weissenbach to write:

If Heaven had endowed him with no other gift than his heart, that alone would make him one in whose presence many would have to rise and bow.

Beethoven's love for this nephew seems almost as morbidly exaggerated as his hatred of the boy's mother—that is, unless one were to go so far as to accept literally the Master's statement in his letter of September 6, 1816, to Dr. Kanka:

I am truly the bodily father [*Ich bin wirklich leiblicher Vater*] of my late brother's child.[3]

If these words, which have apparently escaped comment, should be taken at their face value they would turn the half-mad solicitude and almost ridiculously inflamed love of a bachelor uncle for a nephew into the natural love of a father for a son to whom, through his own fault, he had given an impossible mother.

But telling against any literal acceptation of this apparent

[3]Kasper Anton Karl van Beethoven married Johanna Reiss, May 25, 1806, and little Karl was born October 4, 1806.

confession of paternity is a marginal entry in a Sketch Book of 1816:

Karl betrachtest du als dein eigenes Kind (You look upon Karl as your own child).

This is a much less flat-footed proposition than the former. One must also take into account a statement about Karl's mother in his letter to Bernard (1819):

I hear that she gets 480 fl. W. W. annually from Hofbauer, for, as I hear, he holds her child to be his, it is probably true.

During the litigation, one of the courts discovered that, despite the "van" in his name, Beethoven was not of noble birth. So he was turned over to a plebeian court. An apocryphal tale runs that, when questioned, the Master pointed to his head and heart exclaiming: "My patent of nobility is here and here!" For this there is unfortunately no authority. But in a letter to Piuk he wrote:

The talk turned on the little word *van*, and I had pride enough to declare that I had never bothered my head about my nobility (*"dass ich mich nie um meinen Adel bekümmert"*).

This was a somewhat disingenuous statement, seeing that there was no technical nobility for him to bother his head about. Over the change of venue he was furious and hotly protested against being forced to take his chances there. "I do not belong among these plebs!"

Schindler relates that when his noble friends learned about the little word "van," they were chilled and disillusioned. So that "Vienna became too small" for him. If true, this statement disengages as deep an irony as the incident of the Master's imprisonment for vagrancy when he was composing the *Missa*.[4]

But, however deeply such vexations struck in, they could not dry up the springs of his humour. He sent Steiner a note about something done by Tobias Haslinger (nicknamed "The Adjutant"), which is as purely musical a witticism as the wordless one which opens the Eighth symphony.[5]

The shameful performance of the Adjutant has been entered in the register (though not in the organ-register.) If it were, what a bad sound would issue thence?

Ex. 134

In these days of Stravinsky, Hindemith, and Carillo, it is hard to see how any musical joke could sound much more anachronistic.

A trifling compensation for his woes at this time was Vienna's graceful act, about December 1, 1815, in giving him the freedom of the city.

July and August had been devoted to the two sonatas for violoncello and piano in C and D major (Op. 102, Nos. 1 and 2). Certain of their traits mark the authentic, if still tentative, beginning of the third period.

(1) An uncompromising disregard of mere sensuous charm. A roughness verging at times on brutality. An indif-

[4]See p. 376.
[5]See pp. 321–322.

ference to practical concert effects, entailing on the listener many hearings and much strenuous good-will between first acquaintance and wholly appreciative enjoyment.

(2) A novel plasticity of form, especially in the C major, the manuscript of which was labelled "*Free Sonata.*" This consists of two movements, each subdivided into slow and fast sections, with the dreamy *Andante* theme

Ex. 135

which opens the work as if it were a motto, reappearing later with refrain value.

(3) A fugal tendency, as shown in the *finale* of the D major. This is the first strict fugue in the forty-seven sonatas the Master had thus far written. And it is the first of the nine fugues which form such a gloriously characteristic feature of the third period. Thirty years' study of this rough-hewn movement, as violoncellist and critic, has never altered the writer's conviction that its brutality, inflexibility, and lack of poetic relief make the first fugue of the nine the worst of them.

(4) The *Adagio con molto sentimento d'affetto* of the D major, the deepest movement and the only full-sized *adagio* in all of the violoncello sonatas, is filled with the brooding religious exaltation so characteristic of the Master's final years.

The A major piano sonata (Op. 101), written at about

the same time, has little of the dry crabbedness of opus 102. Indeed, the sensuous lump-in-the-throat beauty of the first movement has provided an inexhaustible inspiration (and loan office) for a host of Romantic composers from Schumann, Mendelssohn, and Brahms down. It even offers us in this phrase

Ex. 136

The horns of elfland faintly blowing.

But the A major has in common with its violoncello neighbours—among other things—a canon in the Trio of the March, where sound is as ruthlessly sacrificed to bleak sense as in the *finale* of the D major; also a fugue—a better one; and a depth and nobility of feeling in the *Adagio,* akin to that in the slow movement of the last violoncello sonata.

Although the human voice was less adapted than any other medium to the expression of Beethoven's genius, his chief work in the unfruitful year 1816 was a group of *Lieder. An die ferne Geliebte* (To the Distant Beloved) (Op. 98) was destined to have a momentous effect on the evolution of the art. It was Beethoven's loftiest flight in lyric song.

True, in setting these lines, he was as iconoclastic towards poetic rhythms and the delicacies and subtleties of the fragile music of vowels and consonants, as musicians since the dawn of song have almost invariably been. Nor were his tones as expressive of the sense of the argument as those of many later song writers. Perhaps he felt that a good poem needs no musical bush; whereas, if the poem is bad, no composer can make it better. At any rate he did the natural thing for a great master of absolute music to do: instead of setting the lines he tried to set what was between them.

But other composers before him had done this too. What made *To the Distant Beloved* a red-lettered milestone in the history of music was the fact of its being the first real song cycle. Here the Master continued his work as emancipator by freeing the song tribe from solitary confinement in individual cells.

During this dark period, 1816–1817, Beethoven was plagued almost beyond endurance by the rapid approach of total deafness; by those questions of food and shelter which were always to him more recondite than triple counterpoint, concealed subjects, or reversible canons; and by the truly damnable business of getting young Karl away from his mother, the "Queen of the Night."

This is the fashion in which, on the margins of his Sketch Books, *Le Grand Sourd* communed with himself:

1816

Submission—submission! Thus may we win something even in the deepest misery, and make ourselves worthy to have God forgive our shortcomings.

Fate, show your force! We are not lords over ourselves. What is determined must be, and so let it be!

He who is burdened with an ill which he cannot alter, which

is bringing him closer and closer to death and without which his life would have lasted longer, must remember that he might have been killed even sooner by assassination or other causes.

Live in your art alone. Limited as you now are by your hearing, this is the only existence for you.

Follow the counsel of others only in the rarest instances. In a matter that has already been considered, to whom can all the circumstances be as clear in consciousness as to oneself?!

Just as the State must have a constitution, so must the individual have one of his own.

1817

Peace and freedom are the best of all things. True friendship can be founded only on the union of similar natures.

One of his friends, a poet named Kuffner, came this summer to live near him in Heiligenstadt. The two often went together to Nussdorf for fish suppers, either to the Sign of the Rose, or nearer the source of supplies. In a Conversation Book a year before the Master's death we find Kuffner's handwriting:

Do you remember the fisherman's house in Nussdorf, where we sat till midnight on the terrace under the full moon, before us the rushing brook and the swollen Danube? I was your guest.

During one of these suppers, the poet seized his opportunity when the Master was feeling at peace with the world to ask:

KUFFNER:—Tell me frankly, which is your favourite among your symphonies?

BEETHOVEN:—(In great good humour) Eh! Eh! The *Eroica*.

KUFFNER:—I should have guessed the C minor.

BEETHOVEN:—No; the *Eroica*.

On August 21, 1817, just as his hearing was at times near the vanishing point, the Master mailed this bitter cry to his sick friend Zmeskall:

I am often in despair and would like to end my life. . . . God have mercy on me, I regard myself as good as lost. . . . If the condition does not change I shall next year be not in London but in the grave.—Thank God the rôle will soon be played out.—

The reference to London meant that the Philharmonic Society had renewed its offer of 300 guineas if Beethoven would come across the Channel with two new symphonies. And he had accepted. If carried out, this plan might have solved his financial problems for the rest of his life. But, as he seldom did first-class work to order, the result might possibly have been a repetition of the unfortunate "*Battle*" symphony episode.

The event did honour to his artistic conscience. While his English friends impatiently awaited the promised works, he let the sketches of the D minor symphony lie in his desk while he sent this word to Czerny:

Just now I am writing at a sonata which shall be my greatest.

It was the one in B flat (Op. 106), known as the *Hammerklavier*. This enormous work occupied him, off and on, until March, 1819. It is as long as a symphony, as brilliant and difficult as a concerto. It makes more strenuous demands upon the instrument, the performer, and the listener than any other composition of the Master.

To clothe these gigantic limbs in such inadequate vesture as piano makers carry in stock is attempting to force Samson into rompers. This is ideal music, but "not for the sensual ear," and fit only for a Brobdingnagian keyboard. It seems to ask of the interpreter more than is possible for human nerve and sinew, brain and emotion to supply. Among the scores of times the writer has heard the *Hammerklavier* sonata played he can recall but one performance which came within appreciable distance of adequacy, and that took place among the favouring conditions of a Beethoven festival at Bonn.

But even if some yet undreamed-of super-virtuoso were to give a perfect reading of this work upon the most superb instrument of a Twenty-first Century Steinway, and our spirits responded eagerly to the privilege, the flesh would still be weak.

We can savour to the full the heroic strength and noble tenderness of the opening movement. We can enjoy the puckish fantasy and Ariel-like winsomeness, the "nods and becks and wreathèd"—but somewhat wistful—"smiles" of the second movement; and are seized anew with the conviction that we are hearing the most luscious of Beethoven's piano *scherzos*.

Reverently we enter into the ethereally poignant tragedy of the *Adagio sostenuto*. The Master's just quoted remark to Zmeskall recurs to us:

God have mercy on me, I regard myself as good as lost.

Von Bülow has set a true word beneath the last page of this *Adagio*:

The pain that tears the heart no longer has the word here, but—as it were—tearless resignation rigid as death.

In this superhuman passage of the *Hammerklavier*, Beethoven triumphantly stands the test of the supreme artist—even in death we are in beauty. This corruption is swathed in the incorruption of loveliness.

But we have gone too fast. For only halfway through the immensity of this movement something happens. We have been too long under an intense strain. Exhausted nature baulks and begins to falsify beauty, just as it falsifies the miracle of sunset playing on the clouds that half fill the Grand Canyon, as observed after fourteen hours in the saddle. Though the movement is in strict form and every note has its unimpeachable reason for being, the listener is so weary by the time he reaches the middle that, from there on, much of the music sounds to him as though Beethoven, plunged into the depths of an amorphous daydream, had remained too long submerged.[6]

Then comes a titanic three-voiced fugue with a subject ten bars long. It involves the greatest effort Beethoven ever demanded of the listener to his sonatas. It is terribly stark, furiously bleak music. Mr. Sullivan calls it "the expression of the final refusal of annihilation, even if no hope and no object be left in life."[7]

By this time the hearer is too spent to appreciate much more than the immensity of the subject, the mastery with which the poet hides the scholar in its manipulation, the heavenly relief of the singing D major episode *sempre dolce*

---

[6] The tired hearer is reminded of the Master's notorious absent-mindedness and wonders whether he were composing these passages the afternoon when he asked the waiter for his bill without having ordered any food.

[7] *Beethoven: His Spiritual Development*, p. 209.

e cantabile following a terrific climax and after one of the most dramatic measure's pauses in all music.

As the monster fugue rages on and on, apparently intent on shattering to bits not only the piano and the struggling virtuoso, but the form of the sonata itself, the weary listener finds himself feebly resenting this brutal whirlwind, coming, as it does, after the ineffable poetic dream of the *Adagio*. But on the way home he asks himself what could have provided a more convincing close to this mighty work. Another piece in sonata-form? Variations? A rondo? No! A thousand times no! And he is driven to the conclusion that the Master was right as usual. Nothing besides a fugue, a ruthless hurricane of a fugue, could have said a fitting last word to such an *allegro,* such a *scherzo,* and such an *adagio.*[8]

During this life one does not expect to see the day when the *Hammerklavier* shall be adequately performed, on an adequate instrument, to adequate listeners. But if there be a next world, and if the report of its being a musical one be true, one hopes to hear the composer of this work, purged long since of Hydean dross, play it upon an instrument as far removed from the piano as the piano is now removed from its ancestor, the primitive harp of David.

---

[8]This work might perhaps be played, like *Parsifal,* with long intermissions for recuperation and an interval after the *scherzo* for dinner!

Charter XXXVII

THE EMANCIPATOR EMANCIPATED

IN 1818, during his summer at Mödling, Beethoven received a present. It was a Broadwood pianoforte from the English makers. Scratched beside the keyboard were the names of England's leading virtuosi: Cramer, Knyvelt, Kalkbrenner, Ferrari, and Ries. The instrument was admitted by the Austrian authorities free of duty.

Beethoven was delighted. In his most elegant French he wrote a letter of thanks, promising to regard the piano "as an altar on which I shall present to the divine Apollo the highest offerings of my spirit" (*"Comme un autel, où je déposerai les plus belles offrandes de mon esprit au divin Apollon."*)

Unfortunately this gift came too late to be of much practical use to the Master, for his hearing was now almost entirely gone. When told that the Broadwood was out of tune he replied with the characteristic suspicion of the deaf: "That's what they all say. They would like to tune it and spoil it; but they shan't touch it." Woe, however, to any piano that Beethoven himself touched! A contemporary reports that at this period the Master attacked the keyboard so savagely he broke from twenty to thirty strings each time he played. And a few years later, to show Stein that certain strings needed replacing in this very instrument, he actually hammered its keys with a bootjack.[1]

The same suspicion and violence which he showed towards his pianos was often turned against his servants. In 1816 he gave Peter Simrock pencil and paper and told him to write down everything personal or confidential, as the servant was an eavesdropper. But when Simrock called again a few days later, the Master said: "Now we can talk, for I've given my servant five gulden, a kick in the rear, and sent him to the devil." In connection with one of these domestic dramas some unidentified hand wrote in one of the small tablets called Conversation Books the following

---

[1] This may have been the very utensil which Schuppanzigh saw put to another novel use in 1823. "Milord" came into the deaf man's room unobserved. Beethoven had his back to the door and was using a bootjack as if it were an enormous tuning fork, striking it against the wall and then holding it close to his ears to try and detect the after vibrations. It throws an unpleasant light on the fat man's character that he retailed this pathetic incident "with humour and sarcastic observations." (Frimmel, *Beethoven Handbuch*, Vol. II, p. 163.)

sage counsel: "Don't beat her! You might have trouble with the police."

Communication with the Master had now to be carried on by means of these Conversation Books, in which the deaf man's answers are, naturally, seldom found. A page transcribed from one of them (November–December, 1819) will give some idea of the intellectual quality of the usual talk that went on in his rooms.

Goethe says the spot on which a good man has set his foot remains consecrated for all time.
To-day he cut open his frozen toe.
Roast veal (Kälbernes) *with some ham and tongue.*
If only everyone could understand and appreciate your love for your nephew.
The dog is missing.
If you lose the book they'll lock me up.
For all eternity.
There are fresh oysters.

When inspiration seized him he would run out of doors, hatless and coatless, perhaps before dawn, and wander about the fields and woods in an oblivious frenzy of creation. Often he returned late at night, cold, wet, and famished. In 1820 Wilhelm Müller called on him at Mödling. The housekeeper said that Beethoven had gone out walking early and he might return that evening—or perhaps in three days. After such exposure he was capable of the inconsistency of objecting to rooms opening upon a garden, because "garden air is precisely the worst sort for me"!

Small wonder his health suffered. In the years from 1818 to 1823 he complained of gout, rheumatism, jaundice, pain in the ears, and failing eyesight. It is sad to think how much torture, how many unborn masterpieces, and how many decades of life he might have saved by observing the most elementary physical prudence.

Small wonder that many thought the worst of his intelligence. In 1819 Zelter wrote Goethe:

Some say he is a fool. That is soon said: God forgive us all our trespasses!

The following year Beethoven, in all seriousness, invented a delightful euphemism for his own language when violent and abusive. It was a gem of rationalization. "Now and then," he remarked to Wilhelm Müller, "I let drop a hearty, free word. On that account people think me mad." Perhaps his often childlike impracticality may have influenced what people thought. On September 27, 1821, the author of "Man, help thyself!" wrote to an unknown correspondent in great distress for aid in selling one of his bank shares. But on the wrapper he scribbled:

You'll easily see what kind of commercial genius I am. After the enclosed letter was written, I talked over this matter of the share, with a friend. He showed me at once that one has only to cut off a coupon, and therewith the whole matter is at an end.

This helpless side of the man—the side which had to do with everything nonmusical—comes out vividly in his correspondence. Reading it, one thinks of him as a sort of Nineteenth Century Don Quixote, three parts sane, super-Sanchoed, first by Krumpholz, whom he nicknamed "My Fool"; then by poor faithful Zmeskall, the "Music Count,"

"Baron Greedygut," "Your Zmeskality"; then by "Papageno" Schindler, the "Samothracian ragamuffin"; then by Holz, that "Splinter of the True Cross."

Alas! Poor Knight! Alas! Poor soul possest!

He and his faithful Sanchos were almost never out of such troubles as normal common sense might easily have averted. He freed music. Himself he could not free from the bondage of his absent-mindedness, his lack of practical common sense, and his dangerous temperament.

But the writing was a different matter. In all his chief works from now to the premature end we find his faculties working with such a glorious freedom as scarcely any other artist has ever attained. This is not to say that he was fluent. Beethoven was never that on paper; least of all in these later years, when he was increasingly bothered by inertia in beginning a new composition. But once the momentum was up he found himself stimulated, not hampered, by the formal, technical side of his art. He could freely utter his profound mind and pour out his great heart, because he was now at last an emancipated artist, in full command of his medium.

The three sonatas which end the immortal series of thirty-two for piano are in remarkable contrast to that monumental concert piece, the *Hammerklavier*. They are intimate and personal, in a sort of string quartet style, with a tinge of improvisation. They have forgotten both the virtuoso and his ways, and the old strict outlines of sonata-form. In fact, they are called sonatas only by a somewhat liberal stretch of courteous imagination. All three were done in the intervals of toil upon the *Missa Solemnis,* which was begun in 1818. And they have much in common with that gigantic work.

The E major sonata (Op. 109) was written in 1820. It is a fantasia sonata, lyrical in mood. The passionate unrest of the sonata-form *prestissimo* which does duty as *scherzo* heightens the happy grace of the opening movement and the calm, serene, reassuring loveliness of the closing variations.[2]

Ex. 137

Andante molto cantabile ed espressivo.
mezza voce.

Behrend[3] calls the A flat (Op. 110, written in 1821) a "memory sonata." Sir George Grove pointed out the resemblance of measures 5—8 of the first movement

Ex. 138   1821

Sonata Op. 110

---

[2] The present writer's own feeling about the theme of these variations may be inferred from his selection of it to stand beside Bach's B flat *Choral Prelude* in the "*Pure Beauty*" section of *The Poetry Cure with Music and Pictures,* 1927.

[3] William Behrend, *Ludwig van Beethoven's Pianoforte Sonatas,* 1927, p. 182.

to themes from four of Beethoven's earlier works.

He went farther and traced this theme back to Haydn's fifty-eighth sonata.

Riemann pointed out the resemblance of the beginning of the introductory measures

to the start of the variation theme of the foregoing E major sonata.[4] And others have remarked that the second theme of the *Allegro molto* is like the old popular song *"Ich bin liederlich."*

But no one seems to have noticed two other curious resemblances. While the right hand, beginning at the fifth measure of the first movement, is calling up a flood of memories of Haydn and of Beethoven himself (Ex. 138), the left actually intones in the bass

Ex. 144

the four opening bars of the *finale* of the *"Jupiter"* symphony

Ex. 145

Allegro molto

(which Mozart derived from one of his five favourite Bach fugues, the E major). And Beethoven even goes so far as to imitate Mozart's six following notes, although transposing his own a semitone higher. Mozart to left of him, Haydn to right of him, Bach behind him! It is hard to look upon this meeting of the four masters as purely accidental.

---

[4]See Ex. 137, p. 369.

One shrewdly suspects that Beethoven's right hand knew what his left hand was doing.

The fugued *finale* contains an even more entertaining memory. If one takes the clarinet tune of the fugato of the *Eroica* Funeral March (bars 135–140), divests it of passing notes, and transposes it for purposes of comparison to the key of this *finale*, one has the following:

Ex. 146

which is nearly the theme of the opus 110 fugue.

Ex. 147

Loans hidden thus artfully have as protective a colouration as that insect named the "walking-stick."[5]

The *Allegro molto* of the A flat sonata, despite its grimness, has gipsy-like gestures which point down the years to the Hungarian rhapsodies of Liszt and such movements of Brahms as the *finale* of the G minor piano quartet. Its first phrase

---

[5] At Munich in the summer of 1927 Herr Wilhelm Furtwängler conducted from memory a prodigious performance of the *Eroica*. Afterwards the writer asked him if he knew that the fugue of the A flat sonata was concealed there. In his forceful Rooseveltian way he swore that such a thing was impossible. Did he not know every note of the symphony by heart? But when the writer produced a pocket score and pointed out the place his surprise and delight were equally forceful.

Ex. 148

seems like a scherzification of the beginning of the short
Arioso dolente.

Ex. 149

This *Arioso* is the grievously poignant utterance of a man
on the downward slope, deaf, ailing, suspicious, mateless,
who felt unjustly neglected as an artist and convinced that
all the world was banded against him as a man.

The *finale* is one of the most satisfying contrapuntal
pieces in all the sonatas. It is as if the monumental majesty

of Bach and the poetic magic of Brahms had met midway. Beethoven had remarked to Holz[6] not long before the composition of these last sonatas:

There is no art in making a fugue. In my student years I made them by the dozen. But imagination also claims its rights. And nowadays into the time-honoured form there must enter a truly poetic element.

This element takes such masterly possession of the A flat fugue that it persists even while the theme is being eruditely stood on its head (in *L'inversione della Fuga*).

There could be no more fitting end for the great thirty-two than the C minor sonata (Op. 111). This two-movement work has no *scherzo*, but each movement offers a supreme example of its own type. Beethoven created both of these types, and his supremacy in them has never since been threatened.[7]

The principal theme of the *Allegro con brio ed appassionato*,[8]

Thundering like ramping hosts of warrior horse,

is one of the most portentously powerful melodies in music. While the *Arietta*, with a naïve simplicity as of folk music, makes one think of those words of St. Paul:

I will come to visions and revelations of the Lord. I knew a man in Christ above fourteen years ago, (whether in the body, I cannot tell; or whether out of the body, I cannot tell: God knoweth:) such an one caught up to the third heaven. And I

[6]See p. 27.

[7]See pp. 499–500.

[8]See the transposed Ex. 330, p. 593.

knew such a man . . . how that he was caught up into paradise, and heard unspeakable words, which it is not lawful for a man to utter. Of such an one will I glory.

Here is the opening portion of the sublime theme

Ex. 150

This movement brings the last sonata to a perfectly satisfying completion. Any addition is unthinkable. Yet poor Schindler is said to have asked Beethoven why he did not write a brilliant fast ending. And the publisher, too, made it clear that this was what he had expected.

Nobody can justly blame them. For even after the lapse of a century it remains true that the listener who can easily cope with the earliest piano sonatas at a first or second hearing requires literally years of persistence, good-will, and sympathy in order to comprehend the thirty-second.

From the sublimities of the C minor to the ridiculous was but a step. Early one morning in 1820 Beethoven rose with his mind full of the sonatas and the *Missa*, slipped into a ragged old coat, and set out for a hatless walk. By evening he was famished and had lost his way. Still deep in thought, he was arrested as a vagabond.

"I am Beethoven," he declared.

"Sure, why not, indeed?" mocked the policeman. "You're a tramp, that's what. Beethoven doesn't look like that."[8a]

He was put in jail for the night, but made such a hullabaloo hour after hour that he forced them to get the police commissioner out of bed, who aroused the musical director of the Wiener Neustadt, who identified the turbulent jail-bird as Beethoven. Whereupon the man who had not only received the freedom of the city but free lodging at the expense of the city was sent home in state by the burgomaster in the magisterial coach.

Perhaps as a salutary consequence of this farcical episode the Vienna policemen of to-day know more about musical celebrities than they did in 1820. One moonlight evening last year a Viennese lady undertook to show the writer Beethoven's famous place of residence, the Pasqualati House. But it did not look like the familiar pictures.

Recourse was had to one of Vienna's famously cultured and polite policemen. He smiled and said that the building

---

[8a] This idealist among policemen resembled such painters as Neugass, and such writers as M. Romain Rolland, who have insisted on attributing to the squat, ugly, and highly human little Master, a Jovian front, a Roman toga, and the character of a seraph.

was Schubert's Dreimäderlhaus. Then he led the way around the corner to No. 8 Mölker Bastei. And with a gallant "Kiss the hand!" to the lady and "I have the honour to recommend myself" to her escort, left them to a study of the tablet commemorating the birth of the Fourth, Fifth, and Eighth symphonies, the Rasoumowsky quartets, and the Violin concerto.

Such is real fame. One tries to imagine what response would issue from a Parisian gendarme, a London bobby, or one of New York's "finest" if asked, respectively, about the home of César Franck, Milton's tomb, or Poe's cottage.

Ignaz von Seyfried reported at first hand, in the florid style of his day, the Master's intensely concentrated mode of life.

From the first sunbeam to dinner time, the whole morning was consecrated to mechanical toil, namely writing his music down. The rest of the day was given over to thought and the ordering of his ideas. The last mouthful had scarcely entered his lips when—in case he had no longer excursion in mind—he began his usual promenade. That is to say, he ran on the double-quick a couple of times round about the city as though he were being stung. Whether it rained, snowed, or hailed, whether the thermometer showed sixteen degrees of cold, whether the north wind puffed his cheeks out and blew his icy breath across Bohemia's frontiers, whether the thunder roared, the lightning's zigzag cut the air, a gale howled, or Phoebus' heat rays fell direct on the skull;—what difference did all this make to the consecrated one who carried his God in his own heart and for whose spirit, perhaps, in the very midst of the elements' uproar, the mild springtide of paradise was blooming?[9]

[9]Translated from A. Leitzmann, *Ludwig van Beethoven, Berichte der Zeitgenossen*, 1921, Vol. II, p. 47.

"Only the artist," Beethoven once wrote, "or the emancipated scholar carries his own happiness about inside himself."

In 1821 Sir John Russell visited Vienna, saw Beethoven, and wrote vividly about him:

His eye is full of turbulent energy. His hair which seems to have remained for years out of touch with comb or scissors, shades his broad brow in an abundance and disorder with which only the snakes about the Gorgon's head can be compared. . . . Friendliness and affability do not lie in his character except when in a circle of trusted intimates. . . . Even his oldest friends must always obey his will as though he were a spoiled child.

At this time, reported the Englishman, Beethoven never played the piano for people unless he were tricked into it. Sir John and Beethoven both dined one evening with a close friend of the latter. At a preconcerted signal everyone left the musician and his host alone together. Now the composer could hear music better than speech. While carrying on a written conversation with him about finance the clever friend touched the piano keys as if by accident, then began to play one of Beethoven's own compositions, intentionally making such glaring blunders that Beethoven finally condescended to stretch out his hand and correct one of them. Once on the keys his hand remained there. On some pretext his friend left the room. Beethoven absent-mindedly sat down at the piano, played a few desultory chords, and gradually lost himself in a half hour's improvisation. Of course the whole company listened breathlessly in the open doorway.

The enthusiasts were carried away [wrote Sir John]. For the uninitiated it was all the more interesting to notice how the music translated itself from the man's soul to his features. . . . His facial muscles swelled and his veins stood out; the doubly wild eye rolled in twice as fine a frenzy, the mouth twitched, and Beethoven looked like a sorcerer who feels himself overpowered by the very spirits whom he has conjured up.

In 1822 Rossini, the popular musical idol of the day, visited the Master whom his own reputation had thrown somewhat into the shade. Beethoven received him pleasantly enough, described himself as *"un infelice"* (an unhappy one), and advised Rossini that he would be doing violence to his destiny if he tried his hand "at anything but opera *buffa.*"

Overcome by Beethoven's apparently wretched poverty the generous "Swan of Pesaro" tried to raise a subscription for him. But everyone declined with much the same remark: "He is a misanthrope, cranky, and can't keep friends."

After this call Beethoven remarked: "Rossini is a good scene-painter. . . . He would have been a great composer if . . ." and he roughly outlined the painful and humiliating discipline which the Italian's music teacher should have applied to an inconsidered portion of his anatomy. However, despite his low opinion of Rossini as an absolute musician, Beethoven occasionally condescended, as we have seen,[10] to imitate his cruder popular effects.

In November, 1822, *Fidelio* was revived; and soon conquered, and held a high place in the affections of the

---

[10]See pp. 173–174.

German-speaking peoples. Beethoven tried to conduct the dress rehearsal. But he was now so deaf that he repeatedly threw everything into confusion. No one dared approach him until Schindler ventured to hand him a note: "I beg you not to go on; will explain at home."

Like a flash Beethoven sprang into the parterre saying only, "Out quickly!" and fairly ran to his house. Schindler relates that

he threw himself upon the sofa, covered his face with both hands, and stayed so until we sat down at table. But not a sound did he utter during the meal. His whole figure was the image of deepest melancholy and despondency.

A tragic situation: his last direct *rapport* with his public roughly snapped. But he was suffering from something even less supportable. As Mr. Grace points out:

One cannot but feel that the real tragedy lay in the fact that at this period, when his powers were at their height, he was so beset with hindrances (many of them avoidable) as to be unable to make the most of his gifts. Probably he alone was fully aware of the discrepancy between his powers and the quantity of his output; and the knowledge must have been an added touch of bitterness to a cup already full.[11]

This knowledge it was that gave the agonizing poignancy to the *Arioso dolente* of the A flat sonata and to that music which was presently to cry to heaven from the opening movement of the *Choral* symphony.

---

[11] *Beethoven,* p. 142.

Chapter XXXVIII

HE FREES THE MASS

Mass in D, Begun 1818 — Intended for Rudolph's Enthronization Ceremony, 1820 — But not Finished Until 1823 — An Unecclesiastical and Unvocal Writer — His Personal Creed — His Detachment from Earth, 1819 — Missa Begun as an Occasional Work — Music with a Purpose — Handicaps to Composition — Comparative Failure of Kyrie, Gloria, *and part of* Sanctus — *Power and Beauty of* Credo, Benedictus, *and* Agnus Dei — *A Barefaced Plagiarism — Hints of Military Music — The Finest Melody in the* Missa — *Evaluation as a Whole — Defensive Rationalization — Beethoven Frees the Mass*

IN ORDER to write true church music, look up and go through all the church chorales of the monks etc.

Beethoven scribbled this reminder in a Sketch Book of 1818. He had just heard that the Archduke Rudolph was in a year or so to be made Archbishop of Olmütz. So he started his Mass in D (Op. 123) with a view to having it performed at the installation ceremony. This ceremony took place almost two years later, but the *Missa Solemnis,* as he called it, was far from ready. Beethoven toiled on it more or less continually for half a decade.

The delay was probably fortunate for the success of Rudolph's ceremonial. His composer friend was decidedly neither an ecclesiastical nor a vocal writer. When he wandered half a dozen paces into either of these fields he became as submerged in his own purely instrumental thoughts as the day he started to accompany the van of his furniture into the country and promptly forgot all about it.

For vans, voices, and churches his sympathies did not blaze brightly. The reason he made things so uncomfortable for all three was not lack of knowledge but lack of the love which breeds consideration. "Singers," he once remarked coldly, "ought to be able to do anything, except bite their own noses!" Hence the fatiguing length of the *Missa* and its loose adaptation to the precise time-table of the church service. Hence those ghastly difficulties for the wretched sopranos, there and in the *Choral* symphony, which made Fräulein Unger call him to his face "tyrant over all the vocal organs," and which made a perfect performance of these works almost unheard of—even in the days before our present high pitch came into fashion. In this connection there is much significance in Beethoven's casual remark: "When I think of a theme, it is always for some instrument."

It was unfortunate for this department of Beethoven's work [writes Mr. Grace] that he lived in a bad choral period when the idiom was secular and operatic, and the beauty of unaccompanied singing seems to have been unrealized.[1]

Beethoven was not as close to the Mass text as many suppose. In his ignorance of Latin he had to have the words translated for him into German. Though he was religious

---

[1]*Beethoven*, p. 287.

in the sense that he had constructed his own religion, his heart did not warm to the less spiritual aspects of ecclesiasticism. There were even affirmations in the *Credo* which he must have actively disbelieved. So it is hard to see how he could have entered into the composition of the *Missa* with that whole-hearted, enthusiastic conviction which is a necessary antecedent for the greatest works of art.

The leading items of Beethoven's personal credo were: self-reliant strength, goodness, beauty as shown in nature and art, and a supreme Being who exemplified and fostered all these. Through the finer parts of the *Missa* such a belief blazes forth in a personally Beethovenian way.

Realizing perhaps that a task like this presented peculiar difficulties to such a man as himself, he plunged into it with a kind of desperate abandon. In a Sketch Book he admonished himself: "Once more sacrifice to your art all the little things of social life. O God above all!" "When I am alone," he once remarked, "I am never alone." And these words apply peculiarly to this period. Schindler testified that never before or after had he seen the Master so detached from earth as in 1819.[2]

Towards the end of August, accompanied by the musician Johann Horsalka, still living in Vienna, I arrived at the master's home in Mödling. It was four o'clock in the afternoon. As soon as we entered we learned that in the morning both servants had gone away, and that there had been a quarrel after midnight which had disturbed all the neighbours, because as a consequence of a long vigil both had gone to sleep and the food which had been prepared had become unpalatable. In the living-room,

---

[2]Ed. of 1860, Vol. I, p. 270.

behind a locked door, we heard the master singing parts of the fugue in the *Credo*—singing, howling, stamping. After we had been listening a long time to this almost awful scene, and were about to go away, the door opened and Beethoven stood before us with distorted features, calculated to excite fear. He looked as if he had been in mortal combat with the whole host of contrapuntists, his everlasting enemies. His first utterances were confused, as if he had been disagreeably surprised at our having overheard him. Then he reached the day's happenings and with obvious restraint he remarked: "Good housekeeping, this! [*Saubere Wirthschaft!*] Everybody has run away and since noon yesterday I haven't had anything to eat!" I tried to calm him and helped him to make his toilet. My companion hurried on in advance to the restaurant of the bathing establishment to have something made ready for the famished master. Then he complained about the wretched state of his domestic affairs, but here, for reasons already stated, there was nothing to be done. Never, it may be said, did so great an art work as is the *Missa Solemnis* see its creation under more adverse circumstances.

Beethoven felt that this Mass was his best composition. And nearly all of his biographers have agreed with him and with one another in declaring it the crown, or something near it, of the Master's career—worthy to stand with Bach's B minor Mass at the summit of all choral compositions. It is time to forget what anyone has ever said about the *Missa*, to hear it with one's own ears and scrutinize it strictly on its own merits according to the light vouchsafed us to-day.

Judged by both outer and inner standards this was started as an occasional work. It was begun as a compliment to his rich patron the Archduke, a man to whom Beethoven in his letters often referred contemptuously as "the weak cardinal," and the like. Such outer incentives for composition almost never resulted in Beethoven's best. Think of the pedestrian triple concerto, written for this same Rudolph. Think of the *"Battle"* symphony, *King Stephen*, *The Ruins of Athens*, the Scotch Songs, and *The Glorious Moment*. All of these compositions give a Beethoven lover a gone feeling, and make him perhaps recall that comforting declaration of Mozart's: "He who judges me by my bad works is a knave!"

Subjectively, as well, much of the *Missa* suffers the blight of the occasional. Beethoven wrote Andreas Streicher, September 16, 1824:

> During the work on this Grand Mass my main purpose was to evoke in both the singers and the auditors religious sentiments and to instil them permanently.

If this was true it goes far to explain the comparative failure of something like one half of the work. Can one possibly imagine Beethoven confessing that his main purpose in writing things like the *Eroica* or the C sharp minor quartet was ethical, philosophical, religious, or anything but purely musical?

Besides these handicaps the composer was sick much of the time between 1818 and 1823. He was distracted by the wretched business of Karl, and by hopeless domestic affairs which were aggravated *crescendo* by the morbid suspicions natural to almost total deafness. These circumstances may abundantly account for the comparatively commonplace *Kyrie*, and for the lack of spontaneity and magic in the *Gloria*. The culminating point of the latter, the *In gloria Dei patris*, is merely the work of a capable fugue-smith who has, however, hammered the thing out cold. There are no sparks.

The only wonder is that, starting with these formidable handicaps, he should have been able, by the time he arrived at the *Credo*, to brush them all aside like so many midges. The *Crucifixus* and the *Et vitam venturi* fugue

Ex. 151

Allegretto ma non troppo

et vi-tam ven - tu-ri sae - - - cu li, a - -

are as gripping and overpowering as anything he ever did for the voice. For sixteen pages the *Sanctus* is undistinguished. Then it breaks into the *Benedictus* with its soaring violin obbligato—that unsurpassed progenitor of the most ethereal, celestial pages of Schubert, Wagner, Brahms, Franck, and Richard Strauss.

The *Agnus Dei* confronts us with an amazing barefaced plagiarism

Ex. 152

pa - cem, do - - na no - bis pa -

from the *Hallelujah* Chorus of *The Messiah*.

Ex. 153

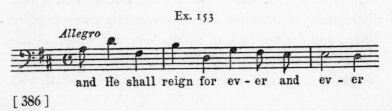

Allegro

and He shall reign for ev - er and ev - er

This fact might lend comfort and countenance to the jazz pickpockets of a century later—especially to the writer of that best-selling popular song of a recent year, "Yes, We Have No Bananas," who likewise helped himself to part of the *Hallelujah* Chorus. Perhaps in this instance Beethoven was too much overpowered by his curious conviction that Handel was the greatest composer who had ever lived, to succeed in transmuting Ex. 153 into his own coin. And the result was an ugly rift in the unity of the Mass.

Yet this same *Agnus Dei* contains what is, in the writer's opinion, the loveliest music of all. Its most moving portion begins with the motto "Petition for Internal and External Peace." There are subtle hints of military music, delicate enough to suggest to those hearers who have poetry in their souls symbols of spiritual dangers, struggles, and triumphs. They are also plain enough to have shocked the horny-minded literalists into indignant protest against the impropriety of martial strains in a Mass.

But Beethoven's sense of propriety in the *Agnus Dei* was exquisite. He felt that an exciting close on a note of triumph or splendour would be inappropriate. So with his almost unerring instinct for endings he made an *"innig"* end, with the finest melody in the Mass. It is one of the most superbly beautiful and haunting tunes that he or anyone else ever conceived.

Ex. 154

do - - - na no - bis pa - cem,

M. D'Indy suggests that part of its penetrative force lies in the curious arrangement by which none of the nine notes stands on a degree previously heard. But it must be a small part, if one may judge from the many weak melodies of which the same is to be said.

Despite the marvellous qualities of its best portions, the *Missa Solemnis*, taken as a whole, stands in the author's opinion on a plane somewhat below its composer's best sonatas, quartets, and symphonies. It stands considerably below that choral Abou Ben Adhem, the B minor Mass of Bach, whose name leads all the rest. And it stands below Bach's *St. Matthew Passion*, and, yes, below *The Messiah*.

Those who have accepted the Master's own estimate of the *Missa* should take into account that this creation cost him more time and trouble than any of his other spiritual children; that artists are notoriously unreliable judges of their own productions; and that a cripple, reared with difficulty, is usually its mother's favourite child.

"From the heart—may it speak to the heart" are the unusual words which stand at the top of the score. The composer "doth protest too much." There is no need for any such statement with the *Eroica* Funeral March or the Violin concerto or the B flat trio or the two last sonatas or the ten last quartets. Perhaps Beethoven had some unformulated misgiving about the qualifications of half of his *Missa* to speak to the heart. Perhaps this motto represents a bit of what the psychologists would call defensive rationalization. Beethoven, as is well known, told Rudolph that having the *Missa* performed at his enthronement as Archbishop would give the composer the happiest day of his life. This protestation should not be taken too literally. It should be collated with his letter to Franz von Brentano, November 28, 1820, about "the weak cardinal who has got me into this morass and does not know how to help himself." And it should be read in connection with the scores of polite but palpable fibs which he wrote over a period of three decades to this most generous and consistent of his patrons.

Though half of it was comparatively weak, the *Missa* continued that work of liberation which its creator had carried on in much of his instrumental music. The tardy appearance of a Bach cult, which delayed the publication of Bach's vocal works until the middle of the Nineteenth Century, conferred upon Beethoven the honour of actually freeing the Mass from its traditional confinement within the boundaries of a particular church. He even liberated it from the confines of ecclesiastical convention itself, and made it free of a region until then almost untrodden by composers—that land of true religion, wide as the human race, where the individual stands in immediate relation with the infinite life of which he is a spark.

Chapter XXXIX

MR. HYDE AND THE HELL-HOUNDS

Bad Faith with Publishers — Palliations — Did Beethoven Have a Higher Private Moral Code?—Weak Case for the Defense — Solicits Private Subscriptions for Missa — Misrepresentations to Zelter — Letter to Goethe, February 8, 1823, Unanswered — Schindler Established as Factotum, 1822 — Liszt's Début, 1823 — Diabelli Variations, 1823

Now comes a distressing matter. At the time when Beethoven's Dr. Jekyll had just finished such other-worldly music as the *Et vitam venturi*, the *Benedictus*, and the *Dona nobis pacem*, and was turning his thoughts to the sublimities of the Ninth symphony, Mr. Hyde flew into a bustle of pernicious activity along worldly lines.[1]

We have already heard how he said to the remonstrant "Falstaff" in the Rasoumowsky period, "Does he really suppose I think of his puling little fiddle when the spirit speaks to me and I compose something?" Now, in the above, Mr. Hyde could honestly have substituted for "his puling little fiddle" "my puling little publishers." For he was playing faster and looser with these so-called 'hell-hounds who licked and gnawed his brains' than he had just played with

---

[1] In *Dr. Jekyll and Mr. Hyde,* Thistle ed., 1901, p. 352, Stevenson's hero-villain wrote of the principles of evil and good within him: "It was the curse of mankind that these incongruous faggots were thus bound together—that in the agonized womb of consciousness, these polar twins should be continually struggling."

the sopranos by making them at one point enter the *vitam venturi* (or almost enter it) on four high B flats.

We shall not go into the details of these sordid business dealings. Are they not written in the books of the chronicles of Thayer? It will suffice here to give the summary in his third volume, for which Krehbiel, the American editor, accepted responsibility (p. 51 ff).

Careful readers of this biography can easily recall a number of lapses from high ideals of candour and justice in his treatment of his friends and of a nice sense of honour and honesty in his dealings with his publishers; but at no time have these blemishes been so numerous or so patent as they are in his negotiations for the publication of the *Missa Solemnis*—a circumstance which is thrown into a particularly strong light by the frequency and vehemence of his protestations of moral rectitude in the letters which have risen like ghosts to accuse him. . . . He was never louder in his protestations of business morality than when he was promising the mass to four or more publishers practically at the same time, and giving it to none of them; never more apparently frank than when he was making ignoble use of a gentleman, whom he himself described as one of the best friends on earth, as an intermediary between himself and another friend to whom he was bound by business ties and childhood associations which challenged confidence; never more obsequious (for even this word must now be used in describing his attitude towards Franz Brentano) than after he had secured a loan from that friend in the nature of an advance on a contract which he never carried out; never more apparently sincere than when he told one publisher (after he had promised the mass to another) that he should be particularly sorry if he were unable to give the mass into his hands; never more forcefully and indignantly honest in appearance than when he informed still another publisher that the second had importuned him for the mass ("bombarded" was the word), but that he had never even deigned to answer his letters. But even this is far from compassing the indictment; the counts are not even complete when it is added that in a letter he states that the publisher whom he had told it would have been a source of sorrow not to favour had never even been contemplated amongst those who might receive the mass; that he permitted the friend to whom he first promised the score to tie up some of his capital for a year and more so that "good Beethoven" should not have to wait a day for his money; that after promising the mass to the third publisher he sought to create the impression that it was not the *Missa Solemnis* that had been bargained for, but one of two masses which he had in hand.

With this should be compared Beethoven's statement in a letter to the publisher Peters, June 5, 1822:

I love straightness and uprightness and am of the opinion that one should not discredit the artist, for alas! it is unfortunately true that however brilliant the outer aspect of fame appears, it is not granted him to be the daily guest of Jupiter on Olympus; unfortunately, in spite of his resistance, common humanity drags him all too often from these pure ethereal heights.

In mitigation of sentence on Mr. Hyde it should be remembered that money was harder for Beethoven to come by at this time, that deafness, ill-health, and many cares and distractions made him peculiarly susceptible to dubious "practical" counsel; made him morbidly suspicious of those with whom he had business dealings; made him produce more slowly and laboriously just when he was engaged on his larger works, and that his desire to keep and lay by money for his beloved nephew had become an obstinate obsession.

An instance of how he rationalized this altruistic avarice occurs in a letter to Peters (July 26, 1822):

I must consider his [Karl's] future, as we are neither Indians nor Iroquois [*sic*] who, as is well known, leave everything to the *lieben Gott*.

Mr. Sullivan comes to the defense of Beethoven by arguing that, while the Master did not recognize the claims of "business morality," he had a higher code of his own.[2] It was the sort of "artistic morality" shown by his threatening to kick General Kyd downstairs for having offered him £100 if he would compose a symphony in his own earlier manner. No doubt such a case of æsthetic rectitude can cover a multitude of business sins; somewhat as the sportsmanship, sincerity, and freedom from cant that characterize the post-war generation more than compensate for its selfishness and bad manners. And in the main our hero's musical conscience was upright and exalted.

But Mr. Sullivan overlooks the fact that, most of the time, Beethoven honoured the claims of business morality to such an extent that he must have had at least a theoretical respect for them. And he must have blunted the teeth of remorse in a very human way. After his dishonest lapses towards the publishers he probably rationalized, as the rest of us do, by telling himself that all was fair in the struggle with these "hell-hounds." And he probably even persuaded himself that the London Philharmonic was legitimately to be treated like the publishers.

In lauding Beethoven's "artistic morality" Mr. Sullivan

[2]*Beethoven: His Spiritual Development*, p. 188 ff.

also forgets the sheer artistic immorality of such works as the *"Battle"* symphony, the *Polonaise* (Op. 89), and those shoddy overtures which he fobbed off upon the Philharmonic.

Mr. Sullivan roundly declares: "Whatever moral canons Beethoven violated he did not violate his own." But how then may we account for his continual reactions of sincere remorse, when, as so often happened, he realized that he had treated his friends shabbily?

No, such a whitewashing cannot entirely convince us. But the author, for one, is glad that Beethoven was no alabaster saint who scrupulously observed all his own moral canons. We should never have had such gloriously human music from a saint as we had from this Dr. Jekyll. And on hearing his greater pages the importance of Mr. Hyde dwindles almost to insignificance.

When all is said, no very strong case can be made out for the defense. Even the sympathetic Dr. Deiters, Thayer's German editor, after putting all the extenuating circumstances before the jury of posterity, felt himself bound to add:

We pay the tribute of our profoundest sympathy for Beethoven in these circumstances; we know sufficiently well the noble impulses of his soul in all other fields; we are aware of the reasons which compelled him to try anything which promised to better his conditions; but the conscientious reporter cannot ignore facts which lie notoriously before him, and, hard as it may be, cannot acquit Beethoven of the reproach that his conduct was not in harmony with the principles of strict justice and uprightness.

Perhaps none but those who have suffered the plight of total deafness can feel more sympathy than repugnance in following the business history of the *Missa*. There is nothing like ear trouble for curdling the milk of human kindness. It can easily persuade a victim that the universe is in league to deride and defraud him, and that almost anything the minority may do is justifiable in such a lopsided war.

In his keenness for money the man who had freed the composer from the patronage system—even while he himself was profiting therefrom—and established him on a professional basis went back on his excellent principles. He postponed publication of the *Missa* and obsequiously solicited private subscriptions for it, at 50 ducats each, from those potentates whom he was fond of describing as "the princely rabble" and worse.

Keats may have been right in saying that beauty is truth; but it does not follow that the creator of beauty is always truthful. The Master's letters to Zelter offering the *Missa* to the Berlin Singakademie show rather crude prevarications. They intimate that the Mass would never be published in the ordinary way; also that this whole composition, unthinkable without the orchestra, "could be almost performed entirely *a la capella* . . . and there is already a movement in it which is entirely *a la capella*."

February 8, 1823, the same day as his first letter on this subject to Zelter, Beethoven wrote Goethe bespeaking his influence towards having the court of Weimar subscribe, and stating that the Mass would not be published in the ordinary way "for the present." Now Goethe was a close friend of Zelter's and may have discovered the discrepancy between these two statements about publication. At any rate, he had never forgiven Beethoven for the trick played on him at Teplitz. We know that Goethe fell suddenly and seriously ill on February 17, 1823. But even after his recovery a month later he treated Beethoven's letter to the same silence which he had meted out six years before to an unknown lad of twenty. This lad was named Franz Schubert. He had sent the *Erlkönig*, in a book of other manuscript settings of Goethe's lyrics, with a bashful request to dedicate them to His Excellency.

By 1822 Anton Felix Schindler, who had first met Beethoven eight years before, had become firmly established as his private-secretary-without-salary. He was tall and lean, a figure of comedy when he laid down the law in his nasal voice and with the angular gestures of a semaphore.

Naturally he never laid down the law to Beethoven, but used to annoy him with all manner of inept questions such as: "Will you tell me, in a few words, how to become an orchestral conductor?"

"Do you imagine," was the exasperated reply, "that a conductor can be improvised?"[3]

No wonder he called his famulus an irksome "appendix."

In April, 1823, Czerny's pupil, Franz Liszt, a twelve-year-old boy, gave his first public concert. On Liszt's own authority the world has long believed that Beethoven came, heard, wept, rushed upon the stage, and publicly kissed

---

[3]*Kölnische Zeitung*, June 28, 1845.

him, uttering complimentary prophesies. But the records of the Conversation Books and of contemporaries strongly suggest that this story was fabricated. It is doubtful whether Beethoven attended the concert. Even if he had, he could not have heard one note. And mere dumb show would scarcely have stirred him to the point of making such an emotional scene in public.

That same year Beethoven furnished a vivid illustration of the poet's chief function, which is to reveal the significance of the seemingly insignificant—to show forth the beauty, not of holiness, but of the apparently ugly. He performed a conjuring feat which recalls how he founded an important figure in the *Credo* of his Mass in C upon the absurd fumblings of a village violoncellist.[4]

A Viennese publisher called Diabelli, having written a waltz of the most perfect insipidity, invited a large number of composers, among them Schubert and Beethoven, to collaborate by contributing one variation each for his volume. Schubert accepted. Beethoven growled that he never collaborated; besides, he didn't want to write a variation on a cobbler's patch (*Schusterfleck*). Then he looked at the foolish thing again, burst out into a great laugh, and straightway fell to composing. It may have tickled his sense of humour that the tune was so much like the *scherzo* of a trio in E flat which he had written at the age of fifteen and never published.[5]

---

[4]See p. 266, note 9.

[5]It is worth noting that when this work was published in 1830, Diabelli was one of three old friends of Beethoven's to sign a guarantee of its authenticity. Perhaps he had based his own tune upon its *scherzo*.

Enthusiasm waxed, and he sent word to the publisher offering to write a whole set himself. Diabelli was delighted and offered him 80 ducats for six or eight variations.

"All right," said Beethoven, in high good humour. "He shall have variations on his cobbler's patch!" He had them—thirty-three in all.

This astonishing piece is a monument to Beethoven's learning, his resourcefulness, his humour, his rhythmical genius, his cosmic breadth,[6] but not throughout to his inspiration. Herr Ernest says a true word.[7] We miss here the evidence of that *"schaffenstarke Passivität,"* that "might of creative passivity," which underlies his supreme work. One feels too that in writing these variations the deaf Master was Utopian and intended them for a theoretical virtuoso playing a theoretical piano. But he was only recoiling *pour mieux sauter.*

---

[6] "Those incredible Diabelli variations . . . the whole range of thought and feeling, yet all in organic relation to a ridiculous little waltz tune." (Huxley, *Point Counter Point,* 1928, p. 294.)

[7] *Beethoven,* p. 395.

Chapter XL

THE CHORAL SYMPHONY

Choral Symphony, Begun before 1817, Finished 1823 —
Long Incubation Period — 1818, Memorandum for Ninth
and Tenth Symphonies — Fusion of the Two Schemes —
Echoes — Initial Difficulty in Composing — The Program
Question — Beethoven's Three Most Original Contribu-
tions — First Movement — Scherzo — The Kettledrum
Joke — Origin of First Subject — Adagio-Andante —
Choral Finale — Skill in Selecting Words — Merits and
Defects of Hymn to Joy

FOR three decades Beethoven carried about in his head part
of the Ninth symphony. Such long preoccupation recalls
the half century during which Goethe brooded and toiled
over *Faust*.

As has been already noted, it was the Master's custom to
write his symphonies in pairs. In an 1818 Sketch Book he
scribbled, among studies for the *Hammerklavier* sonata,
the following memorandum:

Adagio cantique; sacred song in a symphony in an old mode
(We Praise Thee, O God—alleluia), either to stand alone, or
as introduction to a fugue. The whole second symphony to be
based, perhaps, on its melody. The singing voices to enter in
the last piece, or as early as the *Adagio*. Orchestra, violins, etc.,
to be increased tenfold in the last piece. Or the *Adagio* repeated
in a certain manner in the last piece, the singing voices being
then first introduced little by little. In the *Adagio* the text of

a Greek myth—*Cantique-Ecclesiastique*—in the *Allegro*, festival of Bacchus.

It appears that these two symphonies were to be called "The English" and "The German." They were to contrast the worship of the pagan gods with that of Jehovah. The second was to have a vocal termination in an old mode. The first was to have a *finale* commencing with a glorious sweeping tune which, as we shall see, met a different fate. And there was to be an anagram movement based on Bach's name—perhaps as a contrast to the "festival of Bacchus."

When these paired ideas fell into the active volcano of Beethoven's unconsciousness tremendous seethings, fusions, and eruptions took place. The two dream symphonies melted and ran into one. But the pagan gods and the Bach anagram were violently rejected. The old mode and the sweeping *finale* tune were shot forth for later use in the A minor quartet (Op. 132). Various reminiscences of early work flowed in to replace them. And the Ninth symphony began to take definite form.

There are more memories in this symphony than in even the "memory" sonata in A flat.[1] The Trio of the *scherzo*

Ex. 155

opens with a third-period version of the corresponding part of the Second symphony.[2] This was taken from the venerable church tune on which *Non nobis* was founded.

Ex. 156   WM. BYRD, C. 1590

Non   no - bis,   Do - mi - ne, non   no - bis

In the last eleven notes of its final theme, moreover,

Ex. 157

Cello & Viola *p*   *cres.*

the writer has chanced upon a smiling echo of the countryside atmosphere of an old English ballad, "My Man John,"[8]

Ex. 159

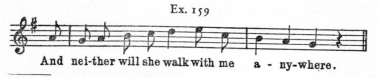

And nei-ther will she walk with me   a - ny-where.

---

[2] See the transposed Ex. 298, p. 584.

[8] The writer's friend Mr. Carl Engel contributes the suggestion that this echo may have been a by-product of Beethoven's recent study of British folk-songs, many of which he arranged. While Miss Marion Bauer points out that Humperdinck made charming use of the same tune in the Forest Scene of *Hänsel und Gretel:*

Ex. 158

Gretel (Sehr ruhig)

Ein Männ-lein steht im Wal-de ganz still und stumm,

which may conceivably have been inserted as a gracious gesture to the land Beethoven had long admired from afar and for whose leading orchestra he was about to write the following inscription on the manuscript copy of the symphony:

> GRAND SYMPHONY WRITTEN
> FOR THE PHILHARMONIC SOCIETY
> IN LONDON
> BY LUDWIG VAN BEETHOVEN

Here we are pleasantly reminded of that youthful Anglomania which he probably acquired by contagion from his early patron Prince Lichnowsky.

The august opening theme

Ex. 160

of the *Allegro ma non troppo* is the *Storm* theme from the *Pastoral* symphony (at bar 23), raised to the *n*th power.

Certain other memories appear to have been overlooked. The opening of the second subject of the *Allegro ma non troppo*

Ex. 161

is taken almost literally from bar 100 of the *Allegro ma non troppo* in this same *Pastoral*. (See Ex. 308, p. 587.)

Another reminiscence is more subtle and interesting than a direct quotation. The writer stumbled upon it through Sir George Grove's footnote statement:[3]

Dr. Charles Wood has pointed out to me that the bass of the first two bars [of the *Adagio's* first subject] is identical with that of the beginning of the slow movement in the *Sonate Pathétique* (Op. 13).

In studying Beethoven's sketches[4] for the movement with this hint in mind, it was noticeable that one of these sketches actually began in the treble with the first five notes of the *Adagio* of the *Pathétique*.

Ex. 162

&c.

(The reader must supply his own treble clef and pair of flats.)

[3] *Symphonies*, p. 362 n.
[4] Nottebohm, *Zweite Beethoveniana*, p. 177, 2d example.

Comparing the final version of the two tunes, one saw that not only was the bass identical for three bars, but even the treble coincided in the third. It became apparent that the *Pathétique* might contain one of those hidden melodies which Beethoven had so often mined out of the interior of existing ones. We have already seen how he performed this feat in the *Allegretto* of the Seventh symphony,[5] the recapitulation of the first movement of the Eighth symphony,[6] and elsewhere. When the key and time signature of the *Pathétique* phrase had been transposed to conform to those of the *Choral* phrase, the surmise was found correct. The two go together even more smoothly than Dvořak's *Humoresque* goes with *The Suwanee River*.

Ex. 163

Ex. 164

[5]See p. 308.
[6]See pp. 323–324.

Skeptics are urged to try the pair as a duet for two pianos.[7]

In composing the *Choral* symphony Beethoven left its slow movement until the last. It was as though he despaired of finding any *Adagio* subject worthy to follow that puissant *Allegro* and that incomparable *scherzo*. Illness and trouble were making his ideas come more deliberately.

"You see," he confessed to Rochlitz in 1822, "for some while past I have not been able to write easily. I sit and think, and think, and get it all settled; but it won't come on the paper, and a great work troubles me immensely at the outset; once get into it and it's all right." This strange new handicap of initial inertia may explain why opus 125 ventured to climb upon the back of opus 13 to get up a few measures' momentum.

Less concretely than in the examples just cited, the opening movement of the Ninth recalls two earlier symphonies. The brooding chaos of the first measures is a third-period version of that prettier, smaller Haydn-oratorio chaos of the introduction to the Fourth symphony; while the main part of the movement is a mature, almost superhuman re-creation of the emotion surging in the terrific conflict that starts the Fifth. Only we feel that the latter conflict is raging in the soul of one who has now risen to the stature of a supreme conqueror.

---

[7]After this had been written the following footnote came to light, on p. 148 of the Bülow and Lebert edition of the sonatas (Schirmer):

"To the best of our knowledge no one has yet remarked the striking affinity of the theme of this movement, even with reference to its external melodic structure, to that of the loftiest *Adagios* of grandest scope from the Master's last period;—we mean the *Adagio* of the Ninth symphony, written almost a quarter of a century later."

It is distressing to find such learned musicologists as Herr Bekker solemnly and elaborately deliberating on questions like: "Where did he [Beethoven] find subject matter for his new work [the Ninth]?"[8] All of the numerous poetic programs which have been written for the *Choral* symphony, including Richard Wagner's impassioned rhapsody, can have—thanks be!—no more than a subjective validity for those who conceived them. Otherwise music would be something pathetically less than the infinite art.

Strip the Ninth of arbitrary interpretations. Remember that using the old idea of the Schiller Joy tune as a *finale* was a questionable afterthought which Beethoven later disavowed. And all that is left as a common programmatic denominator is much the same emotional scheme which Beethoven had often before used—notably in such masterpieces as the *Egmont* and *Leonore* overtures, the E minor quartet, and the Fifth symphony. It is *per aspera ad astra*, through struggle to triumph, passing by way of mystery, naïve trust, humour, abandon, reassurance, consolation, religious ecstasy, love, etc.

Three parts of this symphony are first-magnitude examples of what we shall find[9] to have been Beethoven's three most original contributions to music: the opening movement of titanic struggle, the Dionysiac *scherzo*, "that huge spout of life,"[10] whirling the listener to undreamt regions of humour, abandon, and fantasy; and the visionary slow movement of mystic delight.

---

[8]*Beethoven*, p. 188.
[9]See pp. 499–500.
[10]In Mr. Lawrence Gilman's vivid phrase.

In the Ninth symphony these three are superbly represented and balanced. The opening subject of the first movement, founded on the D minor triad,

Ex. 160

is colossal, although it by no means bestrides the whole
mighty symphony, as some writers insist.[11]

This herculean main subject with the eerie twilight of
the starkly elemental introduction, the extraordinary richness of subsidiary matter, the sudden surprising gleams of
tenderness, the terrific passage with the long *tympani* roll
at the start of the recapitulation where "the Dark Tower
of Childe Roland's encounter looms before us out of the
swirling spiritual mists,"[12] the coda's dirge over a chromatic
basso ostinato that seems crushed beneath the weight of universal woe—all this would clearly constitute the strongest,
noblest page of Beethoven if it were not for the opening of
the C sharp minor quartet, the *Et vitam venturi* fugue in
the *Missa*, and the first half of the *Eroica*. Perhaps it is, in
any case.

Though the first movement is rivalled by that of the
Eroica, the *scherzo*

---

[11] See Paul Bekker, *Beethoven*, p. 193.
[12] To quote Mr. Gilman's interpretation again.

Ex. 165

stands absolutely unrivalled among *scherzos*, and but little below any other movement whatever. There is one curious matter-of-fact reason for the power the *Molto vivace* has over us. At the right tempo, each four-measure group of twelve notes constitutes, according to the psychologists, approximately the largest musical unit which the human mind can absorb as a single impression.

This masterpiece of variety in unity, this "miracle of repetition without monotony," as someone has called it, is made up to a large extent of the dotted three-note phrase with which it opens.

Ex. 166

Such economy of material is very unusual even for an arch-economist like Beethoven.

After the first repeat, where the rhythm changes from groups of four to groups of three bars, there is a piece of deliciously subtle humour: *Ritmo di tre battute* (Rhythm of three beats) is the elegant Italian stage direction. The rank bassoons waggishly lead off. Then the kettledrums, no longer able to contain themselves, start the three-bar group four times with a loud, self-important

Ex. 167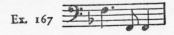

Mr. Grace writes charmingly about this passage:[18]

The drums, hollow of tone and slightly lacking in definition of pitch, change the humour from the polite to the broad. It is as if, impatient of their traditional rôle of mere rhythm-makers, and jealous of the busy bandying of the theme between other parts, the drums said, "Let us take a hand," promptly take it, and find themselves after all unable to improve on the feat with which they started in at the opening of the movement—i. e., the delivery of the first three notes of the theme.

The fifth time, however, they come in with total unexpectedness after *four* measures, but *diminuendo,* as though shaky in their minds.[14]

At the *première* of the Ninth symphony, the quick and creative Viennese listeners were so thrilled and excited by the humour of this passage that their applause quite interrupted the performance.

The three-note phrase underlying this movement is said to have come to Beethoven in a flash, as he went out of the dark into a dazzling light. And upon many a hearer it has a similar effect of abrupt nocturnal illumination. Then suddenly, with the Trio, he finds himself in the sweet and common daylight of an English countryside.

We have it on Czerny's authority, however, that the first subject of this *scherzo*—please look again at Example 165—occurred to the composer not in coming out of the dark but on hearing sparrows twittering in a garden. Assuming that

---

[18]*Beethoven,* p. 276.

[14]This proceeding, as Professor Donald Tovey points out, in his analysis of the Ninth, apparently reëstablishes the original four-bar grouping, though it really does nothing of the sort, because the fifth drum entry simply comes on the second bar of the three instead of on the first.

the deaf composer could have heard them, the sparrows may have had a voice in the nervousness of the hide-and-seek fugato part, and the garden itself in the rustic simplicities of the Trio.

The *Adagio-Andante* is one of the holiest, purest out-pourings of exaltation in the whole domain of mystical music. It is far more akin to the *Benedictus* of the *Missa* than to the *Adagio* of the *Pathétique*, where, as we have seen,[15] the first subject was found like a statue embedded in a block of translucent marble.

After two dozen measures we bring up against a double bar. Most unexpectedly the time signature changes to 3/4 *Andante moderato.* The key signature turns from B flat into D, and the second fiddles fervently intone a tune which Beethoven originally sketched to start this movement as an *Alla Menuetto*, then discarded, and finally brought back for a second subject, to the delight of nephew Karl, who scribbled in one of the Conversation Books, "I'm only glad that you've put in the beautiful *Andante*."

Herr Bekker cleverly suggests that "the two themes of the *Adagio* are comparable to the two female figures in Titian's well-known picture, 'Sacred and Profane Love.' "[16] This may have resulted from Beethoven's original idea of contrasting symphonies, one Christian, one pagan. For the Ninth, as we have seen, came from a fusion of both plans.

In this *Andante* subject Beethoven's sympathy for the downtrodden, and the democracy of the feelings he was

---

[15]See pp. 403–405.

[16]*Beethoven,* p. 185.

about to express concerning Joy, caused him to take compassion on those peons of the orchestra, the second violins,
and assign them one of the most luscious tidbits in the work.
It is touching to hear with what a fevour of gratitude and
enthusiasm these poor fellows fall upon the tune—an enthusiasm which even the most magnetic or savage conductor
can scarcely restrain within the bounds of anything like the
piano enjoined by Beethoven.

This movement is kind to another sort of player as well.
The short, poignant dirge in D flat (bars 133–136)

Ex. 168

has for a century served as a fountainhead of inspiration to improvising church organists.

Beethoven's own description of opus 125 as "Symphony with Final Chorus on Schiller's ode 'To Joy,'" shows that he himself regarded the last movement as an addendum to the first three. Let us say at once all we can in its favour.

Less than half of Schiller's elaborate drinking song was used here. For Beethoven realized that some of the rejected stanzas lapsed into a sophomoric audacity which came rather close to the sacrilegious. For example

> *Lasst den Schaum zum Himmel spritzen!*
> *Dieses Glas dem guten Geist!*

> (Let the foam to Heaven go spurting!
> Lift this glass to the Good Spirit!)

which is as who should say: "*Prosit*, God!"

The composer's skill in selecting the right words to form a whole of far greater dignity than the original poem would have done credit to a poet of no mean power. Feats like this, and scores of remarkable passages in his letters, suggest that his literary ability has been underestimated. In one sense Debussy was mistaken when he wrote "Beethoven was not literary for two sous."[17]

There are two superlatively great things about the choral *finale*: the Joy theme itself,

---

[17]Quoted in J. de Marliave, *Les Quatuors de Beethoven*, 1925, xv.

Ex. 169

and the second intermediate theme of this huge cantata-rondo, beginning at the 595th bar, *Andante Maestoso,* through the *Adagio ma non troppo, ma divoto.*

Here Beethoven's studies in the Gregorian chant[18] bore more fruit than in all of the *Missa* to prepare for which he looked through the "church-chorals of the monks."

Those who have followed the long and painful evolution of the Joy theme through the Sketch Books, may more fully appreciate the force of Richard Wagner's remark:

Beethoven has emancipated this melody from all influences of fashion and variations of taste, and has raised it into a type of pure and lasting humanity.

It has the simple force, the limpid beauty, the generic quality of the greatest folk music. The tune haunted the

[18]See p. 381.

imaginations of those on whom Beethoven's mantle fell.[19]

The *Andante Maestoso—Adagio* section of the *finale*, just mentioned, has need of all the noble qualities it can muster. For it follows a sort of fife and drum corps march of an offensive triviality somewhat reminiscent of the *"Battle"* symphony. By the time this is reached Beethoven has been such a ruthless "tyrant over all the vocal organs" that the wretched sopranos have most of them stopped singing to begin screeching. And not long after this the work expires in a *prestissimo* amid the lamentable howls of these now agonized females, and what Mr. Ernest Walker has computed to be "one hundred and twenty-seven rapid bangs on the big drum and cymbals."[20]

The reliable Czerny told Jahn that, after the first per-

---

[19]Schubert put something very like it into his last symphony (C major),

Ex. 170

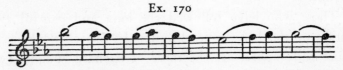

and Brahms let its accents be heard in the *finale* of that C minor symphony, which Von Bülow honoured by naming "The Tenth."

Ex. 171

At one of the early rehearsals of this symphony a certain nobleman ventured to call Brahms's attention to the resemblance. The exasperated composer ran true to his notoriously ungracious form. *"Das hört jeder Esel!"* ("Every donkey can hear that!") he growled.

[20]*Beethoven*, p. 56.

formance, Beethoven emphatically declared he was dissatisfied with the *Hymn to Joy* and wished to write another movement without vocal parts, to take the place of this failure. In the present writer's experience only two conductors have given the *Choral finale* so supremely as to make him cease for the moment to agree with its composer's severe verdict. But Signor Toscanini and Mr. Stokowski are men so creative that they can ennoble the tinsel tawdriness of *Ein Heldenleben.* They are such invincible bull operators that they can even send the watered stock of *Pini di Roma* soaring.

Such artists are unsettling to the equipoise of the critic But on both occasions, when the excitement of their magic had subsided, the writer reverted to his former conviction. Theoretically it was an inspired idea to reinforce the orchestra with the most natural, popular, and directly human of all instruments, the voice. And the experiment might have worked out with brilliant success if the hearers of that time had been prepared to accept what is gaining ground to-day —the voice as an orchestral instrument, used without dragging in the irrelevant and maltreated art of poetry whenever a singer opens his mouth.

The fatal mistake of the *Choral finale* was the mixture of poetry, the concrete and finite, with music, the abstract and infinite. Schiller's drinking song *de luxe* pulled the music down from the cloud-capped eminence of the first three movements to a humiliating materialistic basis. It imposed upon an art that should be all things to all men a belittling concreteness.

Chapter XLI

HE EMBRACES THE AMATEURS

February, 1824, an Address to Beethoven — His Indecision — Conspiracy of Friends — Announcement of Concert — Rehearsal — Concert May 7, 1824 — Deaf to Applause — A Financial Failure — Accuses Supper Guests of Dishonesty — Breaks Faith with London Philharmonic — Word Portrait by Rochlitz

FOR some years now the wild popularity of Rossini had elbowed Beethoven somewhat into the background—though not so far as the vociferous complaints, fed by his mania of persecution, would have led people to suppose. The great public had begun to cool a little. His old friends, however, were still faithful. When they heard that the Ninth symphony was finished the Lichnowskys, Graf von Fries, Zmeskall, and more than two dozen others sent him a charming round robin, begging him reverentially to let the *Missa* and the Ninth symphony be heard. Here are a few of the less flowery lines.

Shall we tell you with what deep regret we have felt your retirement? Do you need our assurance that, as all eyes turned hopefully towards you, all noticed with sorrow that the man whom we must name as the living mortal most eminent in his own sphere, silently looked on while foreign art pitched its camp on German soil, in the German muse's place of honour? . . . You alone can assure to the efforts of the best among us, a decisive victory. From you the art-union of the Fatherland and the German opera await a fresh blooming, restored youth, and a new mastery of the true and the beautiful over the force which would subordinate to the fashion-spirit of the day even the eternal laws of art. Give us the hope of soon seeing fulfilled the wishes of all those who have ever been reached by the strains of your harmonies.

The composer was pleased. "That is really very beautiful!" he cried in a loud voice. "That gives me pleasure!"

He resolved to give an "Academy." But of late indecision had grown on him. It seemed that he simply could not fix on what he wanted and stick to it. So three of his friends formed a benign conspiracy. As if by accident they met at Beethoven's house and tried to wheedle him into signing a definite plan for the concert.

The suspicious genius saw through them, however, as swiftly as he had discovered the hidden tune in Mozart's theme. Before sunset he dispatched three summary notes:

To the COUNT LICHNOWSKY: I loathe treachery. Visit me no more. Academy is off. BEETHOVEN.

To MR. SCHUPPANZIGH: Let him visit me no more. I give no Academy. BEETHOVEN.

To SCHINDLER: I request you to come no more until I send for you. Academy is off. B——N.

But this was only a passing squall. Successful negotiations were soon resumed. The formal announcement of the concert read as follows:

GRAND
MUSICAL CONCERT
by
MR. L. VAN BEETHOVEN

which will take place
To-morrow, May 7, 1824

in the R. I. Court Theatre beside the Kärnthnerthor.

The musical pieces to be performed are the latest works of Mr. Ludwig van Beethoven.

First: A Grand Overture.

Second: Three Grand Hymns with Solo and Chorus Voices.

Third: A Grand Symphony with Solo and Chorus Voices entering in the finale on Schiller's Ode to Joy.

The solos will be performed by the Demoiselles Sonntag and Unger and the Messrs. Haizinger and Seipelt. Mr. Schuppanzigh has undertaken the direction of the orchestra, Mr. Chapelmaster Umlauf the direction of the whole and the Music Society the augmentation of the chorus and orchestra as a favour.

Mr. Ludwig van Beethoven will himself participate in the general direction.

Prices of Admission as usual.

Beginning at 7 o'clock in the evening.

The Overture was *The Consecration of the House* (Op. 124). The three "hymns" were the *Kyrie, Credo,* and *Agnus Dei* of the *Missa Solemnis*.

On May 6th the last rehearsal took place in the Kärnthnerthor Theatre. The orchestra was filled with famous players like Böhm and Mayseder. At the *Kyrie,* as an eyewitness reports, Beethoven was "quite dissolved in devotion and emotion." After the symphony he "stationed himself at the door and embraced all the amateurs who had taken part"— a proceeding more in the spirit of Schiller's

> *Seid umschlungen Millionen!*
> *Diesen Kuss der ganzen Welt!*
>
> (O you millions, I embrace you!
> Here's a kiss for all the world!)

than was the lamentable private scene which was to occur late the following evening.

The house was packed for the concert. The public bestowed upon Beethoven so much more applause than was usually given even the Imperial family that the commissioner of police angrily yelled: "Silence!"

Let us hope [Mr. Lawrence Gilman pithily remarks] that the memory of this incident brought some consolation to Beethoven two and a half years later, when the King of Prussia palmed off on him a near-diamond ring in return for the Ninth symphony.

There had been but two rehearsals, the third having been omitted in favour of a ballet! Naturally the performance left much to be desired. But Beethoven heard neither its defects nor its beauties. He stood in the centre of the orchestra with his back to the audience, following the proceedings in the score. The word "following" must be taken literally. For a lady named Grebner who, at the age of seventeen, sang in that historic chorus told Herr Felix Weingartner three quarters of a century later, that although Beethoven "appeared to follow the score with his eyes, at the end of each movement he turned several pages together."

The pianist Thalberg, another eyewitness, informed Thayer that the choir and orchestra were directed to watch Beethoven but to pay not the slightest attention to his beating of the time.

Tumultuous applause broke out after the *scherzo*. But Beethoven stood utterly deaf to it, fumbling with his score. Then one of the singers, Fräulein Unger, pulled his sleeve and pointed to the rapturous audience. When he turned and bowed there were few dry eyes in the house.

After the expansion and exaltation of this concert there was an equal and opposite reaction. The box office had taken in 2,200 florins. But after deducting the cost of copying and administration less than 420 florins were left. Beethoven boiled over. He had invited Schuppanzigh, Schindler, and Umlauf, the conductor of the concert, to supper with him at a restaurant with the ominously prophetic name At the Sign of the Wild Man. He had ordered what Schindler called an "opulent" meal. But the company had no sooner sat down at table than Mr. Hyde, harpy that he was, spoiled it all. He poured out a flood of what he had once described as "hearty, free words." In downright terms he accused Schindler and the management of having swindled him.

In vain Umlauf and "Milord Falstaff" sought to point out that all the receipts and expenditures had been checked by the two theatre cashiers and by nephew Karl; that, contrary to custom, the latter had been allowed to act as comptroller. But far from listening to them, the composer of

Seid umschlungen Millionen!

only grew more and more hearty and free.

Finally even the meekness of Schindler could stand no more. Gathering his few poor shreds of dignity about him, and seizing Umlauf's arm, he rushed from the room.

Schuppanzigh [remarks Thayer] remained behind just long enough to get a few stripes on his broad back and then joined his companions in misery. Together they finished their meal at a restaurant in the Leopoldstadt.

Before we turn to the last and most exalted chapter of Beethoven's career we must record one more shabby Hydean trick. For the sum of £50, Beethoven had contracted to write the Ninth symphony for the London Philharmonic Society. He had agreed to give that body exclusive possession of it during eighteen months. At the end of this period the property rights in it would revert to the composer.

The money was paid in December, 1822, soon after the offer had been accepted. Beethoven delivered the manuscript late in April, 1824. On the 7th of the following month he broke faith by having the symphony performed in Vienna.

And adding insult to injury he dedicated the work—to the King of Prussia.

This unpleasant chapter cannot close, however, without a word about Dr. Jekyll. Not long before these events Friedrich Rochlitz wrote:

> He will give his last thaler to a man who has grievously injured him an hour before, and whom he has most violently declaimed against. . . . Once he gets up momentum, witticisms of rough power, droll inspirations, surprising, exciting combinations and paradoxes constantly occur to him. Therefore I say, in dead earnest: he gives you a lovable impression. . . . The dusky unlicked bear has such a trustful and true-spirited way with him, he growls too and shakes his tuftlets of hair so harmlessly and curiously, that even if he were indeed nothing but such a bear and had accomplished none of the things he has, one must needs rejoice in him and take to him.

Chapter XLII

THE CREATIVE LISTENER AND THE LAST QUARTETS

Project of English Trip Revived, 1824 — And Wrecked — Prince Galitzin Orders String Quartets — Preparation Necessary for Hearing Last Quartets — Alpine Blossoms of Experience — Anticipations of Man's Evolution — The Ineffable Residue of Reality — Our Debt to His Deafness — "Ditties of No Tone" — The String Quartet a Fit Vehicle — Invents New Forms — Aids for the Listener — How to Approach This Music

LATE in 1824, the project of the trip to England again came up. The London Philharmonic Society made Beethoven another generous offer. But after haggling with them for £100 more, which they refused, he raised so many difficulties as to wreck this project. This was bad for Beethoven's purse. But we are probably the gainers. If he had gone to London the last five quartets might never have been written.

A century ago wealthy Russian amateurs of music were doing as much for their art as M. Koussevitzky is doing to-day. When, in 1806, Beethoven had begun longing to write again in this form, Count Rasoumowsky had earned the enduring gratitude of all quartet lovers by ordering opus 59. Toward the end of 1822 Prince Galitzin, another Russian enthusiast, chose an equally happy moment. He ordered "two or three string quartets." This commission was heartily welcomed. Beethoven was weary of his long struggle with the text of the *Missa* and desirous of returning to his own field of absolute music—that art which escapes the profanation of concrete programs.

For the experience of hearing the last five quartets the listener should be prepared at least as carefully and seriously as a schoolboy for the university, or a freemason for initiation into the higher degrees, or a child for confirmation. Indeed, more carefully and seriously. For these quartets give a glimpse of an evolutionary stage not yet attained by many human spirits. They reveal the Alpine blossom of experience growing farther above the workaday levels of normal Twentieth Century humanity than most visions of the average scholar or freemason or churchman.

"Behold, I show unto you a mystery!" says the Master. He does not proceed to enunciate an enigmatic intellectual proposition such as "We shall not all die." Rather he sets beating within us the heart of the mystery itself. He actually exhibits to us the incorruptibility of this corruption. He shows forth the mortal in the very act of putting on immortality, and the will of the superman, by a supreme rite of renunciation and resignation, drawing the very sting of death itself.

In treating of the experiences communicated by these quartets, Mr. Sullivan writes:

The great artist achieves a relative immortality because the experiences he deals with are as fundamental for humanity as are hunger, sex, and the succession of day and night. It does not follow that the experiences he communicates are elementary. They may belong to an order of consciousness that very few men have attained but, in that case, they must be in the line of human development; we must feel them as prophetic. Beethoven's late music communicates experiences that very few people can normally possess. But we value these experiences because we feel they are not freakish. They correspond to a spiritual synthesis which the race has not achieved but which, we may suppose, it is on the way to achieving. It is only the very greatest kind of artist who presents us with experiences that we recognize both as fundamental and as in advance of anything we have hitherto known.[1]

It is of Beethoven in this last rarefied phase that the writer always thinks in reading a superb page of Marcel Proust:[2]

There is a unique accent to which those great singers who are the original musicians elevate themselves, to which they return despite themselves, and which is a proof of the irreducibly individual existence of the soul. . . . Every artist seems thus the citizen of an unknown fatherland, forgotten by himself, different from that land whence comes, equipped for earth, another great artist. . . . This lost fatherland the musicians do not recall. But each of them remains forever unconsciously tuned in a certain unison with it; he is delirious with joy when he sings in accordance with his fatherland.

Proust goes on to say that this song is composed of all that

residue of reality which we are obliged to keep to ourselves, which words may not even transmit from friend to friend, from master to disciple, from lover to mistress, this ineffable something which qualitatively differentiates that which each has felt

---

[1]"*Beethoven: His Spiritual Development*," p. 250.

[2] "*La Prisonnière*, Vol. II, p. 73, in that great modern epic, *A la Recherche du Temps Perdu*.

and which he is obliged to leave on the threshold of phrases in which he may not communicate with another, except in limiting himself to exterior points common to all and without interest.

Then the great artist appears,

exteriorizing in the colours of the spectrum the intimate composition of these worlds which we call individuals and which, without the aid of art, we never would come to know. Wings, another respiratory apparatus which would allow us to traverse immensity, would be of no service to us. For if we went to Mars and to Venus still keeping the same senses, they would invest themselves for us with the same aspect as all this which we are able to perceive of Earth. The only veritable voyage, the sole true fountain of youth, would be not to seek new landscapes, but to have other eyes, to look upon the universe with the eyes of another, of an hundred others, to see the hundred universes which each of them sees, which each of them is; and this we may do with [great artists]; with beings like them we truly fly from star to star.

Some such experience of extra-terrestial grandeur awaits the music lover who can acquire ears and brains attuned to appreciate the last quartets of Beethoven. In them the Master attained such other-worldly altitudes that, in connection with this *finale* of his career, one might appropriately reverse the title of Strauss's famous tone-poem, and speak of Beethoven's *"Verklärung und Tod"*—his transfiguration and death. No pin-prick thoughts of his irritability, his avarice, his dishonesty can count for a moment in the atmosphere of the *adagios* of the E flat, the A minor, and the B flat quartets and the fugue which opens the C sharp minor.

We are eternal debtors to his deafness. It is doubtful if such lofty music could have been created except as self-compensation for some such affliction, and in the utter isolation which that affliction brought about. Perhaps that very deafness acted as a sort of protection against the too dazzling intensities of the mystic revelation. It may be that his shrouded hearing was like the veiled vision of him who was warned that he might not "see God and live." At times these quartets seem to have the celestial quality of

The light that never was, on sea or land.

Only three years before they were begun, another great artist, in a distant land, sickening like Beethoven for his deathbed, wrote some lines[8] strangely applicable to this last and supreme work of his loftiest contemporary:

Heard melodies are sweet, but those unheard
   Are sweeter; therefore, ye soft pipes, play on:
Not to the sensual ear, but, more endear'd
   Pipe to the spirit ditties of no tone.

When one has entered into intimacy with them, these last "ditties"—the quartets that were of "no tone" to the Master's poor outer ear, gradually become "more endear'd" than any other mortal music.

Nothing could have been a fitter vehicle for Beethoven's swan song than the string quartet—the most perfect means for conveying absolute music yet discovered. It is made up of instruments strongly individual yet capable of merging

---

[8]John Keats, "Ode on a Grecian Urn."

their personalities into one. These instruments are almost uniquely equipped for pure intonation. They interpose less mechanism between hand and ear than the piano. They form an organism far more intimate and pliable than the orchestra—a perfect medium for the high subjectivity and the rich and independent polyphony of these last utterances.

The old quartet form did not suffice for the intense personalism of this music. So Beethoven invented new forms. In these the tempo changed more often and more capriciously than ever.[4] The usual four movements grew to five—six—and even seven, as if in memory of the rococo *divertimento* and Suite. There was less strictness in the sonata-form movements. Their modelling was not so formally pronounced. The second subject sometimes burst in unprepared. The development grew shorter and more polyphonically intensive (e. g., in the first movement of the B flat quartet). The most astonishing contrasts of naïve folk tunes with the music of philosophical reverie were forged into a whole by sheer sorcery. The voice-leading became wonderfully free and daring. In these quartets there are no neutral passages where the hearer may nod and recover. Every moment he must give all he has; for each note is packed with significance.

The only way to make these quartets one's own is by repeated hearings and much detailed study with score in hand. The excellent phonograph records of them now

---

[4]Not counting *ritardandos*, the quartets of the first and second periods usually change tempo about four times, reaching ten times in the Sixth Lobkowitz and the "*Harp.*" But of the three greatest quartets of the last period the A minor (Op. 132) changes tempo twenty times; the B flat (Op. 130) twenty-one times; and the C sharp minor (Op. 131) no less than thirty-one times.

available[5] are godsends. They are powerful aids in speeding up the processes of comprehension.[6]

But a still more powerful aid is a knowledge of how to draw near them. They should be approached in the humble spirit which Mr. Havelock Ellis advocates as necessary for the comprehension of graphic art.

Schopenhauer long ago pointed out that a picture should be looked at as a royal person is approached, in silence, until the moment it pleases to speak to you. For if you speak first (and how many critics one knows who "speak first"!) you expose yourself to hear nothing but the sound of your own voice. In other words, it is a spontaneous and mystical experience.[7]

---

[5] See Appendix, p. 623.

[6] Readers will find much of help and interest in certain books of detailed analysis: Theodor Helm, *Beethoven's Streichquartette*, 3d ed., 1921 (Leipzig: Siegel); Hugo Riemann, *Beethoven's Streichquartette*, Meisterführer No. 12 (Berlin: Schlesinger); Joseph de Marliave, *Les Quatuors de Beethoven*, 1925 (Paris: Felix Alcan) (English translation, 1928).

[7] *The Dance of Life*, 1923, p. 329.

Chapter XLIII

"LA GAIETE"

LIKE all the last five the E flat quartet (Op. 127) has a
superb emotional unity. The words *"La gaieté,"* scribbled
in the Master's hand, were found in a sketch of its slow
movement. These words might be taken to indicate the mellow, serene happiness of a man who has come out on the
other side of catastrophe to find that he has thereby secured
the most precious of all gifts—a creativeness approaching
the divine. Understood in this deeper sense, *"La gaieté"* may
well be the motto of this ripe work.

This quartet often seems festooned with the gold and
scarlet foliage, and pungently sweet with the bursting
grapes, of autumn. The somewhat crabbed *scherzo* serves as
a dun background to heighten the autumnal glow, like a
premonition of arctic rigours in that

Season of mists and mellow fruitfulness.

It is curious to see how Beethoven's thoughts recurred
to the *Sonate Pathétique* (Op. 13), not only in the *Choral*

symphony[1] and the quartet before it,[2] but also in this subsequent E flat quartet. Like the *Pathétique, La gaieté* has a short slow beginning which is thematically an integral portion of the first movement and comes back twice before its close.

The *Adagio, ma non troppo e molto cantabile* is the supreme part of the quartet and constitutes one of the most lusciously satisfying sets of variations in music.[3] It is natural that echoes of the *Missa Solemnis* should ring through this *Adagio.* For Beethoven worked on both compositions together. Here is a bit of the *Benedictus:*

Ex. 172

which is closely akin to the end of the delicious eighteen-measure theme of the variations.

Ex. 173

---

[1] See pp. 403–405.

[2] See pp. 567–569.

[3] Schumann was obviously inspired by it in the Variations of his string quartet in F major.

To the author's mind there is a certain resemblance between part of the first subject of the first *Allegro*

Ex. 174

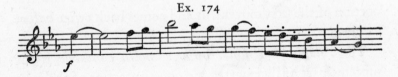

and the jolly second subject of the *finale*

Ex. 175

The opening subject of this *finale*[4] has five notes as the fecund germ of its first part:

Ex. 176

which makes, almost note for note, the same melodic outline as the first five notes (C–F–D–B flat–E flat) of the opening *Allegro*.[5]

The subject continues in dauntless fashion.[6] ➡

Ex. 177

[4]See the transposed Ex. 344, p. 598.
[5]See the transposed Ex. 341, p. 597.

At the start of the *finale's* coda there is a passage through which Beethoven's impishness grimaces. He changed from *Alla Breve* to 6/8 time. But for three measures he managed, by means of trills and confusing triplets, to keep the hearer wildly guessing as to what on earth was happening rhythmically. One imagines the grin of *Schadenfreude* with which the Master conceived this strictly musical prank.

In bringing out the E flat quartet early in 1825 Beethoven was guilty of a pair of shabby tricks. At nearly the same time he promised the first performance both to Linke, the violoncellist of the Schuppanzigh Quartet, and to Schuppanzigh himself. At length "Milord" succeeded in securing it. But he made a mess of the first performance.

In a rage Beethoven showered reproaches upon his poor fat friend and replaced him with a better fiddler named Boehm. He himself attended the rehearsals; and though incapable of hearing a note he watched the bows and fingers so acutely as to be of great help to the players.

At the second performance *"La gaieté"* was given twice, and with such success that various publishers began a brisk

---

[6]Perhaps Brahms, when he began the slow movement of his G minor piano quartet (Op. 25) with the first four notes of Ex. 177, in the same key, and then used the first four notes of Ex. 176 to begin the second half of the great theme—

Ex. 178

Andante con molto

poco f espress.

—recognized this intrepid quality of his original, for he never penned a braver tune.

competition for it. Naturally "Milord's" nose was out of joint. The Conversation Books of those days show entries like:

Schuppanzigh is very angry at Boehm and the others.

. . . . .

Schuppanzigh said he wouldn't have believed you would have done such a thing to him.

It was long before "Milord" forgave the affront.

About this time Carl Holz, the quartet's second violinist, began to supplant Schindler as Beethoven's factotum. He was young, intelligent, charming, had a lively sense of humour, and did the Master good by amusing him and taking him out a little into the world.

He had compassion for the composer's domestic troubles and was alert and clever in helping him out of them.

Beethoven [he wrote with characteristic wit] is an eagle who flies toward the zenith. Attached to his feet, not to his wings, is a cord that hangs to earth. It is firmly held by his housekeeper. Sometimes he abruptly tears himself loose and renews his flight toward the heavens. But if he thinks of earth and fain would stoop toward it, he lets the cord drop. Then she seizes and holds it fast.

Schindler hated Holz as only a bore can hate a wit who has elbowed him out of a privileged position. He called him Mephistopheles. And in the end he triumphed over him. For, shortly before the Master's death, Holz was preoccupied by his marriage and Schindler was again needed. But not before Beethoven had appointed Holz his official biographer. Unfortunately Mephistopheles never took advantage of this authorization. He might have made the first important Beethoven biography a more trustworthy and readable affair than Schindler did.

"Milord" was not the only one in those days to be singed by the blasts of Beethoven's temperament. Wolanek, his Bohemian copyist, endured so many insults that he finally ventured a politely ironic missive in defense of his remaining rags of manhood. He was inclined to overlook Beethoven's conduct with a smile. He wrote:

In the ideal world of tone there reign so many dissonances; why not as well in the world of reality? One firm conviction alone comforts me: that if you had been copyist to those celebrated artists Mozart and Haydn you would have shared a like fate. I only beg you not to confuse me with those wretches of copyists who are glad to be treated as slaves just for a bare existence.

In reply nothing would do but to make the worm who dared to turn feel one hundred per cent. incompetent and contemptible. On every available inch of this remonstrance the Master gave vent to his "hearty, free" fancy in the following endorsements, which may still be studied in the museum at Bonn:

"Stupid fellow, conceited asinine fellow!" he scrawled across the writing, in letters two inches high. Then on the lower margin: "Pay compliments to such a ragamuffin who steals one's money?—better to pull his donkey-ears!"

And on the blank reverse page:

BOTCHING–SCRIBBLER!

STUPID FELLOW!

Yesterday and even before then, it was decided not to have you write any more for me.

Correct the blunders your own ignorance, insolence, conceit and stupidity have perpetrated. This would be more fitting than wishing to teach me, for that is exactly as if a SOW should attempt giving lessons to MINERVA.

BEETHOVEN.

Do YOU do Mozart & Haidn the honour of not taking their names into your mouth.

One cannot help feeling that the poor copyist came out of this encounter first-best by a safe margin.

But let us cheerfully accept the bitter parts of Beethoven with the sweet, recognizing that they were all necessary ingredients of this particular genius. Let us be as large minded as Clara Schumann was about the bearishness of her friend Brahms.

She was always ready to pay the price which the creative artist has a right to ask of the world, as an inconsiderable token of thanks for his gifts, namely: consideration in his hours of creation.[7]

We do not expect a woman in travail to pay close attention to the precepts of the book of etiquette. And men like Brahms and Beethoven were constantly in travail.

When we are repelled by the Master's churlishness, his dishonesty, his priggishness, or any of his other disturbing

[7]Eugenie Schumann, *Errinnerungen*, 1925, p. 247.

traits, let us remember that, as Lord Macaulay remarked about Clive, exceptional men must not be judged by ordinary standards. And let us read again, as a possible antidote for ethical provinciality, these tender, wise, and comprehending words by Reichardt:

It often grieves me to the bottom of my heart when I see this thoroughly good, excellent man gloomy and suffering, although I am convinced, on the other hand, that his most original works can only be created in such peevish, bad-tempered moods. People who are able to enjoy his works should never lose sight of this, and refuse to take offence at any of his outer peculiarities. Otherwise they can never in reality be his true admirers.[8]

---

[8]Leitzmann, Vol. I, p. 103.

Chapter XLIV

THE A MINOR QUARTET

Illness — 1825, Second Galitzin Quartet, A Minor —
Mottos of Slow Movement — Programs — Echo of Arioso
Dolente — Defect of First Movement — Economy in
Allegro ma non Tanto — Harmonic Syncopation — High
Lights

IN APRIL and May, 1825, Beethoven was ill. Inflammation
of the bowels threatened. Nevertheless, he kept hard at the
A minor quartet. This was written second of the last five,
though by mistake it was numbered opus 132. Over the
Molto adagio beginning of the slow movement

Ex. 179

he wrote: "*Heiliger Dankgesang eines Genesenen an die*
Gottheit, in der Lydischen Tonart" (Holy song of thanksgiving to the Godhead, by one recovered from sickness, in
the Lydian mode) ;[1] and over the first *Andante* interlude:
"*Neue Kraft fühlend*" (Feeling new strength).

From this hint it has been easy for the tag makers to
turn the whole quartet into a circumstantial account of
Beethoven's sickness and recovery. According to them the

---

[1]His use here of the Lydian (consisting of the F major scale with B natural) foreshadowed that freer use of the old church modes which has more recently been
stimulated by the influence of Moussorgsky.

first movement shows the illness at its height; the *scherzo,* an exceptionally good day; the *Adagio,* recovery; the March, misgivings and a struggle to keep up appearances; the body of the *finale,* relapse; and its coda, complete rehabilitation.

Readers of *Point Counter Point* will recall that this *Dankgesang* movement was invoked by Spandrell, the murderer and suicide, in order to demonstrate to the toughminded Rampion the existence of God. And Spandrell was as dogmatic about it as Lenz was about the thirty-two dagger thrusts in the *Eroica,* or Herr Emil Ludwig about the festivals and ceremonies in the Seventh.

Ex. 180

Ex. 181

Happily, the literalists cannot spoil such music for all people all the time. To the million who come to the A minor unprejudiced by programs it will convey a million different meanings. And each of these meanings, by the grace of music's infinitude, will be as authentic as Beethoven's fancy mottos for his slow movement were to him when he set them down.

It must be said, however, for the programmatists, that they have derived another hint about the pathological character of the *allegro* from the resemblance of its first tune (Ex. 180) to the *Arioso dolente* of the A flat sonata (Ex. 181)—that memory sonata which, like "the quality of mercy," is blest both in giving and taking. But it is hard to agree that the first movement's emotional tone is as despairing as most of the commentators feel it. The second subject has too much of the joy of creation for despair. But this movement has the same defect as the corresponding portion of the C minor quartet (Op. 18, No. 4)—insufficient contrast between the contours of the first and second subjects.[2] They are too consanguineous with one another and with the main tune of the *finale*.

The *Allegro ma non tanto* is a sort of *scherzo*, chastened by a strong strain of minuet blood on the mother's side. It might appropriately have been christened *Scherzo ma non tanto*. Even for this most thematically economical of all

___

[2] See Ex. 346, p. 599, Ex. 15, p. 68, and Ex. 12, p. 57.

musicians it represents a triumph of economy. Its main portion is built entirely out of a phrase of three notes:

Ex. 182

and another of six:

Ex. 183

In the Trio of this movement Beethoven invented a novelty which was destined to appeal to such lovers of contradiction as Brahms. We have already noticed the whimsical way in which the Master would sometimes displace a phrase out of its natural bar frame, as in the prophetically jazzian *scherzo* of the B flat quartet (Op. 18, No. 6) and the *scherzo-finale* of the G major piano sonata (Op. 14, No. 2). This invention he combined here with another precursor of jazz: harmonic syncopation. The harmony shifts on the unaccented part of the measure a beat before the ear expects the change.

Ex. 184

The most memorable parts of this quartet are the mystic ecstasy of the last *molto adagio* portion of the Song of

Thanksgiving, the forlorn gaiety of the little *Alla marcia*, and the glorious *presto* coda of the *finale*, where the tragic main tune turns minor to major in the spirit of Moody's poem—

> Of loss and doubt and dread
>   And swift, oncoming doom
> I made a helmet for my head
>   And a floating plume.

Chapter XLV

LESS LACK OF FANCY

1825, Word Portrait by Rellstab — Beethoven Complains
of Neglect — Relations with Nephew — Loneliness —
Premonitions of Death — Karl Runs Away — 1825, Third
Galitzin Quartet, B flat — "Quartetto Scherzoso" — Bee-
thoven's "Leibquartett" — Cavatina Cost Him Tears —
Modesty — Contrapuntal Miracles in First Movement —
Influences Wagner — Fairy Music in Andante con moto *—*
The Great Fugue — Writes a New Finale

As BEETHOVEN was preparing in 1825 for a plunge into the
B flat quartet (Op. 130)—the third of the Galitzin series—
he was visited by Ludwig Rellstab, the man who had first
called opus 27, No. 2 the *"Moonlight* sonata." This Berlin
author left an interesting vignette of the man, expressed in
the lush Biedermeyer manner of the period. After remark-
ing the kindly mouth, the jaundiced tone of the complexion,
and the small but eloquent eyes, he went on:

I read on his countenance melancholy, suffering goodness; but
not one hard trait, not one sign of the mighty boldness which
characterizes the rhythms of his spirit could, even in passing, be
noticed.

In spite of all I have said, however, he lacked nothing of that
mysterious magnetic force by which the outward appearance of
great men enthralls us. For the suffering, the dumb burden of
pain which showed forth there, were not due to a momentary
illness. Weeks afterward I saw this same expression, when Beethoven felt in far better health. They were the results of his whole
unique life—destiny.

Young Rellstab confessed that in saying good-bye Beethoven embraced him

in such a heartfelt German fashion [that] my whole heart, glowing with enthusiasm, was lifted up. . . . It was like a dream,—the great immortal Ludwig van Beethoven on my breast. I felt his lips on mine and he must have felt himself bathed by my warm happy tears that welled up unceasingly. And so I left him. I had no thought; only a glowing emotion that surged through my innermost breast—Beethoven has embraced me! And I will be proud of this good fortune to the last day of my life![1]

Towards the end of his career Beethoven complained bitterly that the Viennese were neglecting his works. But the records show that these complaints were as ill founded as his deathbed protestations of extreme poverty, with seven bank shares safely hidden in their secret cubbyhole.

He had a less imaginary grievance in the conduct of Nephew Karl. The lad had grown into a commonplace young man who had inherited his father's littleness and meanness with his mother's frivolity and inability to concentrate. There was no spark of the qualities for which we revere the Master.

The boredom, the exaggerated discipline, the fatuous spoiling, the loneliness, and the interminable harangues of a childhood alone with his uncle had turned out a young fellow who reacted naturally to all this. He had little appreciation of the great man's sacrifices or of his genius. In correspondence he referred to him as "the old fool" and wished only to be well rid of the eternal moralizing.

[1]Leitzmann, Vol. I, pp. 296–311.

In 1823 Karl had begun philosophical studies at the University of Vienna. But after a year and a half he tired of them and was allowed to enter a business course at the Polytechnic Institute.

During the summer of 1825, which Beethoven spent in the suburb of Baden, Karl would grasp any pretext for evading the weekly visit of duty to his uncle. Then Beethoven would seize his pen and pour forth alternate threats, admonitions, and pleadings.

Reading such lines as the following one does not know whether to sympathize more with the misguided genius or the misreared youth. On hearing that Karl had again been seeing something of his mother by stealth the uncle wrote:

If I suffer again the most loathsome ingratitude, nay if the bond between us is severed, so be it, but you will be hated by all unprejudiced people who hear of this ingratitude.

In pathetic contrast to such an ultimatum comes an inarticulate wail of loneliness:

As I live here, you know, with the cold weather besides, the perpetual being alone weakens me still more, for my weakness often actually borders on a swoon, O do not add to my illness, even so the man with the scythe will not grant me much further respite.

Again the mood changes:

God has never forsaken me, some one will yet be found to close my eyes . . . you need not come this Sunday, for true harmony and sympathy will never be between us while you act as you do.

But when Karl ran away, and there was no sign of him for days, the uncle's love burst out with such torrential force as his spirit had shown in the first movement of the *Eroica:*

MY DEAR SON:—

Only nothing further—just come to my arms, you shall hear no harsh words. O God, do not make way with yourself in your misery—you will be received with love as always—we will affectionately talk over what we must consider, what is to be done about the future, on my honour no reproaches, for they would be of no use anyway, from me you need expect only the most loving care and help. Only come—come to the faithful heart of your father.

BEETHOVEN.

[In French]

. . . *Si vous ne viendrez pas, vous me tuerez surement.* . . . (If you do not come you will certainly kill me. . . .)

Plagued as he was in body and mind, Beethoven fortunately could always flee to that "shadow of a mighty rock within a weary land"—his art. Sketches for the B flat quartet overlapped the finishing of the A minor. And so resilient were the resources of his vitality that several of the six movements rank with the most humorous, dainty, and light-hearted of his works.

These elements indeed are so prominent that the question arises whether the B flat does not deserve to be placed beside the Eighth symphony and called the "*Quartetto Scherzoso.*" It is the only quartet which has more than one *scherzo*-like movement. Indeed, it has several. For the *Alla Danza Tedesca* provides much the same sort of relief as a *scherzo.*

The *Andante* is labelled *poco scherzando*. And the *Presto*, or *scherzo* proper, is one of the most delicious bits of pure humour in the whole realm of absolute music.

Of course, when one considers the introduction, the serious portions of the witty first movement,[2] the *Cavatina* with its tender passion, and the ponderous, mystic solemnity read by most interpreters into the Great Fugue which originally served as *finale*, one feels that "*Quartetto Scherzoso*" might, after all, scarcely do. That is, until one hears such a light-hearted, almost sportive reading of the Great Fugue as Mr. Harold Bauer's[3] and remembers that the Master's last act was to write a new, jocund *finale* for this quartet, full of *scherzoso* quality, in which now and again the lower strings echo the drolly skipping octaves for bassoon from the *finale* of the Eighth symphony, as if to underline the quartet's kinship of wit with the "*Sinfonia Giocosa*."

The creation of such high-spirited movements by a man in Beethoven's physical and mental extremity is one of the strangest and most affecting anomalies in the history of the arts. He had a special affection for this work. He called it his "*Leibquartett*," a term of familiar endearment which our language lacks, and needs. Indeed, not a few of its pages represent the most intimate emotional self-revelations which he has left us.

At the very end of his life the Master confessed that each time he recalled the melody of the *Cavatina* it stirred him

---

[2] Aldous Huxley labels this movement: "Majesty alternating with a joke." (*Point Counter Point*, 1928, p. 293.)

[3] When he takes a part in his own two-piano arrangement of this composition.

deeply and cost him tears. Surely, in the stammering accents
of that portion of it marked *"Beklemmt"*

Ex. 185

one seems to catch the anguished, eloquently fragmentary
style of such documents as the Heiligenstadt Testament, the
letters to Amenda and Wegeler announcing his deafness,
and that written to "The Immortal Beloved."[4]

"Mephistopheles" Holz once ventured the opinion that
the B flat was the greatest of his quartets. But, with exceptional modesty, Beethoven answered:

Each in its way. Art demands of us not to stand still. You
will find there a new way of voice-leading [part-writing] and,
thank God! there is less lack of fancy than ever before.

Beethoven was right about the voice-leading. The art of
contrapuntal part-writing for four instruments has never

[4]This was the movement which Joseph Joachim chose to play as his farewell to the
Beethovenhaus at Bonn.

The writer remembers with what a thrill of pleasure he recognized, amid the
puzzling confusion of a Sketch Book in the Prussian State Library, its ethereal opening
melody, suddenly standing out from the page. In this instance, by exception, the first
notation revealed it in virtually the form familiar to us to-day.

advanced in line or space since he conceived those highly compressed thirty-eight bars of development in the first movement. Into the three measures of the following example the Master succeeded in packing no less than five distinct motives:

Ex. 186

and he fused them with the utmost smoothness into a superb whole.

To the eye this example looks meagre enough. But here, none the less, may be found: both parts of the double first subject (a and b); two two-note motives from the second and fourth bars of the Introduction (c and d).

Ex. 187

And finally a new, hidden violoncello tune (e),[5] mined out of the conglomerate and owning allegiance, in its upward leap of an octave, to the second subject.

Ex. 188

sotto voce

How artless and innocent the little development passage, Ex. 186, appears; yet how artful and deep it is! It represents the height of the craft.

A close study of such *tours de force* helped and inspired Richard Wagner to pen pages like that in the prelude to *The Mastersingers*, where he kept all three of his main themes unostentatiously and smoothly going together. And about pregnant music like this the Bayreuth master wrote:

Here there is no longer anything added, there is no more framing of the melody, but all has become melody, every voice in the accompaniment, every rhythmical note—yes, even the pauses themselves!

So much for Beethoven's remark to Holz, quoted above, about "a new way of voice-leading." For light on that superb bit of understatement concerning "less lack of

---

[5] Remember Beethoven's other hidden tunes, which have often been mentioned.

fancy" the reader is referred to such a sympathetic performance of the *Andante con moto*

Ex. 189

as the London String Quartet gives on the stage or the Lener Quartet on the phonograph. Once he manages to know it well—and this is no light task!—he will find it an even more exquisite sort of fairy music than its prototype—the prototype of all its kind, the *Allegretto* of the Eighth symphony. This *Andante* marks, if people only knew, the most seven-leagued stride ahead in all the annals of fairy music. It may, however, be a long time before people do know; because it is hard for humanity, in the present stage of evolution, to sustain life at the rarefied heights where we now encounter Beethoven.

> For he on honey-dew hath fed,
> And drunk the milk of Paradise.

The B flat quartet is less copiously reminiscent than most of its immediate predecessors. In the subtlety and smoothness of its inter-movement thematic liaison work it shows an arresting gain.[6]

For the last hundred years most music lovers who could bear to listen at all to the Great Fugue which Beethoven wrote as the original *finale* of the B flat quartet have looked upon it as a thing of stern and almost unapproachable grandeur. When first played, what were taken to be its

[3]For the sake of the nontechnical reader both of these fascinating subjects are under sentence of banishment to Part II, pp. 527–528 and 560–563.

cryptic, sibylline utterances were sayings too hard for even the most sympathetic and devoted contemporaries of the Master. The work completely baffled even those talented Viennese listeners who, at the first performance of the *Choral* symphony, had been so feelingly responsive to the humour of that now famous kettledrum manœuvre in the *scherzo* and had burst forth into jubilant applause.

This sort of fugal ending to a quartet was a century ahead of the most enlightened performers and listeners in that audience.[7] They criticized, complained, and agitated until the publisher, in alarm, begged Beethoven to write a new *finale*.

The trouble with the Great Fugue has always been that its extraordinarily crabbed and cruel technical difficulties usually make it sound dry and dully ponderous in performance. Whereas Mr. Harold Bauer's half jest contained a large element of truth when he remarked to the late Oscar G. Sonneck: "The Great Fugue is more like a glorified polka-*scherzo*. People play it as if it were profoundly mystical, which it is not. They put philosophy into it instead of music."

Wonderful to relate, the man who had withstood the frenzied demands of embattled singers to revise the *Missa* and the *Choral*, gave way to the critics of the Great Fugue. He put his tongue into his cheek and, almost on his deathbed, as his last composition, wrote an *Ersatz-finale* that a child, though bouncing a ball, might understand.

---

[7]Even so intelligent a modern critic as Mr. Ernest Walker (in *Beethoven*, 1920), labelled it "practically unintelligible" and scored its "uncouth inconsequence."

But he did not connect it with the rest of the quartet, as he had connected the Great Fugue, by his customary thematic liaison work. He had been through that arduous labour once, and enough was enough. Its absence lends colour to the theory that he dashed down these pages in a somewhat cynical mood. Or perhaps he was too nearly spent to summon up pressure high enough for making this afterthought thematically an organic part of the quartet. The Great Fugue was published by itself as opus 133.

We are drawing near the last page of the story. But one supreme work is still before us.

> The best is yet to be,
> The last of life, for which the first was made.

Chapter XLVI

"SPANGY" IN THE BLACK SPANIARD'S HOUSE

1825, Moves to Black Spaniard's House — Renews Intimacy with Von Breunings — "Trouser Button" — Relics — Frau von Breuning — An Embarrassing Escort — Unconsciousness of Discord

In the fall of 1825 Beethoven moved, for the last time, to lodgings in the "Black Spaniard's" house. This structure was so called because it had been built by Benedictine monks from Spain. The Black Spaniard's House. How neatly it fits young Ludwig's childish nickname of "Spangy"!

The man who had once been *"der Spangol,"* or the little Black Spaniard of Bonn, chose his new house as if such a name might have power to bring glimpses of those youthful clouds of glory which had been so prematurely obscured by the vapours from Father Johann's bottle. Something, at any rate, brought them back. For here he was soon to write that swan song, the C sharp minor quartet, whose second, fourth, and fifth movements look at us with young eyes of limpid innocence, and whose other movements—we may imagine—repeat: "Whosoever shall not receive the Kingdom of God as a little child, shall in no wise enter therein."

In the Black Spaniard's house he was to meet an untimely end at the height of his powers, with his Tenth symphony lying sketched in the desk—all done but the writing. As if exhilarated by the new home he spoke gaily of dwelling "on the heights of Black Spain," whence the vision roves across "barbaric Baden." Which is very much as if a cliff-dweller on Riverside Drive, New York City, should claim that his vision roves across barbaric Englewood.

Here Beethoven found himself the neighbour of his boyhood friend Stephan von Breuning and renewed the old intimacy. He became extremely fond of Gerhard, the twelve-year-old son of Stephan, nicknaming him "Hosenknopf," or Trouser Button (because he stuck so close to father), and Ariel (because he was so light on his feet). When the lad took up the piano Beethoven prescribed the Clementi method as preferable to that of Czerny and made Gerhard a present of it. At the Von Breuning home in Vienna the writer handled this precious volume and the kindly letter that went with it. The grandson of "Hosenknopf" showed him a magnificent nutwood desk which had been Beethoven's only fine piece of furniture. Also the funny little painted clock with iron weights, which always hung in the Master's kitchen, but which made such an eager and continuous racket that the Von Breunings had to stop it. Such a timepiece could be tolerated in action only by a very deaf person. If Herr von Breuning's forbears had as much charm as this young palæontologist-entomologist, one can well understand why Beethoven was attracted to them.

Frau von Breuning saw to the fitting up of Beethoven's kitchen and engaged his servants. In return the gallant

Master once accompanied her a long distance to a public bath. Emerging an hour later she saw with astonishment that he was waiting for her in the street.

This may have been an unwelcome attention. For his laugh was sudden, powerful, and piercing; his gestures, angular and eccentric. He was completely indifferent toward strangers. His speaking voice was loud. So that passers-by often stopped in their tracks, taking him for a madman, and the street boys followed him hooting. Of course Beethoven, deaf and absorbed, had no more idea that he was embarrassing the lady than why she hesitated to eat at his table. The truth was that she did not find the Master's neglected clothing and his eccentric behaviour appetizing.

Gerhard's sister Marie reported to Thayer:

Beethoven often told my mother that he longed greatly for domestic happiness and much regretted that he had never married.

The lady sometimes teased her husband to make Beethoven play. But Stephan always replied tenderly:

He doesn't like to do it, and I don't want to ask him, because it might pain him not to hear himself.

When he did, though, it sometimes gave exquisite pain to others. Rellstab tells how, by a trick, he induced the Master to press the keys of his Broadwood.

"I struck a chord lightly . . . in order to make Beethoven turn around. . . . 'That is a beautiful gift,' said Beethoven, . . . 'and it has such a beautiful tone,' he continued and moved his hands towards the keys without taking his eyes off me. He gently struck a chord. Never again will one enter my soul so poignant, so heart-breaking as that one was! He struck the C major triad with the right hand and B as a bass in the left, and continuing to gaze uninterruptedly at me, repeated the false chord several times in order to let the sweet tone of the instrument reverberate; and the greatest musician on earth did not hear the dissonance!"[1]

It may be, however, that Rellstab's sorrow was super-erogatory. Perhaps the composer of that up-to-date Twentieth Century piece, the Great Fugue, was deliberately trying the effect of polytonality on the critic. Perhaps the forward-looking mind which was already interested in steam and aviation agreed with the creator of *The Faërie Queene*,[2] that

> Dischord ofte in music makes the sweeter lay.

---

[1] Translated from Leitzmann, Vol. I, pp. 307–308.
[2] III, II, 15.

Chapter XLVII

THE MASTER'S MASTERPIECE

Le génie de l'artiste est comme toutes les grandes choses du monde: un acte de foi et d'amour.
—PAUL BOURGET, *Address on His Admission to the Académie*.

C Sharp Minor Quartet Completed, 1826 — Its Pre-eminence — Sketches — "Cribbed," yet "Spanking New" — The Author's Own Reaction — "Twenty Minutes of Reality" — From Heaven to Earth — The Opening Fugue —"Consciousness Surpassing Our Own" — An Expressionistic Allegretto — A Mighty Compensation

EARLY in 1826 Beethoven finished that quartet which he called his greatest, the C sharp minor (Op. 131). After many flunctuations of taste, the author has come to feel that Beethoven was right, and that this quartet is his greatest, with the A minor (Op. 132), the E flat (Op. 127), and the F major (Op. 59, No. 1) pressing one another in close competition for second place.

The Master took extraordinary pains with the C sharp minor. The preliminary sketches for it bulk huge beside the portly completed manuscript. Studying them in the Prussian State Library in Berlin, one is filled with something like awe at the infinite pains lavished by this dying man, and the infallibility with which revision progressed from the commonplace first thought to the inspired last thought.

In August, 1826, he sent the manuscript to Schott &

Sons, his publishers. On its title page he scribbled "*Zusammengestohlen aus Verschiedenem Diesem und Jenem*" (Cribbed together variously from this and that).[1] Schotts took fright and wrote, reminding Beethoven of their stipulation that the work must be an original one. To this the Master replied that the expression "*zusammengestohlen*" (cribbed together) had been only a joke, and the quartet was "spanking new" (*funkelnagelneu*).

"Spanking new" it unquestionably was. But was the "*zusammengestohlen*" inscription no more than a humorous lie?

Perhaps not quite. The more one studies this music the more miraculously "cribbed together" it appears. Many of its tunes were born and reared through childhood elsewhere.

The subject of the opening fugue

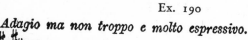

Ex. 190

is enough like that of the C sharp minor five-voiced fugue in Bach's *Welltempered Clavichord* to be its son. But, curiously enough, its component parts can be traced to Beethoven's own earlier works. As we shall see, Herr Bekker points out that the start of the introductions to the (earlier)

---

[1] The winning understatement of this inscription recalls Brahms's way of describing his MS. symphonies, when he first mailed them to friends, as "a bundle of little piano pieces."

A minor quartet and to the Great Fugue were perhaps echoed in notes 2 to 5 of the C sharp minor fugue.[2]

The germ of the first *Allegro*

Ex. 191

comes straight from the *Allegro ma non tanto* of the A minor quartet.

Ex. 183

The theme of the *Andante moderato* variation

Ex. 192

is drawn, with only slight alterations, from a pregnant phrase of the opening movement of this same A minor quartet:

Ex. 193

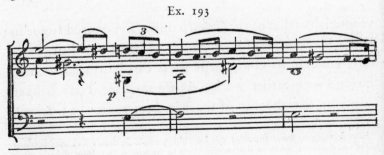

[2]See pp. 573–574.

The lone scrap of melody in the enigmatic *Allegretto* variation

Ex. 194

is borrowed from the *finale* of the A major sonata (Op. 101):

Ex. 195

In the *scherzo,* with its atmosphere of naïve and playful childhood, it is appropriate to find a quotation from the youthful quartet in G major (Op. 18, No. 2) whose first movement ends its main theme thus:

Ex. 196

Twenty-six years later this tune reappeared in the C sharp minor quartet at the place marked *piacevole,* but this time without its rococo trappings and wearing simple greatness as a child's light garment.

Ex. 197

The tune of the short sixth movement

Ex. 198

is not only related to that of the Bagatelle (Op. 26, No. 1)

Ex. 199

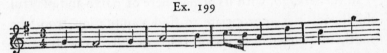

but also to the venerable Hebrew melody, *Kol Nidrei,* which antedates the Ninth Century.

Ex. 200

Last, the motto of the *finale*

Ex. 201

comes almost note for note from Mozart's *Fantasie* sonata in C minor.[3]

Ex. 202

This, in its turn, echoes the theme of J. S. Bach's *Ricercata* organ fugue in C minor from *Das musikalische Opfer*.

Here are nine "cribbings together" of thematic material from other compositions, not counting the inevitable source-motive[4] in fugue and *scherzo* which had already appeared more than a hundred times in his earlier works. Surely these are enough to lend a substratum of seriousness to the joke "*zusammengestohlen*," as well as to shed an additional lustre of the miraculous on the perfectly honest claim that the quartet was "spanking new." For, of course, the point of all this is not how he borrowed, but how magically he disguised, improved, and renewed his borrowings.

For a detailed study of the inter-movement thematic liaison work in the C sharp minor the reader is referred to Riemann,[5] who indeed carries his analogies to the length of declaring that the main themes of the second and seventh movements as well as the initial motto of the latter are rewritings of the subject of the opening fugue.

More than any other work of Beethoven, this quartet represents to the writer the gradual and painful acquisition of a taste long denied. For many years he had taken part in

[3]For this observation the writer is indebted to his friend Mr. Gustave Reese.
[4]See p. 601, (transposed) Exs. 352 and 353.
[5]*Beethoven's Streichquartette*, p. 147 ff.

playing and hearing it without much more response than annoyance at its length and obvious harshnesses. Not until after prolonged study, score in hand, of the phonograph record of the Lener Quartet, and hearing it repeatedly played in concert, did he begin to think it one of the supreme things in all art. It took him thirty years to realize that the C sharp minor uniquely blends the pure and unerring intuition of the child with the maturest experience of the supreme genius.

Without in the least offering a personal view of this quartet as the only valid one, he feels it may be of a certain interest to mention that, though the work affects him variously according to mood and tense, most often its first part offers him, in a language far more veridical than any words, the illumination of the mystic vision. Its "twenty minutes of reality" communicates directly, without recourse to such awkward conventions as the worn counters of speech, the secrets of the universe. He feels himself a completely balanced and integrated being. And he sees everything at a glance as an inevitable progress of clearly unified cause and effect. The past, present, and future are made to form one pure ring of burning light. There is "no more death, neither sorrow, nor crying, neither shall there be any more pain; for the former things are passed away."

Richard Wagner held the *scherzo* of this quartet to be the *chef d'œuvre* of all music. It stirs us with faint echoes from the Master's actual youth, now thirty years gone. It suggests that little *scherzo* which twice interrupted the second *Adagio* of the Serenade for string trio (Op. 8). But it is strangely touching to notice that the opus 8 *Presto* sounds prosaically grown-up in comparison with that of opus 131, where one may overhear the mirth of such inno- cent and exuberant play as the "young-eyed cherubim" might enjoy on the shores of the jasper sea.

The last two movements bring a stirring change. Turning abruptly from the subliminal, they seem—to one listener at least—to intimate secrets even more important to the sons of Earth. They whisper that no man may gaze with impunity into the untempered brightness of the infinite. That we, whose ancestors so recently swung gibbering from branch to branch, are not yet intended to linger with the children of light on the plane of eternal bliss, neglecting our earthly home, like absentee landlords, to feast upon supernal glories. Those painful, resolute footsteps of the *finale's* heroic march fall on the ear like heartening exhor- tations to live out this phase of existence fully and coura- geously if we would develop the momentum of spirit necessary for the next.

When Richard Wagner declares that the opening fugue[6] is "perhaps the most heavy-hearted thing that has ever been said in tones," the writer fails to follow him. Its serenity, elevation, and fullness of life seem incompatible with melan- choly. This fugue is beyond sorrow and joy, beyond good and evil, almost beyond ugliness and beauty.

Nowhere else in music [writes Mr. Sullivan] are we made so aware, as here, of a state of consciousness surpassing our own,

[6]See Ex. 190, p. 459.

where our problems do not exist, and to which even our highest aspirations, those that we can formulate, provide no key.

The experiences Beethoven here communicates

may belong to an order of consciousness that very few men have attained, but, in that case, they must be in the line of human development; . . . they correspond to a spiritual synthesis which the race has not achieved but which, we may suppose, it is on the way to achieving.[7]

This quartet was Wagner's chief inspiration in creating "the music of the future." And to-day, with *Tristan* and *The Ring* to its credit, it remains music of the future in a far deeper sense than any page left us by the seer of Bayreuth.

One is constantly surprised by new evidence of its forward-looking spirit. Study, for instance, the brief *Allegretto* which constitutes the fifth variation of the fourth movement. This cryptic page, which says little directly but suggests much by veiled indirection, is like some expressionistic story of to-day. Without apparent coherence or progression, without narrative or argument—almost without matter itself—it conveys a surprisingly significant and coherent account through shreds and patches of naïvely natural suggestion. This was a new style in the music of 1826. And, though the Marcel Prousts and the Virginia Woolfs have made an accepted and honoured place for the new style in literature, these notes of music are almost as fresh and novel and mysterious to-day as when they were first set down on paper.

[7] *Beethoven: His Spiritual Development*, p. 239.

For people of charm and endowment the world always baits snares. It was rare good fortune for us that Beethoven should have evaded these snares and come safe through to the time when deafness shut him more and more away from distractions and temptations and provided him with a terrible affliction which he had to redress by such mighty compensations as the C sharp minor quartet. A stroke of miraculous luck[8] for this none too lucky planet! In all probability we shall not look upon its like again.

Soon after presenting this gift to the world the Master received a shock that, in a few days, made him look like a man of seventy.

---

[8] In view of the striking superiority of the music which Beethoven wrote after 1818, one is inclined to endorse the proposal of Mr. Harvey Grace that all composers should be made deaf!

Chapter XLVIII

THE "MADMAN" AT GNEIXENDORF

Karl Goes from Bad to Worse — Lays Hands on His Uncle — Attempts Suicide — Decides to Be a Soldier — Beethoven Takes Him to Gneixendorf, September, 1826 — A Trying Guest — Homely Brother Johann — Beethoven's Habits of Composition Too Much for Cook — The Vine-Dresser Valet's Account — What the Natives Thought of Him — "A Bissel Stada!" — Friction

BEETHOVEN's desperate and pitiful attempts to make some sort of contact with humanity by rearing a worthy heir concentrated all the terrific power of his passionate affection upon one quite ordinary young man. Karl nearly died of it. He could not stand the perpetual change from suspicion and angry upbraiding to sentimental coddling. Holz came in one day and found the young fellow actually laying forceful hands on Beethoven.

Karl made debts. He neglected his studies and his uncle. Then he took to stealing. Finally he tried suicide *à la Werther*, among the picturesque ruins of Castle Rauhenstein. At the last moment his nerve partially failed, and two shots resulted in only one scalp wound.

This deed produced in Beethoven the old alternations of emotion: first fury at Karl's ingratitude; then a fervour of thankfulness for his escape, followed by the unconditional but temporary surrender of a loving heart.

Karl told the examining magistrate that he had tried to kill himself because his uncle tormented him too much. "I grew worse because he wanted me to grow better"; which is a reaction perfectly natural in an unwisely handled youngster.

He decided now to be a soldier. Baron von Stutterheim offered to take the boy into his regiment. In return he received from the grateful uncle the dedication of the C sharp minor quartet.

But before Karl put on the uniform his telltale scar must heal. So, on September 28, 1826, uncle and nephew went for a visit to brother Johann's four-hundred-acre estate at Gneixendorf. The name of this village reminded Beethoven's occasionally sensitive literary ear "somewhat of the breaking of an axletree."

His hatred of his sister-in-law, his deep distaste for Karl's growing friendliness with this same Aunt Therese, his suspicion, his irritability, his invalid's diet, and his eccentricities must have made him a difficult guest.

But Johann, too, must have been a trying house companion. He was an ignorant and unmusical but pretentious person who felt that, as the brother of the great composer, he must act the part of a musical Brahmin. After forcing himself to look knowing during several performances of the great E flat quartet, it developed that he had no idea he had ever before heard it. His near presence must have been trying to such a sensitive man as the Master. In one of the Conversation Books of this period we read a jotting in young Karl's hand, discreetly meant for Ludwig's eyes alone, which may be euphemistically translated: "The brother is odoriferous!"

The Conversation Books also give us many a quaint touch of Johann's homely quality; as when he calls the violoncello by its long outlawed name, *Bassettl,* and by even the corruption of this old word, *Passedel.*

Johann was hard put to it to provide Ludwig proper attendance. The latter composed at a table, waving and stamping the tempo with hands and feet while he hummed and shouted what to himself, at least, represented tunes. This was too much for the cook, who made his bed. She was overcome with mirth. And Beethoven drove her out with "hearty, free words."

Then Johann tried one of his vine dressers as valet. Michael Krenn was more discreet. When he could no longer contain himself he rushed away and exploded with laughter at a safe distance. This peasant has left us a vignette of the composer in labour.

At half-past five he was up and at his table, beating time with hands and feet, singing, humming, writing. At half-past seven was the family breakfast and directly after it he hurried out of doors, and would saunter about the fields, calling out, waving his hands, going now very slowly, then very fast, and then suddenly standing still and writing in a kind of pocketbook. At half-past twelve he came into the house to dinner, and after dinner he went to his own room till three or so, then again in the fields till about sunset. At half-past seven he came to supper, and then went to his room, wrote till ten, and so to bed.

The neighbours as well as the servants felt that the strange stranger was not quite right in his head. He shouted and gesticulated so wildly as to stampede the same yoke of oxen twice in one day. Their driver asked Johann the name of the fool who had done this. "My brother." "A pretty brother, that he is!" exclaimed the peasant.

The picture of Beethoven at Gneixendorf following the inner gleam as he stormed across the fields, waving his arms like a windmill and roaring out unintelligible fragments of the last quartet to the consternation of the yokels, reminds us of Old Peter in that gem of Gilbert's *Bab Ballads*, "The Perils of Invisibility":

> At night, when all around is still,
> You'll find him pounding up a hill;
> And shrieking peasants whom he meets
> Fall down in terror on the peats.

It is recorded that one countryman, when the terrifying stranger appeared and made his yoke of oxen plunge, yelled, "*A bissel stada!*" which means in the local dialect, "Go a bit easy there!" This injunction neatly represents the typical reaction of average humanity to the waywardness of genius. If the Master had indeed gone through life "*a bissel stada*" he might never have quickened the heartbeats of either oxen or men.

Ludwig accompanied Johann on two different visits. The first was to the house of his surgeon, whose wife took the composer for a servant, spoke patronizingly to him, and gave him a jug of wine. The second was to a syndic who had as clerk an ardent Beethoven enthusiast.

SYNDIC: Who do you suppose that man was who stood so long by the door?

CLERK: He may be an exceptional case. But if you had not treated him so politely I should take him for an idiot.

Explanation and consternation. How were these simple folk to realize that he whom they held to be a fool or a madman was a great genius in parturition over a beauty full of the peace that passes understanding?

To Karl, life with this wild man, for whom he had now lost every spark of gratitude and affection, was rapidly growing unendurable. Witness his outbreak in one of the Conversation Books. Beethoven had evidently been scolding him for his reluctance to return to Vienna. The nephew replied:

If you want to go, good; if not, good again. But I entreat you once more not to torment me as you are doing; you might regret it, for I can endure much, but not too much. You treated your brother in the same way to-day without cause. You must remember that other people also are human beings. . . . I only want to be alone for a little while.—Will you not let me go to my room?

How the two unfortunate men grated upon each other's nerves can be read between the lines.

Chapter XLIX

RETROSPECT IN F MAJOR

Die Wirklichkeit wird zum Traum. Die Träume werden Wirklichkeit.[1]

October 30, 1826, Last Quartet Finished — Reason for Its Brevity — The Merchant of Venice — Op. 135, a Retrospect — "The Midway" Forecast — Origin of "Muss es sein?" — The Housekeeper Theory — Dembscher and the Canon

AT GNEIXENDORF, on October 30, 1826, Beethoven's last complete work, the quartet in F major (Op. 135), was finished. It consisted of four short movements. Only one other quartet of his, the G major (Op. 18, No. 2), can be performed in as brief a time. According to Holz the Master purposely kept down its length. He had bargained with Schlesinger for 80 ducats, but felt that the publisher had overreached him by sending 360 florins instead. "If a Jew," he exclaimed, "sends amputated ducats he shall have an amputated quartet. That's why it is so short."

All this about the Jew and the ducats, this insistence on the letter of what was nominated in the bond, reminds one of *The Merchant of Venice*. And when we hear the music, its easy mastery, its part-writing as lightly poised and balanced and transparent as the arcades of the Doge's Palace,

---

[1] (Reality turns to a dream. Dreams become reality.) (Gustav Frenssen, *Otto Babendieck*, 1926, p. 1289.)

its crisp autumnal colouring, the freakish quality of the Gobboesque *Vivace*, the folk-tune flavour here and there, and the golden sunset glow that suffuses the *Lento assai*

Ex. 203

Lento assai

with idyllic poetry, we sometimes may still think of Shakespeare's masterpiece.

The F major is in the nature of a retrospect. The Master has fought his fight. Now he looks back over the arduous road he has travelled. In the confident happiness of the first movement, the sparkling vivacity of the second, the deep, brooding peace of the third, the firm but smiling resolution of the last, we see the stranger of Gneixendorf leaning on his staff and looking back toward the distant Danube. It reminds him of that Rhine of his boyhood, beyond which beckoned those castles in Spain.

And fragments of music float up the deep vista to lend him resolution for the facing of whatever may be before him. In snatches he hears the *Adagios* of his first quartet and of the Rasoumowskys, the Episode in the first movement of the *Eroica*, the beginning and end of the Fifth, the slow movements of the "*Emperor*" and of the "*Archduke*," the *Arietta*, the commencement of the *Choral*, the immortal C sharp minor fugue, the *Dankgesang*, the *Et vitam venturi*.

"It will stand," he murmurs. And on his face burns for a moment the transfigured look that no man ever surprised there. Then a surge of pain obliterates it and he hurries back to the Wasserhof to see what mischief Karl is up to.

The F major is less "cribbed together" than any of the other last quartets.[2]

It is appropriate that this last work of the Master's should have had an eye to the future as well as to the past. At the 104th bar of the *finale* there is a curiously plain prophecy of that dusky tune which was to become so popular at the World's Columbian Exposition sixty-seven years later, and was to be christened *"The Midway."*

The *Muss es sein?* motto of this same *finale*

Ex. 204

was destined to suggest, almost note for note, the opening of Liszt's *Les Préludes;* and, far more gloriously, the start of César Franck's symphony in D minor.

The idea is current that this motto and its answering companion,

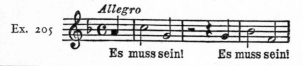

Ex. 205

___

[2]For Beethoven's use of his great source-motive in the *Lento* and *finale,* see pp. 602–603.

which are collectively entitled *Der schwer gefasste Ent-schluss* (The Difficult Resolve), arose from the Master's struggles with the demon of avarice (more serious than comic) during those painful moments every Saturday night when the old witch who kept house for him appeared to pull her eagle to earth by his cord—and demand the weekly house money.

Helm saw the conflict in the sick Master's revolt against the conventional necessity for ending the quartet with a fourth movement. But its true origin can be traced to an ardent amateur named Dembscher.[3] Dembscher wanted to have Boehm play the B flat quartet (Op. 130) at his own home. Unfortunately he had neglected to subscribe to Schuppanzigh's series in which this work had been first performed. He asked Beethoven for the loan of the manuscript. For once in his life the Master showed a little consideration for his bulky friend. He refused on account of Schuppanzigh's feelings.

Thayer[4] relates that

Dembscher stammered in confusion and begged Holz to find some means to restore him to Beethoven's good graces. Holz said that the first step should be to send Schuppanzigh 50 florins, the price of the subscription. Dembscher laughingly asked, "Must it be?" (*Muss es sein?*) When Holz related the incident to Beethoven he too laughed and instantly wrote down a canon:

---

[3]He was the violoncellist to whom Brother Johann referred as playing the *"Passedel."* See p. 470.

[4]Vol. III, p. 224.

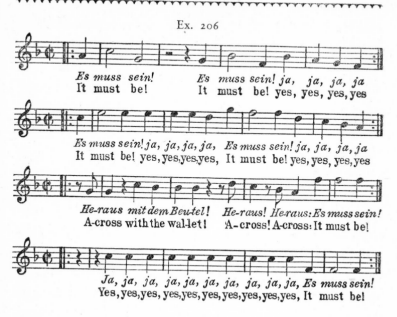

Ex. 206

Es muss sein!   *Es muss sein! ja, ja, ja, ja*
It must be!   It must be! yes, yes, yes, yes

Es muss sein! ja, ja, ja, ja,   *Es muss sein! ja, ja, ja, ja*
It must be! yes, yes, yes, yes,   It must be! yes, yes, yes, yes

He-raus mit dem Beu-tel!   *He-raus! Heraus: Es muss sein!*
A-cross with the wal-let!   A-cross! A-cross: It must be!

Ja, ja, ja, ja, ja, ja, ja, ja, ja, ja, Es muss sein!
Yes, yes, yes, yes, yes, yes, yes, yes, yes, yes, It must be!

And out of this burlesque *jeu d'esprit*—just as the *Allegretto* of the Eighth symphony had grown out of the canon to Maelzel—grew the F major's serious, but not too serious, *finale*.

THE DIVINE COMEDY IS FINISHED

ON DECEMBER 2, 1826, the weather was severely inclement. But Beethoven had determined to take Karl to Vienna forthwith, and nothing could hold him back. Either from riding in a crude open vehicle or sleeping in a cold and wretched inn that night, he caught a chill and arrived "indisposed."

In two days Holz sent for Dr. Wawruch,[1] who found symptoms of inflammation of the lungs. These he soon overcame, but on the eighth day a relapse was brought on by a fit of rage. The cause was unknown, but it was prob-

---

[1]Thayer scotched the libelous tale of Schindler that Karl was too much interested in billiards to call the doctor and sent the billiard marker instead, who at first forgot the commission.

ably directed against either Karl or Johann. This paroxysm caused an attack of summer cholera, also jaundice, hard nodules in the liver, and dropsy.

The dropsy necessitated four tappings. But even during the operations Beethoven was his usual humorous and brilliant self. The first time the surgeon made the incision and applied the tube for the water to gush out, the patient observed whimsically: "Better from my belly than from my pen." Then, turning to Dr. Seibert: "Mr. Professor, you remind me of Moses smiting the rock with his staff."

With the rudimentary medical knowledge of a century ago, ignorance and carelessness combined to make that sickroom a cruel and disgusting place for a man to live or die in. Vermin came to complete the wretchedness.[2]

By the fourth operation Beethoven had lost hope. But still he had the wit to murmur: "My day's work is done. If there were a physician who could help me his name should be called Wonderful." This quotation from *The Messiah* alluded to the gift of Handel's complete works which his friend Stumpff had sent from London to cheer the Master's last days.

Young "Ariel" von Breuning used to bring the heavy folios and stand them on the bed against the wall. Beethoven was delighted. As he turned the pages words of admiration often burst from his lips. "I have long wanted these," he told the boy, "for Handel is the greatest, the ablest composer that ever lived. I can still learn from him."

In a Conversation Book some visitors scribbled: "Your

---

[2]Many of the nauseating details are given in Thayer, Vol. III.

quartet which Schuppanzigh played yesterday did not please." When they had gone the Master tersely remarked to "Ariel," who had found the entry: "Some day it will please them." He told the lad that he used his best judgment and would not permit himself to be carried away by the opinion of the moment.[3] "I know that I am an artist," he added simply.

Time hung so heavily on the patient's hands that, as the Conversation Books show, he even tried to learn elementary arithmetic from Karl, but soon gave it up. As usual, he devoted much anxious thought to that young man's financial future. This preoccupation and the anti-mathematical cast of his mind may help to condone the false representations of poverty and extreme need which he made at that time to the London Philharmonic Society through Stumpff, Sir George Smart, and Moscheles—against the friendly protests of Von Breuning and Schindler. They pointed out that Beethoven could not honestly plead poverty while he owned bank shares worth 7,441 florins. They declared that the fact, if known, would look ugly. But Beethoven insisted that he wished to leave this little fortune to Karl intact— and sent the letter. London took prompt action on February 28, 1827. The sick man was soon overjoyed at hearing from Moscheles:

The Philharmonic Society resolved to express their good will and lively sympathy by requesting your acceptance of £100

---

[3]One remembers how, deep in composing the Eighth symphony, he wrote to Amalie Sebald: "What people say means nothing, they are only people; usually they see in others only themselves, and that is just nothing; away with this, the good, the beautiful needs no people. Independent of external aid, here it is. . . ."

sterling, to provide the necessary comforts and conveniences during your illness.

When the money was brought, Rau the banker suggested delivering it in two instalments.

I found poor Beethoven in a sad way [he wrote to Moscheles], more like a skeleton than a living being. . . . He acknowledged to me openly that he considered this money as a relief sent from heaven; and that 500 florins would not suffice for his present wants. I therefore gave him, according to his wish, the whole sum at once.

Beethoven left an estate which, allowing for the difference in purchasing power between 1827 and 1929, would to-day be worth about $8,800. Yet Sonneck attacked all adverse critics of the Philharmonic incident on the ground that they "naïvely overlook a determining psychological factor. In Beethoven's eyes his seven bank-shares did not exist for him; in his eyes . . . they belonged to nephew Karl, his sole heir. To have touched these for his own comfort would have been considered by Beethoven unpardonable thievery. One may disapprove of this excess of consideration for Karl's future welfare, but it was sincere. Hence, from his point of view Beethoven, logically enough, could not but look upon himself as a poor man."[4]

But Sonneck overlooked the fact that it is far from honest to proclaim one's self destitute while in possession of property, even though one may be filled with a burning desire to transmit this property posthumously. Suppose, for example, that some reader of these pages had accumulated a secret food supply, enough to sustain life for several years,

[4]*Beethoven Letters in America*, 1927, p. 37.

and that he nevertheless begged food from friends and strangers abroad on the ground that he was starving. Could he be cleared of a charge of obtaining food under false pretenses, even though he had set his heart on leaving the entire hoard to a relative? Sonneck wrote: "to have touched these would have been considered by Beethoven unpardonable thievery." But he forgot that Beethoven had already sold one of his accumulated shares on an occasion when he was particularly pressed for money;[5] and that, when on the point of selling another, he found he needed only to cash the coupon.[6] No, the sort of mental falsification of accounts which Sonneck attributed to Beethoven cannot fully relieve the dying Master of the charge of dishonesty; although his fault dwindles when we consider the ridiculous disparity between an estate of approximately $8,800 and the incalculable treasures he bequeathed to us.

As a rule, the greater the artist, the less he rationalizes about the quality of his own creations. He glosses over few misgivings on this subject. But he is human—often more so than most people—and has to strike a balance somewhere. So he usually compensates for his austere æsthetic probity by rationalizing his private life even more extravagantly than the average man.

The lofty artistic rectitude of the last sonatas and quartets, symbolized by the Kyd incident,[7] probably allowed

---

[5] According to records in the National Bank, Vienna, for July 13, 1819, Beethoven originally bought eight, not seven, bank shares. (Dr. Max Reinitz, *"Beethoven als Bankationär,"* in *Neue Freie Presse,* May 28, 1916.)

[6] See p. 367.

[7] See p. 393.

Beethoven to make peace with his conscience for throwing a heavy stool at the servant's head and for obtaining money from the Philharmonic through false representations.

As Dr. Max Friedländer aptly says:[8]

The virtue of lofty natures is unminted gold which does not pass current in the business of daily life. Such men bless peoples more easily than individual people. It is more natural for them to bestow seed-corn than bread. Such a soul is no watering-can for the refreshment of someone's favourite gillyflower, but a stormy flood that quenches the thirst of wide fields and lofty oaks.

To everyone's relief, on January 2, 1827, after another quarrel with his uncle, Karl left Vienna and joined his regiment at Iglau. On the 3d Beethoven drew up a will making the young man "sole and universal heir" of all his property. A note to Schindler, probably written late in February, shows that the great mind had even then begun to grow confused. Schindler had evidently been laid up by some mischance.

About your accident, since it has happened, as soon as we see one another.—Without inconvenience I can send to you by somebody, accept this;—here is something Moscheles, Cramer; without your having received a letter, there will be a new occasion to write you Wednesday and lay my affairs to his heart, if you are not well by that time one of my . . . can take it to the post against a receipt.—*Vale et fave.*—There is no need of my assuring you of my sympathy in your accident—do take the food from me, all given from the heart—Heaven be with you.

Your true friend
BEETHOVEN.

---

[8]In an unpublished lecture.

It is not certain, but highly probable, that the shy and retiring Schubert visited Beethoven during these last days. Hüttenbrenner states that he took him to the house a week before the end and the sick man sent out word: "Let Schubert come first." At any rate, some copies of his songs were among the last things Beethoven enjoyed. And the Master is reported to have exclaimed: "Truly the divine spark dwells in Schubert." When eighteen months later the younger man finished the unfinished symphony of his own career the name of Beethoven was almost constantly on his lips.

The codicil to the Master's will, dated four days before the end, is the last thing we have in his handwriting.

Beethoven's Last Written Words.
Municipal Collections, Vienna.

Verbatim, it reads:

> Mein Nefffe Karle Soll alleini=[ger]
> Erbe sejn, das Kapital
> meines Nachlasses soll jedoch
> Seinen natülichen oder testamen=
> tarisch (isch?) en Erben zufallen.
> Wien am 23=März 1827
> luwig van Beethoen

[Translated:] My nep(p)hew Karle shall be so[le] heir, the capital of my estate shall however revert to his natu[r]al or testamentar(y?)y heirs.

> Vienna the 23 March 1827
> luwig van Beethoen

In signing it he was not fully conscious and had to be supported by Johann and Von Breuning. Notice the misspellings and duplications—mute testimonies to his condition.

The famous phrase *"Plaudite amici, comoedia finita est"* (Applaud, friends, the comedy is finished) was probably half-conscious half-quotation from several other famous deathbeds. There is some question as to whether Beethoven pronounced that lambent bit of sarcasm after receiving the Host or after a long consultation of physicians.[8a] A number of biographers, with more feeling for drama than for history, have assigned to the Latin phrase the rôle of the Master's last words. But one must believe Schindler's statement that his last authentic utterance, spoken at one o'clock on the afternoon of March 24th, was about nothing more

---

[8a]In the latter case, the author of *The Doctor's Dilemma* may well envy him this anticipatory specimen of Shavian irony. *"Plaudite"* was, of course, the conventional closing formula of Latin comedy.

momentous than a present of old Rhine wine from Schott, the publisher: "Pity, pity—too late!"[8b]

Towards evening began two days of almost uninterrupted delirium.

The strong man lay [wrote Gerhard von Breuning][9] completely unconscious . . . breathing so stertorously that the rattle could be heard at a distance. His powerful frame, his unweakened lungs, fought like giants with approaching death.

Late on the afternoon of March 26, 1827, there was a flash of lightning and a sharp peal of thunder. The then unconscious Master raised himself high in bed, as if answering the thunder. His eyes opened wide. He clenched and lifted his right hand, remained in this attitude for several seconds—and fell back dead.[9a] That clenched hand seemed to say:

I was ever a fighter, so—one fight more,
The best and the last!

Ironically enough, it happened that none whom Beethoven loved, neither Wegeler nor Holz nor the Von Breunings nor Karl, were there at the end to close his eyes; and that of the two present one was an acquaintance from out of town named Hüttenbrenner and the other his ancient enemy and sister-in-law Therese.

[8b]It is good to have this human touch in place of the *Plaudite*, etc., just as it is good to know that Goethe's last words were not the grandiose and apocryphal "More light!" but a tender phrase addressed to his son's wife: "Give me, then, your little paw!"

[9]*Aus dem Schwarzspanierhause*, p. 108.

[9a]Significantly, the last piece of tonal defiance—the last musical gesture of challenge on the part of this heroic fighter who had once cried out that he would seize fate by the throat—had been the opening movement of the *Choral* symphony, whose main subject was taken from the Thunderstorm in the *Pastoral*.

THE DIVINE COMEDY IS FINISHED

In the opinion of modern science, the immediate cause of Beethoven's death was cirrhosis of the liver. Long and vainly the friends searched for the dead man's fortune— not without some regrettable mutual suspicions and recriminations. Finally Holz pulled at a nail which stuck from an old cabinet. A secret drawer fell out. And there lay the seven bank shares, with the letter to the "Immortal Beloved" and a portrait of the Countess Therese von Brunswick.[10]

The friends also found the English £100, untouched. Like the wine, this gift had come too late. At first the Philharmonic asked for its return. But when Moscheles begged that it should go to Karl "in honour of the great deceased," the Londoners handsomely consented.[11]

The funeral on March 29th befitted the man who had set music free and had made a professional out of that lackey, the composer. For Beethoven's burial the schools of Vienna were closed, and the military were called out to hold in check a throng of twenty thousand.[12] The city was alert to do him honour.

Schubert, Hummel, Seyfried, Kreutzer, Czerny, and the faithful old quartettists Linke and Schuppanzigh were

---

[10]Nobody realized that Beethoven's papers would one day be worth fortunes. When the holograph score of the Fifth symphony was put up at auction it brought six florins.

[11]This whole action by the members of the Philharmonic, after the exasperating dishonesty shown them by Beethoven, is an admirable example of British sportsmanship. The wheel has recently come full circle through the graceful gesture of the Beethoven Association of New York in contributing £100 to the endowment fund of the London Philharmonic Society.

[12]To his pauper's grave only three people had followed Mozart—and those but a part of the way.

among the torch carriers and pallbearers in the procession to the cemetery at Währing.

Forty-five years later the body was exhumed and re-buried in Vienna's Central Friedhof. There in that greatest of all musical pantheons, near the tombs of Mozart, Gluck, Hugo Wolf, Schubert, and Brahms, he lies. Over him rises an obelisk significantly marked in bronze by that ancient emblem of divine creativeness, the serpent biting its own tail. This encloses a butterfly—mute witness to the immortality of man's re-creative genius.

Chapter LI

HOW BEETHOVEN FREED MUSIC

A Versatile Emancipator — Established Composer on Professional Basis — Democratized and Universalized Music — No Disparagement of Bach Implied — Cultivated Nuance — Developed the Continental Concert — Matured the Art — Freed Form — Helped to Liberate Harmony — Created New Technic for Keyboard Instruments — Emancipated Modulation — Took Music Out-of-Doors — Freed It from Cloistered Outlook — The Luther of Church Music — And of the Dramatic Overture — Rid Music of Exhibitionism — Fought Venality — Developed Mechanism of Piano — And of Orchestra — Dissolved Time-Honoured Identity of Composer and Interpreter — Made Music More Self-Contained —Encouraged Rise of Creative Listening — Beethoven the Chief of Many Liberators

THROUGHOUT this book Beethoven has functioned as a versatile emancipator. We have seen him, by sheer personal magnetism, force of will, and intensity of genius, liberate the art of music from the long-standing indignity of being carried on by lackeys. We have seen him establish the composer's vocation upon a professional basis. No longer, thanks to Beethoven, would a musical genius sup, like Mozart, at the servants' table, or, like that unhappy lad, be kicked from the hall or discharged at a moment's notice. The poor boy from Bonn was the first composer to attain the dignity of seeing his symphonies printed in score.[1]

We have seen Beethoven deliver the music of his day from the ignominious rôle of obsequious hanger-on of the fashionable world and make it a universal thing—a materialization of the utmost range of the human mind and spirit, omitting none of the peaks and abysses. We have followed this imperious figure as he emancipated personality in music, detonating in his scores such a profound charge of thought and passionate emotion that the world still vibrates with the shock.

Let it be noted that such claims as these imply no disparagement of the stupendous achievements of Johann Sebastian Bach. For, although, in our own day, Bach's works have had for the modern composer perhaps as potent a liberating influence as Beethoven's, some unhappy fate decreed that his influence was to remain merely potential during the lifetime of the Father of Music, and until long after Beethoven's death.

In this heroic campaign Beethoven did not scorn the most apparently trivial details. A factor in the triumphant emergence of personality in music was his minute and painstaking labour in developing nuance, through the extension and invention of dynamic symbols and other marks of expression.

He took Continental music from the salon to the concert hall; from the castle to the cottage, and made it the most democratic thing in the æsthetic world.

[1]Hermann Kretzschmar, *Gesammelte Aufsätze über Musik.*

> Through Beethoven melody has become emancipated from the influence of fashion and fluctuating taste, and elevated to an eternally valid type of pure humanity.
>
> —RICHARD WAGNER.

> To him we owe the absolute emancipation of instrumental music from the trammels of polite artistic society . . . his hand . . . gained for us the full measure of spiritual democracy which is our artistic heritage to-day.
>
> —ERNEST WALKER.

> The sum of his message was freedom, artistic freedom, political freedom, personal freedom of will, of art, of faith, freedom of the individual in all the aspects of life.
>
> —PAUL BEKKER.

> Freedom above all.
>
> —BEETHOVEN.

The Man Who Freed Music

He loosed this already grown-up art from the incongruous nursery and gave it a rightful place—for the first time on equal terms—among its adult brethren. For this act Richard Wagner paid him tribute:

Through these last, and to us still unknown works of our wondrous master [Beethoven's posthumous quartets], of all others, the power of musical expression has taken a direction from which the music of earlier periods was often bound to hold deliberately aloof; I will here call that direction *the tenderly and deliberately passionate,* through whose expression music has first raised herself to an equal height with the poetry and painting of the greatest periods of the past. While with this expression Dante, Shakespeare, Calderon, and Goethe, like the great masters of painting in Italy and the Netherlands, took fee of every portrayable object in the world and man; and while it was this that first enabled them to paint the world and man: in music there had ruled an axiom which openly degraded her as a branch of Art, an axiom borrowed from the purely physical pleasure, the purely sensuous entertainment to be found in her.[2]

Beethoven liberated form, not from law, but from the specious compulsions of superficial and modish laws. He did much to free musical forms from slavery to the clogging conventions of formalism, and to give them that profound inner necessity through which they have ever since carried conviction. Nor was he wrecked on the reef of amorphism which has meant destruction to so many romanticists.

As a practical harmonist he broke ground for the skyscraper of Twentieth Century piano harmony. Philipp Emanuel Bach's innovation, the monodic style, had been used by Haydn and Mozart in their stand against the old polyphony. Beethoven's personal genius assimilated and hall-marked the contributions of these men and created a new harmonic, or chordal, technic for keyboard instruments. What was tentative, experimental in Haydn developed into Beethoven's characteristic idiom.[3]

He also freed modulation, brushing aside numerous hampering rules and enriching his harmonic scheme to match the liberty he had won in other departments.

This first great nature lover among composers took the

[2]In his report to King Ludwig II of Bavaria upon the establishment of a German music school in Munich.

[3]As early as the *finale* of the F minor sonata (Op. 2, No. 1) the *Largo et mesto* of the D major (Op. 10, No. 3) and the introduction of the *Pathétique* (Op. 13).

art out of the study, purged it of whatever smell of the lamp still clung to it, and gave it the run of meadow and forest.

He freed music from that cloistered outlook which ignored the march of events in the outside world of action, as Palestrina, Bach, and Haydn had ignored them.

By his choice of texts he presented vocal music with the freedom of the world of great literature—a pioneer accomplishment.

Through the accidental circumstance that the B minor Mass of Bach was not published until years after Beethoven's *Missa,* our hero became the Luther among composers, extricating the Mass from the bonds of convention and dogma.

He released the dramatic overture from subservience to that hybrid thing, opera; and the concerto orchestra from its abject servility as a mere accompanist to the solo part.

More than any previous composer, he rid music of the exhibitionistic taint of virtuosity for virtuosity's sake, and the reproach of composing to the order of outer compulsion rather than from inner necessity.

His ingenuity helped to throw open to the piano and the orchestra a new world of richness and sonority. The accident of his deafness freed the art in another way, by decreeing a divorce between composer and virtuoso and smashing the harmful old convention that the creative musician must necessarily fritter away his energies in interpretive work.

Perhaps his supreme achievement as emancipator was the exertion of a more potent influence than that of his greatest predecessors towards freeing music from the shackles of literature, whose servant it was in the beginning. By pouring into music a wealth of suggestive factors which made it so much more opulent and self-contained than ever before, he made it easier for the imagination of the ordinary listener at length to escape from the weakening incubus of cliché programs and, under the stimulus of this powerfully independent art, to fashion its own poetic interpretations.

Beethoven did more than any other composer has ever done toward realizing that utopian dream of the day when "all men shall be poets." It was scarcely his fault that mistaken inferences drawn from the *Pastoral* symphony, and from the regrettable *finale* of the *Choral* (which, too late, he himself regretted), should have led to a new enslavement of music by the poetic idea. Happily our own day is witnessing a fresh revolt from this degradation. The true lover of music must rejoice that, from the time when centenary thoughts of the Master commenced to hold the minds of all musicians, the world currents of thought and inclination seemed to begin setting away from the compromise relativities of opera and program music toward the pure absolutism of Bach, Brahms, Franck, and Beethoven.

Beethoven found the art of music narrowed to the pastime of a special class. He made it broadly human. He left it superhuman. Of course he was far from being the only man who ever freed music. In many ages and lands the art has been enslaved and has found its liberators. But the most potent of all these was Beethoven.

Chapter LII

WHAT BEETHOVEN MEANS TO US

A Supreme Master of Construction — Novel Architectonic Method — Made Forms "Internal" — Developed Them — Closely Knit Structures — Lengthened Sonata and Symphony — Multiplied Movements — The Germ-Motive — The Source-Motive — Modified the Rondo — And the Fugue — Three Greatest Contributions — The Titanic Allegro — The Scherzo — The Mystical Adagio — Treatment of Variation Form — Originality — Dramatic Power — Unexpectedness — Lavish Vitality — Economy — Concentration — Large Calibre — The Beethoven Religion — Beethoven as Physician — Conscientious Idealism — Trough and Crest — Fluctuations of Fashion — A Gift from Nature

A CENTURY after his death, why does Beethoven stand as the central—if not the chief—figure in music?

For one thing, because he was perhaps an even greater master of construction than the men who made the frieze of the Parthenon, Macbeth, the Sistine frescos, the B minor Mass, and Chartres Cathedral.

By forcing himself to sketch the plan of a movement before he had its subjects more than dimly in mind, he brought into music an architectonic idea hitherto foreign to it. This is the way masters of the other arts often work. The novelist and dramatist frequently start with the plot and build up their architectural plan before the characters take on life or the setting emerges. The painter finds it natural to determine his colour scheme and emotional outline before he knows exactly what figures are to appear in his fresco. The sculptor blocks out the important bony planes of his bust before focussing on details of features or drapery.

For a composer this way of working requires more concentrated imagination than for any other artist. But it is capable of accomplishing inestimable results. When Beethoven adapted to music this commonplace method of the other arts he performed a creative exploit of the first importance.[1]

We have seen how he took the charming, graceful, polished forms handed down to him by Haydn and Mozart, purified them of their superficial formalism, filled them instead with his own generous and fiery spirit, and made them "internal as well as external."[2] "His emotions," writes Mr. H. L. Mencken, "at their highest flight were almost godlike; he gave music a sort of Alpine grandeur."

In sonata-form movements we have watched him make a clean sweep of the star-play of "brilliant passages," the "dish-clatter" of bridge-work, and the cut-and-dried sort of development in which the hearer knew all too well what was coming next because it advanced and retreated like certain armies in the late war, "according to a prearranged plan." We have followed his iconoclastic progress as he remodelled the anticlimactic "cracker-box" type of re-

[1]For a most readable discussion of this subject see Newman, *The Unconscious Beethoven*, p. 115 ff.

[2]See Sir Hubert H. Parry's article: "Form," *Grove's Dictionary*, 3d ed.

capitulation which vainly tried to raise two laughs with the same story. And we have watched him replace it with a new and unpredictable version of the exposition. We have marvelled as he took the ancient coda, which brought the old-fashioned movement to a close as briefly and formally as the word "*finis*," and made of it a glorious and significant thing that sometimes rivalled all the rest of the structure in size, interest, and splendour. This coda exploit was much as though he had found a cathedral consisting of nothing but a large entrance portal, a nave, and a bricked-up transept, in the east side of which there was a tiny door for egress. It was as though he had converted this door into a tremendous breach and had then completed the cathedral with an apse generous and radiant as the choir of Beauvais.

We have seen Beethoven growing all his life progressively farther from the rococo procedure described by Sir Hubert H. Parry:

Prior to Beethoven, the development of a long work was based upon antitheses of distinct tunes and concrete lumps of subject representing separate organisms, either merely in juxtaposition, or loosely connected by more or less empty passages.[3]

But the Master progressively changed all this. Until, in the last sonatas and quartets,

the material is so continuous and unified that we are barely conscious of the passage from one theme to another. Sometimes the structure is so closely knit that even the searching eye of an analyst is defied.[4]

[3]Article: "Sonata," *Grove's Dictionary*, 3d ed.
[4]Grace, *Beethoven*, p. 214.

This, however, was by no means all that Beethoven did to form. He began with sonatas as long as the Mozart symphonies; went on to make symphonies twice as long as these; and finally, in the *Hammerklavier* and the C sharp minor, lengthened the sonata and the quartet to correspond. Taking a cue from the suite of Bach's day, he increased the prescribed number of quartet movements to six or seven. In a word, he regenerated the formalism of sonata-form and made it a thing of enhanced beauty, vitality, and expressiveness.

Meanwhile he carried his audience along with him; for by some fortunate chance this man appeared at just the moment when music lovers had begun to find their way about in the neatly demarcated sonata-form of rococo days and sighed for more difficulties to conquer.

Those readers who look into Part II, chapter LIV, may follow in detail the development of Beethoven's skill in the use of that interlocking thematic device we have called the germ-motive, by which he, first of composers, brought about complete inter-movement unity in long works.

This development of inter-movement liaison had important results. It led to such unified one-movement sonatas as Liszt's B minor, and to that suppression of pauses between different sections of symphonies which, combined with the influence of the *Pastoral*, ended in the one-movement symphonic poem.

In Part II, chapters LV and LVI, will be found studies of Beethoven's equally remarkable use of what we have called source-motives which lent thematic unity to his life work.

Beethoven changed for the better almost every form he touched. Even such a trivial and crystallized affair as the rondo he diversified, made more spacious, and endowed with elasticity, bringing it closer to sonata-form.

But he was not quite so successful with the strict fugue. He experimented at combining this with other forms. These experiments were seldom entirely happy, because the foreign matter introduced for relief tended to injure the fugue's essential one-ness and make it too diffuse. Yet, after all, this originality was sometimes justified by magnificently satisfying examples, such as the *finales* of the Third Rasoumowsky quartet and of the A flat sonata, the *Et vitam venturi* from the *Missa,* and supremely by the perfect opening of the C sharp minor quartet.

Of all Beethoven's concrete contributions to the art of music three were most original and powerful. There was (1) the first movement of titanic and elemental struggle (*Eroica, Serioso* quartet, Fifth, *Choral*).

There was (2) the *scherzo* of tumultuous humour and Dionysiac exultation or of elfin wit (*Eroica,* First Rasoumowsky, *Hammerklavier, Choral*). He did not invent the name *scherzo.* Haydn first quickened the minuet and called it by this attractive name. But Beethoven took what was handed him; broadened, deepened, elevated, and generally rebuilt it physically, intellectually, and emotionally into one of his most brilliantly original creations.

There was (3) the ethereal slow movement of mystic exaltation (*Choral*, B flat trio, Twelfth, Thirteenth, and Fifteenth quartets, *Benedictus* of *Missa*, and C minor sonata, Op. 111). His supreme *adagios* in variation form decidedly outnumber those in song form.

Beethoven's treatment of the variation-form is singularly interesting: it may be briefly described as a gradual advance back to the methods of Bach . . . in [his] colossal "Goldberg" variations (founded solely on the bass of the theme), which reaches its climax, in Beethoven's works, in the late pianoforte variations on a waltz of Diabelli. In this final aspect of the variation-form the merely melodic connection is secondary or indeed frequently non-existent: harmony and structure are the chief essential points, and though these may be altered to almost any extent, yet there is always, so to speak, the same intellectual thread running through the whole; and in place of the old rigid and merely decorative ideal, we have an ideal of unity in diversity, of the same subject presented in continually shifting and new lights.[5]

Beethoven was elementally original. Whenever the spirit moved him he could squeeze blood out of bricks. And he made rubies of the blood, and platinum of the residue of the bricks, and organized these products into miracles of design that would have put Benvenuto Cellini to shame. He could find laughter, beauty, and wonder in his own blaze of farcical fury over the loss of a groschen. (And he was capable of real fury, as well, on such an original provocation.) He could make an evolutionary epic—or the crack of doomsday—out of the peep of a small bird which was all but inaudible to his deaf ears.

---

[5]Ernest Walker, *Beethoven*, 1920, p. 159.

Mr. John Middleton Murry's statement about the simple originality of Jesus might apply, almost word for word, to Beethoven.

His qualities were all new: his quickness of apprehension, his profound simplicity of speech, his astonishing power of revealing an abysm of meaning through a transparent phrase—these appear before us in a combination so harmonious that we take them, as it were, for granted. They seem natural; and they are natural. Nothing is so new as a new naturalness, none so difficult to apprehend. A new simplicity is the most baffling of all human achievements, and the most perdurable.[6]

One reason why the musical embodiment of Beethoven's emotions was more original than that of his predecessors was this: He thought more deeply than they, and his music represented that deeper thought sublimated into feeling.

This music was an unprecedented thing under the sun. In spite of its liberal use of borrowed thematic material, it differed astonishingly from other music. The contrast was almost as sharp as if a winged man had suddenly begun beating his majestic pinions and flashing his irised mail above the stupefied picnickers in the Viennese *Prater*.

It was not merely [writes Mr. W. J. Turner] that music had been more formal in shape, more restricted in content, but that nobody before Beethoven had lived in his music, had imaged his life so fully in music. Earlier composers, Monteverde, Palestrina, Bach, Handel and Mozart, no doubt lived to some extent in their music. But we do not get from it the same impression of personality.[7]

---

[6] *Jesus, Man of Genius*, 1926, pp. 162–163.
[7] *Beethoven*, 1927, p. 31.

A strong factor in Beethoven's originality was his dramatic power. This was best shown when unhandicapped by librettos, in overtures like *Egmont*, *Coriolanus*, and those named *Leonore*. The Master could condense more drama into four notes and a pause than Lord Tennyson could get into four acts, a prologue, and an epilogue. He could imply the momentousness of true dramatic suspense and conflict not only by the opposition of *mf* to *ff* and of *sf* to an abruptly following *mp*, but by the contrast with each other of phrases, subjects, sections, movements, and whole works within a group.

In these ways he was a tremendous innovator. And his dramatic sense even extended beyond nuance to a remarkable use of the symbols of literary expression. For example, in a letter to Schindler, 1823, he referred to his next of kin in these terms: "my brother?!"

The unexpectedness of Beethoven—even at the fiftieth repetition—is one of the major clues to his power over us. For he is so extremely unforeseeable, yet after all so inevitable, that we more easily forget how his music goes than in the case of other composers. He tricks us, artfully holds us in harrowing suspense. By implication he strews between the lines of his staves the impalpable largesse of wisdom, of delicate allusion and sheer loveliness, for us to ferret out as we may. He tickles our curiosity by offering two alternative solutions equally plausible, only to settle on a third, undreamt-of but utterly convincing. He mocks our tender emotion by drumming on the keys with the shaft of his ruthless quill and the flat of his great paw. When we embark with him on some foaming tide of Gargantuan fun he leaves us abruptly in the lurch.

> And our sincerest laughter
> With some pain is fraught.

He is always surprising, perennially unpredictable. A chief reason why he charms us so completely is that almost every musical expedition on which he allows us to accompany him turns into a hidden treasure hunt—in the right spot.

He left [declares Dr. Dyson] thirty-two piano sonatas and nine symphonies, yet the more intimately they are known the less can one hazard even a guess as to what the thirty-third sonata or the tenth symphony would be like. They would be Beethoven, and that is but the statement of a formal enigma. How many movements they would have, and which would be which; what would be the psychological mood of any or all of them either in detail or as a whole; whether the theme would be slight and the handling sublime; whether there would be an orgy of rhythm or a feast of melody, or both; whether they would follow an old form or invent a new one; all these are matters on which nothing intelligible can be said. He would state, in some new and surprising way, ideas which so soon as they were grasped would seem to be as inevitable as they were unaccountable. We talk somewhat glibly of sonata-form and attach it to the name of Beethoven. There never was a greater deception. It is no doubt possible to extract from his movements two themes and a coda, and to say that here is, or might be, or should be, a double bar, and so forth. But it is often equally possible to extract three or four or five themes, though what will be their order of importance is beyond anyone to lay down. . . . The late sonatas and quartets are admitted to be beyond formal classification. He was descended in a measure from Haydn and Mozart, but it is none the less true that the moment we recognize his models we lose him. The things he himself said were just those that had no place in his inherited architecture. Beethoven is the creative iconoclast.[8]

He had that infectious intensity, that almost superhuman vitality characteristic of the great. His canvases suggest as profuse a lavishness of life as those of Rubens and Rembrandt, of Balzac and Dante and Shakespeare. Yet they are never centrifugal. They reveal instead the economy and concentration of a New Testament parable.

Whatever he may have sometimes been as a man, when it came to music Beethoven was nearly always big. It was not his way to let the notes hide the melody or the details conceal the essentials. What artist of smaller calibre could have stood like a colossus with one foot in classicism and one in romanticism, taking the best of each and fusing them into that higher thing which we have called "Beethoven-ism"?

Ever since he scrawled those memorable words beneath Moscheles's piano score of *Fidelio*,[9] Beethoven's "Man, help thyself!" spirit has been a growing inspiration to humanity. Since the Great War a strong movement has actually started in Germany and Austria towards a modern religion of strength and self-dependence, with Beethoven as its founder.

But even if he should fail as a prophet and the founder of a new religious order, he is already recognized as a potent

---

[8]*The New Music*, 1923, pp. 121–122.

[9]See p. 349.

physician. There is in his music something for everybody, everywhere, always. He is the healer, friend, and consoler[10] of humanity. If we are sad, tired, agitated, dull, wakeful, blue, bored, faint-hearted, oppressed by ugliness; if we suffer from a torpid imagination or from having the world too much with us, we may find in his music a richer variety of effective antidotes than in that of any other composer.[11] And, having found, we may echo that closing line of Miss Millay's sonnet: *On Hearing a Symphony of Beethoven:*

Music my rampart, and my only one.

After taking a Beethoven cure one understands why this man was the chief consoler and fortifier of the Central Powers in the Great War and of those Allies who were so large-minded as not to let national bitterness taint the world of beauty. One is not surprised to learn that the Bolshevists adopted Beethoven's as the official music of their movement. And one grasps more fully the truth in that remark of his to Bettina: "He who truly understands my music must thereby go free of all the misery which others bear about with them." Would that the poor physician had been able to heal himself!

As a healer he will be found 99 per cent. Jekyll and 1 per cent. Hyde. Like the ideal man of medicine, this man

---

[10]Readers of Proust's great novel will recall that, on the death of the hero's grandmother, her sisters telegraphed the single word "Beethoven." What piece did they have in mind? Was it the *Cavatina*, or the slow movement of the *Pathétique*, *"Apassionata,"* Second Rasoumowsky, *"Archduke,"* or *Choral? (Le Coté de Guermantes,* Vol. II, p. 34.)

[11]See chapter, "The Musical Pharmacy," in *The Musical Amateur,* 1911, and "Directions" and musical recipes in *The Poetry Cure with Music and Pictures,* 1927; both by the author.

almost never spared himself. With incredible faithfulness and courage he kept pouring out his force through his pen until the music was as good as it could be made. As Voltaire said of another artist, "He laboured at every new work as if he had his reputation still to make." The mass of sketches for the C sharp minor quartet alone is staggering to contemplate, especially when one notices the amount of splendid material he set down and then rejected as not good enough. His six false starts on the fourth movement alone make a thrilling object lesson on the conscientious idealism of genius and on the steadfastness and desperation of effort which often goes to the making of immortal things.

Naturally no man's work can be all best; otherwise there would be none of those contrasts on which the very nature of the superlative depends. His personal life was a succession of trough and crest, and his work more or less followed suit. One might graphically show the comparative quality of the nine symphonies by some such arrangement of type as this:

$$1 \quad 2 \quad 3 \quad 4 \quad 5 \quad 6 \quad 7 \quad 8 \quad 9$$

Viewing his whole life work in the large, one can roughly discern something of the same periodicity, though in *largo* time, which one sees in the *presto agitato* ups and downs of his relations with his much-enduring friends. Though his works were not written in the strict order of their opus numbers, these numbers nevertheless form a chronological sequence roughly correct enough for a bird's-eye view. Of Beethoven's first one hundred numbered works (with the single exception of the glorious opus 60's) the successive groups of ten, taken as wholes, oscillate from weaker to stronger and back to weaker. The groups beginning with Op. 10, 30, 50, 70, and 90 all contain better music than those beginning with Op. 1, 20, 40, and 80.

After the Napoleonic Wars a new generation arose which preferred to Beethoven the more easily comprehended music of Italy. The German Master was partially shelved as *vieux jeu,* only to regain his popularity after some years. A century later, in the United States, a similar thing happened to him. During the Great War the "Hun" Beethoven was taboo. And even after peace came the fashion-worshipping youngsters regarded him as a fossil. But before the centenary of his death he was again in high favour. The Beethovens can afford to disregard the fluctuations of fashion and to say, as the Master remarked when told that his work did not please: "It will please some day." Such a person is not for a day "but for all time." He is not for a nation but for all people. To him might better be applied the words of the Chevalier de Boufflers about Voltaire: "This man is too great to be contained in the bounds of his country; he is a gift from nature to the whole earth."

PART II

BEETHOVEN'S WORKSHOP

Chapter LIII

THE BORROWING ALCHEMIST

Prospecting Adventures in Beethoven — True Value of Such Researches — Beauty in the Making — Plagiarism vs. Genial Appropriation — Choice of Subject Matter for Part II — Beethoven Borrows from Haydn and Mozart — From Himself — Foreign Folk Tunes — From Himself — The Rust Imposture — Mozart Fathers the Joy Tune — Echoes in the Last Quartets

PART II is a study of Beethoven's creative processes. It has been written for the musical reader. All others are counselled to skip the next four chapters.

There are few more engrossing, thrilling, or rewarding forms of adventure than a prospecting expedition through the works of Beethoven, in search of indebtedness, loans, inter-movement, and inter-work relationships. Sometimes —though rarely—these are found on the surface. But the most exciting and rewarding discoveries are of those deeply and subtly hidden facts which call for stubborn exertion with spade, pick, and pan.

The writer would again disclaim any fatuous idea of "explaining" a piece of music in tracing the origin or other relationships of its themes. The interest and value of such studies lie in the light they shed on the richness, economy, and variety in unity of Beethoven's creative processes.

These pages show how successfully, how almost unrecognizably, this man could transmute his own earlier ideas and those of others, then use them not only in locking together the parts of a single movement or composition, but to compass scores of works as well into a larger unity.

The study of beauty in the making is valuable both in itself and for the fresh illumination it sheds on finished works of art. Writing of the creative processes of Coleridge, another great and unfortunate genius, one of the foremost scholars of our day declares:

> It is because the worth of beauty is transcendent that the subtle ways of the power that achieves it are transcendently worth searching out. . . . For a work of pure imagination is not something fabricated by a *tour de force* from nothing, and suspended, without anchorage in fact, in the impalpable ether of an imaginary world. No conception could run more sharply counter to the truth.[1]

Beethoven was one of those rare men who could miraculously steal a tune and then invest it with dazzling novelty. The writer would no more dream of belittling the originality of such a feat than of attempting to "explain" a sonata or symphony. He agrees with Anatole France that the old distinction between plagiarism and genial appropriation for re-creation might well be revived and furnished with expressive designations, for our present vocabulary is inadequate to deal fairly with such matters.

It is absurd, this quibbling about plagiarisms which the vainglorious Nineteenth Century, with its notorious mania for

[1]John Livingston Lowes, *The Road to Xanadu*, 1927, p. 240.

originality, has invented. Formerly all subjects belonged to everybody and each took his property where he found it. Most certainly the idea of plagiarism existed, but it meant theft committed without talent or intelligence, the clumsy disfiguring of what was taken. In this sense,—the only true one, and which forbids a writer to do less well than his predecessors,—all of us are plagiarists if we amount to anything. . . . According to the merit of each one you can tell almost in advance if he is really a plagiarist. [France is now giving the word its usual derogatory sense.] Sardou is, fatally, because he borrows, and Shakespeare never was, although he stole infinitely more than the other. He struck the entire world for a loan, did Shakespeare! But he had a way with him! The whole thing lies there.[2]

That, as a borrowing alchemist, Beethoven had quite as much of "a way with him" as Shakespeare had, the reader of Part I may already have noted in connection with such works as the Fifth, Seventh, and Ninth symphonies, the *"Memory"* sonata (Op. 110), and the C sharp minor quartet.

The subject matter of Part II was chosen more with a view to freshness than comprehensiveness. Without wholly neglecting the discoveries of Grove, Nottebohm, Helm, Riemann, Marliave, Cassirer, Ernest, Frimmel,[3] and others, the available space has been chiefly given to those discoveries made by the writer and his liberal friends, which have not yet been announced in print.

Beethoven's predecessors wrought very much in the generous spirit of the old mastersinging cobbler of *Rothenburg*

---

[2]Nicolas Segur, *Conversations avec Anatole France*, 1925, p. 53.

[3]An able article on this subject will be found in Frimmel's *Beethoven Handbuch*, 1926, Vol. I, p. 11.

ob der Tauber. An inscription on the front of his house is still to be deciphered.

> *Im Hause meiner Väter*
> *Klopf ich allhier das Leder,*
> *Und Mache meinen Reim dazu,*
> *Ich sorge nicht wer's nach mir thu'.*

> . . . .

> (Here in the house of my *paters*
> I hammer and hammer on leather,
> And thread my rhymes together,
> Careless of imitators.)

If Bach, Handel, Haydn, and Mozart were "careless of imitators," who was Beethoven to refuse such bounty? Light-heartedly and light-fingeredly he took his tune where he found it.

This chapter will not attempt to exhaust the subject of Beethoven's thematic indebtedness to his predecessors and to himself. A full treatment of this interesting field might call for additional volumes.

The opening theme of the F minor piano sonata (Op. 2) can be traced back, as we have already seen on p. 222, to the *finale* of Mozart's G minor symphony. Because this arpeggio motive was a favourite with the Mannheim school of composition it was known as the "Mannheim rocket." But, as it can be traced still further back, to the first piano sonata in F minor of the Hamburg master Philipp Emanuel Bach, perhaps it should be known instead as the "Hamburg rocket." Note that these sonatas are in the same key.

The *finale* of the C minor string quartet (Op. 18, No. 4) owes an unpayable debt to Haydn's famous *Gipsy Rondo;* and, as we have seen,[4] one of "Papa's" best Sunday tunes, from his fifty-eighth sonata, is clearly recognizable in the Trio of the minuet of the A major quartet (Op. 18, No. 5).

Ex. 207

In the opening *Allegro* of the First symphony, the bridge-work between the first and second subjects evokes a vision of scissors, paste, and Mozart's *Don Juan* overture. While the beginning of the *Andante cantabile con moto* is a not wholly legitimate scion of the *Andante* in the same composer's G minor symphony.

It made small difference to Beethoven whether his tunes originated with one of the old masters or with a band of gipsies or his own earlier self. The *Eroica* Funeral March opens

Ex. 26

---

[4] See pp. 369–370.

with more than a suggestion of the most forceful *Allegro* he had, up to 1804, given to chamber music, the start of the C minor quartet (Op. 18, No. 4).

Ex. 208

The theme which opens the *Pastoral* symphony[5]

Ex. 209

appears to have been taken from an old Slavonic folk tune.[6] And strangely enough this same tune is to be found in one of the *Grands*, or wordless songs, of the cattle drovers of Auvergne. Stranger still, M. Canteloube has discovered[7] that the oboe solo at bar 91 of the *Pastoral scherzo* closely resembles an old Auvergne *bourrée*; while the Trio's rough

[5]See p. 262.

[6]See F. X. Kuhac's collection of folk songs, Agram, 1878–1881.

[7]J. Canteloube, *Beethoven et l'Auvergne, Le Courrier Musical*, Feb. 1, 1927.

country dance is curiously like a certain *Montagnarde* of that land.

Earlier in this book it has been asserted that the *"Geister"* trio (Op. 70, No. 1) "sounds like a sort of abridged edition *de luxe"* of the D major sonata (Op. 10, No. 3). Both present the contrast of a magnificent and gloomy D minor *Largo* set between more cheerful, fast movements in D major. The first movements of both begin with themes similar enough to be first cousins. Compare that of the *"Geister"*

Ex. 87

with the opening of the sonata.

Ex. 210

Both commence with resolute unison passages of four bars, the first notes of which run D–C sharp–B–A.

Notice that this theme in the sonata (see Ex. 210) ends with an upward scale like that in the first tune of the trio's *finale* (see Ex. 90). The earlier theme (Ex. 210) apparently held both of these later ones (Ex. 87 and 90) in solution. This sort of relationship also holds, though more distantly, between the first subject of the trio's *finale*

Ex. 90

and the *Menuetto* of the sonata.

Ex. 89

When he wrote the new work Beethoven must, for some reason, have been saturated with the old one. He even used a figure that had occurred once only, and then as if by accident, in the recapitulation of the sonata's first movement.

Ex. 211

This recurs almost identically, and with increased importance, in the trio's *finale*.

Ex. 212

The inter-relation of the E flat trio (Op. 70, No. 2) and the E flat sonata (Op. 31, No. 3) has already been mentioned.[8] An additional reason for not making this trio a sonata, as the composer seems to have at first intended, may have been this: He felt that the fast 6/8 movement in each work piled up the resemblance. And he must have seen that the *Allegretto ma non troppo* of the trio

Ex. 213

<hr />

[8] See p. 229.

was too similar in contour and style to the already popular *Menuetto* of the sonata.

Ex. 214

This resemblance between opus 70 and opuses 10 and 31 is but a single rather marked example of Beethoven's growing habit of harking back to his pre-*Eroica* themes and remoulding them "nearer to the heart's desire." The older he grew, the more he seemed to enjoy working over his early ideas. In the *scherzo* of the C minor string trio (Op. 9), this tune—

Ex. 215

is surely a foretaste of the way in which the *finale* of the *Serioso* quartet (Op. 95) was to open.

Ex. 216

(Transposed for comparison)

But the Master also enjoyed echoing his own recent themes. Notice how in the "*Emperor*" concerto at bar 19

[520]

of the first movement the oboes and bassoons bring in a quasi-reminiscence of the second theme of the Violin concerto's first movement. And in the next bar (20) the piano has an echo of another theme in the same movement. At that time Beethoven must have been full of his beautiful, three-year-old violin piece.

It is curious to observe that the *"Archduke"* trio (B flat, Op. 97) begins

Ex. 217

with the Hero theme of the *Eroica* symphony, if one disregards in Ex. 217 the purely auxiliary third note. See also how the end of the second subject of the *"Archduke's"* first movement

Ex. 218

recalls the opening of the First Rasoumowsky quartet:

Ex. 219

In his *Beethoven*[9] and in his editions of T. W. Rust's music M. D'Indy stated that Beethoven had borrowed material from the older composer. Among other particu-

---

[9]Pp. 19, 21.

lars he specified that "the *Adagio* of the sonata for violin and lute [written in 1791], by Rust, bears an astounding resemblance to the melody of the superb *Andante* which forms the middle [*sic*] movement of the trio Op. 97."

Here is the beginning of the Rust movement:

Ex. 220

And Beethoven's *Andante* starts as follows.

Ex. 221

At first glance, this assuredly looks like borrowing. But if the distinguished French musician had studied the original sketches of the B flat trio and followed there the slow, painful evolution of the immortal theme from some such crude and alien inception as this:

Ex. 222

etc.

(the reader must supply the treble clef and two sharps, because the Master was far beyond such details), he would have seen that Beethoven had reached his goal independently. For him to have deliberately copied Rust's _Adagio_ would have been a curious parallel to the aged Velasquez's act if he had deigned to crib the idea of Guido Reni's canvas[10] for that Venus and Cupid which is now one of the chief treasures of the National Gallery.

The Master's indebtedness to Rust, however, has been disproved much more definitely than the Sketch Books could disprove it. Since the publication of M. D'Indy's _Beethoven_ and of his noteworthy prefaces to the modern editions of this so-called pioneer, the researches of Neufeldt have demonstrated that the blameless old T. W. Rust has been turned, in his grave, into an impostor. It now appears that his grandson Wilhelm (one of J. S. Bach's successors as cantor of the Thomas Kirche in Leipzig) deliberately doctored his grandfather's naïve music so that T. W. Rust should seem to have been thematically a most important

---

[10]Now in the Alte Pinakothek in Munich.

precursor of Beethoven and of Wagner; with the result that M. D'Indy was completely duped by the most impudent and amusing imposture in the history of music.[11]

In the first violin part of the *Vivace* of the Seventh symphony

Ex. 223

the writer stumbled upon a phrase which is the ghost of a snatch from the *Egmont* overture.

Ex. 224

This suggests how, when composing the Seventh symphony in 1812, the Master's mind was still obsessed by his labour of love over *Egmont* two years before.

As this chapter was being revised, Miss Marion Bauer kindly contributed a discovery—the probable source of the D major Joy theme in the *Choral finale*.[12] It is the Trio of the *Menuetto* from Mozart's *"Haffner"* symphony (D major, Köchel No. 385)

Ex. 225

[11]The reader may find full information about the sensational episode in T. de Wyzewa, *Beethoven et Wagner*, 1914, p. 173.

[12]See Ex. 169, p. 413.

The *"Haffner"* was composed in 1782. Beethoven probably heard it in the most impressionable part of his youth; and he was blessed with a tenacious memory.[13] He must have had the tune in mind, consciously or unconsciously, when he wrote those songs which were to be the forerunners of the Joy tune. *To Hope*,[14] besides starting with the same melodic progression as Ex. 225, is likewise written in 3/4 time. And *Mit einem gemalten Band*[15] even echoes the third and fourth bars of the Mozart melody, which fall away in the *finale* of the *Choral*. In its power and breadth and almost epic "folk" quality the Joy tune contrasts so strongly with its dainty aristocratic ancestor, the *"Haffner"* tune, that one is reminded of Lenz's remark: "Between Mozart and Beethoven came the French Revolution."

Notice the consanguinity between the exciting march which takes the place of a *scherzo* in the A major sonata (Op. 101), and the *finale* of the C sharp minor quartet (Op. 131), and the *Alla marcia* of the A minor quartet (Op. 132). All three of these movements were destined to make an almost obsessionary impression upon the sensitive minds of Schubert and Schumann.

The second subject of the opening *Allegro* of the A minor quartet

Allegro   Ex. 226

---

[13]Mozart, for his part, had borrowed the melody from Sandrina's aria, *"Una voce sento al core,"* in his own early opera *La Finta Giardiniera*. Even if Beethoven had never heard it in the symphony he assuredly had in its embryonic form in the opera.

[14]See Ex. 281, p. 573.

[15]See Ex. 282, p. 573.

recalls the end of the *Allegro con brio's* first subject in the
D major violoncello sonata (Op. 102):

Ex. 227

Allegro con brio

(Transposed for comparison)

The *scherzo* of the E flat quartet (Op. 127) starts with
a recitative-like enunciation of the theme

Ex. 228

which apparently fathered the recitative passage for the
lower strings at bar 92 of the A minor quartet's *Allegro*.

Ex. 229

The curious fact has been apparently overlooked that
Ex. 228 is the same tune as the bracketed portions of Ex.
229, but with the accents and time-values shifted.

Another recitative is also reminiscent. When one remembers that Beethoven originally sketched the glorious
main tune of the A minor's *finale* to end the Ninth symphony, one cannot wonder that it should be introduced by
a recitative recalling those given out by the double basses
when they usher in the *Hymn to Joy*.

The theme of the *Andante* interludes in the slow movement of the A minor quartet is actually an echo of "one

of the German dances written for the Ridotto balls fully thirty years before."[16] This dance is the eighth in A major. Probably through a misprint, Thayer finds it echoed not in the slow, but in the "first" movement. In the *Allegro* a memory of the great A flat sonata has already been noted.[17]

The B flat quartet (Op. 130) gives, in the transition between the first and second subjects of its opening *Allegro* (at the 41st measure),

Ex. 230

a reminder of the second subject of the *"Harp"* quartet's corresponding movement.

Ex. 231

There is also a parallel between the latter work and the C sharp minor quartet. The *Adagio* of the *"Harp"* quartet,

Ex. 232

---

[16]Thayer, Vol. III, p. 215.
[17]See p. 440.

at the second *espressivo*, gives a foretaste of the breathless, inarticulate anguish of the *Cavatina's* "*Beklemmt*" portion.

Ex. 185

Starting at bar 38 of the first movement of the F major quartet (Op. 135), the accompaniment figure

Ex. 233

in triplets gives a quotation from the F major *Pastoral* symphony—an echo of the start of the *Peasants' Merry-making.*

And the *Es muss sein* theme

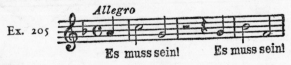

Ex. 205

of the *finale* of this last quartet reverses the beginning of
the great A flat sonata fugue

Ex. 234

But let us turn from Beethoven's borrowings to the vastly
more interesting subject of his constructive alchemy.

Chapter LIV

BEETHOVEN INVENTS THE GERM-MOTIVE

Germ-Motive vs. Source-Motive — New Meaning of the Word "Idea" — Beethoven Feels His Way — A Consciously Used Device — Treatment of Germ-Motive in Part I — Progenitor of Leitmotif — Early Experimentation — First Elaborate Use in Pathétique — C Minor Quartet — Violin Sonatas A Minor and F Major — Second Symphony — "Kreutzer" Sonata — Eroica — "Appassionata" — C Minor Symphony — Serioso Quartet — B Flat Trio — Eighth Symphony — A Masterpiece of Camouflage — Beethoven Describes His Own Creative Processes — Initial Germ-Motive in Last Sonatas — Choral Symphony — Last Quartets

To INSURE full understanding of this and the following chapters it is well to recall the distinction between a "germ-motive" and a "source-motive." A germ-motive is a musical phrase which recurs, more or less disguised, in different movements of a composition to lend the whole thematic unity. A source-motive, on the other hand, is a phrase which recurs more or less identically in a number of distinct compositions.

To illustrate: A scrap of tune may—though rarely—confine itself to the retail business of being a germ-motive, like phrase (e) beginning the Eighth symphony.[1] Or it

---

[1] See p. 547 ff.

may—almost as rarely—specialize in the wholesale trade of being a source-motive, like the phrase from *Adelaide*.[2] Or, as usually happens, it may carry on both wholesale and retail activities simultaneously, like the rhythmical source-*cum*-germ-motive that opens the C minor symphony,[3] or the triad that begins the main movements of all the other symphonies except the Sixth and Seventh.

Though the writer has been obliged by the poverty of the existing technical vocabulary to coin the expressions germ-motive and source-motive, the nature of what they denote has long been understood. Sir Hubert H. Parry has written vividly upon the function performed by the germ-motive.

Before Beethoven, the development of a long work was based upon antitheses of distinct tunes and concrete lumps of subject representing separate organisms, either merely in juxtaposition, or loosely connected by more or less empty passages. There were ideas indeed, but ideas limited and confined by the supposed necessities of the structure of which they formed a part. But what Beethoven seems to have aimed at was the expansion of the term "idea" from the isolated subject to the complete whole; so that instead of the subjects being separate, though compatible items, the whole movement, or even the whole work, should be the complete and uniform organism which represented in its entirety a new meaning of the word "idea," of which the subjects, in their close connexion and inseparable affinities, were subordinate limbs. This principle is traceable in works before his time, but not on the scale to which he carried it, nor with his conclusive force. In fact, the condition of art had not been sufficiently

---

[2]See p. 575.
[3]See pp. 152–154 and 540.

mature to admit the terms of his procedure, and it was barely mature enough till he made it so.[4]

In learning to handle the germ-motive, Beethoven felt his way slowly and cautiously, very much as he did in acquiring the technic of any new means of expression, like the quartet, the symphony, or the Mass. He made small systematic use of subtly camouflaged versions of identical germ-tunes, in any type of composition, before he had gone a considerable way in the mastery of that particular vehicle. For example, he did scarcely any inter-movement liaison work before the eighth of the thirty-two piano sonatas, the last of the six trios, the fourth of the ten violin sonatas, the eleventh of the sixteen string quartets. In his symphonies he began earlier, with the Second. But it should be borne in mind that he deferred this composition until his thirty-second year. His vocal writing shows fewer traces of thematic interlocking. Perhaps he felt that the text gave it unity enough.

In reading the manuscript of this book the late Oscar G. Sonneck noted:

I believe that what you call the principle of the germ-motive, one of the fundamental characteristics of Beethoven's creative style, was consciously used by him for the sake of organic cohesion. Of course, Beethoven's having acquired it does not mean that he applied it pedantically to every composition. He probably applied it or not according to occasion, character of work and fitness of things. However, its absence in any work, does not argue against his having acquired such structural principles,

---

[4]Article: Sonata, *Grove's Dictionary*, 3d ed., pp. 828–829.

and against their *deliberate* application, when he considered that advisable.

Throughout Part I of this book the germ-motive has played an important rôle in connection with such highly integrated compositions as the *Sonate Pathétique,* the *Eroica,* the C minor and *Choral* symphonies, and the "*Quartetto Scherzoso*" (B flat, Op. 130). Even if this invention did not represent one of the most important artistic advances ever made in the direction of economy of material and variety in unity, its distinction as the father of the Wagnerian leitmotif would alone entitle it to the dignity of a separate chapter.

By long practice Beethoven learned to conceal his inter-movement liaison devices so deftly that he could join his materials into an organic whole without letting any mortar appear between the stones. The more subtly he performed these secret *coups de maître* the more thrill they impart to their discoverer. The germ-motives which the writer has been fortunate enough to find in the *Eroica* and Eighth symphonies, the *Serioso* and the "*Archduke*" have given him more pleasure than stumbling upon the prophecy of the A flat sonata fugue in the *Eroica,* or the B–A–C–H anagram in the Second Rasoumowsky quartet. For the latter discoveries were more in the class of curious facts, while the former proved to be aids in deepening the understanding, appreciation, and enjoyment of these works by turning new light on the marvellous economy and unity of their variety.

One of the Master's earliest experiments with the germ-motive took place in the First sonata (Op. 2, No. 1), where the middle section of the *finale* is a modification of the "Mannheim rocket" subject[5] which begins the opening movement. But his first elaborate use of this device was the somewhat obvious one which has already been noted in connection with the *Sonate Pathétique*.[6]

In the C minor quartet (Op. 18, No. 4) Beethoven used an even simpler unifying device than the patent and literal tune-repetitions of the *Pathétique*. This mechanism was to recur in important works like the "*Kreutzer*," the "*Appassionata*," the last sonatas, and the *Choral* symphony. It consisted merely in starting the several main divisions of a composition with the same interval. The first three movements of the C minor quartet begin with a rising fourth (G–C). In a sense both intermediate sections of its rondo-*finale* open similarly. Indeed, in the first and third movements the correspondence is carried even further. For both of these begin with the progression G–C–E flat. This sort of unifying device is so rudimentary that it might perhaps be more suitably called a sub-germ-motive.

As this book goes to press Miss Marion Bauer discovers[7] that the opening phrase of the A minor violin sonata (Op. 23), C–D–E–D–C–B–A is a germ-motive. It recurs in the first themes of the *Andante scherzoso* and of the *finale*.

---

[5]See the transposed Ex. 82, p. 222. Also p. 514.

[6]See pp. 53–55.

[7]Too late to admit of engraving the musical examples.

The same friend finds another germ-motive running through the first subjects of each movement in the *"Spring"* violin sonata (F major, Op. 24).

Although there are attempts in Mozart's G major trio (Köchel No. 496) and his D major quartet (Köchel No. 575) at a thematic interlocking of movements, and although we take into account the liaison work in Beethoven's C minor quartet[8] these violin sonatas occupy in their own sphere the same innovative position which the *Pathétique* holds in piano music and the Second symphony in orchestral. They mark the first mature, elaborate, and fully successful employment of the germ-motive in chamber music.

As we have already seen,[9] the Second symphony employed the triad source-motive extensively as a germ-motive. It also used two lesser germ-motives—and used them much less openly than the triad.

Melodically speaking, the first two measures of the *Larghetto*

Ex. 236

are closely imitated by the third and fourth measures of the *scherzo*:

---

[8]See p. 534.
[9]See pp. 110–111.

Ex. 21

for the upper D in the third bar of Ex. 21 is so orchestrated as to be the melodic note of that chord. The first four measures of Ex. 236 go on to provide material for the opening of the Trio of the *scherzo*.[10]

Ex. 237

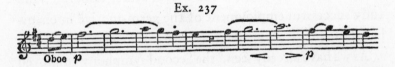

There is small finesse about the *"Kreutzer"* sonata's simple interlocking device. This whole work is built largely on a two-note phrase.[11] The second note falls or rises the interval of a second. This germ-motive first appears (marked by a bracket) in the fourth bar of the slow Introduction,

Ex. 238

---

[10]Ex. 237 was to sire the first half of the Trio of the *Choral* symphony's incomparable *scherzo*. (See pp. 400–401.)

[11]As Mr. Louis von Gaertner has kindly pointed out to the writer.

and soon after in inverted form. It leads off the opening *Presto,* inverted in the treble

Ex. 239

but normal in the bass.

The second subject begins with the phrase first rising, then falling.

Ex. 240

A large part of the variation theme is made up of these two notes, in both forms;

Ex. 241

while the same may be said for the opening subject of the *finale.*

Ex. 242

Notice how, at its first occurrence, the motive simultaneously goes up in the violin and down in the piano, while the second subject, like that of the earlier *Presto*, starts with two successive announcements of the phrase, but both times falling.

Ex. 243

Not until the *Eroica* period did the Master learn how to fuse together the parts of a great work so subtly that the means disappeared and only the artistic end—a mysteriously convincing unity—remained apparent. In an earlier chapter[12] we have seen Beethoven arrive at the Hero theme by first telescoping the *Prometheus* theme, and then making the whole symphony revolve around this fundamental tune.

Notice how the *Eroica* is founded almost as completely as the Second upon that germ-source-motive, the triad. Turning back to chapter XVI one may see that this chord

[12]See pp. 126–131.

underlies examples 25, 26, 28, 30, 46, 51. While the *Prometheus* theme itself (Ex. 31) seems like an elaborate prelude and postlude to its own triad E flat–G–B flat.

The "*Appassionata*" shares with the "*Kreutzer*" its thematic countersign, the rising or falling interval of a second.[13] Throughout its opening *Allegro assai* much is made of the end of the first subject with its rhythmic premonition of the Fifth symphony in the bass.

Ex. 54

The beginning of the variation theme consists of little else but the "countersign"—the interval of a second.

Ex. 55

---

[13]For this fact the writer is indebted to his friend, the Dutch composer, Mynheer Julius Roentgen.

And the first subject of the finale—merely its beginning is quoted—

Ex. 244

rigorously follows suit.

The Fifth symphony, like the Second, uses a favourite source-motive as germ-motive. The Second keeps to the triad and the *Pathétique* motive. The C minor is loyal to the triad and the so-called "*Fate*" motive.

Ex. 77

In the first movement this rhythmic formula is absent from but three of the thirty pages of score. It recurs like a faint promise of hope at the 23d bar of the variations. It is hurled in what might be a defiant personal assertion from the 19th measure of the *scherzo*. It raises its voice in something like a frenzy of victorious exuberance at bars 44 and 65 of the *finale*; and reappears in that miraculous echo of the *scherzo* (at bar 160) which seemed to Beethoven's envious contemporary, Spohr, the only part of the Fifth worthy of unreserved praise.

The *Serioso* quartet (F minor, Op. 95) is a masterpiece of secret interlocking. Compare with the first subject of the opening *Allegro con brio,*

Ex. 110

the eight-note motto which introduces the slow movement.

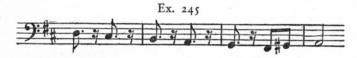

Ex. 245

Omit the first two notes of Ex. 110, and Ex. 245 is seen to be a slow variant of it.

Then consider that memorable fugato, the second subject of the *Allegretto ma non troppo*

Ex. 108

(which, by the way, reminds one of a passage in the slow movement of the C major Rasoumowsky). Prune away its passing notes and it becomes a chromatic variant, as Riemann pointed out,[14] of Ex. 245. And its beginning and end

---

[14]*Streichquartette*, p. 96.

are also seen to be developments of a characteristic little
motive from the closing part of the first movement's exposition (bar 52).

Ex. 246

These three notes also furnish the stuff of the coda.

A tempestuous *Allegro assai vivace ma serioso*, does duty
for a *scherzo* in this serious work. After the two spasmodic,
baulky false starts, and the two long pauses which serve as
introduction, the first bars

Ex. 247

might conceivably be taken as a scherzification of the descending portion of Exs. 110 and 245, while the last three
notes of these examples are echoed at the notes D flat–E flat–
F flat in the chorale-like tune of

Ex. 109

The little ascending motive just mentioned, now transposed and modified into B flat–C–D flat, reappears in Part II of the long tripartite first subject of the *finale*.

Ex. 248

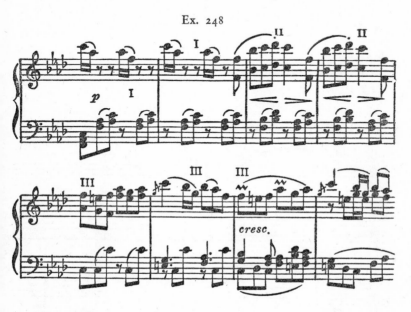

Herr Ernest considers[15] that bars 5 to 8 of that short, happy ending, the final *Allegro*, are a mere jazzing up, so to speak, of the first two measures of Ex. 248 (Pt. I). And Riemann[16] traces a few subtle and minute resemblances between the first three movements. With these exceptions, curiously enough, the inter-movement relationships, which weld the *Serioso* into such a strongly unified personality, seem to have escaped the notice of the commentators. Since the *Pathétique* we have met with no composition but the

[15]*Beethoven*, p. 528.
[16]*Streichquartette*, p. 99 ff.

Eroica that observed such a rigid four-movement economy of material or was thematically so tied up into a single homogeneous parcel.

In the *"Archduke"* trio (B flat, Op. 97) the liaison work, though more varied than in the *Serioso*, is no less skilfully concealed.

The first and second subjects of the first movement run as follows:

Ex. 249

At the start of the *scherzo*

Ex. 250

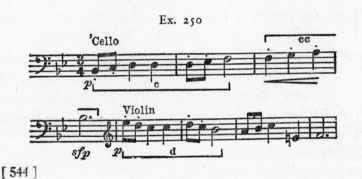

notice how (c) is derived from the last five notes of (a) in
Ex. 249 and (cc) from (a)'s last four notes. Each bar of
(c) also sounds very much like (ab) upside down, while
(d) imitates (ab) with lopsided approximateness.

The beginning of the *scherzo's* Trio

Ex. 112

is an elaboration of the last four notes of (a) in Ex. 249.
It is as if (a) were a snowy hill and Ex. 112 a climber who
slipped back a step for every other step up.

In the *Andante con moto*

Ex. 251

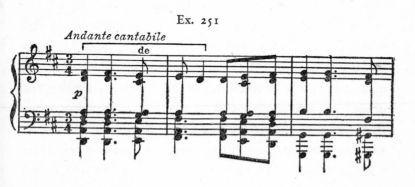

the progression (de) of Ex. 251 amounts to the tune (ab)
in Ex. 249, with a suitable change of rhythm. And the

whole melodic scheme of Ex. 251 may be found summarized in Ex. 250 by humming the second bar of (d) before the first bar of (d).

At the start of the *finale*

Ex. 252

disregard the passing notes of (e), Ex. 252, and notice that the phrase comes from the first three notes of (a) in Ex. 249. The phrase (f) bears a family resemblance to (b), Ex. 249, while the whole of Ex. 252 follows the general contour of Ex. 250.

This enumeration has far from exhausted the germ-motive work in the "*Archduke.*" We can only hope the reader himself is as far from exhaustion.

The Eighth symphony is a surprising example of the skill which Beethoven had now developed in the use of his inter-locking invention. With self-effacing thrift he built the greater part of this work out of the seemingly careless and unsophisticated seven bars with which the symphony opens. In the case of the *Eroica*[17] and the "*Archduke*"[18] we have seen how he could group more than one germ-motive into a single subject. His easy mastery of complicated liaison

---

[17]See chap. XVI.
[18]Pp. 544–546.

work grew until he created the long, apparently naïve opening of the Eighth symphony

Ex. 253

as a sort of "host," if one may term it so, for a swarm of little germ-motives. Or perhaps one might better call the start of the *Allegro vivace* the Alma Mater of a blithe crowd of whistling students. Notice how the four-note phrase marked (a) in the melody just quoted reappears all through the opening portion of the second subject.

Ex. 124

Look again at Ex. 253 and observe that out of the equally short phrase marked (b) is evolved the closing part of the second subject (after the first bar of Ex. 254)

Ex. 254

See the growingly intensive economy of material in the dotted rhythm of bar 1, Ex. 254, which is conjured out of (d), the two middle notes of (b) (Ex. 253).

Consider the hidden spun-sugar-and-white-mice tune,[19]

Ex. 125

which Beethoven, that genial conjuror, produced by sleight of hand from the mouth of the recapitulation. And see how the four-note phrase ending bar 4 is simply (a) standing on its head; a statement which holds just as true of the notes

[19]See pp. 323–324.

marked (aa) in the second subject of the *Allegretto scher-zando.*

Ex. 255

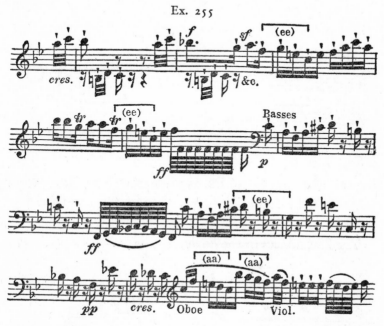

Not content with this, the *Allegretto* phrase marked (ee) closely echoes (e) of Ex. 253.

In its opening measures

Ex. 256

the Minuet is no less faithful to that same Alma Mater example (253). See how (ff) echoes (f), how (cc) copies

(c), and (gg) is true to (g). While at the beginning of
the Trio

Ex. 257

the (a), (b), and (e) of Ex. 253—marked here (aa), (bb),
(ee)—will be found at home, though the last-named is
inverted.

The first subject of the *finale*,

Ex. 258

though curiously and ingeniously disguised, gives at (hh) the first six notes of Alma Mater's opening phrase (h). The most ingenious part of the disguise consists in transposing F, the last note of (hh), surprisingly to the octave above by ascending a sixth instead of descending a third. Concealing this virtual identity of the opening themes of the *Allegro vivace* and of the *finale*—themes which are apparently in utter contrast—was one of the most consummately deft strokes of camouflage among all the brilliant feats which Beethoven performed with germ-motives. Except for F sharp instead of F, phrase (dd), Ex. 258, is an echo of (a), Ex. 253, first inverted and immediately afterwards normal. So that this first subject of the *finale* actually turns out to be the Alma mater tune (Ex. 253) rewritten, but so cleverly masqued that it has apparently escaped detection for one hundred and seventeen years. The joke-loving Master must have been immensely pleased with himself when this witty stroke of dissimulation occurred to him.

The second subject of the *finale*

Ex. 259

reminds us with its four diatonic notes (aa) of (a) (Ex. 253). And it reminds us of (i) with its drop of a fifth at (ii).

The third subject

Ex. 260

begins, (jj), with four approximate statements of (j).
The new and unauthorized melody in the coda,

Ex. 126

which we have already discussed,[20] turns out to be simply
the (k) of Alma Mater, begun on a different degree of the
scale, normal in the bassoon and simultaneously upside
down in the oboe.

Now let the reader turn back to that apparently naïve,

[20]On p. 324.

care-free, thoughtless opening tune, Ex. 253, and see with what thoughtful but unobtrusive thrift almost every bar of it has been used again and again in the course of the composition. If Beethoven had written nothing but this one symphony, such inter-movement liaison work as we have just considered would of itself place him among the foremost masters of construction who ever bore the name of artist.

It is doubtful if any composer with a less prodigious and trustworthy memory than the Master could have performed such an exploit as this welding together of the Eighth symphony. What Beethoven told Louis Schlösser in 1823 about his own habits of composition throws light on the power and scope of this memory—although the Sketch Books bear witness that the Master depended more on his pen for recording and developing ideas than the following passage would seem to imply:

I carry my thoughts about with me long, often very long, before I write them down. In doing this my memory stands me in such good stead that even years afterwards I am sure not to forget a theme that I have once grasped. I alter some things, eliminate and try again until I am satisfied. Then begins the mental working out of this stuff in its breadth, its narrowness, its height and depth. And as I know what I want, the fundamental idea never deserts me. It mounts, it grows in stature, I hear, see the picture in its whole extent standing all of a piece before my spirit, and there remains for me only the labour of writing it down which goes quickly whenever I have time for it. For I sometimes have several pieces in hand at once, but am perfectly sure not to confuse them. You will ask me where I get my ideas. I am not able to answer that question positively.

They come directly, indirectly; I can grasp them with my hands. Out amid the freedom of nature, in the woods, on walks, in the silence of night, early in the morning, called forth by such moods as in the minds of poets translate themselves into words, but in mine into tones which ring, roar, storm until at last they stand as notes before me.[21]

After such complicated feats as he performed with the germ-motives in the *Serioso*, the *"Archduke,"* and the Eighth symphony Beethoven seems now to have reverted for a rest to easier and more overt methods of liaison. In the *Hammerklavier* sonata (Op. 106) he fell back on the simple plan for securing thematic unity which he had used in the *"Kreutzer"* and *"Appassionata"* sonatas. He began all of the four movements with the germ-motive of a rising third. An incident shows the importance he attached to the sort of initial unity thus secured. When the plates were already engraved he discovered that the *Adagio* did not conform. So he sent the present first measure posthaste to Ries for insertion.

Curiously enough this same germ-motive of a third begins all three movements of the next sonata, in E major (Op. 109),

Ex. 261

Vivace, ma non troppo. Sempre legato.

Ex. 262

Ex. 137

while the interval of a fourth figures prominently in the outside movements of the A flat (Op. 110), in both principal subjects of the C minor (Op. 111) and in the Ninth symphony as originally planned. The Master's taste in intervals was evidently broadening with age. If he had lived the allotted span we might have had a series of works based on the fifth.

In the *Choral* symphony complexity and subtlety of interlocking treatment returns. For here only one of several germ-motives is represented in the device of beginning each movement with a falling fourth.

Notice it in the principal subject of the first movement.

Ex. 160

In the *scherzo* consistency is kept by beginning with the characteristic dotted figure first on D then on A, a fourth below.

Ex. 166

The main subject of the *Adagio molto* also commences with the interval of a falling fourth.[22] The *Choral finale* was an afterthought and does not conform to this scheme. But the melody of the *finale* of the A minor quartet, which Beethoven at first intended to use here,[23] begins with the same countersign as the others. Here is the curious original form in which this melody appeared in the Sketch Books.

[22]Ex. 163, p. 404.
[23]Its finished form as far surpasses Ex. 263 as Ex. 80. p. 221, surpasses Ex. 79.

Ex. 263

In the first *Allegro* there is a significant little motive at the close of the development—this time a rising fourth

Ex. 264

which is almost literally echoed near the beginning of the *Adagio's* coda.

Ex. 265

The preparation for the second subject of the *scherzo* is enough like the slow (4-bar) B major melody at bar 110 of the opening *Allegro* to help inter-movement unity.

The *Andante* part of the slow movement begins

Ex. 266

with a major version of the same melodic progression as in
that part of the *scherzo* theme marked here with a bracket,

Ex. 267

and in a motive from the first movement (see Ex. 161),
and in the Joy theme, bars 2–3.

Ex. 169

This Joy theme[24] is plainly foreshadowed in the second
subject of the first movement

Ex. 161

and at the beginning of the Trio of the *scherzo*

[24]See pp. 412–415, 524–525 and 572–573.

Ex. 155

It is more subtly hinted at in the third and fourth bars of the *scherzo's* first subject (see Ex. 267) and in the first three of its second subject.

Ex. 268

The Ninth symphony is filled with examples of Beethoven's two favourite types of melody: the scale tune and the chord-arpeggio tune. E. g. the last six themes above are all of the scale type. From which it is evident that M. D'Indy claims too much in stating[25] that "all the typical themes of the symphony present the arpeggios of the chords of D or B flat; . . . one might, therefore, consider this arpeggio as the real cyclic theme of the Ninth symphony." But this does not hold good of any of the second subjects, or of the Trio of the *scherzo*. And it is only true of the Joy theme for an expert rationalizer who gets out of it what

[25]*Beethoven*, p. 114.

he brings to it. M. D'Indy even strains to the point of treating as passing notes all those in the Joy theme which inconvenience his arpeggio theory. And he then proposes that these "secondary notes . . . might be taken to symbolize the fraternal clasp of hands united by the love of mankind"! No such extravaganza, however, is needed to demonstrate the thematic unity of the Ninth.

In the E flat quartet (Op. 127) Riemann pointed out close parallels between the closing section of the variation theme (see Ex. 173, p. 431) and the second subject of the first movement; and between the beginning of the variation theme and the *maestoso* motto which starts the quartet. This learned musicologist also felt that the first part of the *scherzo*

Ex. 228

is a modification for *scherzo* purposes of this variation theme. Some analogy doubtless exists, though its apprehension requires rather more than the "bit of good-will on the hearer's part" which Riemann engagingly bespoke. It needs an alert musical imagination. But then, so does every part of this tremendous composition.

In connection with the *"Quartetto Scherzoso"* (Op. 130) the old *Sonate Pathétique* is once more brought to mind, not thematically, but in the way this quartet later on recalls its own slow Introduction. The style in which this manœuvre is accomplished in the sonata, as compared with that in the quartet, gives us a measure of Beethoven's artistic growth. There the Introduction was brought in more formally and mechanically, somewhat as themes from earlier movements are injected into the *finale* of Dvořak's *New World* symphony. Here parts of the Introduction recur again and again throughout the first movement with subtle organic inevitability. The former's opening chromatic passage

Ex. 187

is heard once more, with but little disguise, in the last bar given in Ex. 185, of the *"Beklemmt"* portion of the *Cavatina*.

Ex. 185

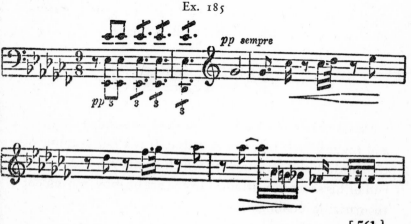

This begins with a faltering tune somewhat like the last three bars of Ex. 187.

The enchanting melody of the *Andante con moto, ma non troppo* pops like a fairy from a peasecod out of the lower voices of its own short Introduction. As we shall see in chapter LVI, it is nothing but a source-motive which runs through most of Beethoven's works, turned end for end.

This movement looks

> . . . before and after,
> And pines for what is not,—

and creates the little *presto* second movement out of itself, significantly enough in its own relative minor.

If we regard the first D flat of this *Andante con moto's* germ

Ex. 189

as an Introduction, and disregard the two 32ds as passing notes, and change the rhythm a bit, we have

Ex. 269

which is the germ of one of the most irresistibly fetching and roguish little *scherzos* in music. It is a fair example of the subtlety and inevitability which Beethoven had, by the end of his short life, attained in the art of inter-movement thematic dovetailing.

The second subject of the first movement has two measures (marked in Ex. 270 with a bracket, the highest notes of which echo Ex. 269)

Ex. 270

whose melodic contour resembles an important part of the second main subject of the Great Fugue which originally served as *finale* for this quartet.

Ex. 271

All but the final one of the last five quartets have this trait in common. They start with either an Introduction or a principal theme which recurs with more or less frequency in the body of the work. The upper notes of the Introduction of the A minor (see Ex. 283, p. 573) come back in the *Alla Breve* part of the *scherzo,*

Ex. 272

And its bass part is suggested by those sixths yearning upward in the *ritornelles* which act as preludes and postludes to the chorale of the *Adagio*. It is suggested as well in the first two notes of the *scherzo* (see Ex. 182, p. 441).

In this quartet Beethoven seemed to rely entirely on the Introduction and on the source-motive to be studied in chapter LVI, for inter-movement liaison work.

There is space to describe only two uses as germ-motives of the fugue subject of the C sharp minor quartet (Op. 131).

Ex. 190

Adagio ma non troppo e molto espressivo.

These are two amusing anagrams. In his book on the Beethoven quartets Bargheer pointed out that if the first three notes of the first subject of the sixth movement of the C sharp minor

Ex. 198

Adagio quasi un poco Andante.

are read backwards they give the beginning of Ex. 190. While Helm discovered that by arranging the first four notes of the *finale's* second subject

Ex. 273

in the order 4–2–1–3 one likewise produced the beginning of Ex. 190.

One may well believe that Beethoven played these tricks deliberately. This prodigious improvisator, this demon for toiling over his material, was not the man to ignore any of its implications, no matter how finely drawn. Besides, one sets at rest any lingering doubts about the latter anagram being unconscious by seeing how the Master rewrote it in the coda:

Ex. 274

From the number of germ-motives which the writer has been fortunate enough to find in Beethoven's music within the short span of four years it may be inferred that there are large numbers awaiting discovery by more painstaking seekers.

Chapter LV

SOME SOURCE-MOTIVES

Source-Motives in Part I — Thrift and Resource — "Certain Musical Pets" — Pathétique Source-Motive — Its Modern Uses — Four Quarters and a Dotted Half — A Motive from Op. 14, No. 2 — Joy Source-Motive — Great Fugue Motive — Adelaide Motive — Triad Habit

From the beginning of his career Beethoven used the same source-motive in numbers of different compositions, in such a way as to produce among them a sense of thematic solidarity.

In Part I we have already considered certain small source-motives, such as the sequence of fourths[1] that joins the Fifth Lobkowitz quartet, the *Pathétique*, D major, and A flat sonatas. And we have seen the more ambitious "Fate" motive[2] of the C minor symphony connecting a larger group of compositions.

The longer one studies Beethoven's use of this device, the more he must admire the uncanny thrift and resource that could thus make a limited stock of basic ideas appear illimitable.

In saying that his stock was limited the writer would by no means imply that it was small. Here he cannot agree

---

[1] See pp. 56–57. Too late to mention in Part I, this source-motive was found in the fugue theme of the A flat sonata, (Op. 110, see Ex. 147, p. 372), and near the end of the exposition of the D major sonata (Op. 10, No. 3, first movement).

[2] See pp. 152–154.

with the late Oscar G. Sonneck, who noted on the manuscript of this book: "Isn't the real explanation of such things the fact that every composer, during his whole career, surrounds himself with certain musical pets? They become a habit, good with one composer, bad with others; —the difference between manner and mannerism. *Cum grano salis*, the baggage of every composer contains, at bottom, only a very few distinctly different ideas. These he breeds in endless variety,—or endlessly without variety."

Beethoven did not spread one idea over several compositions through poverty, but because he was actuated by the instinctive economy and constructive insight of the true artist. We shall see that his stock of basic themes which we call source-motives consisted of more than "a very few distinctly different ideas."

If one may judge from the high quality of the works for whose use he reserved it, the familiar germ-motive[3] of the *Sonate Pathétique*

Ex. 275

was also one of Beethoven's favourite source-motives. Like most of his other source-motives, this fragment of tune was not original. It had been used by many of his predecessors, notably by Johann Sebastian Bach in the subject of his A minor organ fugue.[4]

[3]See beginning of Ex. 7, p. 55.
[4]"*Eight Short.*"

So far as the writer is aware it occurs first among Beethoven's works (as E–A–B–C) in the first subject of the *Adagio con espressione* of his C minor string trio (Op. 9, No. 3). Next, as we have seen,[5] it is found, scattered freely, in the form of the first true germ-motive, through the entire *Sonate Pathétique*.

Soon after it appears as the first four notes (A–D–E–F) of the *"Romeo and Juliet"* Adagio *affettuoso* in the F major quartet (Op. 18, No. 1).

The *Larghetto* of the Second symphony starts with this source-motive transposed to the major.[6]

Ex. 236

But the development section of this movement commences at bar 100 with the pattern in its original minor form (E–A–B–C).

The strange, morbid slow movement of the Third Rasoumowsky quartet (C major, Op. 59, No. 3) commences with the same E–A–B–C, like the scherzo of the A major violoncello sonata (Op. 69). While Part II of the first subject of the *Serioso* quartet's *finale*

[5]See pp. 53–55.

[6]The first four measures of Ex. 236 were destined to inspire the Trio of a much later *scherzo*—that in C sharp minor (Op. 39), by Chopin.

[568]

Ex. 248

throws off its gray-whiskered mask—and its last note—and turns out to be no other than this same germ-motive of the youthful *Pathétique*—F–B flat–C–D flat.[7]

The third theme of the *"Harp"* quartet's rondo-*Adagio*

Ex. 232

[7] Well-known modern uses of this motive occur in both of the Brahms *Rhapsodies* (Op. 79), at the start of the same composer's B flat sextet Variations (Op. 18) and at the words "But nevermore," in that part of Liza Lehmann's *Persian Garden* beginning "Myself when young."

gives this source-motive in its major form. So does the "*Beklemmt*" portion of the *Cavatina*

Ex. 185

from the "*Quartetto Scherzoso*" (Op. 130).

The *finale* of the A major violoncello sonata

starts with a phrase which is a source-motive more by rea-son of its rhythmic and harmonic scheme than through any strict melodic repetitions. It consists of four quarter notes with suspension in the tonic, followed by a dotted half. We meet it again in the first theme of the F sharp major sonata (Op. 78),

[570]

Ex. 93

and in the opening of the *"Archduke"* trio (Op. 97).

Ex. 276

This motive was taken up by Beethoven's successors, as in the famous *finale* of the César Franck violin sonata,

not to mention such minor pieces as the *finale* of Bargiel's Third trio. (See also p. 181, Ex. 59, first two bars.)

The *finale* of the C major violoncello sonata, which is the only part of opus 102 offering anything like the relief of playfulness or gaiety, starts with a bright tune

Ex. 278

which may have inspired the opening *Allegro* of an overture in the same key, written seven years later, *Die Weihe des Hauses* (Op. 124),

Ex. 279

and may, in turn, have been inspired by memories of the *scherzo* of the G major sonata (Op. 14, No. 2).[8]

The Joy tune in the *Choral* symphony[9] represents one form of a source-motive, traces of which are found scattered through Beethoven's work over a period of thirty years. In the first part of a song, *Seufzer eines Ungeliebten und Gegenliebe* (composed about 1795) a version of this motive begins in the minor. The tune of the second part of this song, *Gegenliebe,* transposed here for convenience of comparison,

Ex. 280

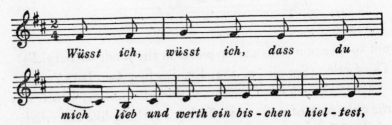

was used, 1808, in that weak up-beat to the famous Joy *finale,* the Choral Phantasie (Op. 80).

---

[8]Note that the second full bar of Ex. 278 is identical with the first half bar of Ex. 279; and that the first six notes of 278 correspond exactly with the first six notes of the opus 14 *scherzo.*

[9]See Ex. 169, p. 413.

In 1805 a song *To Hope* (Op. 32)

Ex. 281

and in 1810 *Mit einem gemalten Band* (Op. 83)

Ex. 282

announced still more distinctly the Joy source-motive. We have seen[10] with what brilliant results it was turned into a pervasive germ-motive in the *Choral* symphony.

The A minor quartet (Op. 132) starts with an echo of the original *finale* of the "*Quartetto Scherzoso*" (Op. 130). The first four notes of the Introduction's bass melody

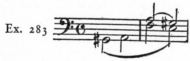

Ex. 283

---

[10]See pp. 558–559.

remind one strongly of the Introduction to the "*Scher-zoso's*" Great Fugue *finale,* studies for which had already been made.

Ex. 284

The writer had no sooner noted this discovery than his elation was dashed by finding that he had been long since anticipated by Nottebohm.[11] Herr Bekker points out that the first four notes of the bass tune in Ex. 283, if one transposes the F–E an octave lower, give the start of the C sharp minor fugue (transposed for comparison),

Ex. 285

minus the first note, and come with bar 1 reversed in the *finale* of that tremendous composition. Herr Bekker feels that this motive thus becomes "the leading idea of the whole group of Beethoven's three greatest quartets, and recognition of this fact throws new light on the composer's train of thought."[12] With Herr Bekker's claim that this is the leading idea of opuses 130, 131, 132 it is hard to agree, in view of the fact that a source-motive described in the following chapter of this book appears in these three great

[11]*Zweite Beethoveniana,* p. 5.
[12]*Beethoven,* p. 329.

quartets not four but twelve times.[13] Beside such emphatic iteration the Great Fugue idea seems subsidiary.

Beethoven's most popular song, *Adelaide*, contains a modest source-motive.

Ex. 286

This reappears in the 36th bar of the *"Harp"* quartet's *Adagio*.[14]

Ex. 287

And here it is again in the *Andante con moto* of the *"Quartetto Scherzoso,"* as it suddenly winked at the author one day out of bar 29:

Ex. 288

We have already remarked Beethoven's liberal use of the triad as a germ-motive in such works as the Second, *Eroica*, and *Choral* symphonies. Beethoven lived in an age in which

---

[13]It recurs nineteen times in the last five quartets.
[14]As discovered by Miss Marion Bauer.

it was as natural for composers to use the triad and the diatonic scale for subject matter as it is for the composers of to-day to use chromaticism, polytonality, and atonality. It was natural for Beethoven to found much of his music on chord-arpeggio and scale progressions. The astonishing thing is that he could use these simple patterns over and over so often and yet be so rich and resourceful as to conceal the frequency of his essential repetitions.

All through life he had the triad tune habit. Both opus 1 and opus 2 began with chord-arpeggio tunes; and so did the last movement he ever finished, the new *finale* of the *"Quartetto Scherzoso."* The triad habit, however, was especially marked during the central part of his career, beginning with the *Entrata* of the Serenade (Op. 25), running on through the *scherzo* of the E flat Fantasia sonata (Op. 27, No. 1), the openings of the C minor violin sonata (Op. 30, No. 2), and of the first two movements of the D minor piano sonata (Op. 31, No. 2). This source-motive carries through the first *Andante* of the *Prometheus* music (Op. 43), the openings of *Adelaide* (Op. 46), the *"Kreutzer"* (Op. 47), *The Praise of God in Nature* (Op. 48, No. 4), and the *"Appassionata"* (Op. 57). The triad runs through the two middle movements of the F major and the first movement of the E minor quartet (Op. 59, Nos. 1 and 2), and the *finales* of the G major and D major concertos (Op. 58 and 61). The Fifth and Seventh symphonies, the *"Emperor"* concerto, the *"Harp"* quartet, the wind sextet, and *Fidelio* are full of it.

It is fitting that Beethoven, the heart of music, should

have built so much of his life work upon the bed rock of this compact source-motive. In so doing he also emphasized for succeeding generations the basic principle of the art—economy of material.

On the part of certain types of musician the writer has noticed a curious reluctance to believe that Beethoven consciously used the source-motive. True, they are bound to admit that he consciously used the germ-motive in such obvious places as the Fifth symphony, and that these uses were triumphs of constructive skill. But they hold that the conscious employment of the same motive in different works—no matter how subtly disguised—argues an unworthy strain of artifice. How the conscious use of a favourite motive in various movements of the same work can be artistic, while its use in various movements of different works is artificial, they do not explain.

This inconsistency is perhaps based on a conservative bias against any new light shed on the processes of the creative minds of old. The long-accepted ideas about them have crystallized almost to the rigidity of religious dogmas, and any others are branded at sight as sacrilegious. The less creative critics seldom realize clearly that not until the final stage of the composition of a work—as Beethoven's Sketch Books bear witness—does artifice flower into art. Oftentimes the more spontaneous the final product appears, the more of conscious calculation has gone to its making.[15]

---

[15]See Professor Lowes' illuminating words, p. 512.

Chapter LVI

A CHIEF SOURCE–MOTIVE OF BEETHOVEN

"If we are rifling the urns where the dead bones of fact have long quietly rested, it is because the unquenchable spirit which gives beauty for ashes is there not wholly past finding out."
—JOHN LIVINGSTON LOWES, *The Road to Xanadu.*

Economy of Material — Variety in Unity — Originality and Uniqueness not Claimed for Motive — Fertility of Creative Resources — Relative Frequency of Motive in His Symphonies, Sonatas, Etc. — Was Its Use Conscious? — Devices for Concealment — The Formula Stated — Traced through Entire Life Work — Its Protean Nature — Conscious Employment — Beethoven as an Improvisator — Improvises on This Motive — Inter-Resemblance of Certain Uses — Newman's Three Notes — His Theory of Beethoven's Unconsciousness — Employment of Source-Motive by Other Composers — Object of This Chapter — The Anagram Idea — Implications

WE HAVE already seen how and why Beethoven used the source-motive. In order to realize more vividly his grasp of two principles basic to art—economy of material, and variety in unity—let us trace in detail through his whole life-work one of his favourite source-motives. The writer is far from claiming that Beethoven invented this particular pattern of notes or from positively asserting that it was used by him with unique frequency. The object of the present chapter is merely to demonstrate how richly fertile were his creative resources.

From long before opus 1 down through opus 135 we shall see him recurring to the pattern nearly one hundred and fifty times for main themes in most of his chief works. This motive occurs in all of his symphonies, in at least twelve out of sixteen quartets, fifteen out of thirty-two piano sonatas, seven out of ten violin sonatas, three out of five violoncello sonatas, and three out of six piano trios. Often it also appears as a germ-motive, repeated several times in the same composition, to give the work inter-movement unity.

The reader's first reaction to such a statement may perhaps be a conviction that if Beethoven actually did use a single idea to the extent described he must have done it unconsciously. For reasons to be given later, the writer holds the contrary view. But whether the Master used the formula consciously or unconsciously, and to what extent other composers may have employed it, are questions which in no way affect the interest or importance of the subject.

It is astonishing and inspiring to see how this greatest of all constructionists could continually utilize the same fairly simple design for almost half a century; yet each time make it so new that the existence of the pattern seems never to have been noticed.

With inexhaustible fertility of resource Beethoven disguised this pattern by changes of accent, rhythm, tempo, tonality, harmony, counterpoint, mode, and instrumentation; by phrasing, diminution, augmentation, turning it upside down or end for end, or both, and beginning it on each degree of the scale.

In essence this source-motive, like so many of Beethoven's themes, is a scale-tune. It consists of a fall of four consecutive notes, joined by a rise of three. In its simplest, crudest form it appears as the opening phrase of the G major sonata for violin* and piano (Op. 30, No. 3)—given twice.[1]

Ex. 289   1802

Observe that this source-motive in Ex. 289 is exactly coextensive with a figure in the first theme of the sonata. As we shall see, Beethoven seldom employed the pattern in this obvious way. Often he made of it an inconspicuous part of a motive, or made it overlap two adjacent ones. If it had been his habit always to let the formula neatly correspond with some figure or motive in his subject-matter, the device would have been instantly apparent to his contemporaries and would have resulted in an intolerable monotony.

The reader may feel that such a motive as this would

---

*Mr. Carl Engel contributes the brilliant suggestion that this source-motive is perhaps a souvenir of "Spangy's" violin-playing years; for it is the typical violin finger-exercise.

[1]For convenience of comparison all examples in this chapter are quoted in C major or A minor. The source-motive is indicated by a bracket, ⌐   ⌐ . The letter (a) shows that the motive is turned end for end; (b) that it is upside down; (c) that it is both end for end and upside down.

often inevitably be formed in the course of purely scale-wise melody-building. Perhaps; but even so, its frequent inevitability would reflect all the more lustre on the resourceful genius of any composer who hid the fact of its use so often and so successfully. Naturally, if the pattern we are considering occurred simply in passage work, it could be dismissed as merely incidental to the fall and rise of scale passages. But almost every one of the following examples shows it as some significant portion of a main subject in which every note is instinct with momentous meaning.

For the interest of following Beethoven's growing skill in devising new disguises for the formula, the examples will be given in chronological order, with dates of composition, in so far as these have been determined.

This pattern occurs in one of Beethoven's earliest compositions. For, although the second *Bagatelle* is marked opus 33, its first draught was, in all likelihood, written at the age of eleven. The first Trio of this little *scherzo* starts with the source-motive end for end—marked (a)—and followed at once by a normal version of it.

Ex. 290   1782 [?]

In an incidental way it comes into the E flat trio—the first number of Beethoven's first opus, almost as though it had been inserted as a playful afterthought. Just before the

Trio of the *scherzo*, the violoncello discovers this formula hidden in the first subject,

Ex. 291   1795

and brings it out as plainly as it was to appear in the *Lento assai* of the last quartet (see Ex. 354).

Disguised by a minor key and a repeated third note, it figures in effective contrast to Ex. 291, in the first subject of the first movement of the C minor trio (Op. 1, No. 3).

Ex. 292   1795

The beginning of the *scherzo* of the C major piano sonata (Op. 2, No. 3) starts it, though a third higher, in a manner reminiscent of the second and third measures of Ex. 291.

Ex. 293   1796

The opening of the *finale* of the C minor string trio (Op. 9, No. 3) is melodically so like Ex. 292, and rhythmically so like Ex. 293, that it seems incredible the resemblance should have escaped detection for more than a century and a quarter.

[582]

Ex. 294   1798

The *Sonate Pathétique* (Op. 13), in the second subject of the first *Allegro,* varies the smooth design with phrasing, shakes, and repeated notes.

Ex. 295   1799

A dotted quarter gives it a quite new complexion in the *finale* of the G major string quartet (Op. 18, No. 2).

Ex. 296   1800

In the theme of the variations which open the A flat sonata (Op. 26), compression within a single bar, a grace note and a rapid finish constitute as effective a disguise as any by which Sherlock Holmes astounded his faithful Schindler, Dr. Watson.

Ex. 297   1802

The Trio of the Second symphony's *scherzo* brings to the motive a fresh rhythmical pattern.

Ex. 298   1802

The grace note worked so well in Ex. 297 that the Master used it in the theme of the *"Kreutzer"* sonata variations (Op. 47).

Ex. 299   1803

Sheer simplicity of announcement long blinded the writer of these lines to its presence in the second subject, *Allegro con brio*, of the *"Waldstein"* sonata (Op. 53).

Ex. 300   1804

In the *"Appassionata"* (Op. 57) the theme of the variations seems at first to be all harmony and no tune. Yet, when analyzed, the source-motive, cunningly oscillating between treble and bass, amounts to this:

[584]

Ex. 301   1804

And now the Master masquerader resolved on a measure too extreme for even Sherlock Holmes. In the *Leonore No. 1* overture (Op. 138) he turned the motive upside down.

Ex. 302   1805

The idea emerges uncompromisingly in the opening movement of the little known F major sonata (Op. 54), as a large part of the second subject. Compare the use of triplets with that in Ex. 294.

Ex. 303   1806

Here it is in Russian costume, claiming much space in the *Theme Russe* of the Second Rasoumowsky quartet's *Allegretto* (Op. 59, No. 2). With a touch of wit, it sounds frequently, though thrice as fast, in the second violin accompaniment.

Ex. 304   1806

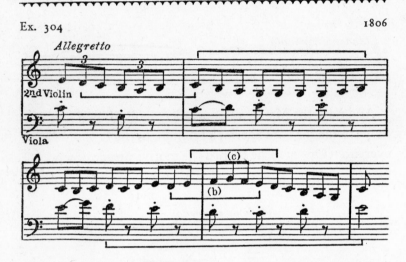

The *finale* of the Third Rasoumowsky quartet in C major
(Op. 59, No. 3) shows the first use of this source-motive
in a fugue. It starts a degree higher in the scale than in
Beethoven's greatest fugue (see Ex. 352).

Ex. 305   1806

This formula might be addressed in the words of the old
song as *"Du überall!"* (Thou omnipresent one!) We meet
it in the opening subject of the Violin concerto (Op. 61),

Ex. 306   1806

and near the end of the Fifth symphony (Op. 67) in the second subject of the *finale*.

Ex. 307   1808

Four times it appears, in appropriately simple rustic guise, during the first three movements of the *Pastoral* symphony (Op. 68). Ex. 308 gives two different uses of it in a single subject (the second of the *Allegro ma non troppo*).

Ex. 308   1808

Ex. 309   1808

Ex. 310   1808

The last three examples offer a clear illustration of the pattern's simultaneous use as source- and germ-motive.

Nothing could well be more obvious than this motive, isolated from its context in the *Adagio* of the *"Harp"* quartet (Op. 74). Yet Beethoven has given it such perfect protective coloration that it melts into the background and almost defies detection.

Ex. 311   1809

In the first movement of the *"Emperor"* concerto (Op. 73) the motive twice becomes a compact half-measure's ornament developed out of the first subject.

Ex. 312   1809

And in the *finale* it shows affinity with Exs. 292 and 294.

Ex. 313   1809

The two following examples veil its identity with naturals in descending and sharps in ascending. The F minor quartet (Op. 95) opens thus

Ex. 314   1810

As we have seen,[2] the chief germ-motive of this quartet is the motto which ushers in the slow movement.

Ex. 315   1810

The more frequently Beethoven used this formula the harder grew the task of disguising his economy as lavishness and making the well-worn source-motive seem new each time. But his skill grew even more rapidly than the need for it. Until the end he was able to mask the old pattern with such increasingly rich variety that in our day an intelligent critic like Mr. W. H. Hadow could sincerely declare in his essay *Beethoven*: "There is no composer who repeats himself so seldom, who makes less use of the formula." Whereas the fact may be that no other composer of first rank ever made more extended use of a formula in his principal subjects than Beethoven.

This point marks the transition to his third period. Henceforth, instead of merely quoting occasional occurrences of the source-motive, all that the writer has found will be printed, in order to show the triumphant way in which Beethoven solved his increasingly difficult problems of camouflage.

The sombreness of the last two examples turns to gaiety in the *scherzo* of the *"Archduke"* trio (Op. 97), at the end of the first subject,

---

[2] See pp. 290, and 541–544.

Ex. 316   1811

and to yearning tenderness in the *Andante con moto*, which disguises the motive by repeating three of its notes and turning the whole end for end.

Ex. 317   1811

Immediately after, it appears in the trifling *Marcia alla Turca* from *The Ruins of Athens* (Op. 113, No. 4).

Ex. 318   1811

Now it comes end for end in the "hidden" violoncello theme at bar 39 of the Seventh symphony's dirge-like *Allegretto*,

Ex. 319   1812

and with a message of reassurance in the major part.

Ex. 320   1812

It lends its voice to the uproarious laughter at the start of the Eighth symphony's *finale*.

Ex. 321   1812

Again, beginning the *finale* of the E minor sonata (Op. 90) it stirs

> . . . the sweet forget-me-nots
> That grow for happy lovers,—

or does anything else of that general nature the hearer likes.

Ex. 322   1814

The song *Merkenstein* (Op. 100) gives the motive again end for end, but how differently from Ex. 317!

Ex. 323   1814

Mer - ken - stein! wo ich wand-le denk ich dein

In the recurrent introduction of the C major violoncello sonata (Op. 102, No. 1) Beethoven apparently threw caution aside and gave, in one even measure, as bald a statement of the formula as we have already seen in Exs. 289, 303, or 308.

Ex. 324   1815

In its D major companion sonata (Op. 102, No. 2) the motive occurs more incidentally, at the end of the first subject of the first movement.

Ex. 325   1815

And in the *Adagio* it appears so much more incidentally still that one almost wonders whether Beethoven's all-seeing musical eye had missed it here.

Ex. 326   1815

Again, as we have noticed in Ex. 308, and shall in Ex. 340, the exuberant Master used it twice in a single subject—the fugue of the A major sonata (Op. 101).

Ex. 327   1816

A slur and triplet lend it distinction in the song *To Hope* (Op. 94).

Ex. 328   1816

A pitiable potboiler for flute and piano (Op. 105, No. 2) reminds one, but not too much, of Exs. 292 and 294.

Ex. 329   1818

Then, in the most dramatic contrast, the source-motive shows that, without its collaboration, the last sonata (in C minor, Op. 111) might not have been the miracle it is. For the familiar pattern looks out at us from a crucial part of the principal subject of the *Allegro con brio,*

Ex. 330   1822

and from the second part of the perfect melody of the *Arietta,* with repeated notes that remind one of another supreme tune, Ex. 317.

Ex. 331   1822

Glancing back over the amazing transformations this little motive underwent in its first forty years, we see it is like Proteus in Greek mythology, who could at will become an eagle, a mountain, an elephant, roaring fire, flowing water, a mole, a dead leaf spinning down the wind, a lion, a tow-headed child, or a cloud no larger than a man's hand.

Observe the care with which Beethoven varied the pattern even in a small, frivolous song, *The Kiss* (Op. 128).

Ex. 332   1822

Compare Exs. 317, 323, and 340 with this treatment of it in *The Consecration of the House* overture (Op. 124), where it occurs once end for end and once upside down.

Ex. 333   1822

The most significant part of the fugue in the *Diabelli Variations* (Op. 120, Var. XXXII) consists of the motive disguised by repeated notes. Notice how the use of the F sharp in the ascending part is reminiscent of Exs. 314 and 315.

Ex. 334   1823

In the second *Bagatelle* (Op. 126) it appears in sixteenth notes,

Ex. 335   1823

and in the fifth it broadens out into dotted quarters. The last two measures give it upside down.

Ex. 336   1823

The *Choral* symphony is full of the motive. It occurs twice in the opening movement: in the hammer strokes of the strong transition phrase between the first and second subjects;

Ex. 337   1823

then in the second subject itself.

Ex. 338   1823

The Trio of the *scherzo*, though notoriously taken from that of the Second symphony (see Ex. 298), makes for the motive, by means of repetition and phrasing, an entirely new rhythmical pattern.

Ex. 339   1823

The Joy theme of the *finale*, like Exs. 308 and 327, contains the motive more than once. The bracket marked (c) shows it upside down and end for end.

Ex. 340   1823

The first subject of the opening movement of the E flat quartet (Op. 127) has for the author a peculiar interest because it was here he first noticed this source-motive, through its resemblance to the end of the fugue subject of the C sharp minor quartet (Op. 131), which is given as Ex. 352.

Ex. 341   1824

At this point Beethoven performed a brilliantly daring feat. He began the motive on the fourth instead of the sixth degree of the scale, on the second instead of the third beat of the bar, and proceeded to use it undetected in the second subject as well as the first, though the time-signature remained the same. He even dared repeat in both subjects the third note of the pattern.

Ex. 342   1824

Not content with this bit of audacity he used the motive again, end for end, in the theme of the variations.

Ex. 343   1824

And in the first subject of the *finale* he let it bob up again, as impudently fresh as if it were conscious of its own entire uniqueness.

Ex. 344   1824

The Master now seemed to grow fonder and fonder of the source-motive. But, as he used it in these last five consecutive quartets, the problems of disguise accumulated rapidly. Notice how in Exs. 345–350 each employment of it resorted to some disguise of as unusual subtlety as that in Ex. 343.

The A minor quartet (Op. 132) is chronologically next in order. The germ of the opening *Allegro*'s first subject is no other than the source-motive upside down and end for end.

Ex. 345   1825

As in the preceding E flat quartet (see Exs. 341 and 342), Beethoven used it in the second subject as well as the first,

here, however, not once but twice. The first time, marked
(b), it is upside down, in almost too-pointed allusion to
Ex. 345.

Ex. 346   1825

The *Molto adagio* theme of the Song of Thanksgiving
also contains it twice, and overlapping—the portion marked
(a) being end for end.

Ex. 347   1825

In this A minor quartet he was consistently topsy-turvy
in his methods of disguise. For the motive comes to light
once more at the end of the main theme of the rondo-*finale*,
upside down and end for end.

Ex. 348   1825

The next example, from the first subject of the *Andante
con moto* of the "*Quartetto Scherzoso*" (B flat, op. 130),
is also end for end.

Ex. 349   1825

Andante con moto, ma non troppo

In the famous *Cavatina* of this quartet Beethoven used the motive still more subtly. There is a measure's introduction by the second violin, on the last beat of which the first violin starts the melody a seventh below. The upper voice of the bracketed portion shows the second violin playing the descending notes of the source-motive and the first violin joining in with the three ascending notes. To make the motive thus overlap and bind together adjacent phrases was a truly Beethovenian stroke of camouflage! And at once he used the overlapping device again, repeating the pattern in the second and third bars, upside down and end for end.[2a]

Ex. 350   1825

Adagio molto espressivo

After these refinements of subtlety the Master ventured out into the open. Compared with the preceding five, his next and last five uses of it were almost childishly obvious.

The Great Fugue (Op. 133) was originally composed as the *finale* of this B flat quartet. The end of the second theme lightly disguises the motive in a dotted rhythm. The F sharp

[2a] The motive also appears in the opening *Allegro* (see Ex. 230, p. 527).

[600]

is another reminder of the germinal motto of the *Quartett Serioso,* Ex. 315.

Ex. 351   1825

In the marvellous fugue subject of the C sharp minor quartet (Op. 131),

Ex. 352   1826

as in the prolongation of the first subject of the *scherzo,*

Ex. 353   1826

the formula begins on the second beat of a 4/4 measure.[3] But the two are completely differentiated by contrasted phrasing and tempos, and by beginning respectively or the sixth and the second degrees of the scale.

Notice how Beethoven's last use of the motive in a slow movement is reminiscent of its early undisguised statements

<hr>

[3]Compare also Ex. 314. For a more or less similar effect see Exs. 325, 327, and 340.

in Exs. 289 and 344. This is the beginning of the *Lento assai* of the F major quartet (Op. 135).

Ex. 354   1826

Lento assai

What plainer revelation than this could he have made of his long-kept secret? Unless it were the literal quotation from Ex. 352, in the *finale* of this last complete work of his.[4]

---

[4]Without pretending exhaustively to complete the list, it may merely be noted that this source-motive is also to be found in the subject matter of the following compositions:

1795	*Das Liedchen von der Ruhe* (start)	Op. 52, No. 3
1796	Piano sonata F minor (Trio of *Menuetto*, bars 3–4; *finale*, episode, bars 16–17)	Op. 2, No. 1
	Violoncello Sonata G minor (*Allegro Molto*, last part 2d subject)	Op. 5, No. 2
	Adelaide (the first word *A-del-a-i-de* is the upward part of motive)	Op. 46
1797	Piano sonata E flat (1st movement, bars 20–21)	Op. 7
	Rondo C major for piano (Main theme)	Op. 51, No. 1
	Serenade for violin, viola, and violoncello (*Marcia*, 2d part; both *Adagios*; theme of variations)	Op. 8
1798	String Trio D major (*Allegretto*, 1st subject; *Menuetto*, bars 4–6)	Op. 9, No. 2
	Violin sonata A major (beginning of *Andante piu tosto Allegretto*)	Op. 12, No. 2
1800	Quartet (*Adagio*, 1st subject)	Op. 18, No. 1
	Quartet (1st movement, 2d half of 1st bar, end for end; theme of variations)	Op. 18, No. 5
	Quartet (*finale*, 1st subject)	Op. 18, No. 6
	Septet (*Adagio cantabile*, 1st subject)	Op. 20
1801	Quintet (1st movement, 2d subject)	Op. 29
	First symphony (*Andante cantabile*, 1st subject)	Op. 21
	Violin sonata A minor (*Presto*, 1st subject, upside down and end for end; *Andante scherzoso*, 1st subject, upside down; *finale*, 1st subject and simultaneously upside down in the bass)	Op. 23
	Violin sonata F major (opening *Allegro*, start of 1st subject; both subjects of *scherzo*, upside down; main subject of rondo-*finale*, upside down)	Op. 24
1802	Serenade (*Andante*, 2d half of theme; *Adagio*, 1st subject)	Op. 25
	Violin sonata A major (start of *Allegro* upside down; theme of variations)	Op. 30, No. 1
	Violin sonata C minor (*Adagio cantabile*, 1st subject)	Op. 30, No. 2

Ex. 355   1826

More than once in the course of the present chapter the reader may have asked himself whether Beethoven used this source-motive consciously or unconsciously. The writer has already stated a belief that his use of it was conscious. Beethoven was the foremost improvisator of his age. One of his

	Piano sonata G major (*Adagio* 1st subject, bars 1–2 end for end, and 5–6; *finale*, 1st subject)	Op. 27, No. 1
	Piano sonata C sharp minor (*Adagio*, bars 12–14 from end; *Allegretto*, 1st 6 bars of 2d part end for end; *finale*, bars 10–11)	Op. 27, No. 2
	Piano sonata D minor (*finale*, 2d subject)	Op. 31, No. 2
	Piano sonata E flat (*scherzo*, bars 10–12)	Op. 31, No. 3
	"*Kreutzer*" sonata (*finale*, 2d intermediate theme)	Op. 47
1803	*Das Glück der Freundschaft*	Op. 88
	Romance G major for violin	Op. 40
1804	*Eroica* symphony (First movement, Episode, violoncello part, bar 284 ff.; Funeral March, second theme; *finale*, bars 365–366 [1st violins])	Op. 55
1805	*An Die Hoffnung* (To Hope) (Notes 4–11)	Op. 32
	Romance F major for violin	Op. 50
	Fidelio (Florestan's aria "In des Lebens Frühlingstagen," bars 2–4. Same in all three *Leonore* overtures; Leonora's aria "Komm, Hoffnung," first 8 notes, end for end)	Op. 72
1806	Fourth symphony (*Adagio*, first subject, end for end)	Op. 60
1808	Fantasie G minor (theme of variations)	Op. 77
	Fifth symphony (*scherzo*, bars 116–117)	Op. 67
	Pastoral symphony (*scherzo*, bars 95–6, end for end)	Op. 68
	Violoncello sonata A major (*scherzo*, 1st subject, upside down)	Op. 69
	Trio E flat (*Poco sostenuto*, 1st 3 bars, first upside down, then normal)	Op. 70, No. 2
	Choral Phantasie (*finale*, Allegro, bars 3–4; *Meno Allegro*, bars 4–6)	Op. 80
1809	"*Harp*" quartet (Second subject of opening *Allegro*; Trio of *scherzo*, bars 80–81)	Op. 74
	"*Emperor*" concerto (*Adagio*, bar 19; *finale* 1st subject, end slightly disguised by chromatic passing notes. A clever masquerade of the motive)	Op. 73
1810	*Mit einem gemalten Band* (bars 2–3)	Op. 83
1825	Canon: "Doctor, close the door to Death."	
(?)	*Rondo a capriccio* (bar 9)	Op. 129

[603]

special gifts was the power to grasp swiftly and unerringly the uttermost implications of any theme. We have seen that, at sixteen, he instantly detected the hidden melody in the subject Mozart gave him for improvisation. As a man of forty we have seen him improvising with marvellous skill from the violoncello part of Steibelt's quintet, which he snatched from the desk in passing and flung upside down upon the piano. His musical reaction period might have been measured by lightning. He was "wax to receive and marble to retain." So that he could remember and accurately reproduce his most lengthy and elaborate improvisations.

There is, indeed, a trustworthy account of his having improvised before friends upon this very source-motive. Castelli[5] relates that in 1819 he attended a banquet in Vienna given by Schlesinger the music dealer. Beethoven was present and, after a great deal of begging, consented to play if he were given a theme. Castelli, who was totally unmusical, went to the piano and with one finger bumped out the following:

Ex. 356

Beethoven laughed, sat himself down and, never once departing from the given pattern, improvised gloriously "for a full hour by the clock."

The reader will at once notice that Castelli's theme is no other than a reversible, two-way version of the source-motive treated in this chapter. One reason for Beethoven's

[5]Ignaz Franz Castelli, *Memoiren meines Lebens*, Vol. III, p. 117. Quoted in Frimmel, *Neue Beethoveniana*, 1890, p. 54.

laughter may have been his ironical recognition of an absurd situation. The tune which was being offered him as an ostensibly brand-new subject was one which he had used for the last thirty-seven years in the principal themes of scores of his works. And his intimate familiarity with this material may also account for the extraordinary length of his improvisation. Every music lover must regret that the piano on which he played that evening was not of the modern recording type.

This was the spirit who brought forth a musical cosmos from a vapid and apparently empty waltz theme, a "cobbler's patch" of Diabelli's,—who wrote the variations of the *Choral* symphony and the E flat quartet. It seems all but incredible that he could have been unconscious of the virtual melodic identity of such phrases as those marked by brackets in the following.

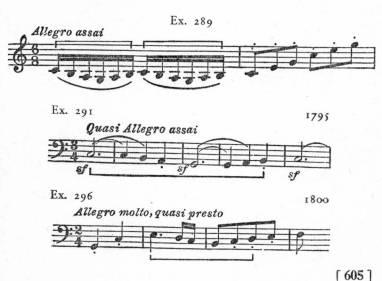

Ex. 289

Allegro assai

Ex. 291   1795
Quasi Allegro assai

Ex. 296   1800
Allegro molto, quasi presto

It is unlikely that those who know Beethoven will seriously contend that the man who was constantly binding his larger works together by means of germ-motives, with the most subtle sort of inter-movement thematic liaison work, as in the *Eroica* and the F minor quartet, would have missed the identity of the source-motive as given in these two examples.

Ex. 352

Adagio ma non troppo

Ex. 355

Allegro

And if he was conscious of this identity, what more likely than that the creator of those infinitely profound variations in the C sharp minor quartet should have been luminously aware of the common source of the most apparently dissimilar examples given above? For instance, Exs. 297, 305, 307, 317, 330, 334, 340, 351, and 355. To believe that such a man could overlook the occurrence of this identical pattern more than a hundred times in the main subjects of his chief works is to strain credulity.

Such considerations, and a study of the originals of a large number of Beethoven's Sketch Books, have convinced the writer that Beethoven habitually incorporated his thematic material so fully into consciousness as to become aware of its farthest implications and possibilities. No doubt the original idea often sprang direct from the unconscious. But his first thoughts were notoriously far from his best. Customarily they were obliged to go through a long and painful period in the *purgatorio* of his active brain before they were ready for the *paradiso* of his perfect work.

In his charmingly written book *The Unconscious Beethoven*[6] Mr. Ernest Newman, the dean of critics, shows how three adjacent notes rise to the emotional climax of many of Beethoven's melodies. This is undeniable. But Mr. Newman also states that the Master used this formula thus, unconsciously and with unique frequency.

It is hard to comprehend how any mind so analytic and so alertly self-critical as Beethoven's could have been unconscious of the significance of a single phrase in any of his principal subjects.

As regards unique frequency one may find these same notes (forming a device which the Germans call an *Anlauf*) ascending to the emotional climax almost everywhere one looks: whether in folk music (*Londonderry Air*); Handel (*Angels Ever Bright and Fair, Largo, Hallelujah Chorus*); Bach (*Air from D major Suite*); Mozart (all four movements of Twenty-second string quartet in B flat); Franck (First movement of *Prelude, Aria and Finale; scherzo* and *finale* of Violin sonata); Wagner (*Siegmund's Love Song*); Dvořak (*Largo* and *finale* of *New World* symphony).

It took ten minutes to compile the above list—in most cases, out of the first pieces of the first music makers that

---

[6]P. 71 ff.

came to mind. In thinking through the work of almost any composer chosen at random one seems to find Mr. Newman's phrase performing its special function, as often as in Beethoven. His study of the three ascending notes seems to the writer valuable—but valuable rather for the light it may shed on Beethoven's conscious mastery of the basic principles of art than for demonstrating the workings of his unconscious mind[7] or the uniqueness of the three notes when used as Mr. Newman describes.

The author has tried to put the subject of this chapter impartially through the same test to which he has subjected Mr. Newman's phrase. Necessarily, any pattern so fundamental to melody as this source-motive, or, for that matter, almost any other scale-tune, is often to be found outside of Beethoven; e. g. in Handel's *Largo*, in the first subject of the slow movement of Tschaikowsky's Fourth symphony and the opening phrase of the Saint-Saëns violoncello concerto in A minor. Mr. Frederick Kelsey has pointed out to the writer a powerful employment of it in the *Faith motif* from *Parsifal*.

Ex. 357

But the motive has probably not been used by other composers with the frequency of Mr. Newman's, because it is twice as long and complicated.

[7]In *The Musical Quarterly*, October, 1927, p. 659 ff., Mr. Carl Engel gave cogent reasons for believing that Beethoven used these three notes consciously.

Suppose, however, that the contrary were proved. Suppose that the four-down-three-up pattern occurred thick as hops in the principal themes of all other composers, ancient and modern. This would not in the least upset the argument of the present chapter, which was written to show the personal grasp of variety in unity, the characteristically opulent economy of this musical Crœsus-cum-Diogenes —quite regardless of the question whether or not other musicians have been similarly gifted.

Why did Beethoven use this pattern with such astonishing liberality? Did he perhaps read in it some private musical anagram? We know that, after his day, Joachim adopted the motto F–A–E which stood for *"Frei aber einsam"* (Free but lonely). We know that Brahms bettered his friend Joachim by adapting this into F–A–F, meaning *"Frei aber froh"* (Free but happy). And that each peppered his principal subjects freely with these anagrams.

It is doubtful if this form of notes

Ex. 358

had any such literary equivalent in the mind of the man who, in spite of the *Pastoral* and *"Battle"* symphonies, did as much as anyone to liberate music from the thralldom of literature. The source-motive formula may have had for him some sort of auspicious association. But whether it was anything which he could formulate in articulate terms, we probably shall never know.

Considering the demonstration of alchemy, economy, variety in unity, and constructive finesse which we have observed in the Master's creative processes, we may reasonably surmise that there are still at large in the sea called Beethoven greater secrets than have yet emerged.

APPENDIX

HOW TO KNOW BEETHOVEN
THROUGH AUTOMATIC INSTRUMENTS

THIS biography will be a failure unless it helps to interest the reader in forming a closer acquaintance with the supreme pages of Beethoven. It would be an irrelevance to set down, concerning this man's art, so many of these groping conventional symbols called words unless they should persuade men to read, hear, perform, and engrave on their minds the melodies and harmonies of the man who freed music. Thanks to the recent progress of invention it is to-day far easier and less expensive to gain an intimate and adequate knowledge of the Master's music than it was during his lifetime—or even before the Great War.

Curiously enough, Beethoven's fortunes were intimately tied up with a crude forerunner of our modern instruments for the reproduction of music. Maelzel's Panharmonicon was one of the earliest known ancestors of the present-day player-piano and phonograph. And for this pioneer invention Beethoven wrote his "*Battle*" symphony, which, despite its ghastly unworthiness, was the first piece by which he won wide popularity. In thus working with Maelzel the Master helped along that emancipation of the unskilled music lover from the necessity for technical proficiency which, a century later, was to be accomplished by automatic instruments. It is good to know that Beethoven had a hand, even though unwittingly, in the epochmaking liberation of the average man from the need for going to a concert when he wants to hear a particular piece of music.

In our own day the best of Beethoven may be played and intensively studied even by those who have never mastered the arduous and complicated craft of finger technic. They merely need access to a good phonograph or automatic piano. In the Introduction the writer has already stated his belief that, "studying these discs and rolls, score in hand, with no limit to the repetition of any desired passage, one can discover, from dawn to dusk, more well-hidden details in a given composition than during a lifetime of casual attendance at concerts."

It is a commonplace that musical performers, from the beginning student to the supreme artist, habitually derive invaluable help from these mechanisms.

A word of counsel to those who have not yet tried mastering the best of Beethoven in this modern fashion. Play the principal themes of a symphony, sonata, or quartet over and over until you have them well in mind. Then see how Beethoven's constructive imagination developed and transfigured these few notes of subject matter.[1] More information about the forms in which Beethoven wrote will be found in the Glossary on pp. 626–635 of this volume.

An attentive use of the improved phonograph and electrically recorded discs will soon bring added enjoyment through growing familiarity with the personalities of the various instruments. Before long even the tyro will, musically speaking, come to tell a hawk from a handsaw by distinguishing the flute from the clarinet, and the bassoon from the French horn.

But do not sit in final judgment on a composition after hearing an old-style disc of it, especially if ground out upon an ancient machine. Although on the one hand the student may derive much benefit and enjoyment from the outmoded apparatus, and although, on the other hand, the latest inventions do not even yet represent the ultimate word in reproduction, it is remarkable how much new richness and how many vital parts of the music—especially the lower tones—are revealed by the

---

[1] The excellent skeleton analyses which begin the pocket scores in the Philharmonia edition point out the germinal tunes on which to concentrate.

new-style phonograph. And the electrical recordings bring out many effects unheard before, besides reproducing far more truly the characteristic tone-colours of such instruments as the oboe, clarinet, piano, and violoncello. Another advantage of the new records is that they are almost uniformly unabridged.

Two recent innovations in this field are particularly useful to those who would like to know the best of Beethoven: the lecture disc by Mr. Leopold Stokowski, introducing the Philadelphia Orchestra's reading of the Seventh symphony; and the brief review of Beethoven's life and works by Sir Alexander C. Mackenzie, printed for the eye upon the two biographical rolls for automatic piano. It is to be hoped that practical educational devices like these may soon come into general use.

The following pages offer a complete catalogue of such of Beethoven's music as has been recorded by three leading American phonograph companies and by three leading American makers of automatic pianos.[2] The first column gives the opus number (when there is one). The second names the composition; the third, the performer. The fourth gives the identifying initial of the make of phonograph record; and the last, that of the autographic piano roll.

Abbreviations Used in the Following List

A	= Ampico.	D	= Duo-Art.
acc.	= accompaniment.	movt.	= movement.
arr.	= arranged by.	Orch.	= Orchestra.
aud.	= Audiographic roll.	rec.	= recorded but not yet published.
B	= Brunswick.	tr.	= transcribed by.
C	= Columbia.	V	= Victor.
cond.	= conducted by.	W	= Welte-Mignon.

---

[2] All the rolls are autograph recordings by virtuosos. It is deeply to be regretted that the nonautographic rolls which allow the amateur player-pianist to project into the performance the moods and tenses of his own personality are now out of fashion and have all but disappeared from the market.

WORKS WITH OPUS NUMBERS

OPUS	COMPOSITION	PERFORMED BY	PHONO-GRAPH	PLAYER
1—No. 3	Trio, C Minor (*Piano part only*)	Adler		D
2—No. 1	Sonata, F Minor (*Piano*)	MacPherson		D
No. 2	Sonata, A (*Piano*)	Bourne (rec.)		D
	(*1st movt. only*)	Suskind		A
	(*Scherzo only*)	Scionti		W
No. 3	Sonata, C (*Piano*)	Hofmann		D
		Stewart		W
6	Sonata, D (*Piano Primo part only*) (*Piano*)	Bauer		D
7	Sonata, E Flat (*Piano*)	Bauer		D
10—No. 1	Sonata, C Minor (*Piano*)	DeGreef (rec.)		D
No. 3	Sonata, D (*Piano*)	Murdoch (rec.)		D
13	Sonate Pathétique, C Minor (*Piano*)	Murdoch	C	
		Bachaus	V	
		Adler		A
		Bauer		D
		Lamond		W
	(*1st movt. only*)	Bachaus		D
14—No. 1	Sonata, E (*Piano*)	Iturbi (rec.)		D
No. 2	Sonata, G (*Piano*)	Murdoch (rec.)		D
18—No. 2	String Quartet, G	Lener	C	
		Flonzaley	V	
No. 3	String Quartet, D Presto (*4th movt. only*)	Lener	C	
		Flonzaley	V	
No. 4	String Quartet, C Minor Allegro (*4th movt. only*)	Lener	C	
		Bauer		D
	Scherzo (*2d movt. only*)	Flonzaley	V	
No. 5	String Quartet, A (*Theme and Var.*)	Bauer		D
		Flonzaley	V	
No. 6	String Quartet, B Flat	Lener	C	
21	Symphony No. 1, C	Henschel and Royal Philharmonic Orch.	C	
22	Sonata, B Flat (*Piano*)	Doguereau (rec.)		D

WORKS WITH OPUS NUMBERS—*Continued*

OPUS	COMPOSITION	PERFORMED BY	PHONO-GRAPH	PLAYER
24	Sonata, F ("Spring") (*Piano and Violin*)	Murdoch, *Piano* } Catterall, *Violin* }	C	
26	Sonata, A Flat (*Piano*)	Landowska		D
		Deering		W
	(*last 3 movts. only*)	Georg Schumann		W
27—No. 1	Sonata, E Flat (*Piano*)	Darre (rec.)		D
27—No. 2	Sonata, C sharp minor	Bauer	V	
	("Moonlight")	Friedman	C	
	(*Piano*)	Lhevinne		A
		Paderewski		W
	(*1st movt. only*)	Paderewski	V	
		Paderewski		D
		Hofmann		D
28	Sonata, D ("Pastoral") (*Piano*)	Friedman		D
31—No. 1	Sonata, G (*Piano*)	Leopold		D
No. 2	Sonata, D Minor (*Piano*)	Mero (rec.)		D
	(*1st movt. only*)	Hallet		W
No. 3	Sonata, E Flat (*Piano*)	Brailowsky		A
		Hofmann		W
34	Six Variations on Original Theme in F (*Piano*)	Kleeberg		W
36	Symphony No. 2, D	Beecham and London Symphony Orch.	C	
46	Adelaide (*arr. by Liszt*) (*Piano*)	Lamond (rec.)		D
47	Sonata, A ("Kreutzer") (*Violin and Piano*)	Menges, *Violin* } DeGreef, *Piano* }	V	
		Huberman, *Violin* } Schultze, *Piano* }	B	
		Sammons, *Violin* } Murdoch, *Piano* }	C	
48	*Die Ehre Gottes aus der Natur* (*Barytone*)	Schorr	B	

WORKS WITH OPUS NUMBERS—*Continued*

OPUS	COMPOSITION	PERFORMED BY	PHONO-GRAPH	PLAYER
49—No. 1	Sonata, G Minor (*Piano*)	Fryer (rec.)		D
No. 2	Sonata, G (*Piano*)	Laffitte (rec.)		D
50	Romance in F for Violin (*Piano Accompaniment*)	Thibaut	V	
		Benoist		D
51—No. 2	Rondo, G (*Piano*)	Schnabel		A
		Howard-Jones		W
53	Sonata C ("Waldstein")	Powell		D
		Carreño		W
54	Sonata, F (*Piano*)	Leginska (rec.)		D
55	Symphony No. 3, E Flat ("Eroica")	Wood and New Queen's Hall Orch.	C	
		Coates and Symphony Orch.	V	
		Lamond		
57	Sonata, F Minor ("Appassionata") (*Piano*)	Murdoch	C	
		Bauer	V	D
		Bauer (aud.)		D
		Levitzky		A
		Schelling		W
59—No. 1	String Quartet, F	Lener	C	
No. 2	E Minor	Lener	C	
No. 3	C	Lener	C	
60	Symphony No. 4, B Flat	Harty and Hallé Orch.	C	
61	Violin Concerto, D	Kreisler and Berlin State Opera Orch. cond. Blech	V	
62	Coriolanus Overture, C Minor	Mengelberg and Concertgebouw Orch.	C	
		London Symphony Orch.	V	
67	Symphony No. 5, C Minor	Weingartner and Royal Philharmonic Orch.	C	

WORKS WITH OPUS NUMBERS—*Continued*

OPUS	COMPOSITION	PERFORMED BY	PHONO-GRAPH	PLAYER
		Ronald and Royal Albert Hall Orch.	V	
		Furtwaengler and Berlin Philharmonic Orch.	B	
		Stoessel		D
	(2 *pianos*)	Suskind and Loesser, cond. Bodansky		A
		Singer		W
	(2 *pianos*)	Singer and Reichmann		W
68	Symphony No. 6, F (Pastoral)	Weingartner and Royal Philharmonic Orch.	C	
	(2 *Pianos*)	Robinson and Singer		W
69	Sonata, A (*Violoncello and Piano*)	Salmond, *Violoncello* Rumschisky, *Piano*	C	
72a	Leonore No. 3 Overture	Wood and New Queen's Hall Orch.	C	
72b	Fidelio Overture	Berlin State Opera Orch.	V	
	Ha! Welch ein Augenblick! (Act I); Hat man nicht auch Gold beineben (Act I)(Barytone)	Bohnen with Orch.	B	
73	Piano Concerto, E Flat ("Emperor")	Bachaus and Royal Albert Hall Orch. cond. Ronald	V	
74	String Quartet, E Flat ("Harp")	Lener	C	

WORKS WITH OPUS NUMBERS—*Continued*

OPUS	COMPOSITION	PERFORMED BY	PHONO-GRAPH	PLAYER
78	Sonata, F Sharp (*Piano*)	Lamond		A
		Scharrer (rec.)		D
79	Sonatina, G (*Piano*)	Hess (rec.)		D
	(*2d movt. only*)	Hess (aud.)		D
81b	Sonata, E Flat (Adieu, Absence, and Re-union) (*Piano*)	Novaes		D
84	Egmont Overture	Mengelberg and Concertgebouw Orch.	C	
		Victor Symphony	V	
		Kohlberg		W
90	Sonata, E Minor (*Piano*)	Schwarwenka		W
92	Symphony No. 7, A	Weingartner and Royal Philhar-monic Orch.	C	
		Stokowski and Philadelphia Orch. with introductory talk by Stokowski	V	
		Strauss and Berlin State Opera Orch.	B	
93	Symphony No. 8, F	Weingartner and Royal Phil-harmonic Orch.	C	
	(*2d movt. only*)	Stokowski and Philadelphia Orch.	V	
95	String Quartet, F Minor (Serioso)	Lener	C	
97	Trio, B Flat ("Arch-duke")	Murdoch, *Piano* Sammons, *Violin* Squire, *Violon-cello*	C	
101	Sonata, A Major (*Piano*)	Hofmann		W

WORKS WITH OPUS NUMBERS—*Continued*

OPUS	COMPOSITION	PERFORMED BY	PHONO-GRAPH	PLAYER
106	Sonata, B Flat (Hammerklavier) (*Piano*)	Cortot (rec.)		D
109	Sonata, E (*Piano*)	Cortot		D
110	Sonata, A Flat (*Piano*)	Cortot (rec.)		D
111	Sonata, C Minor (*Piano*)	Lamond		D
113	Turkish March from "Ruins of Athens"			
	(*Violin, arr. Auer*)	Seidel	C	
	(*Piano*)	Bauer		D
	(*Piano, tr. Rubinstein*)	Hofmann	B	D
	(*Piano, tr. Rubinstein*)	Novaes		W
	(*Piano*)	Rachmaninoff	V	A
123	Missa Solemnis in D (Mass)	Orpheus Choir of Barcelona, cond. Millet	V	
125	Symphony No. 9, D Minor (Choral)	Weingartner and London Symphony Orch. with vocal soloists and chorus	C	
		Coates and Symphony Orch. with vocal soloists and chorus	V	
129	Rondo a capriccio, G Rage Over a Lost Groschen) (*Piano*)	Ney Hofmann		A D
130	String Quartet, B Flat ("Scherzoso")	Lener	C	
131	String Quartet, C Sharp Minor	Lener	C	
132	String Quartet, A Minor	Lener	C	
135	String Quartet, F	Lener Flonzaley	C V	

WORKS WITHOUT OPUS NUMBERS

COMPOSITION	PERFORMED BY	PHONO-GRAPH	PLAYER
Andante in F ("Andante Favori") (*Piano*)	Landowska		D
	Scionti		W
Albumblatt für Elise (*Piano*)	Reisenauer		W
Farewell to the Piano	Bergere		W
Duet in E Flat (*Viola and Violoncello*)	Paul and Rudolph Hindemith	B	
2 Bagatelles (*Piano*)	Peppercorn		W
Six Variations on Duet: "Nel cor piu non mi sento" from "La Molinara," G (*Piano*)	Buell		A
Eight Variations on theme: "Tandeln und Scherzen," F (*Piano*)	Leginska		D
Rondino, E Flat, arr. for violin, Kreisler (*Piano acc. only*)	Charmbury		D
Rondino arr. Kreisler (*Piano*)	Danziger		W
Gavotte, Violin	Kreisler	V	
Gavotte, F (*Piano*)	Bauer	V	
	Bauer		D
Minuet, E Flat (*Piano*)	Fryer		W
	Conradi		W
Minuet, G (*Piano*)	Schnabel		A
(*Piano*)	Leginska		A
(*Piano*)	Fabre		W
(*Piano*)	Daisy Hoffman		D
(*Violin*)	Fradkin	B	
(*Violin*)	Elman	V	
Country Dance No. 1	Gordon		A
Country Dance No. 1 (tr. Seiss) (*Piano*)	Gordon		D
Contra-Danse (*Piano*)	Danziger		W
German Dance No. 1 (tr. Seiss) (*Piano*)	Wilmington		D
German Dance No. 3 (tr. Seiss) (*Piano*)	Powell		D
German Dance C (*Piano*)	Epstein		W
German Dances (*Piano*)	Danziger		W
Ecossaises, E Flat (*Arr. D'Albert*)	Levitzky		A
	Ney	B	

WORKS WITHOUT OPUS NUMBERS—*Continued*

COMPOSITION	PERFORMED BY	PHONO-GRAPH	PLAYER
Ecossaisen	Levin		W
In Questa Tomba (*Song*)	Chaliapin	V	
Ich Liebe Dich (*Song*) (*Piano*)	La Forge		D
Biographical Rolls Nos. 1 and 2	Annotated by Mackenzie (aud.)		D

GLOSSARY

Some Technical Terms Every Music Lover Should Know

APPOGGIATURA: A short note of embellishment suspending or delaying a note of melody.

ABSOLUTE MUSIC: That type of music to which no program or literary interpretation is attached by the composer. Sometimes called pure music.

ACOUSTICS: That branch of the science of physics dealing with the phenomena of sound.

ANSWER: The response to the fugue (q. v.)[1] subject. It resembles that subject but is in another key.

ARIA: One of the more ambitious instrumental forms originally used vocally in the older operas.

AUGMENTATION: Repeating a subject in notes of greater value: halves for quarters, etc. The opposite of diminution.

AUTHENTIC CADENCE: A closing formula consisting of the dominant triad (on the fifth degree) followed by the tonic triad (on the first degree).

BAGATELLE: A short simple composition, usually in song form.

BASSO OSTINATO: A bass part in which the same melodic figure obstinately recurs, as in the Rondo of the *"Pastoral"* sonata, Op. 28, bars 9–16.

BINARY FORM: Two-part form. A movement with two themes.

CADENCE: (From Latin: *cadere,* to fall.) The close (fall) or ending of a phrase, period, part, movement, or work. The harmonic formula by which a phrase or period is ended, giving a sense of temporary or complete finality. Cadences are authentic, plagal, perfect, deceptive, etc.

CADENZAS (Italian for *cadence*): An improvised florid passage usually brought in at or near the end of an instrumental

---

[1] Literally "which see."

movement or vocal aria. In the Eighteenth Century the *cadenza* was the part of the concerto best designed to exhibit the soloist's technical ability, introducing his own development of the subject matter of the movement. Later, not trusting to the powers of the artist, the composer himself wrote the *cadenza*. It is still the custom for composers or performers to compose new *cadenzas* to standard works, such as Kreisler wrote for the Beethoven violin concerto.

CANON: A composition in which a subject sung or played in one voice is imitated note for note in the others, either at the same or at a different pitch. The old-fashioned round is in canon form (e. g., Three Blind Mice).

CAVATINA: A short aria (q. v.). The term is occasionally used for a songlike instrumental piece or movement.

CHAMBER MUSIC: Music meant to be played in a small hall or room by a limited number of soloists, or a group of instrumentalists, such as wood-wind combinations, string quartet, trio, etc., with or without piano.

CHORAL: Psalm or hymn tune. A broad simple song for many voices (chorale).

CHORD: The simultaneous sounding of tones built up in thirds from a given root or fundamental. A three-voiced chord is a triad; four-voiced, a chord of the seventh, etc. To-day chords are sometimes arbitrarily built up in intervals other than the time-honoured thirds.

CHROMATIC SCALE: One which proceeds in half steps.

CODA: A concluding phrase or section added to a vocal or instrumental work, not strictly necessary for completeness, but making a more positive and effective close. It may also occur at the end of a principal section or even of a period.

CONCERTO: In Beethoven's time, an elaborate work for solo instrument and orchestra. In form it is virtually a sonata (q. v.), usually of three movements.

APPENDIX

CONTRAPUNTAL: Pertaining to counterpoint. Contrapuntal forms are canons (q. v.) and fugues (q. v.).

COUNTERPOINT: (Point against point. Point is an old term for note.) Two or more melodies written to sound simultaneously. Polyphonic or many-voiced style. Horizontal music as opposed to vertical or harmonic music.

CYCLICAL FORM: A composition laid out in a series of movements (as a suite or a sonata). To-day we apply the term to inter-movement thematic relation.

DEVELOPMENT: The working out of a theme, subject, or group of subjects by every device for variation, expansion, etc., at the composer's command. The second section in fugue (q. v.) and in sonata-form (q. v.). Also called free fantasia, development section, or working-out portion.

DIATONIC: A scale proceeding by consecutive tone degrees, or a melody containing no tones foreign to the key.

DIMINUTION: Repeating a subject in notes of shorter duration: e. g., quarters for halves, eighths for quarters, etc. The opposite of augmentation.

DIVERTIMENTO (DIVERTISSEMENT): An early instrumental composition usually consisting of more than four movements, and of a cheerful, entertaining character.

DOMINANT: The fifth step of the scale; dominant harmony, the triad on the fifth degree (e. g. the dominant chord of the key of G major is D–F sharp–A).

DYNAMICS: Contrasts between loud and soft, and progressions from one to the other: one of the means of producing expression in music.

ECOSSAISE: A dance of Scotch origin.

ENSEMBLE: A particular combination of instruments or voices, as chorus, string quartet, orchestra, etc. Team-work of instruments or voices. Chamber music is sometimes called ensemble music.

EXPOSITION: The thematic or subject matter set forth in the first part of a fugue or sonata.

FIGURE: A small melodic tone-group or motive.

FIGURED-BASS: A system of numeral-notation of a bass part to indicate the intended harmony. A stenographic method of writing keyboard music. Also called thoroughbass.

FINALE: The final movement of a composition in several movements.

FORM: The plan of a piece of music. The arrangement of material into symmetrical and effective order, as in the rondo, minuet, *scherzo,* sonata-form movement, etc. (q. v.).

FUGATO: A part of a composition built in the manner of a fugue (q. v.) but not carried out with its complication or completeness. The theme begins in one part and is successively imitated by the other parts.

FUGUE (From Latin: *fuga,* flight): An enlarged and elaborately developed canon (q. v.). The highest form of contrapuntal art. A fugue has a subject (q. v.), an answer (the subject repeated more or less exactly a fifth above), a counter-subject (a theme planned to dovetail contrapuntally into the answer), and episodes developed from the subject matter. Sometimes the first part, or exposition, is brought back with the subject inverted (*see* Inversion), augmented (*see* Augmentation), or diminished (*see* Diminution). The stretto (q. v.), in which the subject is shortened by telescoping in order to build up the climax of the composition, is followed by a coda (q. v.) in which there is often a long organ-point (q. v.) before the final cadence (q. v.). As it may be divided into exposition, developing portion, and recapitulation, it may be regarded as the precursor of sonata-form. Fugues are both instrumental and vocal.

GERM-MOTIVE: A musical phrase which recurs, more or less disguised, in different movements of the same composition; used as an interlocking device to lend the whole work thematic unity. (E. g., the motive G–C–D–E flat which runs through the *Sonate Pathétique. See* pp. 53–55 and 530 ff.)

HARMONY: The science which treats of chords—their construction, inter-relation, and logical progression.

IMITATION: An echoing of the theme in other voice-parts but usually higher or lower than the original statement.

INTERVAL: The distance from one tone to another; the difference in pitch between two tones.

INTRODUCTION: A passage or movement at the beginning of a work, leading up to the principal subject (q. v.) or exposition (q. v.).

INVERSION:

(a) Turning the two tones of an interval upside down.

(b) Changing the position of the tones of a chord so that some other than its root serves as bass.

(c) Reversing the intervals of a melodic line so that they go in contrary motion to their original order.

(d) In counterpoint, exchanging the position of two lines of melody so that, e. g., soprano becomes alto, and vice versa.

KEY: Any particular scale or tone series binding the triads of that scale into a unity through relation to a tonal centre which gives the key its name. "Key" and "scale" are used interchangeably. (Key of D.) (*See* Tonality.)

LEITMOTIF: A term first used by Von Wolzogen in connection with the Wagnerian music-drama. A motive intimately identified with some character, situation, or idea in opera. The lineal descendant of Beethoven's germ- and source-motive.

MASS: A choral setting, with or without accompaniment, of certain portions of the Eucharistic service in the Roman Church. Sung in Latin.

MINUET: A dance of French origin originally consisting of two eight-bar phrases in 3/4 time and of moderate pace. A second minuet was added, contrasted in feeling and usually written in three-part harmony, from which it derived the name Trio. Beethoven speeded this form up and altered it emotionally into the *scherzo* (q. v.).

MODE: A type or species of scale. To-day we have the major and minor modes in all keys, corresponding to the major and minor scales. The term was used in Hindu, Greek, and church music (Gregorian and Ambrosian modes).

MODULATION: The process of changing, in the course of a movement, from one key or tonality (q. v.) to another.

MOTIVE, MOTIF: A short melodic figure or note-group used as a structural basis for developing a composition.

MOVEMENT:

(a) Rhythmic motion.

(b) A principal division of a compound or cyclical work, such as a suite or sonata.

ORATORIO: An extended composition for solo voices, chorus, and orchestra, without stage setting or acting, usually illustrating some sacred subject.

ORGAN-POINT: A stationary bass held for a considerable time, over which other voices move freely. (*See* Beethoven's *"Moonlight"* sonata (Op. 27, No. 2), last movement, *Presto agitato*, measures 152–164. Also opus 28, first movement, measures 1–25.)

PLAGAL CADENCE: A closing formula which consists of the triad upon the fourth degree of the scale followed by the tonic triad (q. v.).

PROGRAM MUSIC: A purely instrumental composition to which a detailed poetic program is affixed by the composer.

RECAPITULATION: The restatement of a sonata or fugue exposition (q. v.). Succeeds the development (q. v.) with certain traditional changes in key relations.

APPENDIX

RONDO: A piece derived from the old round dance in which the main theme or subject is frequently repeated, separated by secondary themes, e. g., on the model, ABACA or ABACADA.

SCALE: A definite succession of tones within an octave, written on successive staff degrees. There are many varieties, ranging from the pentatonic, or five-tone scale of the Chinese, Scotch, and many primitive races, and the modal scales of the Greeks and of the Mediæval Church, to the diatonic major and minor, and chromatic scales in use to-day, as well as the whole-tone scale of Debussy, etc.

SCHERZO: Literally the joke movement. Usually the third movement in the larger instrumental works of Beethoven. Consists of two short sections built on three-part song-form (q. v.). The second section is known as the Trio. The typical Beethoven *scherzo* usually begins fast, light, staccato, and in three-part time. Its Trio often brings in contrasting slower, smoother, and mellower music. This is followed by the more or less literal repetition of the first part.

SEQUENCE: The frequent repetition of the same melodic figure, starting on a different degree of the scale.

SONATA: (From Italian *sonare:* to sound; hence a "sound-piece".) An instrumental composition of three or four contrasting and more or less related movements. Most sonatas are for piano, or for piano and another instrument. Trios, quartets, quintets, etc., are really sonatas for groups of instruments. A symphony is a sonata for orchestra. The first movement is customarily in so-called sonata-form. The second, often a slow movement, is generally in extended three-part song-form. The third is usually in minuet or *scherzo* form. The fourth is frequently in rondo form, occasionally in sonata-form. Variation form may be used in any movement of a sonata.

SONATA-FORM: The form in which the first movement of the standard sonata is constructed. It is a development of the three-part song form. The basic material of the typical sonata-form is found in two subjects, each of which may consist of one or more themes closely related by mood and key. The three main divisions of the form consist of:

(1) Exposition:
    (a) First subject in key of tonic, and modulation to
    (b) Second subject in complementary key which is usually dominant, or relative major if (a) is in the minor.
(2) Development: in which these subjects are worked out with much modulation (q. v.), according to the imaginative fertility and technical resource of the composer.
(3) Recapitulation: a virtual repetition of the Exposition with prescribed changes of key (second subject in tonic, etc.).

The following diagram graphically represents the typical structure of sonata-form:

| EXPOSITION | DEVELOPMENT | RECAPITULATION |

SONG-FORM:
    (a) The small, or simple, in two or three parts;
    (b) the large, or extended, in two or three parts.

    (a) is the smallest independent form in use and is so named because it is in the form of a song. Much folk music and many songs are in the small two and three part song forms. The theme from the slow movement of the E major Sonata, Op. 109, is simple, or small, two-part song-form (A+B). Many of the pieces from Schumann's *Album for the Young* and Mendelssohn's *Songs without Words* are in simple three-part song-form (A+B+A). The third part is often a repetition, more or less exact, of the first part, and often a coda (q. v.) is added, e. g., Beethoven's Bagatelle in F major (Op. 33, No. 3).

The large two-part song-forms embrace the old dance-forms such as Allemandes, Sarabandes, also Themes for Variations, e. g., in Beethoven's A flat Sonata, Op. 26, and occasionally an entire Beethoven movement, e. g., the last of his Fourth symphony. Many minuets, *scherzos,* and slow movements are in large three-part song-form, e. g. *Adagio* of F minor sonata (Op. 2, No. 1): A+B+A+Coda.

SOURCE-MOTIVE: A musical phrase which recurs, more or less identically, in a number of distinct compositions and produces in the group an effect of thematic unity. (*See* p. 566 ff., chaps. LV and LVI.)

STRETTO: In a fugue (q. v.) a passage in which the subject and answer are introduced in close succession, so as to overlap and crowd upon each other, producing an effect of climax.

SUBDOMINANT: The fourth degree of the scale. Subdominant harmony, the triad on the fourth degree (e. g. in the key of G major, the subdominant chord is C–E–G).

SUBJECT: A melodic figure or phrase taken as a theme for treatment throughout a composition. Used specifically in a fugue and as a general term in all forms of composition. Opposed to Answer (q. v.).

SUITE: A collection of idealized dance tunes put together in contrasting tempos, rhythms, and moods. Also called partita. A precursor of the form of composition in several movements which finds its highest perfection in the Beethoven sonata. Bach, Handel, Couperin, etc., wrote suites.

SYMPHONY: A sonata for large orchestra.

SYNCOPATION: Shifting the accent to the normally weak or unaccented part of the beat or measure and holding it over the strong or accented part, thus robbing the naturally strong rhythmic position of its normal accent. This rhythmic disturbance is often carried over from one measure to another by means of tied notes. See Beethoven sonata, Op. 27, No. 1, *Adagio* bars 13–16; and *Leonore No. 3* overture, first measures of *Allegro*.

THEMATIC WORK: The development of themes (*see* Development).

THEME: A subject of a composition, or part of a subject.

THOROUGHBASS: Loosely, harmonic composition. Also Figured-bass (q. v.).

TONALITY: All relations between degrees of a scale connected with a tonal centre. A key or mode.

TONIC: The first tone of the scale (for instance, G in the scale of G).

TONIC CHORD: The chord based on the first tone of the scale. e. g., G–B–D in the scale of G.

TRIAD: A three-voiced chord, consisting of a root, third, and fifth. Triads are major, minor, augmented, and diminished.

TUTTI: Denotes the entrance of the full orchestra after passages for individual instruments.

VARIATION: The amplification or modification of a given theme. A form of composition called Theme and Variations.

BIBLIOGRAPHY

The literature of Beethoven is vast. This list includes the more important works published in book form.

BIOGRAPHIES

1838   WEGELER und RIES: *Biographische Notizen über Ludwig van Beethoven.* New ed. by Kalischer, 1906.

1840   SCHINDLER, ANTON: *Beethovens Biographie* (1st ed.). 3d ed., 1860. New ed. by Kalischer, 1908.

1864–77   NOHL, LUDWIG: *Beethovens Leben.* (3 vols.)

1888   WASIELEWSKI, W. J. VON: *Ludwig van Beethoven.* (2 vols.)

1899   CROWEST, F. J.: *Beethoven.*

1903   ROLLAND, ROMAIN: *Beethoven.* Eng. tr. by B. Constance Hull, 1924.

1904   MASON, DANIEL GREGORY: *Beethoven and His Forerunners.*

1907   CHANTAVOINE, JEAN: *Beethoven* (*Maîtres de la Musique*).

1908   DIEHL, ALICE M.: *The Life of Beethoven.*

       MARX, ADOLPH BERNHARD: *Ludwig van Beethoven: Leben und Schaffen.* (2 vols.)

       THAYER, ALEXANDER WHEELOCK: *Ludwig van Beethovens Leben* (Ed. by H. Deiters.) (5 vols. Vols. IV and V ed. by H. Riemann. 2d ed. of Vols. II and III and 3d of Vol. I. ed. by H. Riemann, 1919.)

1911   PAUL BEKKER: *Beethoven.* Eng. tr. by M. M. Bozman, 1925.

1911   D'INDY, VINCENT: *Beethoven.* Eng. tr. by Theodore Baker, 1913.

1913   THOMAS-SAN-GALLI, W. A.: *Ludwig van Beethoven.* 7th ed., 1920.

1920   ERNEST, GUSTAV: *Beethoven.* 3d ed., 1926.

       PROD'HOMME, J. G.; *La Jeunesse de Beethoven.*

1921   THAYER, ALEXANDER WHEELOCK: *The Life of Ludwig van Beethoven.* Edited, revised, and amended

from the original English manuscript and the German
editions of Deiters and Riemann, concluded, and all
the documents newly translated, by Henry Edward
Krehbiel. (3 vols.)

1922   VON FRIMMEL, THEODOR: *Ludwig van Beethoven.*
6th ed., revised and enlarged.

1925   SCHIEDERMAIR, DR. LUDWIG: *Der junge Beethoven.*

1926   DE HEVESY, ANDRÉ: *Beethoven, Vie Intime.*

1927   GRACE, HARVEY: *Beethoven.*

LUDWIG, EMIL: "Beethoven" (essay in *Kunst und
Schicksal*).

TURNER, W. J.: *Beethoven.*

(Undated)   BARTELS, BERNHARD: *Beethoven.*

LETTERS

1901   KASTNER, EMERICH: *Gesamtausgabe der Briefe Beethovens.*

1906–08   KALISCHER, ALFRED: *Gesamtausgabe der Briefe Beethovens.* (5 vols.) (2d ed. by Th. von Frimmel.)

1907–11   PRELINGER, FRITZ: *Gesamtausgabe der Briefe Beethovens.* (5 vols.)

1909   SHEDLOCK, J. S.: *Beethoven's Letters.* (2 vols.) Abridged
edition (1 vol.), 1926, ed. by A. Eaglefield Hull.

1923   KASTNER-KAPP: *Ludwig van Beethovens Sämtliche
Briefe.*

1927   SONNECK, OSCAR G.: *Beethoven Letters in America.*

MISCELLANEOUS WORKS

1870   WAGNER, RICHARD: *Beethoven.* Tr. by Albert R.
Parsons.

1874   VON BREUNING, GERHARD: *Aus dem Schwarzspanierhause.*

1890   TENGER, MARIAM: *Beethovens Unsterbliche Geliebte
nach persönlichen Errinnerunger.* Eng. tr. by Gertrude
Russell, 1893.

1891   KALISCHER, ALFRED: *Die Unsterbliche Geliebte Beethovens.*

APPENDIX

1901   KULLAK, FRANZ: *Beethoven's Piano-Playing.* Tr. by Th. Baker.

1905   VON FRIMMEL, THEODOR: *Beethovens äussere Erscheinung.*

1906   VON FRIMMEL, THEODOR: *Beethoven- Studien.* Pt. I: "Beethovens äussere Erscheinung." Pt. II: "Bausteine zu einer Lebensgeschichte des Meisters."

1908–09   LA MARA (MARIE LIPSIUS): *Beethovens Unsterbliche Geliebte:* Das Geheimnis der Gräfin Brunswick und ihre Memoiren.

   VON FRIMMEL, THEODOR: *Beethovenjahrbuch.*

1909   KALISCHER, A. C.: *Beethovens Frauenkreis.* (2 vols.)

   THOMAS-SAN-GALLI, W. A.: *Die Unsterbliche Geliebte Beethovens, Amalie Sebald.*

1911   UNGER, MAX: *Auf Spuren von Beethovens Unsterblicher Geliebten.*

1913   KERST, F., *ed.*: *Die Errinnerungen an Beethoven.* (2 vols.)

1919   HUSCHKE, K.: *Beethoven als Pianist und Dirigent.*

1920   LA MARA: *Beethoven und die Brunsviks.*

1921   BILANCIONI, GUGLIELMO: *La Sordità di Beethoven, Considerazioni di un otologo.*

   LEITZMANN, ALBERT: *Berichte der Zeitgenossen:* Briefe und persönliche Aufzeichnungen, gesammelt und erläutert. (2 vols.)

   OREL, ALFRED: *Ein Wiener Beethovenbuch.*

1922   SCHWEISHEIMER, DR. WALDEMAR: *Beethovens Leiden.*

1923   VON FRIMMEL, THEODOR: *Beethoven im zeitgenössischen Bildnis.*

   NOHL, W.: *Ludwig van Beethovens Konversationshefte.*

1924   SANDBERGER, ADOLPH: *Neues Beethoven-Jahrbuch.*

1925   LEY, S., *ed.*: *Beethovens Leben in authentischen Bildern und Texten.*

   WALDVOGEL, R. VON: *Auf der Fährte des Genius.*

1926   SONNECK, O. G., *ed.*: *Beethoven:* Impressions of Contemporaries.

1927   ALEXANDRE, ARSENE: *Les Années de Captivité de Beethoven.*

BIBLIOGRAPHY

BOSSE, GUSTAV (ed.): *Beethoven Almanach der Deutschen Musikbücherei auf das Jahr 1927.*
NEWMAN, ERNEST: *The Unconscious Beethoven.*
SONNECK, OSCAR G.: *The Riddle of the Immortal Beloved.*
SONNECK, OSCAR, G.: *Beethoven Letters in America.*
SULLIVAN, J. W. N.; *Beethoven: His Spiritual Development.*

1928 CLOSSON, ERNEST: *L'Élément Flamand dans Beethoven.*
MASON, DANIEL GREGORY: *The Dilemma of American Music.*

THE MUSIC

1852 VON LENZ, WILHELM: *Beethoven et ses trois styles.* New ed., 1909.
1855 VON LENZ, WILHELM: *Beethoven eine Kunststudie.*
1857 OULIBICHEFF, ALEXANDRE: *Beethoven, ses critiques et ses glossateurs.*
1863 MARX, A. B., *Anleitung zum Vortrag Beethovenschen Klavierwerke.* New ed. by G. Behncke, 1912.
1866 NOTTEBOHM, GUSTAV: *Ein Skizzenbuch von Beethoven aus dem Jahre 1801.* New ed., 1925.
1872 NOTTEBOHM, GUSTAV: *Beethoveniana.*
1880 NOTTEBOHM, GUSTAV: *Ein Skizzenbuch von Beethoven aus dem Jahre 1803.* New ed., 1925.
1887 NOTTEBOHM, GUSTAV.: *Zweite Beethoveniana.* (Both vols. reprinted 1925.)
1890 VON FRIMMEL, THEODOR: *Neue Beethoveniana.*
1895 ELTERLEIN, ERNEST VON: *Beethovens Klaviersonaten.*
1897 COLOMBANI, ALFREDO: *Le Nove Sinfonie di Beethoven.*
WEBER, W.: *Beethovens Missa Solemnis. Eine Studie.* New ed., 1908.
1898 GROVE, SIR GEORGE: *Beethoven and His Nine Symphonies.*
1900 SHEDLOCK, J. S.: *The Pianoforte Sonatas.*
1902 MATTHEWS, J.: *The Violin Music of Beethoven.*

1905 WALKER, ERNEST: *Beethoven.* Amer. ed., abridged, 1920.

1906 DE CURZON, H.: *Les lieder et airs détachés de Beethoven.*

PROD'HOMME, J. G.: *Les Symphonies de Beethoven.* 10th ed., revised, 1926.

VON FRIMMEL, THEODOR: *Beethovenstudien.* (2 vols.)

WEINGARTNER, F.: *Ratschläge für Aufführungen klassischer Symphonien.* (Vol. I.) *Beethoven,* 2d ed., 1916. Eng. tr. by Jessie Crosland, *On the Performances of Beethoven's Symphonies,* 1907.

1910 CHOP, M.: *Ludwig van Beethovens Symphonien.*

CHOP, M.: *Ludwig van Beethoven, Fidelio.*

1912 KUFFERATH, M.: *Fidelio de L. van Beethoven.*

MARX, A. B.: *Anleitung zum Vortrag Beethovenscher Klavierwerke.* New ed. by Eugen Schmitz.

1918 SHEDLOCK, J. S.: *Beethoven's Pianoforte Sonatas.*

1918–19 RIEMANN, HUGO: *Ludwig van Beethovens sämtliche Klaviersolosonaten: Aesthetische und formal-technische Analyse mit historischen Notizen.*

1921 CHOP, M.: *Ludwig van Beethoven, Missa Solemnis.*

HELM, THEODOR: *Beethovens Streichquartette.* (3d ed.)

LOWE, C. E.: *Beethoven's Pianoforte Sonatas.*

1922 MERSMANN, H.: *Beethoven. Die Synthese der Stile.*

TOVEY, D. F.: *Beethoven's Ninth Symphony.*

1923–24 EVANS, EDWIN, Sen'r : *Beethoven's Nine Symphonies Fully Described and Annotated.*

NAGEL, WILLIBALD: *Beethoven und seine Klaviersonaten.* 2d ed. (2 vols.)

SCHMITZ, A.: *Beethovens "Zwei Prinzipi": ihre Bedeutung für Themen- und Satzbau.*

1925 MIES, P.: *Die Bedeutung der Skizzen Beethovens zur Erkenntniss seines Stiles.*

CASSIRER, FRITZ: *Beethoven und die Gestalt: ein Kommentar.*

MILNE, A. FORBES: *Beethoven: The Pianoforte Sonatas.*

WETZEL, J. H.: *Beethovens Violinsonaten.* (In progress.)

MARLIAVE, JOSEPH DE: *Les Quatuors de Beethoven.*

BIBLIOGRAPHY

Introduction and notes by J. Escarra. Preface by Gabriel Fauré. Eng. tr. by Hilda Andrews, 1928.

1926 FRIEDLÄNDER, MAX, PROF. DR.: *Beethoven an die Ferne Geliebte.*

HADOW, W. H.: *Beethoven's Opus 18 Quartets.*

HERWEGH, M.: *Technique et interprétation . . . sonates pour piano et violon de Beethoven.*

1927 BEHREND, WILLIAM: *Ludwig van Beethoven's Pianoforte Sonatas.* Eng. tr. by Ingeborg Lund.

(Undated) CZERNY, CHARLES: *Pianoforte Sonatas.* Pt. 4, chaps. II and III.

KRETSCHMAR, HERMANN: *Beethovens Symphonien im Führer durch den Konzertsaal.*

NOHL, LUDWIG: *Beethoven (Musiker-Biographien).* (2 vols.)

RIEMAN, HUGO: *Beethovens Streichquartette.*

WORKS OF REFERENCE

1865 THAYER, ALEXANDER WHEELOCK: *Chronologisches Verzeichniss der Werke von Beethoven.*

1922 RIEMANN, HUGO: *Musik Lexicon.* 10th ed.

1925 NOTTEBOHM, GUSTAV: Ludwig van B., *Thematisches Verzeichniss.* Nebst. der *Bibliotheca Beethoveniana,* von Emerich Kastner, Ergänzt von Theodor von Frimmel.

1926 VON FRIMMEL, THEODOR: *Beethoven Handbuch.* (2 vols.)

1927 GROVE, SIR GEORGE: *Dictionary of Music and Musicians.* 3d ed.

A LIST OF
BEETHOVEN'S PRINTED WORKS

Abbreviations Used in Description

Acc.=Accompaniment.
Alt.=Alto.
Arrd.=Arranged.
Arrt.=Arrangement.
Bsn. = Bassoon.
C.-Bass=Contra-bass.
Cho.=Chorus.
Clar.=Clarinet.
Cor.=French horn.
Eng. H.=English horn.
Fl.=Flute.

Ob.=Oboe.
Op.=Opus.
Orch.=Orchestra.
Pf.=Pianoforte.
Sop.=Soprano.
Str.=Strings.
Ten.=Tenor.
V.=Violin.
Va.=Viola.
Vo.=Violoncello.

Abbreviations Used in Dates

ann.=announcement.
b.=before.
c. = about.
mvt.=movement.

orig. =originally.
prob.=probably.
prod.=produced.
(?) =not certain.

WORKS WITH OPUS NUMBERS

OPUS	DESCRIPTION	DEDICATED TO	COM- POSED	PUB- LISHED
1	Three Trios (E flat, G, C minor) Pf. V. Vo.	Prince Carl von Lichnowsky	1795	1795
2	Three Sonatas (F minor, A, C) Pf.	Joseph Haydn		1796
3	Trio (E flat) V. Va. Vo.		1792(?)	1797
4	Quintet (E flat) 2 V. 2 Va. Vo.	Count M. von Fries		1797
5	Two Sonatas (F, G minor) Pf. Vo.	Frederick William II of Prussia		1797
6	Sonata (D) Pf. 4 hands			1797
7	Sonata (E flat) Pf.	Countess Babette von Keglevics		1797

WORKS WITH OPUS NUMBERS—*Continued*

OPUS	DESCRIPTION	DEDICATED TO	COM-POSED	PUB-LISHED
8	Serenade (D) V. Va. Vo.			1797 ann.
9	Three Trios (G, D, C minor) V. Va. Vo.	Count von Browne		1798 ann.
10	Three Sonatas (C minor, F, D) Pf.	Countess von Browne		1798 ann.
11	Trio (B flat) Pf. Clar. (or V.) Vo.	Countess von Thun		1798 ann.
12	Three Sonatas (D, A, E flat) Pf. V.	Anton Salieri		1799 ann.
13	Sonate Pathétique (C minor) Pf.	Prince Carl von Lichnowsky		1799
14	Two Sonatas (E, G) Pf.	Baroness von Braun		1799
15	Concerto (C) Pf. and Orch. (Really the second)	Princess Odescalchi, née Keglevics		1801
16	Quintet (E flat) Pf. Ob. Clar. Bsn. Cor. Arrd. by Beethoven as a quartet for Pf. V. Va. Vo. Also arrd. as string quartet and marked Op. 75	Prince von Schwarzenberg	b. Apr., 1797	1801
17	Sonata (F) Pf. Cor. or Vo.	Baroness von Braun	b. Apr., 1800	1801
18	Six Quartets (F, G, D, C minor, A, B flat) 2 V. Va. Vo.	Prince von Lobko-witz	1800 (1, 6)	1801
19	Concerto (B flat) Pf. and Orch. (Really the first.) (See No. 151)	Charles Nikl Edler von Niklsberg	b. Mar., 1795	1801
20	Septet (E flat) V. Va. Cor. Clar. Bsn. Vo. C-bass.	Empress Maria Theresia	b. Apr., 1800	1802
21	First Symphony (C)	Baron van Swieten	b. Apr., 1800	1801
22	Sonata (B flat) Pf.	Count von Browne	b. end of 1800	1802

APPENDIX

WORKS WITH OPUS NUMBERS—*Continued*

OPUS	DESCRIPTION	DEDICATED TO	COM-POSED	PUB-LISHED
23	Sonata (A minor) Pf. V.	Count M. von Fries	1800 (1st 2 mvts.)	1801
24	Sonata (F) Pf. V. Orig. No. 2 in Op. 23.	Count M. von Fries		1801
25	Serenade (D) Fl. V. Va. (See Op. 41.)			1802
26	Sonata (A flat) Pf.	Prince Carl von Lichnowsky		1802
27	No. 1 Sonata quasi una Fantasia (E flat) Pf.	Princess Josephine von Liechtenstein		1802 ann.
	No. 2 Sonata quasi una Fantasia (C sharp minor) "Moonlight" Pf.	Countess Giulietta Guicciardi		1802 ann.
28	Sonata (D) "Pastoral" Pf.	Joseph Edler von Sonnenfels	1801	1802
29	Quintet (C) 2 V. 2 Va. Vo.	Count M. von Fries	1801	1802
30	Three Sonatas (A, C minor, G) Pf. V.	Alexander I, Emperor of Russia	1802	1803
31	Three Sonatas (G, D minor, E flat) Pf.		1802 (1, 2)	1803 (1, 2) 1804 (3)
32	Song, "An die Hoffnung" (E flat)			1805 ann.
33	Seven Bagatelles (E flat, C, F, A, C, D, A flat) Pf.		1782– 1802	1803
34	Six Variations on an original theme (F) Pf.	Princess Odescalchi, née Keglevics	1802	1803
35	Fifteen Variations with a fugue, on theme from Prometheus (E flat) Pf.	Count M. Lichnowsky	1802	1803
36	Second Symphony (D)	Prince Carl von Lichnowsky	1802	1804
37	Third Concerto (C minor) Pf. and Orch.	Prince Louis Ferdinand of Prussia	1800	1804

[644]

WORKS WITH OPUS NUMBERS—*Continued*

OPUS	DESCRIPTION	DEDICATED TO	COM-POSED	PUB-LISHED
38	Trio (E flat) Pf. Clar. or V. and Vo. Arrd. by composer from Septet, Op. 20	Prof. J. A. Schmidt		1805
39	Two Preludes, through all 12 major keys, Pf. or Organ		1789	1803
40	Romance (G) V. and Orch.		1803	1803
41	Serenade (D) Pf. Fl. or V. from Serenade, Op. 25, revised by composer			1803
42	Notturno (D) Pf. Va. Arrd. from Serenade. Op. 8			1804
43	"The Creations of Prometheus" Ballet, Nos. 1–16		Prod. 1801	1801
44	Fourteen Variations (E flat) Pf. V. Vo.			1804
45	Three Grand Marches (C, E flat, D) Pf. 4 hands	Princess Esterhazy, née Liechtenstein		1804
46	Song, "Adelaide" (B flat)	Friedrich von Matthisson	1795 (?)	1797
47	Sonata (A) "Kreutzer" Pf. V.	Rudolph Kreutzer	Lastmvt. 1802	1805
48	Six Songs by Gellert for Soprano: "Bitten," "Die Liebe des Nächsten," "Vom Tode," "Die Ehre Gottes," "Gottes Macht," "Busslied"	Count von Browne		1803
49	Two Easy Sonatas (G minor, G major) Pf.		By 1802	1805
50	Romance (F) V. and Orch.			1805
51	Two Rondos (C, G) Pf.	Countess Henriette von Lichnowsky (No. 2)		1797 (1) 1802 (2)

WORKS WITH OPUS NUMBERS—*Continued*

OPUS	DESCRIPTION	DEDICATED TO	COM-POSED	PUB-LISHED
52	Eight Songs: "Urians Reise," "Feuerfarb," "Das Liedchen v. d. Ruhe," "Mailied," "Molly's Abschied," "Die Liebe," "Marmotte," "Das Blümchen Wunderhold"		Most, possibly all, very early	1805
53	Sonata "Waldstein" (C) Pf.	Count von Waldstein	1804(?)	1805
54	Sonata (F) Pf.			1806
55	Third Symphony "Eroica" (E flat)	Prince von Lobkowitz	1804	1806
56	Triple Concerto (C) Pf. V. Vo. and Orch.	Prince von Lobkowitz	c. 1804	1807
57	Sonata, "Appassionata" (F minor) Pf.	Count F. von Brunswick	c. 1804	1807
58	Fourth Concerto (G) Pf. and Orch.	Archduke Rudolph	c. 1805	1808
59	Three Quartets (7th, 8th, and 9th) Rasoumowsky (F, E minor, C) 2 V. Va. Vo.	Count von Rasoumowsky	b. Feb., 1807	1808
60	Fourth Symphony (B flat)	Count von Oppersdorf	1806	1809
61	Concerto (D) V. and Orch. Concerto, Pf. and Orch. Arrd. by Beethoven, Op. 61	Stephan von Breuning Frau von Breuning	1806 1807	1809 1808
62	Overture to Coriolanus (C. minor)	H. J. von Collin	1807	1808
63	Arrt. of Op. 4 as Trio for Pf. and Str.			
64	Arrt. of Op. 3 for Pf. and Vo.			
65	Scena and Aria, "Ah, perfido!" Sop. and Orch.	Countess von Clary	1796	1805

WORKS WITH OPUS NUMBERS—*Continued*

OPUS	DESCRIPTION	DEDICATED TO	COM-POSED	PUB-LISHED
66	Twelve Variations on "Ein Mädchen" (Zauber-flöte) (F) Pf. Vo.			1798
67	Fifth Symphony (C minor)	Prince von Lobko-witz and Count von Rasoumow-sky	c. 1805	1809
68	Sixth symphony "Pastoral" (F)	Prince von Lobko-witz and Count von Rasoumow-sky		1809
69	Sonata (A) Pf. Vo.	Baron von Gleich-enstein		1809
70	Two Trios (D, E flat) Pf. V. Vo.	Countess Marie von Erdödy		1809
71	Sextet (E flat) 2 Clar. 2 Cor. 2 Bsn.		Early work	1810
72	Opera, "Fidelio" or "Wed-ded Love"	Archduke Rudolph	begun 1803	
73	Fifth Concerto (E flat) "Emperor" Pf. and Orch.	Archduke Rudolph	1809	1811
74	Quartet (10th), "Harp" (E flat) 2 V. Va. Vo.	Prince von Lobko-witz	1809	1810
75	Six Songs: "Kennst Du das Land," "Herz, mein Herz," "Es war einmal," "Mit Liebesblick," "Einst Wohnten," "Zwar schuf das Glück," Sop. and Pf.	Princess von Kin-sky	1803 (4) 1810 (1)	1810
	Op. 75 is also marked to an arrt. of Op. 16 as string quartet			
76	Six Variations (D) (*See* Op. 113, No. 4.) Pf.	Franz Oliva	1809(?)	1810
77	Fantaisie (G minor) Pf.	Count F. von Brunswick	1808(?)	1810

WORKS WITH OPUS NUMBERS—*Continued*

OPUS	DESCRIPTION	DEDICATED TO	COM-POSED	PUB-LISHED
78	Sonata (F sharp) Pf.	Countess Therese von Brunswick	1809	1810
79	Sonatina (G) Pf.		b. Dec., 1808	1810
80	Fantasia (C minor) Pf. Orch. Cho. Theme of variations is Beethoven's song, "Gegenliebe"	Maximilian Joseph, King of Bavaria	b. end of 1808	1811
81a	Sonata "Adieu, Absence, and Reunion" (E flat) Pf.	Archduke Rudolph	1809 (1st mvt.) 1810 (2, 3)	1811
81b	Sextet (E flat) 2 V. Va. Vo. 2 Cor.			1810
82	Four Ariettas and Duet for Sop. and Ten., Pf. accomp.: 1. "Dimmi, ben mio." 2. "T'intendo, si." 3. "Che fa, il mio bene" (*buffa*). 4. "Che fa, il mio bene" (*seria*). 5. "Odi l'aura"		1809 (4)	1811
83	Three Songs, Sop. and Pf.: "Trocknet nicht," "Was zieht mir," "Kleine Blumen"	Princess von Kinsky	1810	1811
84	Music to Goethe's "Egmont." Overture. 1. Song, "Die Trommel." 2. Entracte I. 3. Entracte II. 4. Song, "Freudvoll und leidvoll." 5. Entracte III. 6. Entracte IV. 7. Clara's Death. 8. Melodrama. 9. Siegessymphonie		1810	Overture 1811 Rest 1812

WORKS WITH OPUS NUMBERS—*Continued*

OPUS	DESCRIPTION	DEDICATED TO	COM-POSED	PUB-LISHED
85	Oratorio, Christus am Oel-berge ("Mount of Olives") Sop. Ten. Bass, Cho. Orch.		1800(?)	1811
86	Mass (C) Sop. Alt. Ten. Bass, Cho. Orch.	Prince von Kin-sky	1807(?)	1812
87	Trio for 2 Ob. and Eng. H.		1794(?)	1806
88	Song, "Das Glück der Freundschaft" (A)			1803
89	Polonaise (C) Pf.	Empress Elizabeth Alexiewna of Russia	1814(?)	1815 (without op. no.)
90	Sonata (E minor) Pf.	Count M. von Lich-nowsky	1814	1815
91	Orch., "Wellington's Vic-tory, or the Battle of Vittoria"	Prince Regent of England	1813	1816
92	Seventh Symphony (A)	Count M. von Fries	1812	1816
93	Eighth Symphony (F)		1812	1816
94	Song, "An die Hoffnung"	Princess von Kin-sky	1816(?)	1816
95	Quartet (11th) (F minor) 2 V. Va. Vo.	N. Zmeskall	1810	1816
96	Sonata (G) Pf .V.	Archduke Rudolph	1812	1816
97	Trio (B flat) Pf. V. Vo.	Archduke Rudolph	1811	1816
98	Song Cycle: "An die ferne Geliebte."	Prince von Lobko-witz	1816	1816
99	Song, "Der Mann von Wort"			1816
100	Duet, "Merkenstein" (F)		1814(?)	1816
101	Sonata (A) Pf.	Baroness Dorothea von Ertmann		1817
102	Two Sonatas (C, D) Pf. Vo.	Countess Marie von Erdödy	1815	1817
103	Octet, 2 Ob. 2 Clar. 2 Cor. 2 Bsn. (E flat) Original of Op. 4.			c. 1834

WORKS WITH OPUS NUMBERS—*Continued*

OPUS	DESCRIPTION	DEDICATED TO	COM-POSED	PUB-LISHED
104	Quintet (C minor) 2 Vs. 2 Vas. Vo. Arrd. Beethoven from Op. 1, No. 3.		1817	1819
105	Six very easy themes varied, Pf. Fl. or V.		1818—19	1819
106	Sonata (B flat) "Hammerklavier" Pf.	Archduke Rudolph	1818—19	1819
107	Ten national themes with variations, Pf. Fl. or V.		1818—20	1820
108	Twenty-five Scotch Songs for 1 and sometimes 2 Voices and small Cho., Pf. V. Vo.	Prince Anton Radzivil	1815—16	1821
109	Sonata (E) Pf.	Frl. Maximiliane Brentano	1820(?)	1821
110	Sonata (A flat) Pf.		1821	1822
111	Sonata (C minor) Pf.	Archduke Rudolph (by publishers)	1822	1823
112	"Calm Sea and Prosperous Voyage," Sop. Ten. Alt. Bass and Orch.	Goethe	1815	1823
113	"The Ruins of Athens." Overture and eight numbers for Cho. and Orch. For No. 4, *see* Op. 76.	King of Prussia	1811	1846
114	March and Cho. (E flat) from "The Ruins of Athens"			1824
115	Overture in C. sometimes called "Namensfeier"	Prince Anton Radzivil	1814	1825
116	Terzetto, "Tremate" (B flat) Sop. Ten. Bass		1802	1826
117	"King Stephen" Overture (E flat) and 9 numbers.		1811	1815
118	Elegiac Song (E) Sop. Alt. Ten. Bass and Str.	Baron von Pasqualati	1814	1826

WORKS WITH OPUS NUMBERS—*Continued*

OPUS	DESCRIPTION	DEDICATED TO	COM-POSED	PUB-LISHED
119	New Bagatelles (G minor, C, D, A, C minor, G, G, C, C, A minor, A, B flat, G) Pf.		1822 1–6	1821 1823 1828
120	Thirty-Three Variations on a Waltz by Diabelli (C)	Frau Antonie von Brentano	1823 (?)	1823
121a	Variations on "Ich bin der Schneider Kakadu" (G) Pf. V. Vo.			1824
121b	Opferlied, Sop. with Cho. and Orch.		Orig. 1802	1825
122	Bundeslied, (B flat), Sop. Alt. Cho. and Wind		1822–23	1825
123	Mass in D, "Missa Solemnis"	Archduke Rudolph	1818 (or 19)–23	1827
124	Overture in C, "Consecration of the House"	Prince N. Galitzin	1822	1825
125	Ninth Symphony, "Choral" (D minor) Orch. Sop. Alt. Ten. Bass soli and Cho.	King of Prussia	1817–23	1826
126	Six [7] Bagatelles (G, G, minor, E flat, B minor, G, E flat, E flat) Pf.		1823	1825
127	Quartet, (12th) (E flat) 2 Vs. Va. Vo.	Prince N. Galitzin	1824	1826
128	Arietta, "The Kiss," by Weisse.		1822	1825
129	Rondo a capriccio (G) Pf. "Rage over a Lost Groschen"			1828
130	Quartet (13th) (B flat) 2 V. Va. Vo.	Prince N. Galitzin	1825–26 (Op. 133 was orig. *finale.* Present *finale* 1826)	1827

WORKS WITH OPUS NUMBERS—*Continued*

OPUS	DESCRIPTION	DEDICATED TO	COM- POSED	PUB- LISHED
131	Quartet (14th) (C sharp minor) 2 V. Va. Vo.	Baron von Stutter- heim	1826	1827
132	Quartet (15th) (A minor) 2 V. Va. Vo.	Prince N. Galitzin	1825	1827
133	Great Fugue (B flat) 2 V. Va. Vo. Originally *finale* to Op. 130.	Archduke Rudolph	1825	1827
134	Great Fugue (Op. 133) (B flat) arrd. by composer for Pf. 4 hands.	Archduke Rudolph		1827
135	Quartet (16th) (F) 2 V. Va. Vo.	Johann Wolfmayer	1826	1827
136	"Der glorreiche Augen- blick" ("The Glorious Moment"), Cantata, Sop. Alt. Ten. Bass Cho. and Orch., six numbers. Also as "Preis der Ton- kunst ("Praise of Mu- sic"), new text. F. Roch- litz.	The Sovereigns of Austria, Russia, and Prussia, etc.	1814	1836
137	Fugue (D) 2 V. 2 Va. Vo.		1817	1827
138	Overture, (C) known as "Leonore No. 1."		c. 1807	1832

WORKS WITHOUT OPUS NUMBERS

Numbers added by Grove

I. FOR ORCHESTRA OR ORCHESTRAL INSTRUMENTS

NO.	DESCRIPTION	DEDICATED TO	COM- POSED	PUB- LISHED
139	Twelve Minuets			1795
140	Twelve Deutsche Tänze			1795

WORKS WITHOUT OPUS NUMBERS—*Continued*

OPUS	DESCRIPTION	DEDICATED TO	COM-POSED	PUB-LISHED
141	Twelve Contretänze. (No. 7 is dance used in Finale of Prometheus, the "Eroica," etc. No. 11 also used in Finale of Prometheus)		1802 (2, 9, 10)	All 1803
142	Minuet of Congratulation (E flat)		1823	1835
143	Triumphal March, for Kuffner's "Tarpeia" or "Hersilia" (C)		b. Mar., 1813	1819
144	Military March (D)		1816	1827
145	Military March (F)		1809	
146	Rondino, 2 Ob. 2 Clar. 2 Cor. 2 Bsn. (E flat)		Very early	1829
147	Three Duos (C, F, B flat) Clar. Bsn.			1815(?)
148	Allegro con Brio, V. Orch. (C) Fragment of 1st mvt. of a V. Concerto. Completed by Jos. Hellmesberger	Dr. G. von Breuning	1800(?)	1879
149	Musik zu einem Ritterballet		1790	1872

B. FOR PIANO, WITH AND WITHOUT ACCOMPANIMENT

NO.	DESCRIPTION	DEDICATED TO	COM-POSED	PUB-LISHED
150	Sonatina and Adagio for Mandolin and Cembalo (C minor)			
151	Rondo (B flat) Pf. and Orch. Probably finished by Czerny. Perhaps intended for Op. 19.			1829

WORKS WITHOUT OPUS NUMBERS—*Continued*

NO.	DESCRIPTION	DEDICATED TO	COM-POSED	PUB-LISHED
152	Three Quartets (E flat, D, C) Pf. V. Va. Vo. Very early. Adagio of No. 3 is employed in Op. 2 No. 1.		1785	1832
153	Trio (E flat) Pf. V. Vo.		1785 (?)	1830
154	Trio in 1 movement (B flat) Pf. V. Vo.	Frl. Maximiliane Brentano	1812	1830
155	Rondo, Allegro (G) Pf. and V.		1794 (?)	1808
156	Twelve Variations on "Se vuol ballare" (F) Pf. and V.	Eleonore von Breuning		1793
157	Twelve Variations on "See the Conquering Hero" (G) Pf. and Vo.	Princess von Lichnowsky		1797
158	Seven Variations on "Bei Männern" (E flat) Pf. and Vo.	Count von Browne		1802
159	Variations on a theme by Count von Waldstein (C) Pf. 4 hands			1794
160	Air with Six Variations on "Ich denke dein" (D) Pf. 4 hands	Countess Josephine Deym and Countess Therese Brunswick	1800	1805
161	Three Sonatas (E flat, F minor, D) Pf.	Elector Maximilian Frederic of Cologne	Very early	1783
162	Sonata called Easy (C) Pf. 2 movts. only, second completed by F. Ries	Eleonore von Breuning		1830
163	Two Sonatinas (G, F) Pf. Of doubtful authenticity.			
164	Rondo, Allegretto (A) Pf.			1784
165	Menuet (E flat) Pf.		1783 (?)	1805
166	Prelude (F minor) Pf.		1785 (?)	1805

WORKS WITHOUT OPUS NUMBERS—*Continued*

NO.	DESCRIPTION	DEDICATED TO	COM-POSED	PUB-LISHED
167	Six Minuets (C, G, E flat, B flat, D, C) Pf. Perhaps first written for Orch.			1796
168	Seven Ländler Dances (all in D).			c. 1799
169	Six Ländler Dances (all in D except No. 4 in D minor). Also for VV. and Vo.		1802	1802
170	Andante favori (F) Pf. Orig. intended for Op. 53.		1804(?)	1806
171	Six Allemandes (F, D, F, A, D, G) Pf. and V.		1795	1814
172	Ziemlich lebhaft (B flat) Pf.		1818 By request	1824
173	Bagatelle (A minor) Pf.	"Für Elise"		
174	Andante maestoso (C) Pf. arrd. from the sketch for a Quintet and called "Beethoven's Last Musical Thought."		1826	1840
175	Ten Cadenzas to Beethoven's Pf. Concertos in C, B flat, C minor, G, D (arrt. of V. Concerto, *see* Op. 61). Also 2 to Mozart's Pf. Concerto in D minor.			1836
176	Nine Variations on a March by Dressler (C minor) Pf.	Countess von Wolf-Metternich	1780(?)	1783
177	Twenty-four Variations on Righini's air "Vieni [*sic* i.e. "Venni"] amore (D) Pf.	Countess von Hatzfeld	1790(?)	1801

APPENDIX

WORKS WITHOUT OPUS NUMBERS—*Continued*

NO.	DESCRIPTION	DEDICATED TO	COM-POSED	PUB-LISHED
178	Thirteen Variations on Dittersdorf's air "Es war einmal" (A) Pf.		1791(?)	1794
179	Nine Variations on Paisiello's air "Quant' è più bello" (A) Pf.	Prince Carl von Lichnowsky		1795 ann.
180	Six Variations on Paisiello's duet "Nel cor più" (G) Pf.			1796
181	Twelve Variations on minuet (a la Vigano) from Haibel's ballet "Le nozze disturbate" (C) Pf.		1795(?)	1796
182	Twelve Variations on the Russian dance from Paul Wranizky's "Waldmädchen" (A) Pf.	Countess von Browne	1796(?)	1797
183	Six easy Variations on a Swiss air (F) Pf. or Harp			c. 1798
184	Eight Variations on Grétry's air "Une fièvre brûlante (C) Pf.			1798
185	Ten Variations on Salieri's air, "La Stessa, la Stessissima" (B flat) Pf.	Countess Babette von Keglevics	1799	1799
186	Seven Variations on Winter's quartet, "Kind willst du" (F) Pf.			1799
187	Eight Variations on Süssmayer's trio, "Tändeln und scherzen" (F) Pf.	Countess von Browne	1799	1799
188	Six very easy Variations on an original theme (G) Pf.		c. 1800 (?)	1801
189	Seven Variations on "God Save the King" (C) Pf.			1804

[656]

WORKS WITHOUT OPUS NUMBERS—*Continued*

NO.	DESCRIPTION	DEDICATED TO	COM-POSED	PUB-LISHED
190	Five Variations on "Rule, Britannia" (D) Pf.			1804
191	Thirty-two Variations (C minor) Pf.		1806–07	1807
192	Eight Variations on "Ich hab' ein kleines Hütt-chen nur" (B flat) Pf.			c. 1831

III. WORKS FOR VOICES

NO.	DESCRIPTION	DEDICATED TO	COM-POSED	PUB-LISHED
193	Bass Solo "Germania!" Cho. Orch. *Finale* for Treitschke's Singspiel "Gute Nachricht"			1814
194	Bass Solo "Es ist voll-bracht." Cho. Orch. *Finale* to Treitschke's Singspiel "Die Ehren-pforten."			1815
195	"Misere" and "Amplius." Dirge at Beethoven's funeral 4-voiced men's chor. and 4 trombones. Adapted by Seyfried from two of three Ms. Equali for trombones.		1812	
196a	Cantata on the death of the Emperor Joseph II (Feb. 20, 1790) (C minor) Soli, Cho. Orch.		1790	
196b	Cantata (Sept. 30, 1790) "Er schlummert," on the accession of Leo-pold II.		1790	

WORKS WITHOUT OPUS NUMBERS—*Continued*

NO.	DESCRIPTION	DEDICATED TO	COM-POSED	PUB-LISHED
197	Song of the monks from Schiller's "William Tell" —"Rasch tritt der Tod." "In memory of the sudden and unexpected death of our Krumpholz" (May 3, 1817). (C minor) 2 Ten. Bass.		1817	1839
198	Chorus, "O Hoffnung" (4 bars) (G) for Archduke Rudolph		1818	1819
199	Cantata (E flat) Sop. Alt. Bass, Pf.		1823	1867
200	Cantata, "Graf, Graf, lieber Graf" (E flat) Voices and Pf.	Count M. von Lichnowsky		1865
201	Five bars (on the arrival of Herr Schlesinger of Berlin, "Glaube u. hoffe"		1819	
202	Incidental music, "Du dem sie gewunden," written for Duncker's "Leonore Prohaska" (D)		1814	1865
203–222	Many canons and small incidental pieces.			
223	Twenty-five Irish Songs, for 1 & 2 Voices with Pf. V. Vo.			1814–16
224	Twenty Irish Songs			1814–16
225	Twelve Irish Songs			1814–16
226	Twenty-six Welsh Songs			1817
227	Twelve Scottish Songs			1841
228	Twelve Songs of varied nationality, for Voice, Pf. V. Vo.		1815 (2, 6, 8, 11)	1816 (2, 6, 8, 11)
229	Song, "Schilderung eines Mädchens"		1781(?)	1783

WORKS WITHOUT OPUS NUMBERS—*Continued*

NO.	DESCRIPTION	DEDICATED TO	COM-POSED	PUB-LISHED
230	Song, "An einen Säugling"			1784
231	Song, "Farewell to Vienna's Citizens"	Obristwacht-meister von Kövesdy	1796	1796
232	War Song of the Austrians, Solo and Cho. with Pf.		1797	1797
233	Song, "Der freie Mann"		1795 (?)	1806
234	Opferlied, "Die Flamme lodert"		1795 (?)	
235	Song, "Zärtliche Liebe"			1803
236	Song, "La Partenza"			1803
237	Song, "Der Wachtelschlag"		c. 1799	1804
238	Song, "Als die Geliebte sich trennen wollte"			1809
239	Arietta, "In questa tomba oscura" (A flat)		1807 (?)	1808
240	Song, "Andenken" (D)			1810
241	Four settings of Goethe's "Sehnsucht"			1808
242	Song, "Als mir noch"		1809	1810
243	Song, "Welch ein wunderbares Leben"			1810
244	Song, "Der Frühling entblühet			1810
245	Song, "Des Kriegers Abschied"		1814	1815
246	Song, "Die stille Nacht"		1815 or 1816	1816
247	Song, "O das ich dir"		1811	1814
247a	Another setting of above		After Dec., 1812	c. 1840
248	Song, "Dort auf dem hohen Felsen"		1813	1814
249	Song, "Wenn ich ein Vöglein wär"		1816	1817
250	Song, "Wo blüht das Blümchen"		1815	1816

WORKS WITHOUT OPUS NUMBERS—*Continued*

NO.	DESCRIPTION	DEDICATED TO	COM-POSED	PUB-LISHED
251	Song, "Nord oder Sud!"		1817	1817
252	Song, "Lisch aus, mein Licht"		1817	1818
253	Song, "Wenn die Sonne nieder sinket"		1820	1820
254	Two songs, "Seufzer eines Ungeliebten" and "Gegenliebe." (For theme of latter see Op. 80)		1795(?)	1837
255	Song, "Turteltaube'		1809(?)	Prob. 1837
256	Song, "Gedenke mein! ich denke dein"		1820	1844

INDEX

Absolute music, 248.
   defined, 626.
Academies, 34.
Acoustics, defined, 626.
Adagio, mystical, the, 500.
   symphonic, 196.
Adelaide, source-motive, 575.
Adieu, Absence, and Reunion, 241.
   See also Sonata in E flat, Op.
   81a.
Æsthetic radicals, 118.
Albrechtsberger, 26, 27, 28, 29,
   321.
   BEETHOVEN takes lessons from,
   26.
Allegro, titanic, 499.
Amenda, Carl, 25, 43, 85, 332.
Amiel, 263.
An die Hoffnung, Op. 32, 160.
Anagram, B–A–C–H, 185, 186,
   400.
   idea in chief source motive?
   610.
   in Op. 131, 564–565.
"Andante Favori," 150.
Anlauf, 608.
Answer, defined, 626.
"Appassionata" sonata, *see* Sonata
   in F minor, Op. 57.
Applause *versus* tears, 42.
Appoggiatura, defined, 626.
Appropriation, genial, *versus* pla-
   giarism, 512.
Archduke Rudolph, 32, 176, 239,
   242, 291, 381.
   pupil of BEETHOVEN, 198.
"Archduke" trio, *see* Trio in B flat,
   Op. 97.

Aria, defined, 626.
Arnim, Bettina von, *see* Brentano,
   Bettina.
Artaria, 77.
Augmentation, defined, 626.
Authentic cadence, defined, 626.
Automatic instruments, BEE-
   THOVEN'S music on, 615–
   625.
Automatisms, 281.

Bach, C. P. E., 492, 514.
Bach, J. S., 16, 20, 41, 53, 79, 143,
   144, 219, 252, 369, 371, 459,
   490, 567, 608.
B–A–C–H anagram, 185, 186,
   400.
   overture, 168.
Bach's organ fugue in C minor,
   463.
   Welltempered Clavichord, 16.
Bagatelle, defined, 626.
   Op. 26, 462.
   Op. 33, 17, 18.
   source-motive in, 581.
   Op. 126, source-motive in, 581.
Baline, Israel, *see* Berlin, Irving.
Ballantine, Edward, 80.
Ballet, *The Creations of Pro-
   metheus*, Op. 43, 43, 76,
   125.
   variations on theme, 106.
Bargiel, 571.
Baryton, 30.
Bassettl, 470.
Basso ostinato, defined, 626.
Baton, BEETHOVEN'S technic, 147.
Battle of Jena, by Fuchs, 342.

INDEX

INDEX

BEETHOVEN, *continued*

his biographers, puritanism of,
99.

his birth, date of, 8.

place of, 8.

boisterous humor of, 312.

borrows from Haydn, 515.

from himself, 515, 516, 517,
518, 519, 520, 521.

from Mozart, 222, 514, 524.

from folk tunes, 516.

his brave wit during operation,
479.

his breadth of interests, 120.

Broadwood presents piano to,
364.

his brothers, 206.

relations with, 88.

burial of, 487.

business morality of, 393.

catastrophe and courage, 174.

cautious approach to new forms,
63.

a cembalo player, 13.

chief of many liberators, 494.

and classicism, 117, 120, 121.

a classicist, 246.

and Clementi, 204, 205.

codicil to his will, 484.

complains of neglect, 444.

composition, habits of, 3, 470,
553.

conceited? was he, 43.

concentration of, 377, 504.

as a conductor, 147, 380.

his confidence in future, 189.

confident of posterity's verdict,
480.

conscientious idealism of, 505.

BEETHOVEN, *continued*

consecutive fifths allowed by,
144, 145.

construction, a master of, 495.

contributions, his most original,
406, 499.

courage of, 51, 52, 174, 479.

Court of Cassel, offer from, 239.

Court organist, 18.

created new keyboard technic,
492.

creative freedom of, 368.

music freed from composer-
executant tradition, 95.

processes of, 511, 553.

resources, fertility of his, 579.

critics of, 321.

"crown of martyrdom," 168.

cynicism of, 47.

and dancing, 25.

daydreams of, 2, 3.

deaf to applause, 420.

deafness of, 50, 52, 60, 84, 88,
94, 96, 101, 159, 358, 365,
380, 385, 395, 420, 427,
457, 467.

causes of, 96.

effects of, 94.

exaggerates his, 88.

first admission of, 84.

death of, 486.

cause of, 487.

premonition of, 445.

his deathbed, 44, 478–486.

dedication of Op. 2 to Haydn,
41.

defensive rationalization, 388.

defrauds Maelzel, 344.

his delirium, 486.

INDEX

BEETHOVEN, *continued*
  and orchestra, 148, 235, 266.
  origin of name, 4.
  originality of, 500.
  out-of-doors, passion for, 75.
  overreaches the London Philharmonic Society, 303.
  overtures, his best program music, 268.
  and pedants, 321, 322.
  personal creed of, 383.
  personality, 23.
    difficult, 74.
  as physician, 505.
  pianist, last appearance as, 350.
  piano duel with Himmel, 42.
    with Steibelt, 72.
  plagiarisms by, 386, 512.
  and poetic programs, 305.
  popularity, his growing, 158.
  posterity's verdict, confident of, 480.
  poverty of, 341.
    representation of, 480.
  practical jokes, 147, 312, 330, 338, 408.
  praised by Mozart, 19.
  precocity of, 3.
  presence of mind of, 35.
  priggishness of, 317, 319.
  printed works, list of, 642–660.
  productiveness, 270, 271.
  program music, theory of, 268.
  psychological insight of, 144.
  and publishers, 158, 335, 337, 390, 392, 459.
  and punning, 331, 332, 334.
  quality, sustained, of his work, 177.

BEETHOVEN, *continued*
  quarrel with Von Breuning, 145.
  "raptus," 232, 280.
  rebounds from misfortune, 175.
  reburial of, 488.
  receives annuity, 71, 239.
    Broadwood piano, 364.
    Cremona fiddles, 71.
    freedom of city of Vienna, 355.
    golden snuffbox, 41.
  relations with his brothers, 88.
  relics, Clementi method, 455.
  religion, founder of a, 504.
  relishes bad music, 266.
  repels the old, 246.
  resilience of, 88.
  and rhythmic mottos, 191.
  ripening, slow, 20.
  rivals, enmity of, 74.
  Robinson Crusoe costume of, 73.
  and romanticism, 117, 120, 121, 141.
  a romanticist, 246.
  and the rondo, 499.
  and Rossini, 325, 379.
  rudeness to servant, 101.
  Salieri, studies with, 29.
  and Schenck, 26.
  Schubert's visit to, 484.
  self-expression in *Fidelio*, 171.
  self-willed, 29.
  sends for his brothers, 36.
  shares rooms with Von Breuning, 145.
  shocks the reactionaries, 146.
  shows consideration for Rode, 340.
  and singers, 148, 382.

INDEX

INDEX

INDEX

INDEX

INDEX

INDEX

INDEX

INDEX

INDEX

INDEX

INDEX

INDEX